Memorial of
John Slafter

WITH A
GENEALOGICAL ACCOUNT
OF HIS DESCENDANTS
INCLUDING
EIGHT GENERATIONS

Drawn by T. S. Slafter.

Rev. Edmund F. Slafter, A.M.

HERITAGE BOOKS
2016

HERITAGE BOOKS

AN IMPRINT OF HERITAGE BOOKS, INC.

Books, CDs, and more—Worldwide

For our listing of thousands of titles see our website
at
www.HeritageBooks.com

A Facsimile Reprint
Published 2016 by
HERITAGE BOOKS, INC.
Publishing Division
5810 Ruatan Street
Berwyn Heights, Md. 20740

Originally privately printed for the family

Boston:
Press of Henry W. Dutton & Son,
90 & 92 Washington Street
1869

International Standard Book Numbers
Paperbound: 978-0-7884-1570-8
Clothbound: 978-0-7884-5954-2

Drawn by T. S. Slafter.

RESIDENCE OF DEA. JOHN SLAFTER, NORWICH, VT., 1786.

GENERAL INDEX.

ENGRAVINGS.

INTRODUCTION.

THE design of this volume is to give a family record of John Slafter, the emigrant ancestor of all who bear his surname in this country, and of his descendants, extending to eight generations. It has been made as full in dates of births, marriages and deaths as patient and extensive research could make it. No work of this kind can be made absolutely complete. The records of towns are all more or less imperfect, and those of families still more so, and few of the latter are preserved after one or two generations. Lettered gravestones are only occasionally found of a date earlier than 1700, and only a small number of the persons who died during the next hundred years were honored with an inscription. There are, therefore, births, deaths and marriages in all families, of which there is no record existing, and their dates can never be accurately ascertained. Circumstances however often enable us to establish the approximate period, and in such cases I have used some expression indicative of this fact.

In addition to the items of information above stated, some other prominent facts have been recorded, such as the offices held, the military service rendered, the Collegiate course of education pursued, and the learned professions filled. In the earlier generations other facts have been stated which might illustrate standing and character, but I have rarely indulged in anything like personal eulogy. The narrative of Dea. John

Slafter, the first settler of Norwich, Vt., is fuller than any others.
but as he presents a fair type of the New-England pioneer,
of which the family furnishes many examples, the writer trusts
to be excused for exceeding in this instance the limits of his
general plan. It would have been agreeable, both to his feelings
and taste, to write out full narratives of all the adult members
of the family ; but this would have been a life-long labor, and
would have swollen the volume to an impracticable size.
Bearing in mind that the primary aim of the work is to give a
simple family record, laying the foundation on which fuller
narratives may be constructed by any who desire it, the writer
hopes his labors will be satisfactory to those for whom alone the
compilation has been made.

The arrangement, it is presumed, will be found to be obvious
and simple.   Ordinal or consecutive numbers are placed against
those who bear the name of Slafter, under some of its varied
spellings; and also against the names of those whose mother
had the same patronymic. If the name against which the
ordinal stands is other than Slafter, that of the father immediately precedes it, so that there can be no misapprehension.

Some of the names appear twice. In all such cases the
ordinal number at which the name will again occur is placed in
brackets immediately following the name. This reference will
be obvious as soon as the eye falls upon the page.

If it be desired to trace the line of descent, look in the Index
for the name you wish to trace ; against it will stand an ordinal
number. Turn to this number in the body of the work, where
you will find the name, and above it will be found the name of
the parent; at the right of the parent's name, in brackets, will
be a number, for which look in the ordinals, and above this
number, when found among the ordinals, will be the names of
the grandparents; and so continue until the line is traced to the

emigrant ancestor. But the pedigree of each member of the family may be seen at a glance. Immediately after each head of a family will be seen, included in a parenthesis, the pedigree in the Slafter line ; the first name in the parenthesis being either the father or the mother, as the case may be, the second the grandfather, and so on to John, the emigrant ancestor.

It will be proper to say a few words respecting the family name, which in some of the branches has passed through the usual mutations in spelling. A change of spelling is common in the history of New-England names. In some families important changes have taken place, in others they have been slight, while few have withstood all mutation whatever. The earliest records in which our family name is found are in Lynn, Mass., and it there occurs five times, in all of which it is written Slafter.

After the family removed to Connecticut, in the records of deeds and in the town records in Mansfield, Willington and Tolland, the name is generally written Slafter, but in a few instances, Slaughter. Of the five sons of the emigrant ancestor, Anthony had only daughters, and Benjamin had no children. The name has been transmitted by the three sons, Samuel, Moses and Joseph. The descendants of Samuel have all, down to the present time, written it Slafter. The descendants of Moses also have retained the same spelling down to the present generation, but some of them, a few years since, began to drop the f, under the erroneous impression that the name was originally Slater. Joseph, who stands at the head of the third branch, wrote his name Slafter, in a "petition" to the General Court, dated May, 1718, being then an inhabitant of Tolland (see Waldo's History of Tolland, p. 18), and likewise in the same way in the conveyance of land in the same town, as appears by the record in 1764. But in Killingly, where he resided, and in Scituate, R. I., where some of his children were settled, the name in the town records is variously written, sometimes Slaughter, but generally in other ways, as Slatter, Slauter, Slatar and Slater, for which variations it is evident that the clerk of the town is responsible.

Joseph, the eldest son of the above Joseph, and grandson of the emigrant ancestor, resided in Scituate, R. I. He was admitted a freeman at Newport, April 3, 1745, on which occasion his name is written Slaughter. In 1774, when a census was taken in Rhode Island, there were residing in Scituate, as heads of families, Joseph, above mentioned, and three of his sons, viz., Joseph, Jr., who afterward removed to Guilford, Vt. (see No. 299), Abner, who removed to the State of New York (see No. 292), and Abial, who continued in Scituate, afterward Foster, R. I. (see No. 314.) Of the above four families, the name in the census was written Slaughter, and a part of the descendants of Abner still retain this spelling, but the bulk of those descended from these families now write the name Slater.

But while the name was written Slafter in Willington, Mansfield, Ellington and Tolland, in legal documents and on gravestones, there is a uniform tradition that it was commonly pronounced Slaughter, and in the early Church records in Mansfield it is, without any exception, written Slaughter.

Slaughter is an old English name, often met with in all catalogues of English surnames. It was the name of one of the colonial governors of Virginia.

From all the facts which we have been able to collect we do not doubt that the original spelling of the emigrant ancestor's name was Slaughter. After the most careful and patient search, we have not found the name Slafter in any of the lists of English surnames, either ancient or modern. The three letters ugh, coming together, often, in English, have the sound of f, as in cough, tough, rough, laugh, draught, enough. And in the records of Lynn, Mass., and of Mansfield, Conn., and we presume in those of other towns at that period, though not following precisely the same analogy, daughter was often written *dafter*, and persons advanced in age now remember to have heard it pronounced as if so written. It was not therefore unnatural, that the *ugh* should be changed into f, and that Slaughter should come to be written Slafter. The historical facts, as we have seen, appear to corroborate this supposition. The changed spelling, viz., Slafter, appears to have been employed by the emigrant ancestor and by all his children in deeds and legal documents, where the greatest care would naturally be exercised, while in church records, where the name was probably written by the clergyman from the sound, as he commonly heard it pronounced, it was generally written Slaughter. We find no evidence that the name was originally Slater. The tendency in the changes in names, as they grew up gradually in New-England, was to abbreviate and render them more simple in orthography. This end was attained by changing three letters in Slaughter into one in Slafter. But if the name was originally Slater, it must have been changed to Slafter or Slaughter by adding in the one case one letter, and in the other three, thus rendering a short name longer, and more difficult both to write and to pronounce. Such a supposition does not seem to us natural, and moreover is not sustained by the early records. That it was originally the old English name Slaughter, and that the ugh was abbreviated into f, as a matter of convenience, and without probably any distinct intention of changing the name, we see no good reason to doubt. This explains all the facts in the case, and accords with the tendency of that period to the change of names.

The members of the family, down through all the generations, have been, for the most part, landholders, and the vocation of the bulk of them has been that of tilling the soil and of mechanics. Where there has been any important variation from this it has been indicated in the personal record.

In ecclesiastical relations there is the usual variety found in all New-England families. These are so subject to change, that it is difficult, in many cases, to be specific and at the same time accurate. No attempt therefore has been made to indicate the ecclesiastic relations of individuals, except in the case of those who have held some official station.

The author begs to state that in a compilation like this, containing so many thousands of facts, it is impossible not to fall into some errors. No pains have been spared to render the work as accurate as possible, and, while he does not doubt that errors will appear, he flatters himself that as few will be found as in most works of a similar character.

In preparing this Memorial the author has received valuable and essential aid from many of the family, and from others, especially from members of the New-England Historic-Genealogical Society, whose rich stores of local and family history have always been at his service. He begs to express his grateful appreciation of the uniform courtesy displayed by those members of the family, who have so readily taken a part in the voluminous correspondence which it has been necessary to carry on, and to tender to them in this explicit manner his most cordial thanks.

BOSTON, 11 BEACON STREET,
        June, 1869.

THE SLAFTER MEMORIAL.

1. JOHN SLAFTER.

The emigrant ancestor of the family, which is the subject of these pages, whose name we give above, came to this country from Great Britain, a vague tradition says from Wales, as near as can be ascertained not far from 1680. He appears to have settled at Lynn, Mass., and to have reared a family of at least ten children. The records of Lynn are exceedingly meagre, and his name has not been found in them. His residence in Lynn is a matter of direct tradition from his grandchildren, who were born before his death, and who could hardly be misinformed on this point; and, moreover, this tradition is corroborated by the record of the marriage of several of his children in that town.

As early as 1716, he removed to Connecticut, and purchased that year a hundred acres of land on the Willimantic River, in the town of Mansfield. Two years later, he united with others in the joint purchase of a tract of land containing about twenty-eight thousand acres, in the north part of the same town. At the expiration of four years this property was sold. On the second of May, 1721, he made another joint purchase of land on the same stream, about a mile and a quarter beyond the northern limits of Mansfield, being a tract of land included, or supposed to be, in the old township of Windham, where the deed is found recorded. In 1724, the General Court of the Colony of Connecticut was petitioned to set off this tract, together with a part of Ashford, into a new town. His name appears among the petitioners, with those also of his two sons, Joseph and Benjamin. This being unsuccessful, another petition was preferred in 1727. On this appears his own name, and those of his sons, Moses and Benjamin. The ground of the petition is alleged to be the inconvenience and dangerous consequences of being too remote from any place of public worship. "Being sensible," say the petitioners, "of the great loss and unspeakable we are under, by reason of dwelling so remote from the public worship of God, as also of what fatal and destroying consequence our so continuing may be to our posterity, we do, therefore, with an eye to our present comfort and future everlasting felicity, of us and ours, with a desire, also, to advance the interests, and enlarge the kingdom of our blessed Saviour, the Lord Jesus Christ, in this wilderness, and chiefly aiming in all these, at the glory of God, humbly address ourselves to your

1

honors, begging that your honors would so far consider our deplorable state and condition as to find out some way for our relief." This appeal had the desired effect, and the town of Willington was incorporated.

Immediately after the incorporation of the town, he received a deed of his portion of the joint purchase of 1721, which is found recorded among the earliest records of the town. The boundaries as laid down are specially stated to include the "mansion-house of the said Slafter." On this estate he appears to have lived the remainder of his life. The farm is situated on the eastern bank of the Willimantic River, and is about a mile and a quarter above the southern limits of the town. This river runs from north to south, and forms the boundary between Tolland and Willington. Half a mile above the northern limits of the farm, this charming little stream deflects to the east, sweeping round in a graceful curve, forming a complete semicircle, and then resumes its southern course. The railway, which runs along the eastern bank of the river, passes over the river on covered bridges, both at the northern and southern extremity of the semicircle. The lower end of the southernmost bridge rests on the ancient Slafter estate. Easterly from the river's bank, the land rises abruptly, forming an elevation of a hundred and fifty feet in height, as measured by the eye, and then becoming depressed, passes into an undulating plateau. A few rods east of the summit was the "mansion-house" referred to in the deed. It stood in a sunny and protected spot, looking out upon the waters of the nimble Willimantic in their lively flow around the semicircle at the north. The writer visited the spot in 1862. The estate was then owned by Mr. Henry C. Gurley. The "mansion-house" had disappeared, but the walls of the ancient cellar were still in their place. Near by was the decayed trunk of an ancient apple tree, still standing, but in the last stages of decay, the veteran sentinel of more than a hundred years. Its broad base and time-worn aspect indicated that it was planted in the time, and probably by the hand of the emigrant ancestor himself. A few branches were springing from the roots, from which was selected a walking stick, as a memento of the revered ancestor who had the courage and energy to seek a home in the wilderness of America.

At the organization of the town of Willington, soon after its incorporation in 1727, John Slafter was appointed its first grand juror, to which office he was re-elected several years in succession. He was, also, by a vote of his fellow citizens, as appears from the record, clothed with the office of tithingman, an inferior magistracy which has now gone entirely into disuse; but in New England, for a hundred and fifty years, it was esteemed of great local importance. To this officer was committed the guardianship of the Lord's day. His jurisdiction extended over the township, and it was his duty to suppress all secular labor, or travelling except in passing to and from places of public worship. Sometimes, however, he was restricted to the oversight of a certain number of families designated by name. Such persons, therefore, were placed in the office, as, by their wisdom, moderation, dignity and age, were able to exercise a controlling moral influence, irrespective of the legal authority with which they were invested.

Among the early enterprises of the new town of Willington was the settlement of a clergyman. At a public meeting, a vote was passed inviting a certain clergyman to officiate for the term of three months. To this Mr. Slafter took the lead in entering a protest. The ground of his opposition was, doubtless, either a want of satisfaction with the candidate, or disapprobation of any temporary arrangement. For, afterward, at the same meeting, an order was passed for the immediate and permanent settlement of a parish minister. This order, to which he appears to have made no opposition, was carried into effect, and the incumbent remained in the useful discharge of his office till the termination of his life.

Our emigrant ancestor, now probably becoming advanced in years, does not appear again in the records of the town, except as paying taxes for the support of the parish minister.

In 1739, he transferred his estate in equal parts to his two sons, Moses and Benjamin, that part on which the "mansion house" stood being assigned to Moses. Nine years afterward the sons exchanged estates, and a year later Moses disposed of his portion and removed to Ellington, then a part of Windsor, Ct., and Benjamin became proprietor of the homestead. It is presumed that, in the transfer of his estate to his sons, he retained a life interest in it, agreeably to a very general custom in New England, thus securing to the last the home of his earlier years, with the tender ministrations which filial affection alone can render.

In person the emigrant ancestor is said, by tradition, to have been not above ordinary height, with broad shoulders, a powerful osseous frame, overlaid and knit together with strong elastic muscles.

On one occasion, at least, he is reputed to have made proof both of his personal courage and physical strength. During his abode in Massachusetts, the forests were infested with Indians, who made frequent incursions upon the English settlements, often carrying terror and death to the cottages of the emigrants. Returning on one occasion after a brief absence, he found his home invaded by two athletic savages, whose insolent threats and gestures had put his whole household in fear of instant death. Assuming the authority which belongs to the lord of the castle, they were at once ordered to leave. Obedience to this command was haughtily refused. Fastening his eye upon the leader, the second injunction was followed, with the quickness almost of lightning, by a blow from his clenched hand, put forth with all the energy of his powerful frame, which laid the savage prostrate at his feet. The other, awed by this lesson, showed only signs of fear, and with humble promises on the part of both they were permitted to depart, and never afterward ventured to repeat their visit.

The time of his death is not known. As his son Benjamin sold, in 1754, the estate which he had received from him, it is conjectured that his death occurred anterior to that date. He was probably buried in the ancient cemetery in Willington. There are very few inscriptions on the headstones of the early burials, and none is to be found bearing his name. There is a very clear and direct tradition of his great age, of his last illness and death, and of the veneration and esteem in which

he was held in Willington, long after he had passed away. Of his
wife we find no record whatever. The date of the birth of his children, with the exception of Mary and Samuel, is conjectural, and whether
they are arranged in the order of birth in the following list, is uncer-
tain. That he had ten children is evident from the fact, that his son
Benjamin left in his will, the residue of his property, after the decease
of his wife, to his "nine brothers and sisters," or their heirs. The
names of nine of the ten children, with some historical notice, are contained in this memorial. The tenth child may have had no family, and
have left no record. There are, however, many circumstaces which
point to James Shafter, the ancestor of the Hon. Judge Shafter, of California, as the tenth child, but the evidence is not absolute, and his
genealogy is not contained in the body of this work.

The children of John Slafter were as follows. The place of their
birth was probably Lynn, Mass. :—

2.   1. MARY,[11] b. Nov., 1688 ; d. Jan. 12, 1793 ; m. Isaac Wellman.
3.   2. ANTHONY,[16] b. perhaps about 1690 ; d. June 28, 1723 ; m. Mary Eaton.
4.   3. ELIZABETH,[22] b. perhaps about 1693 ; d. probably about 1734 ; m. Thomas Hutchinson.
5.   4. SAMUEL,[23] b. Aug., 1696 ; d. July 31, 1770 ; m. Dorothy Fenton.
6.   5. JOSEPH,[36] b. perhaps about 1698 ; d. about 1787 ; m. Esther ———.
7.   6. SARAH,[41] b. perhaps about 1700 ; m. Samuel Paulk.
8.   7. MOSES,[51] b. perhaps about 1702 ; d. about 1778 ; m. Jemima Scripture.
9.   8. ABIGAIL,[56] b. perhaps about 1704 ; d. March 15, 1738 ; m. Dea. George Sawin.
10.   9. BENJAMIN,[62] b. perhaps about 1706 ; d. about 1760 ; m. Bethia Eaton.

11. MARY,[2] (*John*,[1]) b. Nov., 1688 ; d. Jan. 12, 1793 ; m. Isaac,
son of Isaac and Hannah (Adams) Wellman of Lynn, Mass. Their
intention of marriage was published August 23, 1717. He was grandson of Thomas Wellman, who was in Lynn as early as 1640, and was
the emigrant ancestor of the family bearing this name in New England.
Isaac Wellman resided in Lynn for about six years after his marriage,
when he removed to Norton, Mass., north precinct, where he purchased
a hundred and eighteen acres of land for the sum of £236, lawful cur-
rency of the province of Massachusetts Bay, the deed bearing date of
"this twenty-third day of May, Anno Domini, 1723, in the ninth year
of the reign of our Sovreign Lord George, of Great Britain," &c. In
this deed he is styled Isaac Wellman, Jr., of Lynn precinct. The first
meeting for the organization of the north precinct of Norton, now
Mansfield, was held at his house on Tuesday, August 31, 1731, and the
parish continued to meet there, from time to time, for two or three
years, until a place of worship was erected.

On the 17th of June, 1740, Mary Wellman, widow, was appointed
administratrix of the estate of Isaac Wellman, "lately deceased," and
the division of the property was subsequently made to the widow and
the four children hereafter named. She continued to reside on her
estate in Mansfield, Mass., to the close of her life. In the Mansfield
records is the following entry : "Mary Wellman died January 12, 1793,
in the 105th year of her age ; a religious woman." This is the only
personal comment which we have found in the records, and seems to
have been called forth by the extraordinary age and exemplary char-

acter of this lady. Her age was 104 years and two months. A great-granddaughter of hers is now living, (1869,) Mrs. Jesse George of Wrentham, who, when a child, resided in the same family, and remembers her well, being ten years of age at the time of her death. There are, probably, very few now living, who, with like experience, have seen a person born in 1688. She had five children at the time of her husband's death, one of which died soon after, and the name has not been preserved. Her children, the eldest two born in Lynn, the others in Mansfield, with their descendants, are as follows :—

Mansfield, Mass.

12. 1. ISAAC, son of Isaac and Mary (Slafter) Wellman, b. 1719; d. Dec. 30, 1804; m. Hannah Wellman of Attleboro', Mass., Aug. 4th, 1748.
    1. Peter, son of Isaac and Hannah (Wellman) Wellman, b. Aug. 7, 1750; d. May 28, 1791; m. Hannah Capron of Mansfield, Mass., Feb. 5, 1780. He was in Capt. Hodges' Comp. in 1778, in Rev. War. His children were :—
      (1.) Solomon, son of Peter and Hannah (Capron) Wellman, b. Dec. 21, 1780; d. at Lowell, July 13, 1851; m. Elizabeth-Tripp, dau. of Thomas Leeds of Dorchester, Mass. She was b. Sept. 26, 1791; d Aug., 1849. Their children were :—
        (a.) George, b. March 16, 1810; d. April 4, 1864, at Lowell, Mass. He was the inventor and patentee of a very valuable contrivance used in the manufacture of cotton, called " Wellman's Self-Acting Card Stripper, now adopted by most of the manufacturing establishments in this country and Europe." He m. Louisa Hodges of Walpole, Mass., and had George-Henry and William-Lloyd. *Lowell, Mass.*
        (b.) Eliza-Ann, dau. of Solomon and Eliz. T. (Leeds) Wellman, b. March 25, 1811; m. Dea. John Stetson of Medford, Mass., April 14, 1840, and had 1, Lucinda Maria, b. March 10, 1841; 2, James Henry, b. July 12, 1842, d. July 3, 1863, was in Com. C., 13th Mass. Vol.—he enlisted July 29, 1861, participated in thirteen battles, was killed July 3, 1863, at Gettysburg, and buried there in the Pennsylvania lot; 3, Frank-Lloyd, b. Aug. 21, 1844; 4, Helen-Amelia, b. May 16, 1847.
        (c.) Caroline-Capron, dau. of Solomon Wellman, b. Aug. 23, 1812; m. Josiah Shaw.
Abington, Mass.
        (d.) Lucinda-Boyden, dau. of Solomon Wellman, b. Dec. 3, 1813; d. Jan. 26, 1833.
        (e.) Mary-Elizabeth, dau. of Solomon Wellman, b. Jan. 21, 1815; m. Martin-Bailey Pierce.
Abington, Mass.
        (f.) Clarissa-Maria, dau. of Solomon Wellman, b. Dec. 9, 1817; m. Samuel Burrill, Sept. 28, 1851, and had Mary-Elizabeth, b. Oct. 25, 1852, died June 13, 1859; Henry-William-Gardner, b. Aug. 20, 1854.
        (g.) William-Lloyd, son of Solomon Wellman, b. Oct. 23, 1819; d. April 23, 1845.
        (h.) Henry-Ripley, son of Solomon Wellman, b. March 20, 1821; d. May 14, 1848.
        (i.) Charles-Pynson, son of Solomon Wellman, b.

Dec. 13, 1823; m Elizabeth-Downer Titus
of Colebrook, N. H., Oct. 13, 1847, and had
1, Frances-Josephine, b. March 27, 1849, d.
Feb 11, 1851 ; 2, Charles-Francis, b. July 27,
1852 ; 3, Edward-Coit, b. April 14, 1854.
Lewiston, Me.

(j.) Otis, son of Solomon Wellman, b. Jan. 26,
1827 ; d. in infancy.

(k.) Harriet-Angeline, dau. of Solomon Wellman, b.
March 25, 1828 ; m. John-Adams Floyd.
Abington, Mass.

(l.) Elisha, son of Solomon Wellman, b. Dec. 21,
1830. *California.*

(m.) Lucinda-Jane, dau. of Solomon Wellman, b.
Jan. 26, 1833; m. Freeman Foster, 3d, of
Abington, and had Freeman, b. July 29, 1860.
Winona, Minnesota.

(2.) Hannah, dau. of Peter and Hannah (Capron) Wellman,
b. Jan. 20, 1783; m. Jesse George, of Wrentham,
Mass., April 25, 1805. He was b. Oct. 22, 1783; d.
Sept. 5, 1851. Their children were :—

(a.) Emily, dau. of Jesse George, b. Oct. 7, 1805 ;
m. Joseph Cowell, March 17, 1835, and had
Hiram-Augustus, b. Jan. 17, 1845.
Wrentham, Mass.

(b.) Elizabeth, dau. of Jesse George, b. Nov. 1, 1807 ;
d. July 8, 1834 ; m. Joseph Cowell, (who m.
her sister Emily, 1835,) Nov. 17, 1830. Their
children were Sarah-Elizabeth, b. Nov. 10,
1831, d. March 17, 1847; and Joseph-George,
b. June 30, 1834, who resides in San Francisco, Cal.

(c.) Hannah-Maria, dau. of Jesse George, b. April 8,
1811 ; d. Jan. 31, 1816.

(d.) John-Capron, son of Jesse George, b. Nov. 4,
1813 ; m. 1st, Sarah-Dingley Trouant, April
30, 1840 ; she was b. May 13, 1814, d. April
18, 1851 ; m. 2d, Kate-Richardson, dau. of
Samuel and Cynthia (Whiting) Jardon, April
27, 1865. She was b. in Philadelphia, March
22, 1832. Children by 1st wife, Sarah-Augusta, b. in Marshfield, Jan. 31, 1841 ; Josephine, b. Nov. 13, 1845, and William-Jardon,
b. in Chelsea, Mass., Jan. 30, 1866.
Boston, Mass.

(e.) Lyman-Augustus, son of Jesse George, b.
March 17, 1817 ; m. Harriet-Green, dau. of
Drury Fairbanks of Boston, June 27, 1850,
and had Mary-Bemis, b. June 30, 1854 ; Lyman Fairbanks, b. Oct. 5, 1856 ; Drury-Fair-
banks, b. Nov. 25, 1858. *Boston, Mass.*

(f.) Hiram, son of Jesse George, b. June 23, 1820 ;
m. Elizabeth Wheelock, March 19, 1845, and
had Clara-Elizabeth, b. Aug. 24, 1846 ; Frank-
Augustus, b. Aug. 11, 1848 ; Ella-Frances,
b. Nov. 15, 1849 ; Jesse, b. Nov. 24, 1851;
Harvey, b. June 21, 1855. *Wrentham, Mass.*

(g.) William-Emerson, son of Jesse George, b.
Aug. 11, 1823. *Wrentham Centre, Mass.*

(h.) Catharine-Augusta, dau. of Jesse George, b.
July 20, 1826 ; d. Nov. 19, 1864 ; m. Lafay-

ette Bates, Wrentham, Nov. 27, 1862, and
had Katie-Josephine, b. Aug. 2, 1863, d.
July 28, 1864.

(3.) Deliverance, dau. of Peter and Hannah (Capron) Wellman, b. Feb. 25, 1785; m. Windsor Wheelock of
Mendon, and had

  (a.) Clara-Elizabeth, m. Hiram George. [See (f.)
above.]

  (b.) Charlotte, dau. of Deliverance Wheelock, m.
Marvel Morse, and had Waldo and Maria.
West Thompson, Ct.

  (c.) Nancy.

  (d.) Mary, m. Philip Taft, and had Philip, and perhaps others.

  (e.) Sylvia, m. Nelson Steere, and had Adelbert and
Sarah. *Burrillville, R. I.*

  (f.) Peter, son of Deliverance Wheelock, m. and
had Joseph and Mary. *Woonsocket, R. I.*

(4.) Christiana, dau. of Peter and Hannah (Capron) Wellman,
b. Feb. 26, 1788; d. 1809; m. Harvey George, and
had Mary, who died in infancy.

(5.) Isaac, son of Peter and Hannah (Capron) Wellman, b.
June 8, 1790; m. 1st, Lucinda Boyden; 2d, m. Nancy
Boyden, (sisters,) of Medfield, Mass., and had children; removed to the State of New York; residence
unknown.

2. Ebenezer, son of Isaac and Hannah (Wellman) Wellman, b.
Sept. 22, 1752; m. and had Isaac, Edwin and Sarah; removed
to Brookline, Vt.

3. Mary, dau. of Isaac and Hannah (Wellman) Wellman, b. May
12, 1756; unmarried; removed to Brookline, Vt.

4. Sarah, dau. of Isaac and Hannah (Wellman) Wellman, b. Sept.
19, 1758; unmarried; removed to Brookline, Vt.

13. 2. EBENEZER, son of Isaac and Mary (Slafter) Wellman, b. 1720 or
1721; d. Feb. 11, 1776, in the 56th year of his age; m. 1st, Sarah
Payson of Stoughton, May 28, 1747; m. 2d, Priscilla Day of Stoughton, March 26, 1761. Their children were as follows: 1, Joseph, b.
Dec. 28, 1747; 2, Sarah, b. March 27, 1749; 3, Samuel, b. March 13,
1751; 4, Benjamin, b. March 18, 1753; 5, Mary, b. June 9, 1755; 6,
Judith, b. Feb. 9, 1757; 7, Phebe, b. July 2, 1759; 8, Oliver, b. Oct.
18, 1761; 9, Lucy, b. Nov. 30, 1763; 10, Abigail, b. July 21, 1767;
11, Betty, b. March 24, 1769; 12, Ebenezer, b. May 4, 1772. Oliver
Wellman was in the Rhode Island service in 1777. See Hist. Norton,
p. 403. Joseph Wellman was in Capt. Israel Trow's Comp., 1780.

14. 3. TIMOTHY, son of Isaac and Mary (Slafter) Wellman, b. about 1724;
was in Capt. Isaac Hodge's Comp., in 1776, in Tiverton alarm; see
Hist. Norton, p. 399; in Capt. Silas Cobb's Comp., id. p. 403-4; m.
Rachel Newland of Norton, Aug. 4, 1755.

15. 4. HANNAH, dau. of Isaac and Mary (Slafter) Wellman, b. about 1727.

16. ANTHONY,[2][3] (*John*,[1]) b. perhaps about 1690; d. June 28,
1723; m. Mary, dau. of William and Mary (Burnet) Eaton of Lynn,
Mass., Dec. 12, 1712. She was b. March 23, 1694-5; d. July 20,
1780. Her father removed from Lynn to Tolland, Conn., as early as
1717, and was the first selectman of that town; his descendants are
still to be found in Tolland and Hartford, Ct. Anthony Slafter removed from Lynn to Tolland, probably about 1716. Lands were laid
out to him in 1720, and after his death lands were surveyed and laid
out to his widow. Mary (Eaton) Slafter married 2d, John Scripture
of Coventry, Dec. 30, 1728, by whom she had three children, Mary,

Anna and Daniel. The children of Anthony Slafter, and Mary, his
wife, were as follows :—   *Tolland, Ct.*

17. 1. MARY, b. June 25, 1714 ; m. Joseph Skinner, of Tolland, Jan. 28, 1734,
        who died Oct. 8, 1760 ; she m. 2d, Isaac Holmes, of Ashford, Ct., Oct.
        19, 1761. Her children were, by her 1st husband, viz. : 1, Joseph, b.
        Feb. 23, 1735 ; 2, Eleazer, b. July 28, 1737 ; 3, Mary, b. April 20,
        1739, d. at Stafford, March 15, 1758 ; 4, Dorcas, b. Oct. 21, 1743, d.
        Sept. 16, 1751 ; 5, Eleazer, b. June 7, 1746 ; 6, Lucy, b. June 28, 1750,
        d Feb. 16, 1751 ; 7, Jonathan, and 8, David, (twins) b. Oct. 3, 1753.
                                                             Tolland, Ct.
19. 2. ANNA, b. April 14, 1717 ; m. Simeon, son of John and Abigail (Utley)
        Scripture of Coventry, Ct., Sept. 19, 1738, and had 1, Simeon, b.
        June 19, 1739 ; 2, Ann, b. April 23, 1741 ; 3, Lydia, b. April 21, 1744 ;
        4, Jeremiah, b. Aug. 8, 1746 ; 5, Lois, b. Nov. 28, 1748 ; 6, Irene, b.
        Nov. 10, 1750, m. July 17, 1766, James Allen, and had Levina and
        Cynthia, and removed to Walpole, N. H. ; 7, Abigail, b. Nov. 21,
        1752, m. Nathaniel Ladd, deacon of Cong. Church in Woodstock,
        Ct., and had 1, Nancy, 2, Nathaniel, 3, Abigail, 4, Lavina, 5,
        Ephraim, 6, Berthena, 7, Mason, 8, Betsey, 9, Nancy ; 8, Tryphena,
        b. Feb. 3, 1757, m. Daniel Babcock, Nov. 16, 1775. [See Bond's
        Watertown, p. 971, and Weaver's Windham, p. 53.]   *Coventry, Ct.*
20. 3. DORCAS, b. Oct. 13, 1719 ; m. Ebenezer Heath of Willington, Ct.,
        Nov. 5, 1753. He was an original grantee of the town of Norwich,
        Vt. Their children were 1, Dorcas, b. Feb. 2, 1755 ; 2, Ebenezer, b.
        Sept 25, 1756 ; 3, William, b. Sept. 27, 1758 ; 4, Hannah, b. April
        17, 1762.   *Willington, Ct.*
21. 4. LYDIA, b. Dec. 20, 1722 ; when the estate of her uncle Benjamin was
        conveyed, by his heirs, in 1764, among the signers were "Daniel
        Smith of Windsor, and Lydia, his wife." No further record has been
        found.   *Windsor, Ct.*

22. ELIZABETH,[2][4] (*John,*[1]) b. perhaps about 1693 ; m. Thomas
Hutchinson of Lynn, Mass., May 2, 1711. He was probably son of
Hananiah and Martha Hutchinson, and if so, was b. April 6, 1690.
The records of Lynn are very imperfect, and the births of no children
are recorded. They appear, however, to have had at least one son,
and most likely other children. The intention of marriage between
Benjamin Hutchinson and Mary Breed of Lynn, was entered June 22,
1735. On the 24th of June, the father, Thomas Hutchinson, appeared
and forbade the bans; the reason is not assigned. They appear, however, to have been married, and the following births of Benjamin
Hutchinson's children are recorded, viz.: 1, Benjamin, b. Oct. 2, 1736 ;
2, Mary, b. May 22, 1739 ; 3, Amos, b. July 18, 1743.

23. SAMUEL,[2][5] (*John,*[1]) b. Aug., 1696, probably in Lynn, Mass. ;
d. in Mansfield, Ct., July 31, 1770 ; m. Dorothy, dau. of Robert and
Dorothy (Farrar) Fenton of Mansfield, Conn., Jan. 24, 1721-2. She
was born Sept. 4th, 1700 ; d. Sept. 29, 1783. [See Fenton Genealogy.] His first purchase of land in Conn. was, so far as I can ascertain,
in Tolland, July 4, 1720. In 1723, he appears to have disposed of his
lands in Tolland, amounting to 260 acres, and to have purchased others
in Mansfield, the same year, where he continued to reside the remainder
of his life. His first purchase in Mansfield was a sixty acre lot, of
Robert Fenton, his father-in-law, June 13, 1723, for the sum of £29,
lawful money of New England. Another purchase was of the Rev.

Eleazer Williams, bearing date of March 13, 1727, and "13th of the reign of our Sovreign, Lord George, King of Great Britain," &c., &c. Other small purchases were made, until his farm reached the dimensions of about a hundred and twelve acres. It was situated in the north part of the town, and occupied the south-west angle of what is now known as Mansfield Four Corners. Among the three hundred and eleven tax payers in Mansfield, in 1753, he was among the twenty-two who paid the largest taxes. He was one of the original proprietors of the town of Norwich, Vt., and was the first Treasurer of the Corporation, which office he held several years. He and his wife early became members of the Congregational church in Mansfield, and in its faith his family were carefully educated. His wife was born, probably, in Woburn, Mass., where her father resided several years before he removed to Conn. They were both interred in the ancient cemetery in North Mansfield, and the headstones, now in complete preservation, bear the following inscriptions :—

"Here lies ye body of Mr. Samuel Slafter. He departed this life July 31, A. D. 1770, in the 75th year of his age.

Death is a debt to nature due,
Which I have paid, and so must you."

"In memory of Mrs. Dorothy Slafter, wife of Mr. Samuel Slafter, who died Sept. 29, 1783, aged 83 years.

"Blessed are the dead which die in the Lord."

Their children, all born in Mansfield, were as follows :—
Mansfield, Ct.

24. 1. SON, b. Aug. 1, 1722 ; d. Aug. 3, 1722.
25. 2. DOROTHY, b. July 14, 1723 ; d. in infancy.
26. 3. ABIGAIL,[63| b. Jan. 3, 1724-5 ; d. Nov., 1811 ; m. Joseph Johnson of Mansfield, Ct.
27. 4. ELIZABETH, b July 20, 1727 ; d. June 6, 1775.
28. 5. DOROTHY,|70] b. Nov. 12, 1729 ; d. April 24, 1811 ; m. Hezekiah Johnson of Norwich, Vt.
29. 6. EUNICE,[77] b. Jan. 23, 1731-2 ; d. March 20, 1825 ; m. Thomas Jewett of Norwich, Conn., afterwards of Pownal and Bennington, Vermont.
30. 7. SAMUEL,[88] b. Sept. 21, 1734 ; d. Jan., 1825 ; m. Anna Freeman of Mansfield, Ct.
31. 8. LOIS, b. Aug. 31, 1736 ; d. Sept. 1, 1813, in Norwich, Vt.; unmarried.
32. 9. JOHN,[96] b. May ;26, 1739 ; d. Oct. 8, 1819 ; m. 1st, Elizabeth Hovey ; 2d, Mrs. Priscilla (Hovey) Whittaker. *Norwich, Vt.*
33. 10. ANNE, b. May 28, 1742 ; d. Jan. 2d, 1816 ; unm. *Mansfield, Ct.*
34. 11. ELEAZER,|105] b. March 19, 1744-5 ; d. June 29, 1828 ; m. 1st, Mary Freeman ; 2d, Eunice Fenton. *Mansfield, Ct.*
35. 12. MARY, b. March 30, 1747 ; d. Aug. 8, 1818 ; unm. *Norwich, Vt.*

36. JOSEPH,[9][6] (*John,*[1]) b. perhaps 1698 ; d. probably about 1787 ; m. Esther ——— ; no record of his marriage has been found. The earliest notice we find of him is in 1718, when he was one of twenty-five who subscribed a document sent to the General Assembly of Connecticut, denominated a "petition of us the subscribers, inhabitants of

Tolland, relative to Coventry lands." [See Waldo's Hist. of Tolland, p. 18.] After this he resided sometime in Wilmington, and was a signer of a petition for the incorporation of that town, May 14, 1724. The birth of his daughter Esther was recorded in Willington. On the 24th of Sept., 1724, he purchased a tract of land in Mansfield, Ct., adjoining Samuel Slafter's land on the west, and lying on both sides of the great Cedar Swamp Brook. He sold this property about two years afterward, and removed to Killingly, Ct., where he purchased land in 1735, adjoining land already in his possession. Additions were made in 1742 and 1745. He sold an estate in Tolland in 1764; the deed bears the signature of "Joseph Slafter." At how early a period he came into possession of it, has not been ascertained. No date of his death has been found, but his heirs sign acquittance to title in his real estate, June 16, 1788, and he probably died about that time. His farm was in Killingly, near the line of Scituate, now Foster, R. I. A small burial ground near by, bears the family name, where he, and many of his descendants were, doubtless, buried, but no headstones of the early burials are inscribed.   *Killingly, Ct.*

37.   1. JOSEPH,[121] b. probably about 1721; d. Aug. 13; 1775; m. Hannah
            Covel.
38.   2. ESTHER, b. July 26, 1723; m. Timothy Grover, and was a widow living
            in South Hoosuck, Mass., (?) at the settlement of her father's estate,
            June 16, 1788.
39.   3. JOHN,[138] b. in Mansfield, Ct., 1725-6; d. Feb. 8, 1821; m. Elizabeth
            Handell.
40.   4. ABRAHAM,[129] b. Oct. 7, 1731; d. anterior to 1795, at which date his
            estate was settled. He m. Hannah Adams.

41. SARAH,[2][7] (*John,*[1]) b. perhaps about 1700; m. Samuel Paulk of Tolland, Ct., May 5, 1720, He was probably son of Samuel Paulk of Concord, Mass., who m. Sarah Brabrok, Feb. 13, 1690. [See Middlesex marriages and births, in Library of N. Eng. Hist. Gen. Soc., Boston, Vol. I., p. 200.] The tradition is that Sarah Paulk, the mother of Samuel, with her children, came to Tolland, Ct., her husband having previously died. Her death is recorded in Tolland, as having occurred May 3, 1744, and she is denominated a widow. Samuel Paulk was one of the fifty-one grantees in the deed of the first proprietors of Tolland. He had an allotment of land made to him, May 18, 1719, also Jan. 12, 1721. In 1722, he conveyed a tract of land, situated near Skungamug River, to John Paulk, who is supposed to have been his brother. In 1764, he was an inhabitant of Windsor, Ct., at which time he and his wife Sarah united with the heirs of her brother Benjamin, in conveying his estate. The following were their children:—
                                                        Tolland, Ct.

42.   1. INFANT, b. Feb. 6, 1721; d. same day.
43.   2. MARY, b. Feb. 8, 1723-4.
44.   3. RUTH, b. Feb. 28, 1727-8.
45.   4. NOAH, b. Oct. 31, 1729; m. Rachel, and had (a.) Noah; (b.) Rachel; (c.)
            Isaiah; (d.) Cephas; (e.) Alpheus.
46.   5. SARAH, b. Jan. 31, 1732.
47.   6. ABIGAIL, b. Nov. 15, 1734.
48.   7. SAMUEL, b. April 3, 1737.
49.   8. JOHN, b. Sept. 17, 1739; d. April 23, 1742.
50.   9. JOHN, b. Nov. 30, 1742.

51. Moses,[2][8] (*John*,[1]) b. perhaps about 1702 ; d. about 1778 ; m.
Jemima, dau. of John and Abigail (Utley) Scripture of Coventry, May
13, 1743. She was born March 10, 1724. Moses Slafter signed a
petition to the General Court of Connecticut, asking for the incorporation of the town of Willington, in May, 1727. He was chosen collector
in Willington, Dec. 18, 1740. His father, John Slafter, deeded to him,
Feb. 9, 1739, half of his farm, "with mansion house and barn." With
him, it is probable, the father continued to reside until he removed from
the homestead. He exchanged farms, Jan. 28, 1748, with his brother
Benjamin, whose estate was contiguous. The next year, March 6, 1749,
he sold the farm obtained from his brother Benjamin, and purchased
an estate in Windsor, now Ellington, in "the equivalent," bounded
"north on the Stafford lower line, and south on a highway." Here
he continued to reside till his death, which occurred not far from 1778.
His children were probably born in Willington, except Moses, who appears to have been born after he removed to Ellington.

Ellington, Conn.

52. 1. JEMIMA, b. Sept. 20, 1744; m. John Aldrich, and died young and without children.
53. 2. STEPHEN, b. May 30, 1746 ; d. Jan 18, 1817, in Springfield. Mass. ; unm.
54. 3. ANTHONY,[149] b. probably about 1742 ; d. April, 1826 ; m. Experience Frost.
55. 4. MOSES,[158] b. 1752-3 ; d. May 7, 1839 ; m. Mary Johnson.

56. ABIGAIL,[2][9] (*John*,[1]) b. perhaps about 1704; d. March 15,
1738; m. George, son of Munning Sawin of Watertown, Mass. He
was b. April 2, 1697 ; d. Nov. 7, 1783. He was elected constable by
the town of Willington, Ct., at the first meeting after its incorporation
in 1727. In 1728, he was appointed "to go for a minister." The first
religious services after the organization of the town, were, by vote, appointed to be at his house, and continued to be held there for some time.
He was, for many years, a deacon of the Congregational church in
Willington. After the death of his wife, Abigail Slafter, he married
Anna Farrar, Oct. 23, 1738, and had Lucia, b. Sept. 28, 1740 ; Abijah,
b. April 23, 1742 ; Mary, b. Jan. 17, 1743-4 ; Phebe, b. July 2, 1746 ;
d. June 21, 1748; Isaac, b. Sept. 23, 1748. The following are his
children by his first wife :—

Willington, Conn.

57. 1. GEORGE, b. Feb. 12, 1728; d. March 7, 1826. He resided in Willington, Conn., till 1795, when he removed to the State of N. Y., residing in
Cambridge and Salem, and finally in Danube, where he died, in his 99th
year. He m. Ruth Crocker, April 29, 1776, and had
(a.) Benjamin, b. April 9, 1777, who became a Baptist preacher in 1804,
preached in Willington and Ashford, Ct., Danube and Middle-
field, N. Y. ; in the latter place was settled 25 years; afterward
in Aurora, N. Y., and finally in La Porte, Ind. He m. Sabra
Holman, and had 1, Louisa, who m. Stephen Mix, no children ;
2, Edna ; 3, Hervey ; 4, George, who m. Louisa M. Brayton, and
had Albert B. and Maria S., who reside in Watertown, Wis. ;
5, Albert, a lawyer, resides in Buffalo, N. Y., m. Mary-Ann
Darling, and had Louisa, Julia, Mary, Lucy, Benjamin, James-
Albert ; 6, Morilla, La Porte, Ind. ; 7, Judson, La Porte, Ind. ;
8, Julia, m. Levi Jones, and had Charles, La Porte, Ind. ; 9,
Sabra.
(b.) Elizabeth, b. March 1, 1779 ; d. 1822 ; m. Stephen Curtis, and had

1, Benjamin ; 2, David ; 3, Stephen ; 4, Leroy ; 5, Alanson ; 6, Whiting ; 7, Sylvester ; 8, George ; 9, Eliza. *Springfield, N. Y.*

(c.) George, b. June 6, 1781 ; Baptist minister ; officiated in Stark, Danube, Warren, Ripley, &c., N. Y. ; m. Elizabeth Tennant in 1812, and had 1, Olive-Eliza, b. 1815, m. Platt Webster, 1836, and had Helen, 1837, and Emma-M., 1845, Ripley, N. Y. ; 2, Edna-Maria, 1818, m. Eli Shore, she died 1845, no children ; 3, William-Orlando, 1827, m. Jane-E. Bacon, 1860, and had Franklin-B. *Ripley, N. Y.*

(d.) Edna, b. Jan. 7, 1784 ; d. 1826 ; m. Stephen Curtis, her sister's widower, and had Solomon. *Springfield, N. Y.*

(e.) John, b. April 10, 1786 ; Baptist minister in Cortland and Otsego Cos., N. Y., and in Green Co., Wis.; m. Orrel Tennant, 1813, and had 1, Aurilla, b. 1814 ; 2, Ann-Eliza, 1816, m. Wm. N. Gott, and had Emerette-Augusta and Watson, Green Co., Wis. ; 3, Alvin-John, 1819 ; 4, Clarissa, 1821, m. Albert Tillinghast, no children ; 5, David-M., 1823 ; 6, Ethan-Philander, 1824, m. Lucina Tupper ; 7, Lucinda-Maria, 1827 ; 8, Lorenzo-David, 1829 ; 9, Mary-Jane, 1831 : 10, Maranda, and 11, Marinda, 1834 ; 12, Eleanor-Matilda, 1836 ; 13, Juliette, 1839 ; all reside in N. Y. and Wis.

(f.) Ethan, b. Dec. 15, 1789 ; m. 1st, Eleanor Annis, 1816, 2d, Sarah Osterman, 1832, and had 1, Ethan-Alexander, 1818, m. Lucina Remmington, 1840, and had George-Alpheus, Ripley, N. Y.; 2, Horace-C., 1821, m. Mary-Ann Osterman, 1845, and had Horace-Eugene, 1847, Ripley, N. Y. ; 3, Sarah-Eliza, 1823, m. Delos-G. Tennant, 1843, and had Catharine-E. and Moses-G., Ripley, N. Y. ; 4, John-Alonzo, 1824, m. Catharine-M. Cornish, 1848, and had Charles-Edgar, 1849, Ripley, N. Y. ; 5, Elizabeth-Mary, 1838. *Ripley, N. Y.*

58. 2. ABIGAIL, b. Jan. 28, 1731 ; d. young.

59. 3. MARY, b. Nov. 7, 1732 ; d. young.

60. 4. ESTHER, b. Aug. 20, 1734 ; d. April 29, 1764.

61. 5. ANNA, b. July 15, 1736 ; m. David, son of Edy Hatch of Tolland, and had, in Willington, Ct.,

(a.) George, b. Sept. 29, 1764 ; m. Avis Bicknell, May 20, 1790, and had Roena, b. May 22, 1792.

(b) Solomon, b. Nov. 5, 1766. *Providence, R. I.*

(c.) Lucy, b. Feb. 19, 1768 ; m. Erastus Root.

(d.) Jerusha.

(e.) Anna.

(f.) Sarah.

(g.) Hannah ; m. Eleazer Root of Willington, Ct.

62. BENJAMIN,[10] (*John,*[1]) b. perhaps about 1706 ; d. about 1760 ; m. Bethia, dau. of William and Mary (Burnet) Eaton of Tolland, Ct., Nov. 11, 1744. She was b. in Lynn, Mass., Nov. 3, 1708 ; d. about 1764. She was the youngest of her father's family, and was the only sister of the wife of Anthony Slafter. His name is found with that of his brothers, Joseph, in 1724, and Moses, in 1727, on the petitions for the charter of the town of Willington. To him his father conveyed half of his farm in Willington, in 1739. After the exchange of farms with his brother Moses, in 1748, he appears to have continued on the homestead till 1754, when he exchanged it for an estate in Tolland. His will was made Oct. 20, 1756. In this instrument he leaves his personal estate to his wife Bethia, and his real estate, also, so much of it, at least, as she should need for a comfortable subsistence ; and, at her death, the residue was to be divided equally among his *nine* brothers and sisters, and their heirs. In 1760, his estate was appraised, his

death having occurred, probably, a short time previously. The following articles in the invoice, indicate the simple habits, as well as the intelligence and religious tastes of a plain Connecticut farmer of that day. The list is as follows: " 2 Bibles; Books on Divinity; Powderhorn and Ammunition; Several pairs of leather britches; Warming pan; Pewter; Saddle, bridle and pillion; 2 Wheels for spinning, turning tools and lathe, et cetera." Most of these utensils would hardly be found, at the present day, in the house of a New England farmer. His wife appears to have survived him about four years. The farm was sold by his heirs, May 21, 1764. He left no children. *Tolland, Ct.*

63. ABIGAIL,[3][26] (*Samuel,*[2] *John,*[1]) b. Jan. 3, 1724-5; d. Nov., 1811; m. Joseph, son of William and Hannah Johnson of Mansfield, Ct., July 3, 1746. He was b. in Woburn, Mass., April 28, 1720; d. May 31, 1787. He was brother of Hezekiah Johnson, who m. Dorothy Slafter, and was descended through William,[4] William,[3] Major William,[2] from Capt. Edward Johnson,[1] the renowned author of the History of Massachusetts Bay, printed in London, 1654, commonly entitled, "Wonder-working Providence of Sion's Saviour, in New England." William Johnson sold his estate in Woburn, and removed to Mansfield, Ct., where he died, possessed of a considerable landed property. The children of Joseph and Abigail (Slafter) Johnson, born in Mansfield, were as follows:—

64.   1. ABIGAIL, b. Aug. 30, 1748; d. in Wrentham, Mass., of small-pox, about 1768; unm.
65.   2. RUTH, b. March 22, 1753; d. about 1801; unm.
66.   3. JOSEPH, b. May 2, 1754; d. about 1810; m. Mehitable Farley; no children.   *Mansfield, Ct.*
67.   4. HANNAH, b. July 7, 1755; d. Dec. 26, 1815; unm.
68.   5. WILLIAM, b. July 15, 1759; d Jan. 13, 1816; m. Mary, dau. of Archibald and Margaret (Watts) Knox of Ashford, Conn., April 6, 1787, and had
      (1.) William, b. Feb. 9, 1788; m. Roxa, dau. of Recompence Smith of Tolland, Ct.; resided in Mansfield, Ct., and had
          (a.) Orra-Caroline, b. Sept, 12, 1809; m. Willis Mattoon, April 6, 1834; he d. April 7, 1857. They had 1, Persis-Cassandra, b. Sept. 7, 1835; she m. Frederick-Augustus Baker, Feb. 16, 1866, and had Jessie, b. the 4th, and d. 16th July, 1867, and Harry-Clifton, b. Oct. 30, 1868. 2, Josephine-Henrietta, b. Oct. 18, 1838; she m. Rev. Henry-Lucius Whitehead, Jan. 1, 1861, and had Rolla-West, b. Sept. 17, 1862, and George-Willis, b. July 26, 1864. Mr. Whitehead, in war of rebellion, raised a Com. (of which he was 1st. Lieut.) of volunteer militia, 100 days' men, afterwards incorporated into U. S. service as Com. D., 133d Ohio National Guard, stationed at New Creek, W. Va., Bermuda Hundred, and at Fort Powhatan, on the James River; dis. Aug. 20, 1864; in service 110 days; res. Baltimore, Ohio. 3, Albert-Gilmore, b. Sept. 8, 1840; in war of rebellion he served 100 days in Com. D., 133d Ohio National Guard, raised by Mr. Whitehead, as above; m. Mary-Ann Snoddy, Oct. 3, 1866, and had Willis-Ray, b. Aug. 24, 1867. 4, Erving-Howard, b. Dec. 3, 1845. 5, Alice-Cary, b. March 29, 1848; d. Aug. 17, 1853. 6, Laura-Cowles, b. Aug. 1, 1850.

(b.) Olive-Cornelia, b. Oct. 12, 1810; m. Horace Fenton of
Willington, Ct., and removed to Huntington, Ohio.

(c.) William-Smith, b. Nov. 1, 1813; d. May 10, 1854; m.
Susan-Fellows Hunt; resided at Clintonville, Ohio;
no children.

(d.) Norman-Knox, b. Jan. 18, 1815; d. April 25, 1854; m.
Sophia Porter; no children; residence West Jefferson,
Ohio.

(e.) James-Porter, b. Sept. 10, 1816; m. Hannah Worthington, and had Mary-Lucretia and Cornelia.
Vinton, Iowa.

(f.) Henry-Clark, b. Feb. 5, 1818.

(g.) Charles-Palmer, b. Dec. 9, 1820; d. Sept. 16, 1863; m.
1st, Eliza Case, and 2d, Cynthia Webster.
West Jefferson, Ohio.

(h.) George-Brigham, b. July 11, 1822; m. Cornelia-Grant.
Hartford, Ct.

(i.) Daniel-Merrill, b. Nov. 6, 1824; d. 1846.

(j.) Mary-Elizabeth, b. Jan. 16, 1829; m. John-Stewart
Henderson, and had Mary-Emma and Estella-May.
Dublin, Ohio.

(k.) Princes-Lucretia, b. Nov. 6, 1831; d. 1839.

(2.) Orange, son of William and Mary (Knox) Johnson, b. Feb. 7,
1790; m. Achsa Maynard of Worthington, Ohio, and had
(a.) William, d. unm.
(b.) Mary, b. July, 1823; m. Charles-Francis Sessions.
Columbus, Ohio.

(3.) Chester, son of Wm. and Mary (Knox) Johnson, b. Feb. 4,
1792; d. Nov., 1852; m. Sophia Alison, and had
(a.) Clarissa-Louisa.
(b.) Chester-Knox.
(c.) Sarah-Elizabeth.   *Tiffin, Ohio.*

(4.) Olive, dau. of Wm. and Mary (Knox) Johnson, b. Feb. 23, 1794;
m. Dr. Alanson Norton of Berlin, and had
(a.) Alanson-Carlos-Ward.
(b.) Olive-Princis-Henrietta.
(c.) Devander.   *Big Island, Ohio.*

(5.) Crissa, dau. of Wm. and Mary (Knox) Johnson, b. July 16, 1796;
d. Feb. 8, 1846; m. 1st, Zebina Hanks, and had
(a.) Gardner, d. in infancy.
(b.) Mary-Louisa, who m. Dr. Park Beeman of Sidney,
Ohio. Mrs. Hanks m. 2d, Moses Maynard of Worthington, Ohio, and had
(c.) Devos-Woodward.
(d.) Helen-Gloriana, who m. William-Williams Metcalf of
Washington, D. C.

(6) Clarissa, dau. of Wm. and Mary (Knox) Johnson, b. Dec. 8,
1798; m. Roger, son of Zaccheus Waldo of Mansfield, Ct.,
and had
(a.) Mary-Emeline, b. Feb. 1, 1820; m. Dr. Samuel-Ketch-
um Page, Champaign, Illinois, and had 1, De Witt-
Waldo; 2, Alice-Josephine; 3, Samuel-Calvin-Her-
bert; 4, Victor-Norton.
(b.) Olive-Louisa, b. Oct. 20, 1821; d. Sept. 7, 1839.
(c.) Maria-Wealthy, b. Oct. 12, 1823; m. Calvin-Stebins
Mattoon.   *Washington, D. C.*
(d.) Henrietta, b. May 12, 1827; m. Alpheus Dawkins,
Port Royal, Ky., and had 1, Calvin-Mattoon; 2,
Mary-Bell.
(e.) Harriet, b. May 12, 1827; d. in infancy.
(f.) Norton-Alson, b. June 22, 1830; m. Sarah-Elizabeth
Harvey.   *Mansfield, Ct.*
(g.) Clarissa-Amelia, b. Nov. 29, 1836; d. April 19, 1838.

(h.) Clara-Louisa, b. Aug. 20, 1839 ; d. Sept. 18, 1855.
(7.) Lurancy, dau. of Wm. and Mary (Knox) Johnson, b. Jan. 17,
1803 ; d. Aug. 11, 1849 ; m. John-Palmer Brigham, and had
1, Mary-Lurancy-Palmer ; 2, Lurancy-Johnson. *Tolland, Ct.*
69. 6. JOSIAH, b. March 22, 1762 ; d. in infancy.

70. DOROTHY,[3][28] (*Samuel,*[2] *John,*[1]) b. Nov. 12, 1729 ; d. April
24, 1811 ; m. Hezekiah, son of William and Hannah Johnson of Mansfield, Ct., Jan. 25, 1749-50. He was born in Woburn, Mass., May 12,
1724 ; d. in Norwich, Vt., Dec. 22, 1806. He was brother of Joseph
Johnson, who m. Abigail Slafter, and descended from the renowned
Capt. Edward Johnson. [See No. 63.] He resided for some years in
Mansfield, where some of his children were born, but early removed to
Norwich, Vt., of which town he was an original proprietor, and one of
its earliest settlers. He was a selectman of Norwich in 1765, and for
the next twenty years was prominent in the public business of the town.
He held the office of town clerk, moderator, supervisor, treasurer, assessor, and was of the " Committee of Safety " in the Revolutionary
War. He had a sound judgment and benevolent disposition. He conveyed as a gift to the town, Sept. 22, 1804, about two acres of land on
the Connecticut River, and near the mouth of the Ompompanoosuc, for
a public burial ground ; in this cemetery slumber his own and the re-
mains of his family, together with those of many of the early settlers
of the town. He gave to Dartmouth College, in 1770, a tract of land
in Norwich, containing a hundred acres, to aid in the endowment of
that institution. *Norwich, Vt.*

71. 1. ESTHER, b. March 1, 1751; d. Sept. 26, 1761.
72. 2. HEZEKIAH, b. 1766 ; d. Oct. 24, 1784.
73. 3. DOROTHY, b. —, ——; d. Sept. 16, 1804 ; m. Jeremiah Hedges, Nov.
11, 1784, and resided in Norwich. They had 1, Susannah, b. March
4, 1786 ; 2, Lucinda, b. Dec. 13, 1787, m. Samuel Wright, Dec 27,
1810 ; (?) 3, Ethelda, b. 1790, d. Nov. 5, 1814 ; 4, Leanthy, b. July 23,
1798, m. Joseph Root, and had Lucinda—resided in Norwich, Vt.
74. 4. WILLIAM, b. Dec. 8, 1761 ; d. Dec. 22, 1761.
75. 5. EXPERIENCE, b. May 22, 1769 ; d. June 19, 1792.
76. 6. SAMUEL-SLAFTER, b. Oct. 4, 1771 ; m. 1st, Mary, dau. of David Goodrich of Norwich ; she d. April 12, 1805 ; m. 2d, Lydia, dau. of Capt.
Beeman of Strafford, Vt., and had by 1st wife, 1, Esther, b. June 10,
1793 ; 2, Mary, b. April 26, 1797, who m. Horace Cushman ; by 2d
wife, had 3, Experience, b. Feb. 17, 1806 ; 4, Dorothy, b. April 15,
1807, d. Feb. 11, 1808; 5, Samuel, b. Sept. 15, 1809 ; 6, Lydia, b.
Jan. 12, 1811 ; 7, Warren, b. July 30, 1812 ; 8, Hoyt ; 9, Ormand ;
10, Orpha, b. May 17, 1818 ; 11, Lucy, b. Oct. 18, 1822. Mr. Samuel-
Slafter Johnson resided in Norwich, Vt., where his children were born,
but late in life removed to the State of N. Y.

77. EUNICE,[3][29] (*Samuel,*[2] *John,*[1]) b. Jan. 23, 1731-2 ; d. March
20, 1825 ; m. Thomas, son of Eliezer Jewett of Norwich, Conn.,
—— —, 1758. He was b. Aug., 1736 ; d. May 29, 1812. He was
descended through Eliezer,[5] Eliezer,[4] Jeremiah,[3] and Joseph,[2] who
came to this country in 1638, and settled in Rowley, Mass., and who is
said to have been the son of Edward[1] Jewett of Lincolnshire, England.
He resided in Norwich, Conn., till 1769, when he removed to Pownal,
Vt., and late in life removed to Bennington, Vt. He was very active in
public affairs in the early history of that State. He was a member of

its first Legislature, which met at Windsor, March 12, 1778, and of its adjourned meeting at Bennington, June 4, of the same year, and was placed upon several important committees. He was likewise returned by Pownal, in 1783, 1787, 1788, 1789, 1790, 1791. He was a member of the Convention held at Bennington, Jan. 10, 1791, which ratified the act of Congress admitting Vermont into union with the United States. He was also a member of the Convention of 1793. He was a Justice of the Peace, and was Judge for the shire of Bennington in 1778. He was a Lieut. in the Militia, and was in active service at the battle of Bennington. It is said that, in the midst of the fight, it was announced that the cartridges had given out, whereupon Lieut. Jewett seized a camp kettle, and filling it with powder, dealt it out in a dipper, with his own hand, to the soldiers. At the close of the action he found an unfortunate officer of the enemy wounded and expiring on the field; he gently placed him against a tree, but his cap, belt and sword, no longer useful to him, he bore away. He afterwards learned that the unfortunate officer was the Hessian, Col. Baum, the commander of the expedition. Mrs. Eunice (Slafter) Jewett was a "woman of superior intellect, a Christian in word and deed, of fine manners and of remarkable strength of character." Thus writes her grand-daughter. Their children were as follows:—

78. 1. THOMAS-FREDERICK, b. Nov. 18, 1759; d. Nov. 15, 1820; m. Elsie, dau. of Thomas Green of Bennington, Vt., 1786, and had
    (1.) Eunice, b. May 27, 1787.
    (2.) Levi, b. July 18, 1789; d. June 11, 1863; m. Laura, dau. of Oliver Perry of Woodford, Vt., Jan., 1815; and had
        (a.) Adaline.
        (b.) Finette.
        (c.) Thomas.
        (d.) Sarah.
        (e.) Samuel.
        (f.) Perry.   *Bennington, Vt.*
    (3.) Tryphosa, b. July 3, 1791; m. Loring, son of William Brewster of Weybridge, Vt., Oct., 1818; and had
        (a.) Lucina.
        (b.) Elsie.
        (c.) William.
        (d.) Sarah.
        (e.) Eveline.
        (f.) Lavinia.   *Weybridge, Vt.*
    (4.) Lydia, b. Sept. 24, 1793; d. Sept., 1864; m. Job, son of Thomas Green of Broadalbin, N. Y., Nov., 1823; and had
        (a.) Elvira.
        (b.) Paulina.   *Broadalbin, N. Y.*
    (5.) Laura, b. July 25, 1796; m. Barrel, son of Willard Green of Bennington, Vt., Oct. 26, 1814; and had
        (a.) Cecilia.
        (b.) Sylvester.
        (c.) Polly.
        (d.) Laura.
        (e.) Edwin.   *Bennington, Vt.*
79. 2. SAMUEL, son of Thomas and Eunice (Slafter) Jewett, b. June 5, 1761; d. Oct. 20, 1830; m. Lucy, dau. of Amasa Hungerford of Pownal, Vt., Feb. 23, 1789. She was b. July 3, 1773; d. Jan 24, 1838. He was returned to the Legislature of Vermont, by Weybridge, eighteen

Eng^d by J. Halpin

Jno. Godfrey Saxe

years, and declined any further service ; was the first town clerk of Weybridge, which office he held twenty-six years ; he was a Justice of the
Peace twenty-two years. Their children, all born at Weybridge, were
as follows :—
 (1.) Elizabeth, b. Jan. 8, 1790 ; m. Peter, son of John Saxe, (who
        immigrated from Saxony, Germany, 1733,) of Highgate, Vt.,
        May 17, 1813. He was b. Dec. 15, 1779 ; d. May 27, 1839, in
        Cambria, N. Y. He was returned to the Legislature of Ver-
        mont, by Highgate, 1806 and 1807 ; was town clerk, post-
        master and Justice of the Peace ; was Judge for the County of
        Franklin, Vt., in 1818. Their children, all born in Highgate,
        Vt., were as follows :—
          (a.) Charles-Jewett, b. March 25, 1814 ; d. in Troy, N. Y.,
                Oct. 1, 1867 ; he represented this city in the Legisla-
                ture of 1860 and 1861 ; m. Susan-Maria Baker, Feb.
                22, 1844 ; and had 1, Amelia-Elizabeth, b. Dec.,
                1844 ; d. in infancy. 2, Charles-Hammond, b. Dec.,
                1846 ; d. Oct. 20, 1847. He m. 2d, Ellen Griggs of
                Brookline, Mass., Feb. 22, 1853, and had 3, Charles-
                Griggs, b. Feb. 21, 1855. 4, William-Henry, b. May 3,
                1857. 5, Thomas-Edward, b. July 3, 1860. 6, James-
                Arthur ; 7, John-Alfred, (gemini,) b. Nov. 28, 1863.
                8, Mary-Ellen, b. Dec. 2, 1865.   Troy, N. Y.
          (b.) John-Godfrey, b. June 2, 1816 ; grad. Middlebury Col.,
                in class of 1839 ; received degree of LL. D. from
                same, 1866 ; was admitted to the bar at St. Albans,
                1843 ; State's attorney in Vermont, 1852 ; candidate
                for Governor in that State in 1859 and 1860 ; was five
                years editor and proprietor of the " Burlington Senti-
                nel ; " is a large contributor to American periodical
                literature, and well known as a distinguished humor-
                ous and satirical poet ; his poems have passed through
                one English and thirty-four American editions ; last
                ed. Fields, Osgood & Co., Boston, pp. 465 ; he m.
                Sophia-Newell, dau. of the Hon. Calvin Sollace of
                Bridport, Vt., Sept. 9, 1841, and had 1, John-Theo-
                dore, b. April 22, 1843. 2, George-Brown, b. Feb. 1,
                1846 ; d. Nov. 18, 1847. 3, Charles-Gordon, b. June
                7, 1848. 4, Sarah-Elizabeth, b. Feb. 10, 1850. 5,
                Harriet-Sollace, b. Aug. 14, 1853. 6, Laura-Sophia,
                b. Nov. 13, 1856.   Albany, N. Y.
          (c.) Peter, b. July 27, 1819 ; he was postmaster of Yates,
                N. Y., 8 years. He raised the 62d Reg. New York
                National Guards, of which he was commissioned Col.
                1851, and continued in command five years, when he
                removed from the district ; he m. Sept. 4, 1839, Sa-
                rah-Keith Drury of Highgate, Vt., and had 1, Rollin-
                Peter, b. Aug. 22, 1840. 2, Minerva-Drury, b. July
                4, 1842 ; d. Nov. 7, 1851. 3, Homer-Polk, b. June 5,
                1844. 4, Howard-Martin, b. April 1, 1847 ; d. Nov.
                25, 1863.   Troy, N. Y.
          (d.) James, b. Nov. 9, 1823 ; m. Sarah-Storrs, dau. of the late
                Judge Calvin Sollace of Bridport, Vt., and had, all
                born in St. Albans, 1, Lillie-Sophia, b. Sept. 18, 1852 ;
                2, James-Franklin, b. Sept. 2, 1854 ; 3, William-Hen-
                ry, b. March 31, 1856 ; 4, Ellen-Sollace, b. Feb. 19,
                1858, d. Feb. 1, 1862 ; 5, Fanny-Maria, b. May 6,
                1860 ; 6, Mary-Sollace, b. Feb. 23, 1865.
                                                         St. Albans, Vt.
 (2.) Thomas, b. Jan. 13, 1792 ; m. 1st, Sarah, dau. of William Brews-
        ter of Weybridge, Vt., May 23, 1817 ; she d. Nov. 9, 1818 ; he
        m. 2d, Naomi, dau. of Joel Barber of Bridport, Vt., June 13,
        1819, who was b. Oct. 20, 1794 ; she d. March 29, 1866 ;
        children b. in Weybridge, Vt.   Yates, N. Y.

2

(a.) Samuel-Franklin, b. Jan. 19, 1823 ; d. at Yates, N. Y.,
Oct. 28, 1851.

(b.) Lucy-Abigail, b. July 19, 1824 ; m. April, 1852, Rice-
Montreville Harrington, and had 1, Harriet-Mary, b.
Nov. 16, 1855 ; 2, Thomas-Jewett, b. June 14, 1858 ;
3, Cora-Adel, b. May 8, 1865 ; 4, Carrie-Ethel, b.
Dec. 29, 1867.   *Independence, Iowa.*

(c.) Sarah-Ann, b. April 5, 1829.

(d.) Mary-Roxcina, b. Aug. 26, 1831 ; m. Sept. 6, 1849,
Isaac-Morris Colt, attorney-at law, and had 1, Emma-
Sarah, b. Sept. 26, 1850 ; 2, Thomas-Jewett, b. Sept.
23, 1852, d. Dec. 7, 1855 ; 3, Jessie-Naomi, b. March
23, 1856.   *Yates, N. Y.*

(3.) Samuel, b. Dec. 14, 1794 ; d. Nov. 9, 1850, at San Francisco,
Cal. ; m. Feb., 1827, Marie Xexcrera (anglice Herrera), dau.
of Ignatio and Peuta de la Puente, b. in the City of Mexico,
1805, a near relative of the late Gov. Herrera ; he went to Sa-
vannah, Ga., in 1818, and to Mexico in 1822. In our late war
with Mexico he accompanied our forces to the Capital, giving
essential information as to the roads and topography of the
country. He removed to California, where he died at the date
above mentioned. His widow died there also, April 20, 1867.
Their children, born in Mexico, were :

(a.) Samuel-Ambrose, b. Dec. 7, 1828.

(b.) Adelaide-Brown, b. March 21, 1830.

(c.) Lucy, b. Dec. 9, 1833.

(d.) Carmen, b. April 5, 1835 ; m. March 11, 1859, Angel
Queredo.

(e.) Charles-Joseph, b. Jan. 24, 1838.

(f.) Thomas-M., b. Jan. 10, 1840.   *San Francisco, Cal.*

(g.) George-O., b. March 22, 1842.

(h.) Henry, b. Aug. 17, 1844.

(4.) Philo, b. Nov. 24, 1805 ; he was returned by Weybridge, Vt , to
the Legislature, in 1842, 1843, 1849, and was a selectman of
the same town twelve years ; m. Eliza Landon, April 30, 1829.
Their children, all born in Weybridge, Vt., were :

(a.) Elizabeth, b. Jan. 15, 1831, who m. Oliver-Perry Sco-
vell, May 1, 1856, Lewiston, N. Y., and had 1, Oliver-
Perry, b. Jan. 3, 1859 ; 2, Elizabeth-Eddy, b. Oct. 12,
1861 ; 3, Philo-Jewett, b. May 17, 1865.

(b.) Harriet, b. Nov. 10, 1832 ; m. Silas-Wright Elmer, and
had 1, Crucy-Eliza, b. Jan. 12, 1851 ; 2, Edward, b.
March 27, 1853 ; 3, Howard, b. April 23, 1855 ; 4,
Chester-Philo, b. Feb. 20, 1857 ; 5, Esther-Huldah, b.
July 12, 1859 ; 6, Horace, b. Aug. 5, 1861 ; 7, Harriet, b. Jan. 18, 1864 ; 8, Annie-Belle, b. June 10, 1866 ;
9, Mary, b. May 26, 1868.   *Addison, Vt.*

(c.) Samuel, b. July 13, 1835, Weybridge, Vt. ; m. Sarah-
Ann Foote, Sept. 8, 1858, and had 1, Sylvester-Foote,
b. Jan. 12, 1860, d. Dec. 15, 1868 ; 2, Philo, b. Nov.
3, 1862 ; 3, Abby-Ellen, b. June 8, 1865.
                                    Independence, Mo.

(d.) Edson-Bushnell, b. June 11, 1837 ; resides at Bridport,
Vt. ; m. Mary Ellen Gillett, March 7, 1859, and had
1, Eliza-Sophronia, b. July 26, 1861 ; 2, Lucy-Hun-
gerford, b. Jan. 10, 1868.

(e.) Lucy-Ann, b. Sept. 22, 1840 ; m. Byron-Washington
Crane of Bridport, Vt., Nov. 2, 1868.

(f.) Emma-Caroline, b. Oct. 29, 1843 ; m. Solomon-Jewett,
her cousin, Aug. 16, 1868.

(g.) Silas-Wright, b. Nov. 2, 1847.

(h.) Catharine-Charlotte, b. Feb. 13, 1851.

(i.) Orpha-Landon, b. July 3, 1852.

(5.) Solomon-Wright, b. May 22, 1808 ; was returned by Weybridge

to the Legislature of Vermont, in 1838 and 1839 ; has been
much engaged in the culture and importation of sheep. [See
Swift's Hist. of Addison Co., p. 102.] Has been a frequent
contributor to the Agricultural press ; was Commissioner from
Vermont to the " World's Fair " at London, in 1851 ; has introduced into California, where he now resides, excellent stock,
both sheep and cattle, to the great advantage of that State.
He m. 1st, Fidelia Bell, Jan. 5, 1831; she d. May 20, 1838.
Children :—

    (a.) Thomas, b. Oct. 14, 1831 ; d. in infancy.
    (b.) Louisa-Maria, b. Jan. 19, 1833.
    (c.) Solomon, b. March 13, 1835 ; m. Emma-Caroline, dau.
       of Philo Jewett of Weybridge, Vt., Aug. 16, 1868.
    (d.) Philo-Dennis, b. July 31, 1837. [These two sons are
       in California, Jewett's Ranch, Kern Co., engaged in
       "wool growing," having flocks varying from 10,000 to
       14,000.] Solomon W. Jewett m. 2d, Mary-Catharine,
       dau. of Othniel and Susan (Nash) Jewett, his second
       cousin, Sept. 26, 1838, and had
    (e.) Mary, b. March 6, 1840, who m. Rev. A. Kendrick, St.
       Louis, Mo.
    (f.) Susan-Nash, b. Aug. 9, 1841.
    (g.) Charles-Elam, b. April 27, 1843, who, in War of Rebel-
       lion, enlisted in Com. F, 2d Wisconsin Volunteers,
       April 24, 1861 ; was in battle at Bull Run, July 21,
       1861, received a slight wound ; Second Bull Run,
       Aug. 28, 1862, again wounded ; South Mountain,
       Sept, 14 ; Antietam, Sept. 17 ; Fredericksburg, Dec.
       13, 14, 15, 1862; crossing the Rappahannock, below
       Fredericksburg, April 29, 1863; Chancellorsville,
       May 3, 1863 ; Gettysburg, July 1, 1863, received a
       severe wound, requiring ten months to recover ; was
       commissioned 1st Lieut. of Com. F, 39th Wis. Vol.,
       May 17, 1864, and, with the regiment, was discharged
       Sept. 22, 1864. Is now in the regular army, his com-
       mission as 2d Lieut., 10th U. S. Infantry, bearing date
       Feb. 23, 1866.
    (h.) Martha-Caroline, b. May 5, 1845, who m. Wm.-Phelps
       Nash, Nov. 1, 1866.
    (i.) Fidelia, b. Oct. 3, 1851.
    (j.) Kate-Wright, b. July 27, 1858.
(6.) Charles, b. June 13, 1810 ; grad. Middlebury College, class of
    1834 ; received degree of A. M. at same college ; began the
    practice of law in Niles, Mich., 1836 ; has been prosecuting at-
    torney for his county eight years, County Judge four years,
    Circuit Court Commissioner four years, Judge of Probate four
    years, and a Justice of the Peace ; m. Catharine-Charlotte Sco-
    vell, Jan. 11, 1836 ; resides at Niles, Mich. Children, born in
    Niles, Mich. :—

    (a.) Edwin-Scovell, b. April 29, 1839, who was commissioned
       1st. Lieut. Com. G, 102d U. S. Colored Troops, alias
       1st Michigan Colored Regiment, Oct. 1, 1863 ; com-
       missioned Captain, July 16, 1864 ; was made acting
       Assistant Inspector-General for the Department of
       the South, which office he held till mustered out with
       his regiment, Oct. 30, 1865. He was in battle at
       James Island, S. C. ; at Baldwin, Fla. ; was aid to
       Gen. Potter at Pocotaligo, De Vaux Neck and Honey
       Hill, S. C. He m. Amelia-Virginia Cox, and had
       Charles-Cox, b. Sept. 18, 1863, and Thomas, b. Aug.
       20, 1866.
    (b.) Edward-Saxe, b. July 21, 1842, who m. Sarah-Louise
       Kirch of Conneautville, Pa., Oct. 24, 1866.
    (c.) Ada-Anna, b. March 29, 1847.

(d.) Charles, b. April 1, 1849 ; d. Sept. 7, 1850.
(e.) Charles, b. July 21, 1854.

80. 3. COMFORT, dau. of Thomas and Eunice (Slafter) Jewett, b. Sept. 13, 1763 ; d. in Pownal, Vt., April 12, 1831 ; m. Ephraim, son of Seth Mann of Braintree, Mass., and had

(1.) Eunice, b. July 25, 1782 ; d. Sept. 20, 1860 ; m. Joseph Parker, April 13, 1802. He was b. Nov. 27, 1779 ; d. March 10, 1855. They had

(a.) Hiram, b. June 25, 1803 ; m. Nancy Mason, and resides at Cazenovia, N. Y.
(b.) Tryphosa, b. Oct. 3, 1804 ; m. Lyman Thompson.
                                                    Greenwich, Conn.
(c.) Abel-Joseph, b. Feb. 26, 1806 ; m. Catharine Michael.
(d.) Eunice-Jane, b. June 24, 1808 ; m. Dea. Joseph Myers of Pownal, June 10th, 1827, and had 1, Ruth-Harriet ; 2, Ellen-Victoria ; 3, Eunice-Jane ; 4, Caroline-Eliza ; 5, Joseph Parker,   *Pownal, Vt.*
(e.) Maria-Delia, b. March 15, 1810 ; m. Simeon Myers.
                                                    Pownal, Vt.
(f.) Thomas-Mann, b. June 18, 1812; d. in London, C. W., May, 1866 ; unmarried.
(g.) Caroline-Eliza, b. Aug. 28, 1815 ; m. William-Robert Bates.   *Pownal, Vt.*
(h.) Harriet-Angeline, b. April 1, 1818 ; m. Wanton Hall.
                                                    Pownal, Vt.
(i.) Charlotte-Adeline, b. April 1, 1818, (gemini) ; d. Sept. 18, 1819.
(j.) Joseph, b. June 13, 1820 ; d. Aug. 18, 1823.
(k.) Sarah-Mooar, b. Aug. 26, 1826 ; m. Azel Barkus.
                                                Cazenovia, N. Y.

(2.) Polly, b. Feb. 28, 1784; m. Solomon Bennett, March 4, 1810, and had

(a.) Mary, b. June 16, 1811 ; d. June 25, 1811.
(b.) Jane, b. May 25, 1812 ; m. Daniel Cole, Nov. 18, 1832.
(c.) Oliver-Hazard-Perry, b. March 20, 1814 ; was a member of Williams College about three years ; removed to Tennessee.
(d.) Mary A., b. Feb. 9, 1816 ; d. April 1, 1840.
(e.) Betsey, b. July 1, d. July 4, 1817.
(f.) Solomon, b. June 11, 1818 ; d. Aug. 9, 1819.
(g.) Eliza, b. April 13, 1820.
(h.) Charlotte, b. Sept. 8, 1821 ; d. —.

(3.) Tryphosa, b. Aug. 23, 1789 ; d. June 1, 1863. Her son, Homer-Ephraim Mann, was b. Dec. 14, 1809. She was m. to Dr. Cranmer Bannister, about Jan. 1, 1814, and had

(a.) Juliette-Corrinne, b. Oct. 27, 1814.   *Pownal, Vt.*
(b.) Ruth-Phillip, b. July 26, 1816 ; m. Lewis Lincoln, March 10, 1840, and had Fidelia and Celestia-Tryphosa, who. m. Alonzo Raynor.   *Carbondale, Ill.*
(c.) Tryphosa, b. July 5, 1818 ; d. Nov. 22, 1839 ; m. Orrin Bates, and had Orrin-Cranmer, who died an undergraduate of Williams College.
(d.) Cranmer, b. May 20, 1820; m. in Milton, Mass., Catharine McDermett, and had James-Cranmer. He resides at Santa Cruz, Cal.
(e.) Joseph-Addison, b. March 27, 1822.   *Pownal, Vt.*
(f.) Eunice, b. July 25, 1827 ; d. June 4, 1862.

(4.) Thomas-Jewett, b. ——. He was in the war of 1812 ; m. Betsey Wideman, and had Malinda, Ephraim-Jacob, Thomas, Tryphosa, Elizabeth, Sophia, Eunice, Josiah, Almon, Andrew-Jackson, Joseph.   *Breakabeen, Schoharie Co., N. Y.*

81. 4. EUNICE, dau. of Thomas and Eunice (Slafter) Jewett, b. Aug. 13, 1764 ; d. Sept. 14, 1851 ; m. Solomon, son of Charles and Ruth (Boltwood) Wright of Pownal, Vt., Nov. 19, 1782. He was b. at Fort Hoosic,

near North Adams, Mass., Dec. 28, 1763; d. in Pownal, March 24, 1837. He was representative of Pownal, in the Legislature, in 1796, 1803, 1804, 1815, 1816, 1817, 1821 and 1823; was Judge of the County Court in 1798, 1799, and Chief Judge in 1814, and was also Judge of the Probate Court. He was gifted with a sound judgment and fine natural abilities. He often appeared as an advocate before referees and auditors, and in Justices' Courts, displaying great skill both in management and argument, and sometimes rising to a surpassing eloquence. [See Vermont Hist. Mag., Vol. 1, p. 219.] *Pownal, Vt.*

(1.) Charles, son of the above, b. Aug. 8, 1783; d. Feb. 15, 1819; grad. at Williams College in class of 1803; admitted to the bar in 1807, and was a lawyer of great promise, and at the time of his death, had the largest practice of any lawyer in the county, and stood high in the profession for ability and integrity; m. Eunice, dau. of Moses and Ruth (Dewey) Robinson of Bennington, Vt. He resided in Bennington. After his death his widow married the Rev. John Whiton. His children were:

   (a.) Jane, b. Nov. 3, 1809; m. Rev. Dexter, son of Merrick Hitchcock of Greenfield, Mass., June 13, 1827. He d. in Granville, N. Y., May 1, 1864.

   (b.) Catharine-Janette, b. March 14, 1812; d. Oct. 20, 1813.

   (c.) Thomas, b. Oct. 11, 1814; grad. Williams College in class of 1835; studied divinity at Princeton and Andover; graduated in 1839; was pastor of Pres. church in Wolcott, N. Y, from Oct., 1839, to 1856; m. 1st, Mary-Ann, dau. of Zimri Belden of Guilford, N. Y., Jan. 5, 1842. She was b. Nov. 29, 1820; d. June 21, 1845; m. 2d, Ruth, dau. of Chauncy Smith of Butler, N. Y., Jan. 7, 1847. She was b. May 5, 1815. The Rev. Thomas Wright resides at Feltonville, Mich. Children: 1, Eunice-Whiton, b. Nov. 20, 1842, who m. Dr. Watling of Ypsilanti, Mich.; 2, Mary-Priscilla, b. Nov. 29, 1847; 3, Charles, b. Nov. 26, 1849; 4, Anna-Janette, b. Aug. 17, 1851; 5, Chauncy-Smith, b. June 7, 1853; 6, George-Nutting, b. Nov. 10, 1855; 7, Florence-Belden, b. May 11, 1860.

   (d.) Moses-Robinson, b. April 7, 1818; d. June 6, 1855; unmarried; was in the practice of law at Ithaca, N. Y.

(2.) Thomas-Jewett, son of Solomon and Eunice (Jewett) Wright, b. April 7, 1785; d. April 20, 1813; was an undergraduate of Williams College, of class of 1810; admitted to the bar in 1812; practised law at Bennington, Vt.; unmarried.

(3.) Solomon, son of Solomon and Eunice (Jewett) Wright, b. Jan. 27, 1787; d. Nov. 13, 1865; m. Eleanor Seeley of Williamstown, Mass., and had

   (a.) Mary-Bowdish, b. Oct. 30, 1812; m. Roderick-Beebe Newman, M. D., of New York, and had 1, Delia-Mary-Eleanor; 2, Solomon-Wright; 3, Malvina; 4, Roderick-Henry; 5, Marion.

   (b.) Sarah-Eleanor, b. June 8, 1815; m. Alanson Lincoln, and had Diana-Albina, who m. Augustus-Hubbel Potter.
                                         Pownal, Vt.

   (c.) Sophia-Janette, b. 1818; m. Levi Lincoln, and had 1, Marietta; 2, Melissa-Janette; 3, Eleanor-Wright; 4, Levi-Alanson. *Pownal, Vt.*

   (d.) Eunice-Albina, b. July 29, 1820; m. David-William Gardner, and had Elizabeth-Ann. *Pownal, Vt.*

(4.) Pliny, son of Solomon and Eunice (Jewett) Wright, b. March 19, 1789; d April 8, 1864; m. Finette-Wadsworth of Pittstown, N. Y., and resided at Pownal, Vt. He represented Pownal in the Legislature, in 1856. Their children are:—

   (a.) Charles, b. Oct. 27, 1819; d. Oct. 30, 1848; m. Martha Bradley, and had Martha-Frances, b. June 25, 1840, m. Wm.-H. Frear of Troy, N. Y.

(b.) Joseph-Wadsworth, b. Jan. 8, 1825. He has held various
town offices, is a Justice of the Peace, and was returned
to the Legislature, by Pownal, in 1867.

(c.) Adelaide-Loraine, b. April 27, 1831.

(d.) Solomon, b. Sept. 9, 1837 ; grad. Williams College, class
of 1859; m. Mary Brimmer, and had 1, Harriet; 2, Solomon ; 3, Son.   *Pownal, Vt.*

(e.) Pliny, b. June 27, 1844 ; m. Ellen-Theresa Baker, and had
Charles-Wadsworth, b. Aug. 2, 1864.   *Pownal, Vt.*

(5.) Eunice, dau. of Solomon and Eunice (Jewett) Wright, b. Aug. 4,
1791 ; m. 1st, William Lovett of Pownal, 1810 ; he d. Dec. 27,
1811 ; m. 2d, David Gardner, Nov. 14, 1814 ; he was b. May 18,
1785 ; d. July 31, 1867 ; Pownal, Vt. Their children were :—

(a.) Albina, b. June 22, 1816 ; d. Jan. 17, 1818.

(b.) Armenius, b July 4, 1818 ; d. July 5, 1818.

(c.) Abraham-Brookins, b. Sept. 2, 1819 ; graduated at Union
College in class of 1842 ; attorney-at-law ; representative
in Legislature, from Bennington, 1862-3-4 ; Speaker of
the House the latter year; was elected Lieut. Governor
of Vermont in 1865 and 1866 ; m. 1st, Mary-Jennette
Swift ; m. 2d, Cynthia-E. Brown, and had 1, Anna-Au-
gusta ; 2, Isaac-Tichenor ; 3, Estella-Louise ; 4, Mary-
Jennette ; 5, Arthur-Brown.   *Bennington, Vt.*

(d.) Solomon-Wright, b. Jan. 11, 1822 ; representative in Legislature from Pownal, in 1865 ; m. Abigail-M. Carpenter,
and had 1, Lyman-Carpenter ; 2, Hannah-A. ; 3, George-
Card ; 4, David-Solomon ; 5, Frederic-W. *Pownal, Vt.*

(e.) Samuel-Jewett, b. Nov. 19, 1824 ; member of Legislature
of Vermont in 1855 ; m. Janette-L. Merchant, and had 1,
Abraham-Brookins; 2, Marcus-Merchant ; 3, John-Winne.
                                            Pownal, Vt.

(f.) Augusta-Elvira, b. Oct. 10, 1827 ; d. May 20, 1853 ; m.
Joseph-Ira Carpenter, and had Joseph-David. *Pownal, Vt.*

(g.) Lodieska-Sarah-Russell, b. Dec. 13, 1833. *Pownal, Vt.*

(6.) Ruth, dau. of Solomon and Eunice (Jewett) Wright, b. Feb. 20,
1794.   *Pownal, Vt.*

(7.) Lephy, dau. of Solomon and Eunice (Jewett) Wright, b. Oct. 20,
1796 ; d. Nov. 26, 1840.   *Pownal, Vt.*

(8.) Sophia, dau. of Solomon and Eunice (Jewett) Wright, b. Nov.
15, 1798 ; m. Ezra-Bowma Hoxie of Pownal, Vt., and had

(a.) Timothy-Wright, b. Dec. 1, 1818 ; m. Mary-Elizabeth
Palmer, and had 1, Mary-Alice, b. July 9, 1847, who m.
Dec. 1, 1868, Wilson-M. Fay ; 2, Mendell-Wright, b.
Nov. 1, 1849, d. Aug. 20, 1865 ; 3, Emily, b. May 21,
1852, d. Aug. 4, 1853 ; 4, Henry-Dexter, b. Feb. 15,
1855 ; 5, Helen-Sophia, b. July 9, 1857 ; 6, Walter-Pal-
mer, b. May 23, 1860.   *Boston, Mass.*

(b.) Abigail-Tobey, b. Nov. 12, 1821 ; m. April 7, 1847, Spencer-
Chandler Gurney, b. Sept. 14, 1823, and had Clarinda-Isa-
bella, b. in Goshen, Ms., Feb. 9, 1848. *S. Weymouth, Ms.*

(c.) Elvira-Armenias, b. Nov. 9, 1824 ; d. Oct., 1865.

(d.) Charles-Wright, b. in Rochester, N. Y., March 24, 1828 ;
m. Oct. 7, 1851, Harriet-Dorleske, dau. of John-Reeves
Jones, now of Serena, Ill. She was b. Dec. 18, 1833, in
Williamstown, Mass. Their children are, 1, Harriet-Ar-
dela, b. in Pownal, Vt., Aug. 1, 1852 ; 2, Charles-Wright,
b. in Pownal, July 26, 1854 ; 3, John-Henry, b. in Pownal, Oct. 23, 1855 ; 4, Flora-Sophia, b. in Serena, Ill.,
Feb. 6, 1858 ; 5, Eunice-Ada, b. in Serena, Jan. 14, 1860 ;
6, Mercy-Ethlen, b. in Serena, Oct. 20, 1861 ; 7, Ezra-
Boardman, b. in Serena, Aug. 26, 1863 ; 8, Alberta-Isa-
bel, b. in Serena, Aug. 24, 1865 ; 9, Isaac-Tichenor, b.
in Serena, April 12, 1867 ; 10, Lowell-Hiland, and 11,
Loretta-Ellen, (gemini,) b. in Wallace. Ill., Oct. 22,
1868.   *Ottawa, Ill.*

(e.) John-Henry, b. Oct. 19, 1830. *Dayton, O.*
(f.) Hiland-Hall, b. July 22, 1833.
(g.) Eunice-Jewett, b. July 8, 1836.
(h.) Josiah-Beecher, b. Dec. 5, 1842. *Boston.*

(9.) Isaac-Tichenor, son of Solomon and Eunice (Jewett) Wright, b. July 18, 1802; d. Oct. 12, 1862; m. Delia H. Adams; practiced law at Castleton, Vt.; was Judge of the County Court several terms; represented Castleton in Legislature in 1851, 1852, 1859 and 1860. *Castleton, Vt.*

(10.) Sarah-Russell, dau. of Solomon and Eunice (Jewett) Wright, b. Aug. 31, 1804. *Pownal, Vt.*

(11.) Elvira-Armenius, dau. of Solomon and Eunice (Jewett) Wright, b. July 19, 1808; m. Hinckley, son of John and Mercy (Weeks) Williams of Goshen, Mass., Jan 9, 1833. He was postmaster of Goshen more than twenty-five years. *Goshen, Mass.*
Their children are :—
(a.) Clarinda-Boardman, b. Aug. 31, 1836; m. Lucius-Manlius, son of Lucius and Fanny-Haskins (Shepard) Boltwood of Amherst, Mass.; he graduated at Amherst College in class of 1843; was Librarian of Amherst College from 1852 to 1863; postmaster at Amherst, from June, 1861, to July, 1865; was member of Massachusetts Senate in 1859-60; Assistant-Librarian in Library of Congress one year, 1867-8, and since then Librarian of Young Men's Institute, Hartford, Ct., and so continues, (1869). Their children are, 1, George-Shepard, b, March 2, 1861; 2, Lucius, b. July 27, 1862; 3, Charles-Wright, b. Dec. 6, 1867. *Hartford, Ct.*
(b.) Hinckley-Wright, b. Oct. 8, 1844; d., accidentally killed, Aug. 27, 1864; was an undergraduate of Amherst College in the class of 1866
(c.) Sarah-Russell, b. May 3, 1850.

82. 5. TRYPHENA, dau. of Thomas and Eunice (Slafter) Jewett, b. Dec. 15, 1767; d. Nov. 23, 1843; m. Abraham, son of Michael Dunning of Pownal, Vt., May 3, 1784. He was b. 1765; d. Aug. 22, 1842. Their children were as follows :— *Weybridge, Vt.*
(1.) Samuel, b. Nov. 18, 1786; d. Dec. 18, 1854; m. Abigail-Wallace, and had (a.) Tryphena. (b.) Franklin. (c.) Ocean. (d.) Lafayette (e.) Narcissa. (f.) Josephus. *Castleton, Vt.*
(2.) Fanny, dau. of Abraham and Tryphena (Jewett) Dunning, b. Dec. 6, 1790; m. Dr. Daniel, son of William Spaulding of Castleton, Vt., July 4, 1812. He was b. in Castleton, July 1, 1792; d. in Bethany, N. Y., Oct. 23, 1836. He was a practising physician. She m. 2d, Joseph Rix, Feb. 21, 1848; he d. May 13, 1861, aged 97 years. Her children, all by first husband, were :—
(a.) Mary-Evelyn, b. April 6, 1813; residence Almont, Mich.; m. Henry, son of Benjamin Way of Alexander, N. Y., Dec. 2, 1840, and had 1, Evelyn-Adelaide, b. Dec. 6, 1841; she m. William-Henry Lamb, March 29, 1868, Dryden, Mich.; 2, Olive-Frances, b. June 18, 1844, m. Watson Hallock, Dec. 30, 1864, Almont, Mich.; 3, Loan-Dennis, b. Aug. 3, 1846,—in war of rebellion served seven months in Com. B, 30th Michigan Volunteers, home guard, stationed at Port Huron, enlisted Nov. 11, 1864; 4, Frank-Spaulding, b. Sept 19, 1848; 5, Zoraida-Nancy, b. Oct. 27, 1850, d. Jan. 12, 1860; 6, Mary-Ellie, b. Nov. 16, 1852; 7, Virginia-Florence, b. March 11, 1855; 8, Rosa-Stevens, b. Aug. 30, 1857.
(b.) Benjamin-Franklin, b. Aug. 9, 1823; d. at Giard, Iowa, Dec. 22, 1862; he was sheriff of the county and U. S. "detective;" m. Melissa Marsh, and had 1, Helen, b. Dec. 7, 1841, d. ——, 1844; 2, Arabel, b. Nov. 1, 1843; 3, Walter-Delos; 4, Clayton; 5, Clarence; 6, Franklin; 7, Carl-Saxe, b. Feb., 1863.

(3.) Clarissa, dau. of Abraham and Tryphena (Jewett) Dunning, b. Aug.
19, 1792; m. Conrade Saxe of Highgate, Vt., Feb. 5, 1816, and
had

   (a.) Loan-Dunning, b. Nov. 26, 1816.
   (b.) Horace-Jacob, b. March 21, 1818.
   (c.) Edwin-Abram, b. Nov. 13, 1819.   *Sacramento, Cal.*
   (d.) Clarissa-Eliza, b. June 15, 1824; m. James-Parish Place,
      Jan. 1, 1845, and had 1, Lizzie-Landis, b. April 3, 1846;
      2, Harriet-Saxe, b. Sept. 22, 1848; 3, Sarah Giffin, b.
      Oct. 23, 1850; 4, William-Aubery, b. Nov. 3, 1852; 5,
      James-Conrade, b. Sept. 18, 1854; 6, Charles-Henry, b.
      Oct. 8, 1856   *Highgate, Vt.*
   (e.) Hannah, b. Jan. 16, 1827; m. Zephaniah-Keith Drury,
      Highgate, Vt., Oct. 31, 1849, and had 1, Horace-Saxe, b.
      Feb. 23, 1852; 2, Sarah-Clarissa, b. May 21, 1857; 3,
      Minerva-Saxe, b. Feb. 8, 1866.
   (f.) Harriet Tryphena, b. Feb. 19, 1830.   *Highgate, Vt.*
(4.) John, son of Abraham and Tryphena (Jewett) Dunning, b. April
19, 1794; d. Nov. 20, 1858; m. Mary Conden, and had
   (a) John. (b.) William. (c.) Jane. (d.) Tryphena. (e.)
      Benjamin. (f.) Clarissa, (g.) Charles. (h.) Samuel.
      (i.) Frederic. (j.) Lovina.   *Res. Lockport, N. Y.*
(5.) Loan, son of Abraham and Tryphena (Jewett) Dunning, b. Dec. 23,
1795; d. Dec. 30, 1865; m. Alzina Little, Dec. 31, 1821; resided
at Boylin's Grove, Iowa. They had
   (a.) Susan Frances, b. April 29, 1823; m. Silas Needham, Feb.
      20, 1841, and had 1, Edward-Elmore, b. Jan. 23, 1842,
      who m. Hannah Ensign, May 16, 1862, and had Orlin-
      Hubert and Gilbert,—he enlisted in war of rebellion in
      Comp. E, 32d Iowa Vol., Jan. 1, 1864, discharged April 30,
      1866,—he was in the battles of Fort De Russey, Pleasant
      Hill, Tupelo, Nashville and Mobile, was wounded seriously
      in the face and receives a pension; 2, Melville-Silas, b.
      May 1, 1846; 3, Leslie Benjamin, b. July 30, 1851; 4,
      Lillian-Tryphosa, b. Sept. 12, 1861. *Boylin's Grove, Iowa.*
   (b.) Maria-Aurora, b. Sept. 29, 1824; d. April 15, 1854.
   (c.) Alzina-Eliza, b. July 31, 1827; m. Franklin Brannick,
      Nov. 17, 1846, and had 1, Charles-Franklin, b. Dec. 3,
      1847, who m. Cynthia McKinney, Feb. 7, 1867, and had
      Ephraim-Francis; 2, Norissa-Alzina, b. July 28, 1851,
      d. Nov. 7, 1867, who m. Charles-E. Waist, Dec. 28, 1866,
      and had Norissa-Alice; 3, Francis-Albert, b. June 22,
      1853, d. Sept. 4, 1853; 4, Etta-Maria, b. March 19, 1857,
      d. Nov. 27, 1857; 5, Fremont-Grant, b. March 4, 1864,
      d. Nov. 15, 1865.   *Boylin's Grove, Iowa.*
   (d.) Andalucia-Lee, b. Oct. 13, 1831; d. Nov. 19, 1857; m.
      Thomas Bates, Nov. 23, 1852.
   (e.) Erasmus Darwin, b. April 18, 1835; d. Jan. 30, 1843.
   (f.) Arthur, b. Dec. 18, 1835; d. July 1, 1837.
   (g.) Oscar, b. Aug. 24, 1837; d. Nov. 15, 1839.
   (h.) Franklin, b. April 6, 1839; d. Aug. 12, 1845.
   (i.) Albert-George, b. Jan. 8, 1841; m. Martha-J. Niece, Feb.
      21, 1864, and had Charles-Raymond and Frank-Lewis.
                      Boylin's Grove, Iowa.
   (j.) Abram-Herbert, b. Nov. 24, 1842; m. Emma Hammond,
      Sept. 5, 1864, and had Abra and Harris-Lester. In war
      of rebellion he was in Comp. E, 32d Iowa Volunteers six
      months, and then transferred to the invalid corps on post
      duty at Davenport, Iowa, where he served two years and
      a half.   *Denver City, Colorado.*
   (k.) William-Henry, b. March 14, 1845; in war of rebellion
      was eighteen months in Comp. E, 32d Iowa Vol.; was
      in battle of Fort de Russey, Pleasant Hill, Tupelo, Nash-
      ville and Mobile.   *Res. Boylin's Grove, Iowa.*

(6.) Abraham, son of Abraham and Tryphena (Jewett) Dunning, b. June 1, 1798; d. Sept. 12, 1841; m. Louisa McEving, and had
    (a.) Frederic. (b.) Maria. (c.) Thomas. (d.) Abra-Eliza.
                                                  Weybridge, Vt.
(7.) Frederic, son of Abraham and Tryphena (Jewett) Dunning, b. March 6, 1800; d. Sept., 1859; m. Catharine Zibble, and had
    (a.) Martin-Van-Buren. (b.) Henry-Clay. (c.) Andrew-Jack-
        son.   *Saratoga, N. Y.*
(8.) Erastus-Darwin, son of Abraham and Tryphena (Jewett) Dunning, b. Nov. 7, 1803; d. June, 1847; m Mrs. Lucinda Gamble, and had Emeline-Tryphena; he resided at Vincennes, Ind.
(9.) Tryphena, dau. of Abraham and Tryphena (Jewett) Dunning, b. Nov. 24, 1806; d. March 10, 1847; m. Newell Dustin, and had
    (a.) Morris. (b.) Lewis. (c.) Frances-Tryphena.
                                      Res. Lemomwein, Wis.
(10.) Tryphosa, dau. of Abraham and Tryphena (Jewett) Dunning, b. Sept. 2, 1809.   *Middlebury, Vt.*

83. 6. TRYPHOSA, dau. of Thomas and Eunice (Slafter) Jewett, b. Dec. 15, 1767; d. Jan. 25, 1820; m. Silas, son of Simeon Hathaway of Bennington, Vt. He was b. 1763; d. Nov. 9, 1831; was Judge of County Court and Representative in the Legislature of Vermont. Their children, all b. in St. Albans, except the eldest, who was b. in Bennington, Vt., were as follows:—   *St. Albans, Vt.*
    (1.) Mary, b. March 6, 1788; m. John-Howes, son of Josiah Burton of Manchester, Vt., April 4, 1806. He was b. Nov. 22, 1780; d. May 13, 1852. In the war of 1812 was Lieut. and Adjutant. Their children, all b. in St. Albans, were as follows:—
                                        St. Albans, Vt.
        (a.) John-Augustin, b. Nov. 14, 1806.   *Florence, Ohio.*
        (b.) Albert-Sedley, b. Sept. 21, 1808; d. Dec. 5, 1842, at St. Albans Bay; m. Prudence-Hopson Beardsley, July 10, 1835, and had two sons, who d. in infancy, and Cornelia-Chloe, b. April 5, 1836, who m. Israel-Smith Bostwick, Sept. 20, 1853, St. Albans Bay, and had Arthur Burton, b. June 12, 1854, Milton-Swift, b. July 7, 1856, Cornelius-Albert, b. Dec. 12, 1862, all b. at St. Albans Bay.
        (c.) Oscar-Alexis, b. July 19, 1810.   *Burlington, Vt.*
        (d.) Edgar-Mandlebert, b. Dec. 9, 1812; d. Sept. 17, 1834; Cadet U. S. Mil. Acad. at West Point, of Class of 1834.
        (e.) Mary-Malvina, b. Dec. 22, 1816, m. Marcus-Wells Beardsley, Aug. 4, 1841, and had 1, Charles-Burton, b. April 4, 1851; 2, Frederic-Wells, b. July 2, 1858, all b. at
                                        St. Albans Vt.
        (f.) Carlos-Carlton, b. Jan. 13, 1820; m. Lemira-Sophia Barstow, October 10, 1849, and had, b. at St. Albans Bay, 1, Marcus-Carlos, b. Aug. 20, 1850; 2, Sidney-Barstow, b. Feb. 28, 1853; 3, Theodore-Jarvis, b. July 16, 1855.
                                      St. Albans Bay, Vt.
        (g.) Agnes-Tryphosa, b. Oct. 9, 1821; m. Alanson-Manzer Clark, Sept. 5, 1848, at St. Albans Bay, and had 1, John-Burton, b. June 17, 1850, d. Sept. 23, 1850; 2, Howes-Burton, b. May 13, 1852; 3, Mary-Burton, b. Aug. 16, 1853; 4, Kate-Manzer, b. Sept. 20, 1855; 5, Agnes-Maria, b. July 21, 1861, all b. at St. Albans Bay, Vt.   *St. Albans, Vt.*
        (h.) Josiah-Howes, b. Dec. 27, 1824; m. in Buffalo, N. Y., Lucia-Maria Clark, Aug. 11, 1852, and had 1, Clark-Candee, b. at St. Albans Bay, May 11, 1853; 2, Frank-Vincent, b. at Penn Yan, N. Y., May 29, 1855; 3, Robert-Lewis, b. No. 2, West 39th Street, New York, March 27, 1860.   *New York.*
        (i.) Theodore-Mortimer, b. June 12, 1830; m. Oct. 13, 1853, Harriet-Sophia Lewis, dau. of Chittenden Lewis of Cleve-

land, Ohio, b. Feb. 22, 1832, in Malone, N. Y., and had Charles-Chittenden, b. Aug. 15, 1854, d. Jan. 3, 1855.

New York.

(2.) Tryphosa, dau. of Silas and Tryphosa (Jewett) Hathaway, b. Feb. 20, 1790; d. Nov. 21, 1857; m. Col. Shadrach, son of Shadrach Hathaway of Bennington, Vt., July 10, 1811. He was b. Aug. 18, 1778; d. in Willoughby, Ohio, April 15, 1867. Their children were, all born at *Swanton, Vt.*

    (a.) Melvin-Smith, b. April 12, 1812; m. Persis Beardsley.

        Hudson, Ohio.

    (b.) Laura, b. Feb. 27, 1814; m. 1st, Ebenezer Sprague, Nov. 14, 1839; he d. Aug. 9, 1841; she m. 2d, Ebenezer Brown, Dec. 12, 1844. *Willoughby, Ohio.*

    (c.) Joanna, b. Oct. 1, 1816; m. Zopher Hayes.

        Willoughby, Ohio.

    (d.) Henry-Hiram, b. Jan. 28, 1822; m. Rachel Noax.

        Swanton, Vt.

    (e.) Harriet-Coit, b. Jan. 18, 1824; m. Bradford Lampman.

        Swanton, Vt.

    (f.) Frances, b. May 30, 1829; m. Asahel B. Peters, Dec. 8, 1861. *Willoughby, Ohio.*

(3.) Silas, son of Silas and Tryphosa (Jewett) Hathaway, b. Jan. 9, 1794; d. ———.

(4.) Sophia, dau. of Silas and Tryphosa (Jewett) Hathaway, b. April 30, 1797; m. Silas Pomroy Hannum, March 25, 1821. *L. Original, Canada West.* Their children were

    (a.) Esther-Pomroy, b. Sept, 20, 1822.

    (b.) John-Abner-Burton, b. Sept. 20, 1824; m. Sarah McLeod, March 22, 1848, and had 1, Thomas-Jewett, b. July 19, 1849; 2, Margaret-Sophia, b. June 20, 1851; 3, Esther-Pomroy, b. May 31, 1854; 4, Christy-Ann, b. April 13, 1857; 5, Elizabeth-Janette, b. April 7, 1861; 6, Hannah, b. Feb. 10, 1863. *Ottawa City, Canada.*

    (c.) Horace-Liscomb, b. June 29, 1826; d. Aug. 30, 1858; m. Mary Allen, Jan. 22, 1849, and had 1, Esther-Pomroy, b. Dec. 2, 1854, d. May 13, 1856; 2, Horace-Silas, b. May 2, 1857. *Geneva, Ohio.*

    (d.) James-Milville-Tisdale, b. Dec. 30, 1827; m. 1st, Eliza Burhan, Aug. 22, 1849, and had 1, Eliza-Ann, b. July 2, 1850; m. 2d, Elizabeth Nicholson, Oct. 16, 1856, and had 2, Sophia-Maria, b. Dec. 7, 1857; 3, Frank-Milville, b. Oct. 8, 1860; 4, Minnie-Elizabeth, b. Feb. 8, 1863, d. Aug. 7, 1863; 5, Maria-Elizabeth, b. Jan. 21, 1865.

        Ottawa City, Canada.

    (e.) Carlos-Colborne, b. July 3, 1830; d. Dec. 29, 1832.

    (f.) Thomas-Jewett, b. Nov. 25, 1834; d. May 14, 1838.

(5.) Hiram, son of Silas and Tryphosa (Jewett) Hathaway, b. May 24, 1798, m. Adaline Tullar, Jan. 25, 1831; she was b. Jan. 27, 1805, St. Albans, Vt. Their children, all b. at St. Andrews, Canada, were:—

    (a.) Tryphosa, b. March 16, 1834; d. July 14, 1840.

    (b.) Roderick-Random, b. Feb. 29,1836; m. Elizabeth-Frances Evarts, Dec. 19, 1866. *North Hero, Vt.*

    (c.) Bellesson-Lawrence, b. Aug. 3, 1837; d. Jan. 13, 1862; m. William-M. Hyde, Jan. 21, 1857. *North Hero, Vt.*

    (d.) Oscar-Burton, b. May 10, 1839; d. Nov. 14, 1854.

    (e.) Alice-Tryphosa, b. Oct. 24, 1840; m. Eli-Brooks Mitchell, March, 1859. *St. Albans, Vt.*

    (f.) Ellen-Maria, b. Feb. 1, 1843.

    (g.) Hiram-Henry, b. April 12, 1845.

    (h.) Florilla-Tullar, b. Feb. 14, 1847.

(6.) Helen, dau. of Silas and Tryphosa (Jewett) Hathaway, b. Aug. 22, 1803; m. Sidney-Chamberlin, son of Samuel Burton of

Malone, N. Y., Dec. 16, 1828. He was b. May 26, 1805 ; d.
Dec. 11, 1855, Cleveland, Ohio. Their children were :—
  (a.) Frances-Harriet, b. June 9, 1835 ; m. Richard-Seaton
    Blossom, March 14, 1857 ; he served in war of rebellion
    as orderly sergeant in Company C, 103d Ohio Volunteers,
    one year and a half, sickened and died, January 27,
    1863. She m. 2d, John-Harris Bowman, July 4, 1866,
    Cleveland, Ohio. Her children by 1st husband, are Sid-
    ney-Burton, and Carrie-Louisa.
  (b.) Edgar-Barney, b. Nov. 17, 1836 ; d. April 12, 1857.
  (c.) John-Howes, b. May 5, 1843 ; m. Josephine Doty, Sept.
    16, 1864, Cleveland, Ohio. In "war of rebellion" was
    in Comp. A, 7th Ohio Vols., enlisted May 30, 1861 ;
    wounded at Fort Republic, June 9, 1862, and discharged
    July 25, 1862 ; afterward as Sergeant-Major in 150th Ohio
    Vols., "hundred days' men ;" served full time.
  (d.) Sidney-Chamberlin, b. July 27, 1846.   *Cleveland, Ohio.*
(7.) Thomas-Jewett, son of Silas and Tryphosa (Jewett) Hathaway,
  b. June 10, 1805 ; d. April 26, 1840.   *St. Albans, Vt.*
(8.) Esther, dau. of Silas and Tryphosa (Jewett) Hathaway, b. June
  17, 1807 ; m. John Barney of Swanton, Vt., May 26, 1826. He
  was b. March 18, 1804. Their children, all b. in Swanton, were
  (a.) Byron-Burton, b. July 25, 1828. In the war of rebellion
    he was a sergeant in Comp. F, 7th Vermont Vols.,
    enlisted Nov. 30, 1861, discharged Aug. 3, 1864. He m.
    July 28, 1849, Malinda Marvin ; she was b. Aug. 18,
    1829, and d. Aug. 24, 1858. They had Clara-Marvin, b.
    June 25, 1852 ; Helen-Hathaway, b. Feb. 22, 1855 ; Wil-
    liam-Henry, b. Sept. 11, 1857   *Swanton, Vt.*
  (b.) Helen-Hathaway, b. July 23, 1830 ; d. Nov. 20, 1847.
  (c.) Amanda-Louisa, b. Nov. 26, 1832 ; d. Dec. 24, 1860.
  (d.) John-Hermon, b. July 19, 1840.
  (e.) Jane-Gray, b. June 11, 1845.   *Swanton, Vt.*
84. 7. ELEAZER, son of Thos. and Eunice (Slafter) Jewett, b. Sept. 22, 1769 ; d.
  May 20, 1815. He was County Surveyor, and held various town offices ;
  m. Mary, dau. of John Pratt of Swanton, Vt. She was b. 1775, d. Aug.
  4, 1842.   *St. Albans, Vt.*
  (1.) Eleazer, son of Eleazer and Mary (Pratt) Jewett, b. Dec. 18, 1796 ;
    d. Feb. 6, 1864 ; m. Dorothy, daughter of Jesse Abell of Swanton,
    Vt., March 20, 1826. She was b. Sept. 13, 1806. Their children
    were   *Swanton, Vt.*
    (a.) Jason-Philo, b. Oct. 13, 1827 ; m. Elizabeth-Maria Hol-
      dridge, July 4, 1850. They have an adopted daughter,
      named Mattie-Lasell. He was appointed postmaster
      of Swanton, May 11, 1861, and still holds the office.
            Swanton, Vt.
    (b.) Albert-Burton, b. March 20, 1829 ; m. Achsa Giffin,
      March 20, 1851, and had 1, Frances-Emily, b. June 12,
      1852 ; 2, George-Albert, b. April 25, 1860. He entered
      United States service in war of rebellion, as 1st Lieut.
      Co. A., 1st Regiment Vols. (3 months Reg.) April 27,
      1861, and was mustered out Aug. 15, 1861. He again
      entered the service as Col. of 10th Vermont Vols., Aug.
      26, 1862 ; resigned for physical disability, April 25, 1864.
      Was stationed mostly on the Upper Potomac ; was in the
      battle of Orange Grove, Nov. 27, 1863.   *Swanton, Vt.*
    (c.) Harriet-Maranda, b. Feb. 3, 1831, m. Sanford-Tullar Meigs,
      Oct. 27, 1852.   *St. Albans Bay, Vt.*
    (d.) Eleazer-Thomas, b. Feb. 22, 1833, m. Laura Janes, Feb.
      10, 1862.   *St. Albans Bay, Vt.*
    (e.) Mary-Amelia, b. Feb. 1, 1835 ; d. Jan. 2, 1860 ; m. Robert-
      Lyon Frazer.   *Lawrence, Kansas.*
    (f.) Jesse, b. May 4, 1837 ; d. March 15, 1866. In war of
      rebellion was mustered into U. S. service as 2nd Lieut.

of Comp. C., 5th Vermont Vols., Sept. 5, 1861 ; promoted 1st Lieut., July 9, 1862 ; promoted to Capt. of Comp. K, March 21, 1863 ; resigned for physical disability, May 29, 1863, of which he d. He was in the battles of Lee's Mills, Williamsburg, Golding Farm, Savage Station, White Oak Swamp, Crompton's Gap, Antietam, Fredericksburg, Mary's Heights and Salem Heights. *Swanton, Vt.*

(g.) Erastus, b. April 1, 1839 ; m. Fannie Brigham, Oct. 28, 1863, and had Jessie-Brigham-Jennette. He was mustered into U. S. service in war of rebellion, as 2nd Lieut., Comp. A., 9th Vermont, June 14, 1862, promoted to 1st Lieut., May 24, 1863, resigned Nov. 21, 1864. He was in the surrender of Harper's Ferry, was paroled, and did garrison duty at Chicago, at Yorktown, Portsmouth, Va., and Newbern, N. C. *St. Albans Bay, Vt.*

(h.) Charles-Saxe, b. July 22, 1841 ; m. Louisa Shelton, Jan. 1, 1867. *St. Albans, Vt.*

(i.) Sophia Pratt, b. Aug. 1, 1846.

(j.) Myron-Holly, b. March 13, 1848.

(2.) Mary, dau. of Eleazer and Mary (Pratt) Jewett, b. 1799 ; d. Jan. 2, 1833, unmarried.

(3.) Erastus, son of Eleazer and Mary (Pratt) Jewett, b. July 12, 1801 ; m. Cynthia-Serena, daughter of Israel Robinson of Swanton, Vt., March 25, 1845, and had

(a.) George-Robinson, b. Aug. 2, 1847 ; d. 1849.

(b.) Caroline-Susan, b. April 25, 1849.

(c.) Margaret-Amelia, b. Dec. 22, 1851.

(d.) Abbie-Serena, b. Dec. 14, 1853

(e.) Herman-Franklin, b. June 13, 1860.

(f.) John-Robinson, b. April 15, 1863 ; d. Oct. 13, 1863. *Swanton, Vt.*

(4.) Harriet, dau. of Eleazer and Mary (Pratt) Jewett, b. 1804 ; d. Feb. 3, 1832, unmarried.

85. 8. MARY, dau. of Thos. and Eunice (Slafter) Jewett, b. March 26, 1772 ; d. April 8, 1795 ; m. Col. Joseph Bowdish. He was b. Aug. 8, 1766 ; d. April 18, 1820 ; he was sheriff several years in Franklin County. After the death of his wife, Mary Jewett, he married Amanda Butler, Aug. 17, 1796, and had Mary-Clio, Napoleon-Bonaparte, Amanda-Hannah, Joseph, and Fanny. His children by his first wife, Mary Jewett, were as follows— *Fairfield, Vt.*

(1.) Columbus-Jewett, b. April 16, 1790 ; d. May 30, 1865 ; m. Ruth, dau. of Ephraim Smith of Bennington, Vt., and had

(a.) Pomroy, b. Aug. 30, 1815.

(b.) Lora, b. Oct. 1, 1817.

(c.) Sarah, b. Aug. 7, 1819.

(d.) Joseph, b. March 30, 1822.

(e.) Thomas-Jewett, b. Nov. 18, 1826.

(f.) Henry, b. Sept. 11, 1828. *Weybridge, Vt.*

(2.) Mary, b. Oct. 28, 1792 ; d. Sept. 12, 1800.

(3.) Eunice, b. March 20, 1795 ; d. Sept. 1, 1829.

86. 9. ERASTUS, son of Thomas and Eunice (Slafter) Jewett, b. Sept. 27, 1775 ; d. July 29, 1819. He was thirteen years clerk of the town of Pownal, Vt., and held other town offices ; m. Rachel, dau. of Benjamin Morgan of Pownal. She was b. April 25, 1779 ; d. Aug. 6, 1859. *Pownal, Vt.*

(1.) Mary, b. Jan. 2, 1800.

(2.) Eunice, b. May 21, 1803 ; m. Joseph, son of Seth Keyes of Pownal, Vt., Oct. 26, 1820, Bennington, Vt. Children :—

(a.) Laurette, b. Dec. 10, 1821 ; d. Sept. 11, 1855 ; m. William Rodgers, Oct. 26, 1839, and had 1, Mary-Elizabeth, b. May 27, 1843, Brooklyn, N. Y. ; 2, Eva-Laurette, b. Feb. 10, 1846, Bennington, Vt. ; 3, John-Colt, b. Aug. 1, 1848 ; m. Rhoda-Adaline Hawks, June 25, 1868. *Bennington, Vt.*

(b.) Erastus Jewett, b. April 7, 1825 ; m. Sarah-Jerusha Hall of Stony Creek, Ct., Nov. 14, 1860, and had 1, Henry-

Hall, b. April 11, 1863 ; 2, Rachel-Sonora, b. April 13, 1867. *Bennington, Vt.*
(c.) Anna, b. Sept. 29, 1827 ; m. 1st, John-Brewer Colt of Hinsdale, Mass., June 28, 1847 ; he d. Aug. 21, 1847 ; m. 2d, Henry-Burt Brewer of Wilbraham, Mass., July 4, 1849, and had Henry-Edwards, b. Dec. 12, 1851.
Wilbraham, Mass.
(d.) Sarina-Eveline, b. June 15, 1833 ; m. James-Henry Godfrey, Jan. 7, 1857 ; he d. Oct. 19, 1860. They had 1, James-Franklin, b. Oct. 17, 1857 ; 2, Laurette, b. Sept. 27, 1859.
(e.) Samuel-Brown, b. Aug. 15, 1835 ; m. Mary-Emilia Fuller of Williamstown, June 21, 1868.
(f.) William-McKendree, b. Jan. 15, 1835. He is a physician, graduate New York Medical College, and resides at Georgeville, Canada, P. Q.; m. Susan-Emeline Packard of Georgeville, May 15, 1864, and had Anna-Laurette, b. Jan. 16, 1867.
(g.) Rachel-Jewett, b. July 19, 1844 ; grad. of Wesleyan Academy, Wilbraham, Mass.
(3.) Lucy, b. July 9, 1805 ; m. Eber, son of Obadiah Dunham of Pownal, Vt., Feb., 1824 ; res. Fairfield, Iowa. Their children are :—
(a.) Mary. (b.) Cornelius-Hendrix (c.) Rachel. (d.) Lois-Abigail. (e.) Eunice-Tryphena. (f.) Erastus-Jewett.
(4.) Erastus-Thomas, b. Dec. 27, 1807 ; m. Clarissa, dau. of Eli Carpenter of Pownal, Vt., Oct. 28, 1835, and had
(a.) Charles-Erastus, b. Sept. 8, 1836.
(b.) Ruth-Marion, b. Sept. 5, 1840.
(c.) Julia-Cornelia, b. Dec. 12, 1842.
(d.) George-Thomas, b. Oct. 14, 1856. *Pownal, Vt.*
(5.) Rachel, b. May 4, 1810 ; d. July 4, 1851 ; m. Abraham-Gardner, son of Stephen Fowler of Brunswick, N. Y., July 4, 1835, and had
(a.) Isaac.
(b.) Ammon-Erastus.
(c.) Delilah-Winne, who m. Merritt Barber, an officer, U. S. A., stationed at Vicksburg, Miss.
(6.) Abigail, b. Aug. 3, 1814. *Pownal, Vt.*
87. 10. LOAN, son of Thomas and Eunice (Slafter) Jewett, b. May 4, 1778 ; d. Feb. 8, 1850 ; m. Elizabeth, dau. of Ephraim Smith of Bennington, Vt., Sept. 12, 1800. Their children were :—
(1.) Giles, b. Sept. 12, 1801 ; m. Jane-Ann Powers of Chester, N. Y., and widow of David Northup, Oct. 6, 1859, and had Frank, b. March 30, 1861. *Bennington, Vt.*
(2.) Elizabeth, b. April 13, 1803 ; m. Riley Harrington of Shaftsbury, Vt., March 27, 1836. *Bennington, Vt.*
(3.) Ruth, b. Sept. 20, 1807 ; m. Nairn, son of Benajah Burgess of Hoosick, N. Y., Nov. 16, 1828 ; he was b. Dec. 23, 1824, and had
(a.) Caroline, b. April 2, 1831, who m. Daniel-Webster Percey.
N. Hoosick, N. Y.
(b.) Eliza-Ann, b. May 11, 1833 ; d. April 25, 1865; m. Col. James-Hicks Walbridge, who was Capt. of Comp. A, 2d Vt. Vol., in war of rebellion ; served three years.
North Bennington, Vt.
(c.) Loan-Jewett, b. Sept. 18, 1835.
(d.) Nairn, b. Feb. 18, 1838.
(e) Giles-Jewett, b. Oct. 13, 1840; in war of rebellion was corporal in Comp. A, 2d Vt. Vol.; served three years ; was wounded in battle of the Wilderness.
(f) Edna-Augusta, b. Feb. 29, 1844. *Hoosick, N. Y.*
(4.) Stephen, b. April 8, 1812 ; m. Emeline, dau. of Jesse Downs of Pownal, Vt., and widow of Erastus Morgan, and had Loan, b. Oct. 30, 1850 ; d. Oct. 14, 1865. *Bennington, Vt.*

88. SAMUEL,[3][30] (*Samuel,*[2] *John,*[1]) b. Sept. 21, 1734 ; d. Jan., 1825 : m. Anna, dau. of Nathaniel and Martha (Dunham) Freeman of Mansfield, Ct., March 25, 1756. She d. April 9, 1812, aged 76. She was descended through Nathaniel,[5] Edmund,[4] Edmund,[3] Edmund,[2] from Edmund,[1] the emigrant ancestor, who settled in Sandwich, Mass. See Freeman's Cape Cod, Vol. II., p. 75. He was of the Standing Committee of the Congregational Church to which he belonged in North Mansfield. The title of Lieutenant is given to him in the public records. His children were all born in Mansfield, Ct.

89. 1. DOROTHY,[172] b. Nov. 29, 1756; d. Aug. 11, 1839; m. Nathan Lamb of Randolph, Vt.
90. 2. SAMUEL, b. Jan. 11, 1758. Is said to have been taken prisoner in the second year of the revolutionary war, and to have perished in a prison-ship in New York harbor.
91. 3 SARAH,[178] b. March 24, 1760; d. April 24, 1800 ; m. Amasa Reed of Mansfield, Ct.
92. 4. MARTHA,[187] b. Aug. 24, 1764; d. June 2, 1840 ; m. Nathaniel Nichols of Mansfield, Ct.
93. 5. ANNA,[195] b. March 11, 1766; d. Sept. 18, 1824; m. Samuel Thatcher of Norwich, Vt.
94. 6. ROXA,[199] b. Nov. 29, 1767 ; d. March 17, 1842; m. Daniel Dexter of Clayville, N. Y.
95. 7. NATHANIEL-FREEMAN,[206] b. June 11, 1771 ; m. Martha Topliff of Mansfield, Ct.

96. JOHN,[3][32] (*Samuel,*[2] *John,*[1]) b. May 26, 1739 ; m. 1st, Elizabeth,* dau. of Edmund and Mary (Farwell†) Hovey of Mansfield, Ct.,

---

*1. *Daniel* Hovey, the emigrant ancestor, was at Ipswich, Mass., in 1637. He went to Brookfield in 1668, but returned to Ipswich after about ten years, where he died April 24, 1692, at about 74 years of age. He married about 1642, Abigail, dau. of Robert Andrews, and sister of Thomas Andrews, the Ipswich schoolmaster. Their children were 1, Daniel ; 2, John ; 3, Thomas ; 4, *James* ; 5, Abigail ; 6, Joseph ; 7, Nathaniel.

2. *James,* b. about 1650 ; went to Brookfield with the Ipswich planters of 1668 ; was killed there in King Philip's war, Aug. 2, 1675. [See Coffin's Hist. Newbury, p. 389 ; Hist. Hadley, p. 139.] He married ——— ———, and had 1, Daniel ; 2, *James,* and 3, Priscilla.

3. *James,* b. probably about 1674 ; m Deborah ———, resided in Malden, Mass. ; sold land in Charlestown in 1715, and his homestead in Malden in 1716, and probably removed soon after to Mansfield, Ct. His children's births are recorded in Malden, where they were probably born. His wife died in Mansfield, May 15, 1749. Their children were:—1, James, b. Sept. 24, 1695 ; 2, Deborah, b. April 2, 1697 ; 3, *Edmund,* b. July 10, 1699 ; 4, John, b. Feb., 1700-1 ; 5, Mary, b. Dec., 1702 ; 6, Joseph, b. Feb. 6, 1704-5 ; 7, Thomas, b. Feb. 1, 1706-7 ; 8, Precilla, b. Dec. 11, 1708 ; 9, Daniel, b. Dec. 7, 1710 ; 10, Samuel, b. April 29, 1713, d. March 17, 1713-14 ; 11, Abigail, b. March 15, 1714-15.

4. *Edmund,* b. July 10, 1699 ; resided first in Mansfield, where his children were born, afterward in Norwich, Vt., where he died Jan. 21, 1788 ; m. 1st, Mary, dau. of Isaac Farwell, Feb 8, 1727-8, and had 1, Edmund ; 2, Isaac ; 3, Mary ; 4, Aaron ; 5, James ; 6, William ; 7, Elijah ; 8, *Elizabeth.* He m. 2d, Ann, dau. of Thomas Huntington, April 16, 1747, and had 9, Ann ; 10, William ; 11, Priscilla ; 12, Amos ; 13, Mary.

5. *Elizabeth,* b. June 22, 1744 ; m. John Slafter.

† 1. *Henry Farwell,* emigrant ancestor, Concord, Mass., made freeman March 14, 1639 ; m. Olive ———, removed to Chelmsford ; d. Aug. 1, 1670. His children were *Joseph,* Henry, John, Mary, Olive, Elizabeth, and perhaps James.

2. *Joseph,* b. Feb. 26, 1640-41 ; resided in Chelmsford, Mass. ; m. Hannah, dau.

March 26, 1767; she was b. June 22, 1744, d. Jan. 6, 1811; m. 2d, Priscilla, daughter of Edmund and Ann (Huntington) Hovey, and widow of ——— Whitaker, Oct. 5, 1815. She was a half-sister of his former wife, and was b. April 17, 1751; d. May 1, 1847, being a little past ninety-six years of age. John Slafter was born on his father's estate, which comprised the south-west angle of Mansfield Four Corners. His early education was such as could be afforded by the limited opportunities of a new and thinly settled country. At the age of sixteen, on the breaking out of what is now called the "Old French War," he enlisted as "drummer boy" in a company of Lyman's Regiment, raised and commanded by Capt. Israel Putnam, afterward a Major-General of the Revolutionary Army. He belonged to the party of Rangers under Putnam and the partisan Rogers, which did excellent service in the campaign undertaken for the reduction of Crown Point in 1755. Discharged with the Provincial troops in the autumn, he returned to Connecticut, but the next year enlisted again in the 1st Regiment, 6th Company, Connecticut Volunteers, commanded by Capt. Aaron Hitchcock. He continued in the service, enlisting from year to year, and was at last present at the capitulation of the French at Montreal, Sept. 8, 1760. Three English armies, moving from different points, and from great distances, had most fortunately been able to reach the city at the same time, agreeably to the plan of the commander. Arriving on the 6th of September, on the morning of the 7th, preparations were going forward for a regular investment of the city. The Marquis Vaudreuil, the Governor of Canada, finding himself encompassed by powerful armies, immediately offered a capitulation. While several communications were passing between the commanders, and doubt brooded over the issue, the most intense excitement pervaded the investing army. General Amherst was on the field, and the subject of this notice used to relate that he was so near to him, that he could observe the play of his features, as he gazed upon his watch, and awaited the moment after which, if his terms were not complied with, active operations would immediately commence. And when at length the signal was given that the French had surrendered, such a shout went up from the whole army, reiterated and prolonged, as made the welkin ring again. This was indeed one of the grandest events that had taken place on the Western Continent. An empire was on that day transferred from the French to the English nation.

The town of Norwich (now of Vermont) was chartered by Benning Wentworth, governor of New Hampshire, July 4, 1761. Samuel Slafter, the father of John, being an original proprietor, and being at the first meeting chosen Treasurer of the Corporation, took a deep interest in the settlement of the town. At his suggestion his son John made a journey through the forests of New Hampshire, in 1762, to

---

of Isaac Learned, and had Hannah, Joseph, Elizabeth, Henry, *Isaac*, Sarah, John and Oliver.

3. *Isaac*, b. probably about 1676 or after; m. Elizabeth ———; resided first at Medford, Mass., afterward in Willington and Mansfield, Ct.; he d. June 28, 1753. Their children, whose births are recorded in Medford, were : 1, Elizabeth ; 2, *Mary;* 3, John ; 4, William ; 5, Dorothy.

4. *Mary*, b. Nov. 19, 1709; m. Edmund Hovey, Feb. 8, 1727-8.

examine the territory, and report upon the advantages it might offer as a place of settlement. He found it pleasantly situated on the western banks of the Connecticut, with a good soil, but for the most part of an uneven, hilly surface. He reported it well watered, not only by the Connecticut, but by several small, sweet, clear streams, and by one more important one, called the Ompompanoosuc, an Indian name, signifying "the place of very white stones," whose waters emptied themselves into the Connecticut at the north-eastern part of the town. As he was inclined to engage in the settlement of the new town, the next year (June 7, 1763,) his father transferred to him, as a "token of his affection," all his rights "as proprietor of Norwich." He immediately set out for the new scene of his labors, in company with Mr. Jacob Fenton, his maternal uncle, and Mr. Ebenezer Smith, both of them original proprietors. They took with them a horse, and such implements as were indispensable in beginning a settlement. On arriving at their new possessions, they found themselves alone in an unbroken forest, where the echo of the woodman's axe had perhaps never yet been heard. He first commenced to fell the trees on the river lot, No. 17, which had been assigned to his father's right in the division of the proprietors, which was a mile and a quarter north from the southern boundary of the town. This lot, unlike most others, proved to be a high rocky elevation, reaching to the very shore of the river, difficult of cultivation, unsuitable as a homestead, and was immediately abandoned. A permanent settlement was fixed upon further up the river, opposite the farm of Mr. Timothy Smith, in Hanover, about four miles north of the present seat of Dartmouth College, and where the well-known "rope ferry" was for many years maintained. Here the first "clearing" was commenced, and the first human habitation in the town was constructed. The summer was passed in felling the forest, in burning the wood, and preparing the soil for future culture. In the autumn, when the cold season approached, and nothing more could be accomplished, he returned to his home in Connecticut, and this was repeated four summers, until he married and brought his young wife to his forest home.

An incident occurred during the first summer, worthy of record in itself, and important also as fixing the date of the first settlement of the town. On Wednesday, the 13th of July, Messrs. Slafter, Fenton and Smith left their homes to lend their services for a few days to some friends, who were making a settlement at Lebanon, six or eight miles below. Recent rains had swollen the Connecticut, and Mr. Fenton's horse, in crossing, was compelled to swim for a short distance in the deepest part of the river, which was near the shore to which he was approaching. The horse was carried down the current, and passed under the trunk of a tree, which had fallen into the river, the roots still clinging to the shore. In passing under the trunk of the tree, while leaning forward to avoid being carried from his seat, his horse, rising at the instant, forced him with great violence upon the pommel of the saddle, causing a serious injury of the chest. It was soon found necessary for Mr. Fenton to return, and Mr. Smith and a young Mr. Hovey, who had joined them, accompanied him to his camp in Norwich. They remained with him, doing what they could for him, but the injury proved so serious that he died on Friday of the same week. On Saturday the two young men proceeded down the river on the Vermont side, and endeavored by hallooing, and discharging their muskets, to attract the attention of their friends at Lebanon, and thus communicate with Mr. Slafter, but in this they were unsuccessful. However, on their regaining the camp before night fall, they found that Mr. Slafter had already returned, and been apprised of the sad and unexpected event of his uncle's death. On Sunday morning, assisted by his companions, he proceeded to make preparations for the burial. They peeled the bark from a bass-wood of suitable size, and, with reverent hands and sorrowing hearts, placed their companion within its pure white inner surface, closing it up and making it fast with thongs twisted from the tough bark of the young elm. On the bank of the Connecticut, near to its quiet waters, they placed him in the clean earth to await the resurrection day. A monument of stone was erected, and an inscription placed upon it by Mr. Slafter. This monument remained in its place about eighty years. At length it became broken and somewhat defaced. A portion of it is, however, still preserved, and is now in the possession of one of the grand-children of Mr. Slafter. The date of 1763 is so far preserved as to be clearly identified. The 1 is complete; the upper part of the 7 is gone, so is likewise the perpendicular part of the 6, but the 3 is as distinct as when first chiseled upon the stone. This monument still bears testimony to the year in which this death occurred. But if this evidence were wanting, there is yet another record made at the time, which establishes the date of this occurrence beyond the possibility of doubt. In the book of records of births and deaths in the town of Mansfield, Connecticut, is the following entry:

"Mr. Jacob Fenton* of Mansfield departed this life at Norwich in New Hampshire on ye 15th day of July, A. D., 1763."

The grantees or original proprietors held meetings from time to time, for some years after the incorporation of the town, to make such arrangements as the early settlement of the town, and division of their lands, required. These meetings were entirely distinct from the meetings of the "Town," and their doings were made the subject of a separate record, and are still preserved. At one of these meetings "of the Proprietors of the town of Norwich," held on the 17th day of September, 1770, the following vote was passed:—

"*Voted*, That Mr. John Slafter shall have the privilege of pitching seven rights in the lower meadow, on Ompompanoosuc River; and also Capt. Hezekiah Johnson to pitch six rights in the lower meadow on said river; and Mr. Peter Thatcher to pitch one right and one-half in said meadow; and Mr. Daniel Waterman to pitch four rights in said meadow, on said river; and Mr. James Huntington to pitch one right in said meadow, as a consideration for first coming into the town, and for the burden of first settling said town, being proprietors or purchased."

The inscription upon the monument of Jacob Fenton, the date of his death recorded in the town of Mansfield, and the vote of the proprie-

---

* Jacob Fenton was the son of Robert, the emigrant ancestor, and Dorothy (Farrar) Fenton of Mansfield, Ct. He was the father of Jacob Fenton, who m. Rebecca Cross, and grandfather of Roswell Fenton, who m. Deborah, daughter of Stephen Freeman of Mansfield, and great-grandfather of George-Washington Fenton, who m. Elsie Owen, and great-great-grandfather of the Hon. Reuben-Eaton Fenton, the present (1868) Governor of the State of New York.

tors, plainly prove, first, that the settlement of the town was commenced
in the summer of 1763 ; and, in the second place, that Mr. John Slafter
was regarded, by the proprietors, in 1770, as the first among the first
settlers of the town.   This subject has been here referred to somewhat
at length, as there seems to have been some confusion on this point introduced by the author of " Sketches of the Coos Country."

Mr. Ebenezer Smith does not appear to have continued in his efforts
at a settlement.   Mr. Fenton died the first year, while Mr. Slafter
passed the remainder of his life in Norwich, and must therefore be regarded as the pioneer in the settlement of the town.

He was married in Mansfield, Ct., in the spring of 1767, and a month
after departed with his young wife to his home in the New Hampshire
grants.   A journey from Connecticut, with a family, was at that
time an undertaking of no small moment.   The distance was a hundred
and fifty miles, mostly through the primitive forest, and the road, for
fifty miles at least, was scarcely passable, except for footmen and pack-
horses.   Several families from the same neighborhood were at this time
emigrating to the Coos Country, and they accordingly joined together, and
" made up a pleasant party."   It was decided to "navigate" the Connecticut rather than to encounter the difficulties of an " overland route."
Having provided themselves with log canoes, they embarked with their
" goods," probably at Windsor, Ct.   They left Mansfield on Thursday, the
23d of April, and arrived at their home in Norwich on the 10th of May.
Against the current of the river, which was very strong at that period
of the year, they were not able to make more than eight or nine miles
a day.   On Saturday evenings they moored their craft in some shel-
tered spot, where they remained till Monday morning, devoting the day
to rest, diversifying its consecrated hours by reading together the Holy
Scriptures, and singing sacred psalms.

In several places in the river the rapids, or falls, could not be passed,
and they were obliged to unship their goods and carry them and their
boats around, and reload before they could pursue their journey.   It
was, as we may well imagine, a joyful moment when they arrived at
their destination, and were at home in their rude habitations.   These
were the same as had served during the preceding summers.   But preparations had already been made, and before the frosts of winter approached, Mr. Slafter had built, on the banks of the Connecticut, a comfortable and substantial dwelling.   As mills for sawing timber had not
then been erected within practical distance, the material was fashioned
with the axe, without the use of plane or jointer.   Small trees, of not
more than a foot in diameter, were carefully hewed, halved together
at the intersections, and placed upon a foundation, and tier upon tier
added, until a suitable height had been attained for receiving the roof.
This was formed by placing upon proper rafters, bound together at frequent intervals by ribs or small beams, the thick, impervious bark of the
hemlock, or other trees.   In this way a covering was made, giving complete protection from the rains of summer and the snows of winter.
The floors were formed of plank, hewed and fitted with the axe alone.
Their furniture was of the rudest kind.   Their tables and chairs were
puncheons of basswood, a split log having its faces a little smoothed
with an axe, with legs inserted of suitable length.   Such was the rude
abode of the pioneer.   And who shall say, that of a winter's evening,

when under an intense cold, the expanding ice was heard opening its wide seams, reverberating far up and down the Connecticut, or when the north wind was raging furiously without, whistling its dreary dirge over the chimney top, and piling the falling snow in high banks about his cottage door, who shall say that as he sat, with his young wife, before his ample fireplace, with its blazing maple and hickory, that he did not enjoy as pure a happiness as, in after years, when in affluence, he occupied a spacious mansion, and saw his numerous herds and flocks, and his barns bursting with the harvest of his many productive acres?

On the 4th of May, 1784, Mr. Slafter removed from the structure we have here described, on the banks of the Connecticut, to another part of his estate, two miles inland, where, two years afterwards, on the 8th of June, 1786, he raised the frame of the spacious house, which he occupied the remainder of his days, and which is now (1869) the property of Mr. Peter Johnson.

This house, a drawing of which, by Master Theodore S. Slafter, we have given (see No. 586), was built in the style of the more commodious and expensive houses of that day. Its chimney was an immense structure, in the centre of the house, having three ovens, where the family bread and meats were cooked for the table. About the year 1850 it was modernized by removing the chimney and erecting smaller ones, and by removing the "square roof" and replacing it by the more common "gable." The lofty elm represented in the drawing was planted by Mrs. Elizabeth (Hovey) Slafter, a little before, or soon after the erection of the house. In 1867 this tree measured, at one foot from the ground, 16 feet in circumference; at 6 feet the circumference was 10$\frac{1}{2}$ feet; its branches began to spring at 14 feet from the base; the spread of the limbs, as measured on a line drawn through the centre of the trunk, was 80 feet, or 40 feet on each side. It is an unusually fine specimen of the noble elm, which is undisputably the queen of ornamental trees in New England.

The first meeting for the organization of the town was held in Mansfield, Ct., in 1761, and the annual meetings of the town were held there each year until 1768. At the meeting of 1765 he was chosen selectman for civil affairs. To this office he was repeatedly chosen, the last year he held the office being in 1805, just forty years after his first election to it. He was in some office, by the choice of his fellow-townsmen, in each of the first twenty-five years after the organization, with a single exception. On an average he was elected to one office every year for the period of forty years, and to two offices every other year on an average for the same space of time.

He was entrusted, as one of a committee, by the grantees in 1765, with the duty of allotting and dividing the lands among the proprietors, and laying out highways for the convenience of the settlers, and in 1770 was again appointed to lay out the remaining undivided lands.

When the revolutionary war broke out new and important responsibilities were laid upon him. He was appointed by the "Council of Safety" at Bennington, to take possession of, and confiscate the property of "tories." He was commissioned also to procure a quantity of snowshoes, and hold them in readiness for scouting parties, when it should be necessary to send them out. He laid in powder and other amuni-

tion, and had provisions stored at his own house "against an alarm."
He was one of the Committee of Safety in 1776. In 1782, when a
difficulty arose between the inhabitants in the eastern and those in the
western part of the state in regard to jurisdiction, he was appointed one
of a committee to meet committees of other towns at Thetford, to
ascertain whether a union of the territory west of the Connecticut
river could be effected with the state of New Hampshire, and on what
terms, and to consult upon measures of defence against the enemy.

He was much employed in the administration of justice. As an
arbitrator he was frequently called upon, in connection with one or two
other persons, to settle disputes, and by the confidence reposed in his
judgment, and his conciliating manners, he usually succeeded in estab-
lishing "justice" and "peace" where a civil magistrate would have
inevitably failed.

In ecclesiastical affairs he held from the beginning a prominent posi-
tion. We first find him charged with the duty of levying a tax for the
support of the first minister. Soon after the erection of the first
"meeting-house," he was appointed (in 1782) on a committee to act, as
the agent of the town, in making a settlement with the building committee. And in 1801, when a severance of the pastoral relation of the
Rev. Lyman Potter, after a long ministry, became necessary, he was
called upon to conduct the delicate negotiation. He became a member
of the church at its organization, in 1770, and was early elected a
deacon, which office he discharged for many years, only withdrawing
from it near the close of his life.

In looking over the records of the town, and of the original proprietors, we find him associated in some responsible way, by the suffrage of
his fellow townsmen, with nearly every important measure relating to
education, religion, or prudential affairs, for a period of more than
forty years.

In the settlement of the town there were difficulties to encounter
which at this distance of time we cannot well appreciate. The early
settler had not only to level the forest, and remove the heavy timber
from the soil by burning or otherwise, but he had to do everything with
the simplest implements. There was no blacksmith or carpenter to
call in for repairs. Even the mill for grinding the "family grist" was
at first at Charlestown, a distance of forty miles, and afterwards at
Hartland, about half that distance. This journey cost several days of
severe labor, in navigating the Connecticut with their log canoes, with
several "carrying places" to pass.

The first potatoes raised in Windsor county were the product of
"quarter of a bushel" carried by Mr. Slafter on a foot journey from
Charlestown to Norwich. After a few years these trials gradually
diminished, but others soon took their place. When sheep were introduced they became the prey of wild beasts. To abate this nuisance the
state offered a bounty of eight pounds for the destruction of a wolf or
panther, and half the amount for that of the young of either of these
animals. Mr. Slafter constructed pits for taking the wolf, which proved
eminently successful. An excavation was made in the earth with walls
inclining inward, and so deep that the animal could not leap from the
bottom to the top. It was surrounded by a fence including a small

additional space at one end, on which a lamb was secured, the fence being very high at the end where the decoy was fastened. The hungry wolf, frenzied by the scent of his fancied prey, leaping the fence where it was low, fell to the bottom of the pit, and being unable to extricate himself was compelled to await the approach of his captor in the morning. By this and other means of destruction, the farmers of Vermont removed this obstacle to the raising of sheep, for which this state has now become so distinguished.

On the breaking out of the revolutionary war the settlers of the New Hampshire grants were greatly alarmed by the expectation of Indian raids from the north. Memory summoned at once the names of myriads of kindred and neighbors on the frontiers of New England, who in the past had been victims of the scalping knife, or of the more cruel fate of a hopeless captivity. That these barbarities would be again enacted, there could be little doubt. Mr. Slafter did not therefore deem it prudent that his little family should remain, where, under the cover of the forest, the insidious approach of the Indian could not be foreseen, and which was sure to be followed by the most painful, if not fatal results. It was decided therefore that his wife and two children should retire for safety to Connecticut, where both his and her parents were ready to receive them under their hospitable roofs. On the 5th of July, 1776, the day after the declaration of American Independence was read from the window of the old State House in Philadelphia, the three set forth on the lonely and even perilous journey. The distance was a hundred and fifty miles, mostly through the forests, with numerous streams to ford, and temporary, frail and dangerous bridges to pass. Mr. Slafter himself was compelled to stay behind to gather in the harvest; his noble wife was ready to undertake the journey alone for the safety of the dear ones committed to her care. The Mizpah of that morning prayer, "the Lord watch between me and thee, when we are absent one from another," as the patriarch stood up and gave his parting blessing to his little family, was tender, earnest and affecting. They were set across the Connecticut in their little canoe, and as carriages were impracticable and unknown to use in the forests of New Hampshire, the sturdy horse was brought up, caparisoned with saddle and pillion, and numerous packages of clothing, utensils and food for the way, strapped here and there as best they could be for poise and safety. Behind, on the pillion, was placed the little girl, eight years of age, and the little boy, not quite four, on such a seat as could be arranged in front, and so they set forward on their weary journey. But the two that had been joined as one were not separated, but their hearts were still bound up in each other, her memory reverting to her happy home on the banks of the Connecticut, and he in imagination following her hour by hour through all the stages of that painful journey, and both hearts rejoiced together, and put up the oft repeated thanksgiving to God, that every hour placed their dear ones farther and farther from the threatened danger which they desired to escape. When Mr. Slafter returned to his deserted home, he made this entry: "Norwich, July 5, 1776, Elizabeth, Christiana and Farwell set out for Mansfield, driven off by the fear of Indians." The journey was safely accomplished, and on the 31st of October following she gave birth to a son, the only one of her children not born at her home on the banks of the Connecticut in Norwich.

In 1777, when General Burgoyne made his appearance at Crown Point, the frontiers of Vermont were seriously threatened, and, after the skirmish at Hubbardton, the inhabitants in the western part of the state were left without any protection. The general government had not the means, or was not disposed to offer any assistance. It became a matter of vital importance for the people of the " New Hampshire grants" to raise and support a regiment for their own protection. At this time the state was not fully organized. The civil power was lodged for the time being in the " Council of Safety," appointed by a convention held at Windsor, July 4, 1777. As it was not feasible for the " Council" to levy a tax upon the people generally, the plan was conceived and put into execution by them, of appointing " Commissioners of Sequestration," who seized the goods and chattels of all who had joined the common enemy, and, selling them at public auction, the proceeds were paid to the Treasurer of the Council of Safety, and from a fund thus formed a regiment of Rangers was supported, commanded by Col. Samuel Henrick. In pursuance of these measures Mr. Slafter was charged with the execution of the plan in a district of which the town in which he resided was a part, viz., Norwich, Thetford, Strafford, Hartford, and perhaps one or two other towns. While a considerable revenue by his agency was thus obtained, he executed this unenviable office with so much prudence and moderation, that he did not gain the permanent ill will even of those who were the victims of this severe but necessary measure. He appears, however, on one occasion, to have been in serious danger, though unconscious of it himself at the time. While collecting together the property of one of his "tory" neighbors, the owner was still concealed near the premises, and related afterward, that he levelled his gun at him and was ready to discharge it, but the thought providentially occurred to him, that in case of failure he should sacrifice his own life, as he observed that the Commissioner was himself armed.

The town of Royalton, Vt., though chartered in 1779, had been settled some time previous to that period, and in 1780 had a thriving population, with well stocked farms and comfortable dwellings. On the 16th of October of that year a " raid" was made upon this little settlement by about three hundred Indians from Canada, commanded by Lieutenant Horton, a British officer. Their object was plunder, and a malicious disturbance of the unoffending inhabitants. Besides killing three or four persons, they burned twenty-one dwellings, sixteen barns filled with the year's harvest, destroyed about a hundred and fifty cattle, with many sheep and swine, and took away with them thirty horses, and twenty-six prisoners of war. They made a complete destruction of all the furniture and provisions which they could not carry away. The inhabitants who remained, being mostly women and children, were consequently left entirely destitute of food and shelter. As soon as the intelligence of this calamity to a neighboring settlement reached him, Mr. Slafter, true to the instincts of his generous nature, set about furnishing immediate relief. The family oven was heated, and the whole night was consumed in baking batch after batch of bread, and at earliest dawn he packed it, together with cured meats from his cellar, upon his horse, and led him thus loaded through the forests, over hills and valleys, and streams, for a distance of fifteen or twenty miles, and at the termination of his weary march had the satisfaction, as a good Samaritan, of ministering to these unfortunate victims of Anglo-savage cruelty.

The invasion of Vermont by a detachment of Burgoyne's army under Colonel Baum, which resulted in the battle of Bennington on the 16th of August, 1777, created a general alarm throughout the New Hampshire grants. The citizens flocked with patriotic zeal to the standard of Stark and Warner. Mr. Slafter left his fields, ripening for the harvest, and hastened to give every possible aid in his power, and is said to have acted as an Adjutant in Stark's regiment. He returned to his home after this battle, but again joined the army, and was present at the capitulation of Burgoyne on the 17th of October. He was accustomed to relate that in the French war the king's troops often played Yankee Doodle in derision, and that it gave him a peculiar gratification on this occasion to see his Majesty's troops march to the same tune and lay down their arms.

Mr. Slafter took a deep and practical interest in the subject of education. On the 13th of Dec., 1769, Dartmouth College was chartered by John Wentworth, Governor of New Hampshire, and its location was fixed at Hanover, only four miles from Mr. Slafter's residence. In addition to generous contributions for the erection of the first buildings, he transferred, on the 13th day of Nov., 1770, a tract of land to the Trustees of the College. After referring to the noble franchises and privileges of the Charter, and the generous donations of the Governor, he says, "In consideration of the extensive charity of the design, and in addition to said fund, I, John Slafter of Norwich, in the province of New York, have given, and granted, and by these presents do absolutely give, grant, consign, and confirm to the Trustees of said Dartmouth College, and to their successors in that trust, for the use and benefit of said College, one half of the hundred acre lot drawn to the original of Samuel Slafter, in the 2nd Division of the hundred acres in said Norwich, it being the 16th east of the four mile and a half highway, to have and to hold." This gift to the College must have comprised one-tenth of his landed estate. In private charity he was never found wanting. From his ample stock of provisions the destitute were not sent away unsupplied. The widow and the orphan found in him a sympathizing friend. In business his word was as sacred as his bond. In private and public duties he was prompt and efficient. And while he contributed largely to the happiness of others, Providence conferred upon him that most desirable of gifts, a serene, sunny old age. He was executor of his own will, and had the luxury of seeing his children and grandchildren in the rational enjoyment of his own accumulations. He gave a farm of ample dimensions to each of his four sons, and an equivalent sum of money to his only daughter. Soon after he reached fourscore years his constitution began to yield, and although on the Sunday preceding he was in his place in church, on Friday, the 8th of October, 1819, he passed to the " better land," and on Sunday he was placed in the little cemetery near the mouth of the Ompompanoosuc, and a simple stone marks the place of his rest. The following is a fac-simile of his signature, at the age of 55 years:

The children of John and Elizabeth (Hovey) Slafter were all born in Norwich, Vt., with the exception of John, who was born in Mansfield, Ct.

97. 1. CHRISTIANA,[210] b. Feb. 6, 1768 ; d. Feb. 17, 1815; m. Dr. Richard-
       Crafts Seaver.
98. 2. ASAHEL, b. May 6, 1770 ; d. May 12, 1770.
99. 3. ASAPH, b. May 6, 1770 ; d. May 6, 1770.
100. 4. FARWELL, b. June 13, 1771 ; d. June 22, 1771.
101. 5. EDMUND-FARWELL,[217] b. July 26, 1772 ; d. March 17, 1812; m.
       Clarissa Tolman
102. 6. JOHN,[224] b. Oct. 31,1776 ; d. Nov. 21, 1856; m. Persis Grow.
103. 7. SYLVESTER,[234] b. June 30, 1780; d. May 9, 1850; m. 1st, Mary-
       Armstrong Johnson ; 2d, Anna White.
104. 8. ELIJAH,[245] b. Jan. 9, 1784 ; d. July 29, 1864; m. Olive Grow.

105. ELEAZER,[3][34] (Samuel,[2] John,[1]) b. March 19, 1744–5; d. June 29, 1828 ; m. Mary, dau. of Sylvanus Freeman of Mansfield, Ct., Nov. 23, 1773 ; she was b. Feb. 27, 1754 ; d. April 23, 1795. She was descended through Sylvanus,[5] Edmund,[4] Edmund,[3] Edmund,[2] from Edmund,[1] the emigrant ancestor, of Sandwich, Mass., (see Freeman's Hist. Cape Cod, Vol. 2, p. 75.) He m. 2, Eunice, dau. of Ebenezer and Sarah (Dunham) Fenton of Mansfield, Sept. 10, 1795. She was b. July 29, 1767 ; d. 1848. She was the grand-daughter of Ebenezer and Mehitable (Tuttle) Fenton, and great-grand-daughter of Robert and Dorothy (Farrar) Fenton of Mansfield, Ct. He inherited the paternal estate at Mansfield Four Corners.   *Mansfield, Ct.*

106. 1. MARY, b. July 13, 1774 ; d. July 15, 1774.
107. 2. ELEAZER,[256] b. Sept. 28, 1775 ; d. Oct. 1, 1860 ; m. Mary Burleigh.
108. 3. IRA,[260] b. May 13, 1778 ; d. April 9, 1818 ; m. Joanna Jacobs.
109. 4. SYLVANUS, b. May 24, 1780 ; d. 1858 ; m. Lovina, dau. of Eleazer
        Fenton of Willington, Ct ; she was b. Sept. 14, 1778 ; had no children.
                                                           Cambridge, N. Y.
110. 5. SAMUEL, b. Jan. 20, 1782 ; d. Aug. 1, 1786.
111. 6. CALVIN,[268] b. April 11, 1784 ; d. Sept. 7, 1857; m. Jerusha Dexter.
112. 7. TRYPHENA, b. April 6, 1786 ; d. Sept. 27, 1852; unm.
113. 8. ORIN, b. Dec. 18, 1788; d 1851; unm. He was on the ship United
        States, when she took the Macedonia.
114. 9. SAMUEL,[277] b. April 22, 1791 ; m. 1st, Lydia Fisher; 2d, Mary
        Chatterton.
115. 10. TRYPHOSA,[283] b. March 25, 1793 ; m. Moses Thompson.
116. 11. ASENATH, b. Aug. 18, 1796 ; d. ——; m. Josiah, son of Oliver Janes,
        and had Asenath.
117. 12. JOSEPHAS, b. Oct. 25, 1797 ; d. Sept. 1, 1802.
118. 13. ELISHA, b. Aug. 18, 1801 ; d. Aug. 31, 1802.
119. 14. JULIA, b. Aug. 17, 1803; d. ——; unm.
120. 15. LUCINDA, b. Feb. 18, 1807 ; d. ——; unm.

121. JOSEPH,[3][37] (Joseph,[2] John,[1]) b. perhaps in 1721 ; d. Aug. 13, 1775 ; m. Hannah Covel; he was admitted freeman at Newport, R. I., April 3, 1745. This is the only clue to his age which has been found.
                                                           Scituate, R. I.

122. 1. ABNER,|292| b. Feb. 28, 1743-4 ; m. Sarah Russell.
123. 2. JOSEPH,|299| b. Oct. 10, 1745 ; m. Lois King.
124. 3. ABIAL,|314| b. Sept. 15, 1747 ; d. Aug. 1813 ; m. Anna Adams.
125. 4. SILAS,|320] b. Nov. 26, 1754 ; d. Aug. or Sept., 1825 ; m. Beulah Adams.
126. 5. JOHN,|334] b. 1756 ; d. Feb. 14, 1815; m. Lois Carpenter.
127. 6. HANNAH,|383] b. 1760 ; d. Sept. 1829 ; m. Stephen Slater.
128. 7. SARAH,[344] b. ———; d. Aug., 1808 ; m. William Taylor,

129. ABRAHAM,[3][40] (*Joseph*,[2] *John*,[1]) b. Oct. 7, 1731 ; d. 1795 ; m.
Hannah Adams.   *Killingly, Conn.*

130. 1. JEREMIAH, b. May 11, 1751 ; d. 1807 ; unm.   *Killingly, Ct.*
131. 2. STEPHEN,[383] b. Aug. 1, 1752 ; d. Sept., 1821 ; m. his cousin, Hannah,
       daughter of his father's brother Joseph.
132. 3. ABIGAIL, m. Benoni Page.   *Dutch Hoosick, Albany Co., N. Y.*
133. 4. MERCY, m. Matthew Moffit, and had : 1, Rufus ; 2, Andrew ; 3, John ; 4,
       Abraham ; 5, David ; 6, Matthew ; 7, Thomas ; 8, Joseph.
134. 5. SAMUEL,[372] d. about 1822 ; m. Delana Moffit.
135. 6. ESTHER, m. 1st ——— Thomas, and had : 1, Samuel ; m. 2d, Jacob
       Russell of *Killingly*, and had : 2, Isaac ; 3, Lucy.
136. 7. AMY ; unm.
137. 8. ABRAHAM.

138. JOHN,[3][39] (*Joseph*,[2] *John*,[1]) b. in Mansfield, Ct., 1725 ; d. Feb.
8, 1821 ; m. Elizabeth, dau. of Barachiah Handell. She was born
about 1736, and died in 1826. He sold his estate for Continental
money, which proved worthless.   *Foster, R. I.*

139. 1. ZERVIAH, b. Nov. 1, 1756 ; m. Daniel Walton, and had : 1, Daniel ; 2,
       Hannah ; 3, Prudence ; 4, Anna ; 5, Rebecca.   *Preston, Ct.*
140. 2. BENJAMIN,[366] b. Aug. 28, 1758 ; d. 1812 ; m. Waitie Hopkins.
141. 3. SARAH,|361] b. 1760 ; d. Sept., 1828 ; m. John Maguire.
142. 4. SIMON.   ⎫
143. 5. JOHN.   ⎪
144. 6. ASA.   ⎬ Died young.
145. 7. NATHAN.   ⎭
146. 8. RHODA,[355] b. Feb. 24, 1771 ; d. March 5, 1859 ; m. Willard Shippee.
147. 9. PHEBE, died young.
148. 10. RACHEL, m. John Wood of Scituate, R. I., and had : 1, Lois ; 2, Asa ;
       3, Nathan ; 4, Elizabeth ; 5, Barbara ; 6, Susan ; and removed to
                                                               Delhi, N. Y.

149. ANTHONY,[3][54] (*Moses*,[2] *John*,[1]) b. about 1742 ; d. April, 1826 ;
m. Experience, dau. of Josiah Frost of Ludlow, Mass., Jan. 4, 1769.
She was b. Dec. 17, 1742 ; d. Sept. 17, 1827.   *Springfield, Mass.*

150. 1. MARY, b. Feb. 12, 1770 ; d. about 1828 ; m. Charles Johnson, and had :
       1, Mary ; 2, Charles ; 3, Uriel ; 4, Lodica ; 5, Jasper ; 6, David ; 7,
       Lyman ; 8, Almira ; 9, Jehiel ; 10, Jemima ; 11, Esther ; 12, Swain.
151. 2. EXPERIENCE,[394] b. Jan. 4, 1773 ; d. 1844 ; m. Noah Paulk.
152. 3. MARY-ANNA, b. July 23, 1774 ; d. about 1798 ; unm.
153. 4. ANTHONY,|396] b. about 1779 ; d. Feb. 16, 1850 ; m. Lavina Carpenter.
154. 5. SARAH,|409] b. Jan 21, 1783 ; m. Alpha Frost.
155. 6. DAVID-FROST,|416] b. March 1, 1784 ; d. May 31, 1866 ; m. 1st, Dimmis
       Baldwin ; 2d, Emelia Grow.
156. 7. ZEBULON-WEST,|425] b. Aug. 26, 1785 ; d. March 22, 1862 ; m. 1st,
       Hannah Frost; 2d, Sarah Foster.
157. 8. JEMIMA, b. 1786 ; d. Jan. 17, 1862 ; m. George Gillett of Springfield,
       Mass., and had (a.) David, b. March 18, 1809. (b.) George. (c.)
       Adaline. (d.) James.

158. MOSES,[3][55] (*Moses*,[2] *John*,[1]) b. about 1752 ; d. May 7, 1839 ;
m. Mary, dau. of Capt. David Johnson of Stafford, Ct. She was b.
about 1759 ; d. Feb. 16, 1855. Their children were all b. in Ellington, Ct.   *Ellington, Ct.*

159.　1. JEHIEL,|433] b. Nov. 15, 1778 ; d. June 23, 1860; m. 1st, Mary Weaver;
　　　　2d, Lydia Avery ; 3d, Susan Payne.
160.　2. BENJAMIN, b. 1780; d. in infancy.
161.　3. MOSES,|445] b. Sept 30, 1782; d. Feb. 21, 1863 ; m. Mary Gray.
162.　4. PHEBE,|450] b. March 1, 1784 ; d. Nov., 1850 ; m. Asa Lewis.
163.　5. ADONIJAH,[459] b. Jan. 31, 1787 ; d. Feb. 12, 1865 ; m. 1st, Lura
　　　　Pond ; 2d, Mrs. Rebecca Daggett.
164.　6. MARY,|468] b. March 3, 1789 ; m. Ira Hodges.
165.　7. RHODA,|472] b. July 18, 1791 ; m. Roswell Green.
167.　8. ESTHER,[487] b. May 14, 1793 ; m. Park Rockwell.
168.　9. LYDIA,|492] b. Oct 26, 1795 ;　m. Jesse Willes.
169.　10. SAMUEL,[496] b. June 10, 1797 ; m. Sarah Norris.
170.　11. WILLIAM,|510] b. June 5, 1799 ;　m. Fanny Kellogg.
171.　12. ARIEL,[517] b. June 15, 1803 ; m. Mary Fox.

172. DOROTHY,[4][89]　(Samuel,[3] Samuel,[2] John,[1]) b. Nov. 29, 1756 ;
d. Aug. 11, 1839 ; m. Nathan, son of Nathan Lamb of Hopkinton,
R. I., Jan. 18, 1787.　He was b. in Hopkinton, Jan. 17, 1766 ; d. June
27, 1845.　　　　　　　　　　　　　　　　　　　Randolph, Vt.

173.　1. NATHAN, b. April 13, 1787 ; m. Mrs. Sarah (Johnson) Davenport,
　　　　widow, and had : 1, Lydia; 2, James ; 3, Chauncey ; 4, Zerah ; 5,
　　　　Smalley ; 6, Maria ; 7, George.　　　　Baraboo, Saulk Co., Wis.
174.　2. EZRA, b. Oct. 12, 1789 ; m. late in life ; no children.
　　　　　　　　　　　　　　　　　　　　White Creek Centre, N. Y.
175.　3. DOROTHY, b. June 6, 1791 ; d. Jan. 7, 1861 ; m. John Cleaveland, March
　　　　12, 1821, and had : 1, Milo, b. Oct. 15, 1824 ; 2, Ira-H., b. June 11,
　　　　1827 ; 3, Susannah, b. July 7, 1836.　　　　　　　Braintree, Vt.
176.　4. FREEMAN, b. Nov. 18, 1792 ; m. Aurelia, dau. of Seth Hoyt of New
　　　　Haven, Vt., and had : 1, Ezra-Gould ; 2, Orletus-Hoyt ; 3, Julius-
　　　　Freeman.　　　　　　　　　　　　　　　　Houston, Penn.
177.　5. REUNY, b. Feb. 26, 1795 ; m Amelia, dau. of Stephen Carpenter of Tol-
　　　　land, Ct., afterwards of Montpelier, Vt., and had : 1, Nathan ; 2, Nancy-
　　　　Washburn ; 3, Amelia-Carpenter ; 4, Dinna-Slafter ; 5, William-
　　　　Henry, in the late war was three years in a California Reg.; 6, Phile-
　　　　mon ; 7, Emily-Louisa.　　　　　　　　　　Woodstock, Vt.

178. SARAH,[4][91]　(Samuel,[3] Samuel,[2] John,[1]) b. March 24, 1760 ; d.
April 24, 1800 ; m. Amasa, son of Amasa and Mary (Heath) Reed,
Feb. 4, 1783.　He was b. Jan. 13, 1757 ; d. Jan. 2, 1829.　He was
three years in service in the revolutionary war.　　Mansfield, Ct.

179.　1. JOHN, b. Dec. 20, 1783 ; d. Oct. 30, 1860 ; m. Annah Hitchcock, and had :
　　　　1, Maria ; 2, George-Hitchcock ; 3, Mary-Almira ; 4, William.
　　　　　　　　　　　　　　　　　　　　　　Mansfield Ct.
180.　2. PRECENDA, b. June 14, 1785 ; m. William Gurley, and had no children.
　　　　　　　　　　　　　　　　　　　　　　Mansfield, Ct.
　　　　3. JESSE, b. Sept. 29, 1786 ; m. Priscilla Bingham, and had : 1, Sarah-Ann ;
　　　　2, Charles-Miller ; 3, Mary ; 4, Amasa-Harrison.　Mansfield Ct.
182.　4. ETHELDA, b. Jan. 26, 1787 ; d. Sept. 23, 1844 ; m. Marvin Fenton, and
　　　　had Sarah-Roena.　　　　　　　　　　　　Mansfield, Ct.
183.　5. ROENA, b. Jan. 28, 1790 ; m. Marvin Fenton, husband of her deceased
　　　　sister ; had no children.　　　　　　　　　　Mansfield, Ct.
184.　6. ANNE, b. Nov. 14, 1791 ; d. April 17, 1817 ; m. Peleg-Sandford Coggs-
　　　　hall ; no children.　　　　　　　　　　　　Mansfield Ct.
185.　7. SAMUEL-FREEMAN, b. Sept. 14, 1793 ; m. Patience Sibley, Feb. 14, 1816 ;
　　　　and had : 1, Nancy, b. May 19, 1817, m. James-Madison Chapman,
　　　　Jan 1, 1857 ; 2, Mary, b. April 21, 1819, m. William-Henry Stevens,
　　　　Nov. 1839, and had : William-Henry, Mary, Nancy, Charles, Franklin,
　　　　Flora, James, Nellie ; 3, Precenda, b. March 7, 1821, m. James-Almon
　　　　Orcut, Jan. 1, 1840, and had Ellen and Milton, who is " preparing for
　　　　College," res. Defiance, Ohio ; 4, George, b. May 26, 1824, m. Eliza-
　　　　beth Waite, and had Ellen, Frederick and Franklin ; 5, Charles, b.
　　　　April 16, 1826, m. Harriet Beach ; 6, Cordelia, b. April 25, 1828 ;

7, John, b. July 18, 1830 ; 8, Jane, b. Jan. 2, 1833 ; 9, Roena, b. Jan.
15, 1836.   *Granville, Mass.*
186.   8. MARY, b. Sept. 9, 1795 ; d. April 1, 1808.
186¼. 9. ELSON, b. Nov. 23, 1797 ; m. Ann Taylor ; and had Sarah and others.
                                                              Fowler, Ohio.
186½. 10. JEHIEL-HEATH, b. Dec. 5, 1799 ; m. Martha Chamberlain.
                                                              Uxbridge, Mass.

187. MARTHA,⁴[92] (*Samuel,³ Samuel,² John,¹*) b. Aug. 24, 1764 ; d.
June 2, 1840 ; m. Nathaniel, son of Nathaniel and Anna (Davis)
Nichols of Mansfield, Ct., September, 1784. He was b. March 27,
1760 ; d. May 1, 1832. He served in the war of American Revolution, as a substitute for his father, when fifteen or sixteen years of age ;
stationed at New London and New York ; was in the battle of Long
Island, and of Monmouth, and is said to have served till the end of the
war. He was also in service in the war of 1812, in a Comp. called the
" Silver Grays." He resided at Paris, Rodman, and at
                                    York, Livingston Co., N. Y.

188.   1. ALBION, b. Aug. 8, 1793 ; he was a " minute man" in the war of 1812.
                                                        Grafton Centre, Ohio.
189.   2. ASA-HUNTINGTON, b. in Paris, N. Y., April 29, 1796 ; d. Sept. 28, 1860,
         in Carmel, Mich. He was in the war of 1812, one month ; m. Susan,
         dau. of Samuel Dorris of York ; she was b. in Avon, Jan. 17, 1802 ; d.
         March 10, 1840, in Dayton, N. Y. Their children were b. the eldest
         four in York, the others in Dayton, N. Y. Their children were as
         follows—   *Carmel, Mich.*
         (1.) George-Washington, b. Jan. 22, 1820 ; m. March 13, 1844, Eme-
               line-Eliza, dau. of Alanson Holbrook of Leicester, N. Y., and
               resides at La Grange, Ohio. Their children are—
               (a.) Albert-Albion, b. Nov. 5, 1845.
               (b.) Alva-Asa, b. April 13, 1850.
               (c.) Emeline-Eliza, b. April 29, 1853.
               (d.) Julia-Jane, b. March 1, 1855. All b. in Grafton, Ohio.
         (2.) Esther-Susan, b. Oct. 9, 1821 ; m. March 31, 1844, Waldo
               Munger of Attica, N. Y. Children—
               (a.) Cynthia-Ann, b. March, 1845.
               (b.) Franklin, b. 1847 ; both in Geneseo, N. Y.
         (3.) Enoch-Samuel, b. May 23, 1824 ; m. Aug. 23, 1848, Sarah-
               Amelia Savage of Medina, Mich. She was b. May 28, 1831.
               Their children—
               (a.) George-Enoch, b. Aug. 17, 1851.
               (b.) Fanny-Eliza-Ann, b. April 24, 1854.
               (c.) Stephen-Aaron, b. June 25, 1861.
               (d.) Martha-Caroline, b. July 9, 1865.
               (e.) John-Asa, b. Dec. 27, 1868.   *Charlotte, Eaton Co., Mich.*
         (4.) Eunice-Martha, b. Feb. 25, 1826 ; d. Sept. 25, 1826.
         (5.) Alva-Abion, b. Nov. 11, 1828 ; m. Dec. 31, 1850, Lucy-Ann, dau.
               of George Burt of Penfield, O. Children—
               (a.) Bessie-Emeline, b. Feb. 27, 1852.
               (b.) Susan-Elizabeth, b. March 20, 1854.
               (c.) Cora-Ettie-May, b. Dec. 13, 1863.   *Charlotte, Mich.*
         (6.) Harriet-Martha, b. May 6, 1831 ; m. Aug. 3, 1848, Ira-Addison
               Foster of La Grange, O. ; he was b. June 25, 1827. Children—
               (a.) Esther-Lucy, b. Sept. 10, 1850.
               (b) Addison-Ira, b. Oct. 9, 1853.
               (c.) Charles-Wilber, b. July 24, 1860.
               (d.) Ella-Martha, b. Jan. 22, 1863.   *Charlotte, Mich.*
         (7.) James-Wellington, b. Aug. 4, 1835. In war of rebellion he was
               in Comp. E, 6th Mich. Vols., served three years ; m. Oct. 30,
               1856, Sarah-Ann Smith of Carmel, Mich. Children—
               (a.) Wilbur-Leonard, b. Sept. 24, 1857.

        (b.) James-Elmer, b. July 24, 1862.

        (c.) Clara-Jane, b. July 4, 1868.   *Charlotte, Mich.*

   (8.) Clarissa-Polly, b. June 25, 1838; m. Feb. 14, 1861, Levi-Monroe Sawyer of Bedford, Ohio. Children—

        (a.) William-Spencer, b. April 15, 1862.

        (b.) Charles-Watson, b. Dec. 14, 1863.

        (c.) Sylva-Ella, b. July, d. Dec., 1866.   *Cleveland, Ohio.*

190. 3. ENOCH, b. in Paris, N. Y., June 17, 1798; d. in Milan, O., March 21, 1861; m. 1837, Catharine, dau. of Benj. Horton of Oxford, O.; she was b. at Bellville, N. Y., Aug. 13, 1813. Children, all b. in Oxford, Ohio: *Weston, Ohio.*

   (1.) Martha-Jane, b. Aug. 11, 1838; m. Feb. 23, 1857, Caleb, son of Hiram Root of Milan, O. Their children, all b. in Troy, Wood Co., O.:

        (a.) Kate-Parthenia, b. Nov. 24, 1857.

        (b.) Hiram-Nichols, b. Aug. 6, 1859; d. Feb. 13, 1860.

        (c.) Ettie-Eloise, b. April 11, 1861.

        (d.) Mattie-May, b. April 22, 1864; d. July 25, 1864.

        (e.) Mary-Maude, b. April 22, 1864; d. July 25, 1865.

                        Woodville, Sandusky Co., Ohio.

   (2.) Etta-Hannah, b. Oct. 12, 1839; m. Sept. 17, 1862, Ebenezer, son of Wm. Baldwin of Woodville, O. Children—

        (a.) William-Enoch, b. in Woodville, Nov. 3, 1863.

        (b.) Helen-Martha, b. Nov. 4, 1865.

        (c.) Carrie-Catharine, b. in Lawrence, Kansas, Feb. 21, 1868.

                        Lawrence, Douglas Co., Kansas.

   (3.) Benjamin-Townsend, b. July 29, 1845. In war of rebellion served one hundred days in Comp. F, 145 Ohio Vols.; m. Oct. 28, 1868, Alice Hughes of Milan, O.   *Newark, O.*

   (4.) Albion-Nathaniel, b. March 9, 1850.

   (5.) Horton-Samuel, b. April 12, 1852.

191. 4. ESTHER, b. in Paris, N. Y., Dec. 19, 1800. The compiler is much indebted to her for information relating to the family.

                        Grafton Centre, Ohio.

192. 5. METHERSA, b. in Paris, N. Y., Nov. 25, 1802; m. Feb. 17, 1825, William, son of Jedediah Richardson of York, N. Y.; he was b. in Claremont, N. H., Dec. 18, 1797. Their four eldest children born in York, the others in Grafton, Ohio:—

   (1.) George-Washington, b. Nov. 3, 1827; d. at Natural Bridge, Mexico, June 6, 1847.

   (2.) Miles-Clinton, b. Nov. 16, 1831. In war of rebellion he served six months as mechanic, in Tennessee.   *Charlotte, Mich.*

   (3.) John-Wesley, b. Sept. 22, 1833; d. in Grafton, Aug. 1, 1845.

   (4.) Harriet-Martha, b Jan. 27, 1836; d. in Grafton, April 17, 1845.

   (5.) William-Warner, b. Feb. 3, 1839. In war of rebellion he was in Comp. H, 8th Ohio, and in Comp. F, 128th Ohio Vols.; served 20 months; m. Sept. 15, 1861, Martha, dau. of Charles Broughton of Grafton, O. Children—

        (a.) Netta-J., b. Aug. 9, 1862.

        (b.) William-Washington, b. July 9, 1868; both in Grafton, O.

                        Rawsonville, O.

   (6.) Esther-Jane, b. July 16, 1841; m. June 13, 1861, Charles-W., son of Charles Broughton of Grafton, O.   *Rawsonville, O.*

193. 6. NATHANIEL, b. in Rodman, N. Y., May 7, 1806; m. Sept. 16, 1827, Dorcas, dau. of Benj. Bailey of Leicester, N. Y. She was b. March 29, 1804, in Elmira, N. Y.; d. at La Grange, O., Feb. 19, 1864. Children—

   (1.) Allen-Woolsey, b. in York, July 3, 1828.   *Grafton, O.*

   (2.) Martha-Emma, b. in Dayton, N. Y., July 2, 1831; m. June 25, 1850, Milton Adams of Columbia, O. Children—

        (a.) Mary-Melissa.

        (b.) Martha-Emma.

        (c.) William.   *Eaton Rapids, Mich.*

   (3.) Mary-Ann, b. in Dayton, Dec. 27, 1834; m. Dec. 25, 1852, Orange Adams of Columbia, O. Child—

Ellen-Rosabelle, b. Feb. 27, 1853. *Eaton Rapids, Mich.*

(4.) Rolla-Alonzo, b. in Nunda, N. Y., June 7, 1838 ; he was living at the South when the rebellion broke out, and was forced into the rebel army; he served as 1st Lieut. in 61st Alabama Reg., and Capt. of Comp. H, in same Reg., and staff officer ; he was taken prisoner at Spottsylvania Court House, having served from April 1, 1861 to May 11, 1864 ; he immediately enlisted in United States service, first as orderly sergeant in Comp. II, 1st United States Vols.; promoted to Capt. of Comp. H, and was discharged May 29, 1865 ; length of service one year and five days. He is now in the United States Army, Commissary Department, at Paducah, Ky.

(5.) Ellen-Dorcas, b. in Nunda, Sept. 25, 1843; m. Oct. 29, 1864, Don-Carlos Van Deusen ; he served two years in the war of rebellion; participated in seven battles ; lost his right arm at Vicksburg. Child—

Lincona, b. Aug 5, 1865. *Hinckley, O.*

194. 7. MARTHA, b. Feb. 2, 1809; d. Dec. 8, 1827.

195. ANNA,[4][93] (*Samuel*,[3] *Samuel*,[2] *John*,[1]) b. March 11, 1766 ; d. in Leicester, N. Y., Sept. 18, 1824 : m. Samuel, son of Peter Thatcher of Norwich, Vt., December, 1790. He was b. in Lebanon, Ct., April 5, 1764 ; d. Sept. 9, 1839. He resided in Brookfield and in Barton, Vt., and in Bloomfield, Nunda, York, Geneseo and Leicester, N. Y.

Alfred, N. Y.

196. 1. SAMUEL, b. Oct. 3, 1791 ; was in service in the war of 1812, near Buffalo ; he has held the office of town clerk in Alfred, N. Y., 1840-1, Justice of the Peace in 1843-7; m. Ruth Green, Feb. 15, 1816, and resides in Brockport, N. Y.

(1.) Philena, b. Nov. 15, 1816; m. John-Lincoln Russell, Jan. 1, 1835 ; and had :—

(a.) Charles-Carrol, b. July 18, 1835 ; he was, during war of rebellion, a U. S. Sub-Tr. asury agent in West Virginia ; m. Mary-Virginia Reed, and had Horace.

Racine, Meigs Co., Ohio.

(b.) William-Henry-Harrison, b. July 4, 1840 ; m. Mary Elizabeth Boyce, and had: 1, Lillian Lola, b April 23, 1860 ; 2, Ella-Irene, b. May 22, 1863. He was mustered into U. S. service, in war of rebellion, July 30, 1861, as Capt. of Com. F., 4th West Virginia Vol., was commissioned Lieut. Col. of the same Reg., Aug. 26, 1861, and resigned for disability, Jan. 31, 1863. He was in many skirmishes with guerrillas in West Virginia, and was in command of the Reg. at the fight at Charlestown, Va., Sept. 13, 1862 ; and took part in the destruction of the salt works in the velley of the Kanawha. His Reg. was transferred to the West, and was moving upon Vicksburg, when his health gave way, and by the decisive advice of his surgeon, he resigned. He is now clerk of Alleghany Co., N. Y., having entered upon the office, Jan 1, 1868, for a term of three years. *Belmont, N. Y.*

(c.) James-John, b. Nov. 20, 1842 ; m. Mary-Almira, dau. of Frederick-Plumb Dunning of Belmont, N. Y., Aug. 21, 1864. *Alfred, N. Y.*

(2.) Arminda, b. May 11, 1820; m. Benjamin Maxson, May 16, 1854 ; no children. *Brockport, N. Y.*

197. 2. ELIAS, b. Sept. 23, 1793 ; m. Mary-Delilah Lampson, July 1, 1822 ; she was b. Oct. 20, 1802. *Cuylerville, N. Y.*
They had :—

(1.) Harriet-Matilda, b. Sept. 12, 1823 ; who m. David McEwen, Sept. 29, 1844.

(2.) Amos-Lampson, b. Oct. 12, 1825 ; d. July 11, 1866; m. Jane McCart, Nov. 5, 1860 ; she died March 19, 1864;

    (3.) Lucy-Jane, b. Jan. 4, 1828; d. Sept. 27, 1854; m. Robert Gilbert, Oct. 17, 1846; and had Miles-Hall, b. May 14, 1848; enlisted Feb. 22, 1864; d. at Albany, March 5, 1864.

    (4.) Miles-Wilson, b. April 7. 1830.

    (5.) Bertram-Castner, b. Aug. 1, 1832; enlisted in Com. E., 33 N. Y. Volunteers, April, 1861; d. Oct. 8, 1862, in Harwood Hospital, Washington, and buried in Soldiers' Cemetery.

    (6.) Joseph-Truesdale, b. Sept. 16, 1834; enlisted Oct. 1, 1861, in Com. C., 89 N. Y. Vol., discharged March 24, 1863, for disability, and is pensioned.

    (7.) Filitia-Clarissa, b. April 28, 1838; d. Feb. 8, 1863; m. George Luce.

    (8.) Cereno-Elias, b. June 17, 1840; d. Sept. 21, 1841.

    (9.) William-Washington, b. Jan. 8, 1843; enlisted April, 1861, in Com. E., 33d N. Y. Vol.; died in General Hospital, Philadelphia, Sept. 23, 1862; buried at Cuylerville, N. Y.

    (10.) Piety-Annette, b. June 5, 1845.

    (11.) Mary-Delilah, b. Feb. 22, 1848; d. July 29, 1852.

198. 3. ANNA, b. in Brookfield, Vt., Dec. 26, 1799; d. Aug. 5, 1854; m. William, son of William Potter of Wilbraham, Mass., Nov. 1815; he was b. Nov. 20, 1799; d. April 30, 1863.

Amboy, Illinois.

    Their children were:—

    (1.) William-Thatcher, b. Feb. 17, 1817; in Nunda, N. Y., resides in   *Lowell, Mich.*

    (2.) Samuel, b. Aug, 7, 1820; d. Jan. 3, 1821.

    (3.) George-Washington, b. Nov. 27, 1821.

    (4.) Mary, b. Feb. 17, 1824; in Geneseo, N. Y.

    (5.) Elizabeth, b. July 20, 1826.

    (6.) James-Madison, b. March 28, 1828.

    (7.) Anna, b. Feb. 10, 1831.

    (8.) Henry-Jefferson, b. July 23, 1833.

    (9.) Emily-Jane, b. March 16, 1836.

    (10.) Martha-Louisa, b. Nov. 12, 1838.

    (11.) Dulena, b. Nov. 12, 1840.

199. ROXA,[4][94] (*Samuel,[3] Samuel,[2] John,[1]*) b. Nov. 29, 1767; d. March 17, 1842; m. Daniel, son of Jonathan Dexter of Mansfield, Ct. He was b. Sept. 11, 1765; d. Sept. 27, 1848. Their eldest son was b. in Mansfield, Ct., their other children were b. in Paris, N. Y.

Clayville, N. Y.

200. 1. ASAHEL, b. May 16, 1788; he was Capt. of the Paris Furnace Comp., 140 New York Reg., in the war of 1812, and was in active service six months; m. Susan, dau. of Benjamin Austin of Paris, N. Y., Sept. 27, 1818; she was b. Dec. 12, 1798; d. Oct. 20, 1847. Their children, all born in Paris, N. Y., were

    (1.) Susan, b. Feb. 5, 1820.

    (2.) Lovira, b. Oct. 24, 1821.

    (3.) Emily, b. April 5, 1824.

    (4.) Charles, b. Feb. 15, 1829; m. May 14, 1851, Almira-L. Hammett; she was b. Nov. 5, 1832, and had Charles-Albert, b. June 24, 1857.   *Clayville, N. Y.*

201. 2. TRYPHOSA, b. 1792; d. 1810.

202. 3. DANIEL, b. about 1800; d. about 1822.

203. 4. CHESTER, b. Oct. 5, 1804; m. Ann, dau. of William Williams of Albany; she d. March 23, 1865. They had—

    (1.) Anna-Matilda.

    (2.) Jeannie-Elizabeth, m. Carmer-H. Conklin of Binghampton, N. Y., Dec. 26, 1865.

    (3.) Cornelia-Emily.   *Utica, N. Y.*

204. 5. SAMUEL-FREEMAN, b. Aug. 13, 1806. He was ordained as a Free-Will
Baptist preacher, May 3, 1838 ; m. 1st Caroline Risley, and had—
(1.) Daniel.   (2.) Lucy-Ann.   (3.) Henry.   (4.) Lucy-Ann.
(5.) Emmet.   (6.) Jane.   (7.) Dick-Freeman.   Second
wife, Malvina-Cerintha Daily.   *Clayville, N. Y.*
205. 6. JOHN, d. in infancy.

206. NATHANIEL-FREEMAN,[95] (*Samuel,³ Samuel,² John,¹*) b. June
11, 1771. He is supposed to have been lost at sea ; m. Martha, dau. of
Calvin Topliff of Mansfield, Ct. She was b. July 10, 1776 ; d. Aug.
21, 1839, in Coventry, Ct. Their children were as follows:

207. 1. ACHSA, b. Aug. 14, 1798 ; d. Aug. 17, 1802.
208. 2. MARTHA, b. Aug. 28, 1795 ; m. Henry-Horsford, son of John Corrin
of Liverpool, England, Nov. 30, 1820 ; he was b. Aug. 8, 1796. They
reside in Willington, Ct. Their children, all b. in Coventry, Ct., were
as follows—
(1.) James-Henry, b. April 11, 1822. In the war of rebellion he
enlisted in Comp. A, 25 Conn. Vols., Sept. 15, 1862, and
served as Commissary Sergeant of his regiment. He was
appointed Captain of Comp. G, 75th United States Infantry,
(colored) March 4, 1863, at Baton Rouge, La. He was ordered
before a Military Board, Feb. 25, 1864, "for examination for
promotion for distinguished merit and services," and was commissioned Major of the 84th United States Infantry (colored)
with rank from March 25, 1864, and commanded the Regiment
during the Red River Campaign under Gen. Banks. He received a discharge, on certificate of his Surgeon of physical
inability from "chronic rheumatism," Aug. 11, 1864. He m.
Maria-Ann, dau. of Ralzamon Belknap of Coventry, Ct.,
Sept. 14, 1847, and had Henry, b. in Coventry, Sept. 24,
1848, d. Aug. 14, 1849 ; Arthur-Belknap, b. in Worcester,
Mass., July 5, 1860, and Hattie-Maria, b. at Coventry, Oct.
24, 1862.   *City of New York.*
(2.) Caroline-Martha, b. June 20, 1824 ; d. Aug. 31, 1849.
(3) John, b. March 24, 1826 ; enlisted Oct. 19, 1862, in Comp. K,
162d New York Vols. ; last heard from, May, 1864 ; probably
lost on a vessel returning from New Orleans with discharged
soldiers. Of him, his brother, Major Corrin, says, " We have
no room for doubt but that he was on board the steamer
'Pocahontas,' which was run into by the steamer 'City of
Bath,' off Cape May, on the night of June 1, 1864."
(4.) Mary-Ann, b. July 7, 1829.
(5.) William-Pitt, b. Sept. 28, 1831 ; m. Elizabeth-Fiske Martin,
Oct. 9, 1862. He is now (1868) in charge of City Hospital,
                                     Hartford, Ct.
(6.) Daniel-Webster, b. Aug. 8, 1836 ; d. Aug. 11, 1863, in Coventry.
209. 3. ALVIN, b. July 25, 1797 ; d. Aug. 9, 1797.

210. CHRISTIANA,[97] (*John,³ Samuel,² John,¹*) b. Feb. 6, 1768 ; d.
Feb. 17, 1815 ; m. Dr. Richard-Crafts, son of Nathaniel and Judith
(Treadway) Seaver* of Petersham, Mass., March, 1793. He was b.

---

*1. *Robert Seaver*, or *Sever*, the emigrant ancestor, resided in Roxbury, became
a freeman, April 18, 1637. His children were *Subael*, b. 1639 ; Caleb
and Josiah, (gemini), 1641 ; Hannah, 1650.
2. *Subael Seaver*, of Roxbury, Mass., b. 1639, and wife Hannah, had Robert
b. 1670 ; *Joseph*, b. 1672 ; Hannah, b. 1674 ; Abigail, b. 1677 ; Subael, b.
1679 ; Thankful, b. 1684.
3. *Joseph Seaver*, b. 1672 ; d. in Framingham, 1754 ; m. in Sudbury, Mass.,
Mary Reed, Dec. 10, 1701 ; and had : 1, Robert ; 2, Mary, b. Oct. 5,
1706, m. Christopher Nixon ; 3, *Nathaniel*, b. April 1, 1709 ; 4, Hannah,

Oct. 28, 1767; d. Oct. 5, 1821. He practised medicine in Norwich, Thetford, and Chelsea, Vt., and in Wayne, Me., where he died. Their children were b. in Chelsea, Vt. Dr. Seaver married a second wife, by whom he had children, b. in Wayne, Me. His children by first wife were as follows:

211. 1. JOHN-SLAFTER, b. Feb. 14, 1795; d. Feb. 14, 1795.
212. 2. ELIZABETH-HOVEY, b. Feb. 7, 1796; m. 1st, Joseph Wallis, May 16, 1813, and had: 1, William-Henry; 2, Joseph; 3, Christiana; 4, Sarah-Elizabeth; by 2d husband, Otis Leighton: 5, Lorana; 6, Lewis-E.; 7, Benjamin-Wallace; 8, Cemantha-Almira; 9, Robert; 10, John-Augustus.   *Millbridge, Me.*
213. 3. ALMIRA-CEMANTHA, b. May 16, 1798; d. May 15, 1847; m. 1st, Thomas-Niles, son of James Gray of Gardiner, Me., Dec. 29, 1816, and had
        (1.) Eliza-Norris, b. Oct. 31, 1817, in Monmouth, Me.; m. Thomas Stinchfield, and had
            (a.) John-Allen.   (b.) Almira-Cemantha.   (c.) Ann-Eliza.
            (d.) Ann-Eliza.   (e.) Emma-Josephine.   (f.) Christiana-Baldwin.   (g.) Florence-Elvira.   (h.) Hannah-Etta.   (i.) John-Allen.   (j.) Thomas-Sewall. The 2d, 6th and 7th, only, are now living (1868). She resides at   *Livermore Falls, Me.*
        (2.) Simon-Philip, b. June 5, 1819, in Monmouth, Me. In war of rebellion was in Comp. A, 23d Maine Vols., 10½ months; m. 1st, Aramintha-Pettengill Stinchfield of Leeds, Me., and had (a.) Augusta-Ann.   (b.) Mary-Ella. He m. 2d, Rosannah Redman of Biddeford, Me., and had (c.) Estella-Aramintha.
                                                        Boston, Mass.
        (3.) Almira-Cemantha, b. Sept. 21, 1822; d. Feb. 11, 1840.
        (4.) Richard-James, b. Aug. 28, 1833, n East Livermore, Me. In war of rebellion he was in Comp. C, 6th New Hampshire Vols., two and a half years; and in Comp. A, 1st New Hampshire Cavalry, ten months; m. Harriet-Elizabeth Roberts of Portland, Me., and had
            (a.) Charles Wallis.   (b.) Frederick-Thomas.   (c.) James-Richard.   (d.) Lola-Minnie.   *East Kingston, N. H.*
214. 4. CHRISTIANA-SLAFTER, b. Oct. 5, 1800; d. March 8, 1804.
215. 5, SUSANNAH OAKES,b. Oct. 10, 1802; d. Oct. 24, 1802.
216. 6. JOHN-HOVEY, b. Sept. 4, 1804; m. 1st, Rebecca Lewis; dau. of Tristam Ordway of Greenfield, N. H., Oct. 2, 1831; she was b. Feb. 21, 1803; d. Nov. 8, 1835; m. 2d, Lydia, dau. of John Sawyer of Springfield, N. H., Sept. 18, 1836; she was b. Dec. 26, 1798; d. July 5, 1864; he had by 1st wife:
        (1.) Richard-Tristam, b. Feb. 29, 1832, in Plaistow, N. H.; d. May 22, 1833.
        (2.) Warenzo-Kelley, b. July 19, 1833, in Plaistow; m. Olive-Maria Emery, Nov. 6, 1857; and had:
            (a.) Willis-Woodman, b. Aug. 29, 1859.
            (b.) Henry-Randall, b. Feb. 7, 1863.   *Plaistow, N. H.*

---

b. 1712, m. John Belcher; 5, Elizabeth, b. Jan. 31, 1714, m. Samuel How; 6, Abigail, m. Azariah Walker.
4. *Nathaniel*, b. April 1, 1709; d. in Petersham, 1777; m. 1st, in Sudbury, Rebecca Willis, Feb. 23, 1737-8; and had: 1, Elijah, b. June 16, 1739; 2, Ann, b. Jan. 3, 1740; 3, Josiah-Willis, b. July 18, 1742; 4, Rebecca, b. Feb. 3, 1743 4; 5, Joseph; 6, Mary (gemini), b. Jan. 26, 1746; 7, Catharine, b. 1748, m. Dyer, and 2d, Thos. Mellins, and lived in Petersham. Nathaniel, father of the above children, m. 2d, Judith Treadway of Framingham, and had Luther, Calvin, Fanny, Robert, Betty, *Richard-Crafts*, and John Reed. He is said to have had eight children by his first wife. He resided in Framingham, Westminster, and perhaps in Sterling, and lastly in Petersham.
5. *Richard-Crafts*, m. Christiana Slafter.

(3.) John-Hovey, b. Sept, 9, 1835 ; d. Feb. 18, 1837.
(4.) Jabez-True, b. July 13, 1837, in Greenfield, N. H.; m. Susan-
    Frances Robinson, Oct. 25, 1863, and had (a.) Anna-Gertrude,
    b. May 11, 1864, and (b.) Ida-May, b. March 17, 1867, in Plais-
    tow, N. H.
(5.) Lydia, b. Sept. 11, 1838 ; d. same day.
(6.) Helen-Cemantha, b. July 19, 1840, in Peterboro', N. H. ; m.
    Charles-William Tozier, Feb. 10, 1858, and had (a.) Albert
    Monroe, b. June 15, 1860 ; (b.) Charles-Elsworth, b. April 24,
    1863 ; (c.) John-Franklin, b. Oct. 24, 1865.
                                                    Haverhill, Mass.
(7.) Christiana-Elizabeth, b. Nov. 25, 1842, in Plaistow, N. H.; m.
    James-Wilson Drew, Sept. 28, 1866, and had (a.) George-
    Francis, b. March 28, 1867, in Plaistow, N. H.

217. EDMUND-FARWELL,[4][101] (*John,*[3] *Samuel,*[2] *John,*[1]) b. July
26, 1772; d. March 17, 1812; m. Clarissa, daughter of Peter and
Elizabeth (Hitchcock) Tolman of Guilford, Conn., Aug. 27, 1798.
She was b. June 5, 1778 ; d. Sept. 11, 1821. Their children were
born in Norwich. She m. 2d, Eliphalet Tenney of Corinth, Vt., July
17, 1814.   *Norwich, Vt.*

218.   1. EMELINE,[524] b. Sept. 20, 1799 ; m. James Brown.
219.   2. FARWELL, b. Nov. 30, 1800 ; d. Nov. 30, 1800.
220.   3. ALONZO, b. Oct. 14, 1801 ; d. in Bradford, Vt., Feb. 8, 1864. He began
          the study of law, but soon abandoned it, and devoted many years to
          the art of painting, in which he attained merited distinction. He
          was, however, too sensitive and retiring to place himself in a position
          to be known or appreciated by the public. Many portraits and other
          specimens of his art are to be seen in the dwellings of the opulent in
          the valley of the Connecticut where he resided, and in other parts of the
          country. He wrote many sonnets and other poems in early life, some
          of decided merit, a few of which against his wishes got into print, but
          generally they were not permitted to be even copied from his manu-
          script. He never married ; the last years of his life he spent on his
          farm in Bradford Vt., in the rural retirement which he always greatly
          enjoyed.
221.   4. BLOOMY-FAIR,[535] b. Nov. 28, 1803 ; m. Joseph-Stephens Crooke.
222.   5. SOLON, b. Feb. 7, 1808 ; d. Nov. 24, 1839.
223.   6. ORPHA, b. Feb. 26, 1810 ; d. April 22, 1811.

224. JOHN,[4][102] (*John,*[3] *Samuel,*[2] *John,*[1]) b. in Mansfield, Ct.,
Oct. 31, 1776; d. Nov. 21, 1856, in Worth, Mich. He m. Persis,
daughter of the Rev. Timothy and Phalle (Richardson) Grow of
Hartland, Vt., Jan. 14, 1805. She was b. June 17, 1783. He inherited the paternal estate in Norwich ; was a Justice of the Peace many
years, and was prominent in the affairs of the town, for a long
period, where he exercised a most wholesome influence, holding the
offices of selectman, overseer of the poor, &c., &c. He was also much
engaged in surveying lands from early youth down to the last years of
his life. His children were all born in Norwich. He sold his estate
in 1850, and removed to Worth, Tuscola Co., Mich.   *Norwich, Vt.*

225.   1. PHALLE-RICHARDSON,[538] b. Jan. 1, 1806; d. Aug. 14, 1863; m.
          Naham-Newton Wilson.
226.   2. WILLIAM,[547] b. Oct. 1, 1807; m. 1st, Roisa-Hovey Johnson ; 2d,
          Mary-Pierson (Sutherland) Waters.
227.   3. PERSIS-GROW, b. Dec. 28, 1809; m. 1st, Austin, son of Samuel Hutch-
          inson of Norwich, Dec., 1832 ; he was b. June 30, 1807 ; d. March
          28, 1843 ; m. 2d, John Marsh of Hartford, Vt., Dec. 9, 1845.
                                                       Hartford, Vt.

4

228.   4. ELIZABETH-HOVEY, b. June 5, 1812; d. April 1, 1814.
229.   5 JOHN-FARWELL, b. Nov. 11, 1814; d. Oct. 24, 1847, unm., at Keokuk,
           Iowa.   He was a member of Norwich University in 1837, but did not
           graduate.
230.   6. DAVID-GROW,[555] b. Jan. 1, 1817; m. Ann-Calista Lucas.
231.   7. ALMINA-LOUISA,|556] b. July 25, 1819; m. Paschal Richardson.
232.   8. JUDSON,|560] b. Jan. 3, 1822; d. Dec. 31, 1863; m. Mrs. Fanny Tice.
233.   9. AUGUSTA-MALVINA,[564] b. July 11, 1826; m. Oliver-Paul Tobey.

234. SYLVESTER,[4][103] (*John*,[3] *Samuel*,[2] *John*,[1]) b. June 30, 1780;
d. May 9, 1850; m. 1st, Mary-Armstrong, daughter of Calvin* and
Sarah (Armstrong) Johnson of Norwich, Vt., Jan. 20, 1803. She was
b. March 25, 1783; d. Aug. 17, 1835. He m. 2d, Anna, daughter of
Nicholas and Deborah (Ford) White of Bradford, Vt., April 9, 1836.
She was b. Dec. 21, 1790; d. April 1, 1867. He held various town
offices, such as selectman, assessor, grand juror, and some for many
years in succession. He entered upon the study of medicine in early
youth, but soon abandoned it for agricultural pursuits, which were
better suited to his taste. He took a deep interest in the culture of
fruit, and was the first to introduce choice varieties of apples into that
part of the valley of the Connecticut, where he resided. His ideas on
agriculture he occasionally communicated through the local papers.

---

* *Calvin Johnson*, b. in Willington, Ct., Dec. 20, 1755; d. in Norwich, Vt.,
   Oct. 7, 1843. He was married to Sarah, daughter of John Armstrong of
   Norwich, May 30, 1782; she was born in Franklin, Ct., whence her father
   removed to Norwich, Vt. Calvin Johnson enlisted about the 15th of May,
   1775, in Capt. Solomon Wills' Company, of Tolland, Ct, Col. Spencer's
   Reg., and was stationed at Roxbury and Brookline during the siege of Boston; service seven months. He enlisted for six months in 6th Com., 3d
   Conn. Battalion, June, 1776, repaired to New York, stationed on Governor's Island, and was the last man to leave it when the British landed upon
   it after the Battle of Brooklyn; was at the battle of White Plains, and afterward stationed near West Point. He enlisted Dec., 1776, for three
   months, in 2d Com., 3d Conn. Battalion, and was stationed at Rye, N. Y.,
   and was discharged March 25, 1777. In August of the same year he was
   drafted for three months, and served under Capt. David Johnson; was first
   at Fishkill, then at Esopus with the forces stationed there to prevent the
   British army from going to the relief of Burgoyne, who was then at Saratoga; was again stationed at Fishkill, where he was discharged. In June,
   1779, he was again drafted for three months, and was stationed at New London, Conn. His whole service in the revolutionary war was one year and ten
   months. He removed to Norwich, Vt., where his father, an original proprietor, gave him a hundred acres of land, March 29, 1780, on which he
   continued to reside. His children were: 1. *Mary-Armstrong*, b. March 25,
   1783; 2, Calvin, b. Jan. 14, 1785; 3, Esther, b. Jan. 6, 1787; 4, Samuel, b.
   March 26, 1789. The father of Calvin Johnson was:
Capt. William Johnson of Willington, Ct., b. in Lexington, Ms., April 2, 1725;
   died in Willington, Ct. He married Dorcas Chamberlin, Jan. 25, 1750-1; his
   children were: 1, Seth, b. Jan. 29, 1752; 2, William, b. April 23, 1754; 3,
   Calvin, b. Dec. 20, 1755; 4, Dorcas, b. Jan. 24, 1758; 5, Sarah, b. Sept. 10,
   1759; 6, James, b. Aug. 21, 1761; 7, Anne, b. March 1, 1764; 8, John, b.
   June 1, 1766; 9, Tabitha, b. July 18, 1769; 10, Thankful, b. Feb. 17, 1771.
   The father of Capt. William Johnson of Willington was
William Johnson of Lexington, Ms., who married Ruth Rugg of Lexington, Feb.
   2, 1724-5. She was the daughter of Thomas Rugg, and grand-daughter of
   John Rugg of Lancaster, Ms., who was there as early as 1654. Mr. Johnson
   removed soon after his marriage to Concord, Ms., and about 1738 emigrated
   to Willington, Ct., where he had some years previously purchased a landed
   estate. His children were : 1st, *William*, b. April 2, 1725, in Lexington, Mass. ;
   Abel, b. March 8, 1744-5 ; Elisha, b. Sept. 22, 1748 ; the latter two b. in Ct. ;
   he had other children whose names have not been obtained.

Drawn by T. S. Slafter.

OLD PARSONAGE—RESIDENCE OF SYLVESTER SLAFTER, THETFORD, VT.

He resided for many years on a farm near the centre of the town of Thetford, given him by his father, where all his children, with the exception of two, were born. Late in life he sold this estate, and purchased another in the eastern part of the town, containing 130 acres, and including that given by the town to the Rev. Asa Burton, D. D., and known as the " Old Parsonage." On the settlement of Dr. Burton, the parish, then comprising the whole town, gave to him fifty acres of land, and contributed fifty pounds towards the erection of a house. The " Old Parsonage," now standing and in good preservation, was the result of the contributions of the parishoners, mostly by their personal labor, and was erected in the summer of 1779. Mr. Slafter remodelled it in many of its internal arrangements, but preserved intact one room in it for his own use, and in memory of the distinguished divine for whom it was erected, and whom he greatly revered. He occupied this apartment in his declining years, and enjoyed without weariness the beautiful scenery, which it commands, stretching along the valley of the Connecticut. The exterior of the old parsonage has not been changed. The trees, however, by which it is surrounded, were planted by Mr. Slafter. The drawing from which the engraving, which we here present, was made, was by his grandson, Master Theodore S. Slafter, sketched in the summer of 1867, and is very accurate: see No. 585. Most of the sixty or eighty clergymen, educated by Dr. Burton, found an agreeable home in the old parsonage. We give a fac-simile of Mr. Slafter's handwriting at the age of 60 years. *Thetford, Vt.*

Sylvester Slafter.

235. 1. THOMAS-JEFFERSON,[568] b. Aug. 19, 1803 ; m. Rebecca Seaver.
236. 2. CHRISTIANA-SEAVER, b. Oct. 1, 1805 ;· d. June 15, 1811.
237. 3. SARAH-ARMSTRONG, b. Jan. 9, 1808 ; d. July 31, 1844 ; unm.
238. 4. MARY, b. Feb. 24, 1810 ; d. Sept. 20, 1835 ; unm.
239. 5. SYLVESTER,[572] b. Aug. 16, 1812 ; d. Aug. 23, 1854 ; m. Eliza Read.
240. 6. MARCUS, b. April 24, 1815 ; d. July 20, 1815. *Norwich, Vt.*
241. 7. EDMUND-FARWELL,[576] b. May 30, 1816, in Norwich, Vt. ; m. Mary-Anne Hazen.
242. 8. CHRISTIANA-SEAVER,[577] b. Feb. 1, 1819 ; m. Reuben-Chamberlin Tilden.
243. 9. LYMAN,[582] b. Jan. 22, 1822 ; m. 1st, Mary Taylor; 2d, Mrs. Mary-Ann Green.
244. 10. CARLOS,[585] b. July 21, 1825 ; m. Rebecca Bullard.

245. ELIJAH,[4][104] (*John,[3] Samuel,[2] John,[1]*) b. Jan. 9, 1784; d. July 29, 1864; m. Olive, daughter of the Rev. Timothy and Phalle (Richardson) Grow of Hartland, Vt., Jan. 26, 1809. She was born Jan. 24, 1791; d. April 21, 1854. He resided three years after his marriage in Norwich, Vt., where two of his children were born. After this he removed to Orange, Vt., where the rest of his children were born. In 1828 he removed to Lawrence, N. Y., and in 1856 to Genesee, Mich., where he continued to reside till the close of his life. He had a mechanical turn of mind and was the author of several useful inventions. At nearly eighty years of age he invented a successful corn planter. *Genesee, Michigan.*

246. 1. HERMONA,[588] b. Nov. 14, 1809 ; m. Clark Chandler.
247. 2. CORODEN-HOVEY,[594] b. Jan. 31, 1811 ; d. April 7, 1841 ; m. Maria Maine.

248.   3. CAROLINE, b. July 20, 1813; d. April 7, 1857; m. 1st, Sept. 18, 1836,
Rev. Peter Robinson of Marion, Iowa; 2d, Samuel Hoyt of Parisville,
N. Y.; 3d, Luther Hurlburt of Stockholm, N. Y.; she had by her 1st
husband, Albert-Coroden, b. May 13, 1841, in Lawrence, N. Y. In war
of rebellion he was in U. S. service three years in Com. A, 60th N.Y.
Regt. He was severely wounded at the battle of Chattanooga and
receives a pension; he m. at Adams, N. Y., Dec. 22, 1868, Elvira-
Rhoda Crane.   *Marseilles, Ill.*

249.   4. CHRISTIANA, b June 2, 1815; d. May 31st, 1837.
250.   5. LEVINIA,[595] b. June 2, 1817; m. Jacob Smith.
251.   6. OLIVE-SALOME,[602] b. May 4, 1819; m. Amos-Emerson Smith.
252.   7. TOLMAN-TENNY,[606] b. Sept. 12, 1821; m. Eliza-Miller Waters.
253.   8. ELIZABETH-JANE, b. March 26, 1823; d. July 27, 1825.
254.   9. HELEN-PHALLE. b. Oct. 23, 1827.
255. 10. EDWIN-MAROW,[610] b. Jan. 7, 1830; m. Lominda Palmer.

256. ELEAZER,[4][107] (*Eleazer,[3] Samuel,[2] John,[1]*) b. Sept. 28, 1775;
d. Oct. 1, 1860; m. Polly Burleigh of Mansfield, Ct., May 8, 1796.
She was born Feb. 6, 1777; d. Sept. 20, 1863.   *Willington, Ct.*

257.   1. ARTEMAS,[612] b. Nov. 18, 1796; m. 1st, Hannah Baker; 2d, Mrs. Esther
Buffington.
258.   2. HORACE, b. Oct. 6, 1802; d. Jan. 8, 1807.
259.   3. ALMIRA,[614] b. Dec. 29, 1804; m. Royal-Chapman Eldridge.

260. IRA,[4][108] (*Eleazer,[3] Samuel,[2] John,[1]*) b. May 13, 1778; d. in
Pompey, N. Y., April 9, 1818; m. Joanna, daughter of Samuel Jacobs
of Mansfield, Ct., Dec. 6, 1801. She was born March 13, 1780; d.
April 18, 1857.

261.   1. ZEMIRA-MAHALA,[615] b. Sept. 11, 1802, in Mansfield, Ct.; m. Joel
Bishop.
262.   2. MARILDA,[626] b. in Cambridge, N. Y., July 1, 1805; d. Dec. 10, 1849;
m. Simmons Warren.
263.   3. SANDFORD,[629] b. in New Lisbon, N. Y., July 24, 1808; d. Oct. 23,
1842; m. Elmina Wood.
264.   4. OLIVE, b. May 5, 1809.   *Watervale, N. Y.*
265.   5. ELIZA-PERKINS, b. in Butternuts, N. Y., Nov. 17, 1812. *Watervale,
N. Y.*
266.   6. JESSE-BENNET,[631] b. in Butternuts, March 21, 1815; m. 1st, Ophelia-
Brunette Gage; m. 2d, Henrietta-Maria Holman.
267.   7. MARY-FREEMAN,[636] b in Guilford, N. Y., July 24, 1817; m. Luther-
James Wheelock.

268. CALVIN,[4][111] (*Eleazer,[3] Samuel,[2] John,[1]*) b. April 11, 1784;
d. Sept. 7, 1857, in Portage Co., Wis.; m. Jerusha, daughter of Elijah
Dexter of Cambridge, N. Y., May 25, 1809. She was b. Jan. 23,
1791; d. in Fond du Lac, Wis., March 8, 1861. He resided at different times in Cambridge, Manlius, Pompey, and Cuba, N. Y., and in
Greenwood, Ill.

269.   1. ASAHEL,[647] b. in Cambridge, N. Y., Feb. 28, 1810; m. Electa Pierce.
270.   2. ADELIA-MARIA, b. in Cambridge, N. Y., Feb. 15, 1812.
271.   3. ELIJAH-DEXTER,[653] b. in Pompey, N. Y., Dec. 14, 1814; m. Maria-
Lucretia Lilly.
272.   4. ORIN,[659] b. in Pompey, Feb. 16, 1818; m. Dorcas-Reinshaw Collins.
273.   5. TRYPHENA,[660] b. in Pompey, Feb. 25, 1820; m. Henry-Wallace
Bruce.
274.   6. IRA, b. in Cuba, N. Y., April 15, 1822; d. Sept. 28, 1845; unm.
275.   7. CYNTHIA,[664] b. in Cuba, May 25, 1824; d. Aug. 14, 1845; m. John-
Michael Kull.
276.   8. MARILDA,[669] b. in Cuba, Oct. 23, 1826; d. Jan. 28, 1859; m. Edwin-
Ruthvin Roberts.

277. Samuel,[4][114] (*Eleazer,*[3] *Samuel,*[2] *John,*[1]) b. April 22, 1791; m. 1st, Lydia, daughter of Ebenezer Fisher of Pompey, N. Y., June 3, 1813. She was born Sept. 2, 1793; d. Sept. 14, 1832; m. 2nd, Mrs. Mary Chatterton, dau. of Ezra Elwell of Southeast, N. Y., Dec. 5, 1832. She was b. April 27, 1795. He resided in Cambridge, Pompey, Scott, Homer, Virgil and Ledyard, N. Y., and in 1859 removed to Wautoma, Wis. He was town clerk in Virgil and postmaster, was Deacon of the Baptist Church there for many years, and now (1868) holds the same office in the Baptist Church at *Wautoma,* his present residence. His children were as follows:

278.   1. Antha-Matherson, b. in Cambridge, N. Y., May 29, 1814; d. Sept. 20, 1832.
279.   2. William-Purlee,[643] b. in Scott, N. Y., Oct. 11, 1817; m. Maria Campbell.
280.   3. Arabella-Amanda, b. in Scott, N. Y., Nov. 18, 1819; d. Aug. 26, 1820.
281.   4. Edwin-Philander,[646] b. in Homer, N. Y., Sept. 26, 1821; m. 1st, Sarah-Miranda Johnson; 2d, Helen-Maria Sumner.
282.   5. Harriet-Amanda, b. in Homer, N. Y., Oct. 31, 1824; d. Sept. 28, 1832.

283. Tryphosa,[4] [115] (*Eleazer,*[3] *Samuel,*[2] *John,*[1]) b. March 25, 1793; m. Moses, son of Jerod Thompson of Mansfield, Ct., Sept. 21, 1813; he was b. Sept. 30, 1792; d. Dec. 27, 1832. *Mansfield, Ct.*

284.   1. Lucius, b. June 20, 1814; m. Ann-Caroline Bromley, May 2, 1836; photographer. *Norwich, Ct.*
285.   2. Mary, b. May 22, 1817; m. Dec. 2, 1839, Isaac-Parks Davis, Hartford, Ct., and had:
        (1.) Mary-Jane, b. Aug. 23, 1840.
        (2.) Ellen-Maria, b. Aug. 24, 1842.
        (3.) Walter-Shaffer, b. Aug. 15, 1846. Served in U. S. Navy from Aug. 6, 1862, to Aug. 6, 1863.
        (4.) Emily-Josephine, b. Oct. 12, 1847.
        (5.) Anne-Carrie, b. Dec. 16, 1849. All born in Windham, Ct.
286.   3. Emily, born Aug. 13, 1819; m. 1st, Hiram Spencer, Jan. 1, 1843; m. 2d, Daniel Spencer, and had, (1.) Edwin-Eugene, (2.) Frances-Eliza-beth, (3.) Jared-Aurelius, (4.) Emily, (5.) Sophia.
        Salt Lake City, Utah Ter.
287.   4. Lucetta, b. Nov. 18, 1821; d. Aug. 18, 1835.
289.   5. Mardula, b. March 21, 1824; d. June 27, 1860; m. Orlando-Hallam Godfrey, and had (1.) Charles Henry, (2.) Orlando Hallam, (3.) Gerard-Chapman, (4.) John-Fremont, (5.) Mardula-Elizabeth.
290.   6. Almira, b. April 30, 1826; d. Dec. 18, 1858; m. William-E. Whiting of Hannibal, Mo., and had (1.) Idah-Thompson. *Providence, R. I.*
291.   7. Henry-Eugene, b. June 12, 1831. He enlisted at St. Louis, Aug. 10, 1861, in Com. G, 10th Missouri Vols. He was made Corporal on the day of enlistment, and during the last nine months of his service was Quarter Master Sergeant. He was discharged, Aug. 27, 1864, having served three years and seventeen days. He was in the battle of Pitts-burg Landing, April 6th–7th, 1862; at the siege of Corinth under Gen. Pope; in the battle of Iuka, Mississippi, Sept. 19, 1862, under Gen. Rosecrans; in 2d battle of Corinth, Oct. 3–4, 1862; in the Yazoo Pass expedition; was under Gen. Grant all through the Vicksburg Campaign; in battle of Port Gibson, May 8, 1863; in the battle of Ray-mond, May 10th; Jackson, May 14th; Champion Hills, May 15th; Black River Bridge, May 17th, and forty-seven days in the trenches at Vicksburg. Marched from Memphis to Chattanooga, was in action at Mission Ridge, at Ringold Gap on Nov. 28, 1863; with Gen. Sher-man in the Atlanta Campaign. On the 15th of Aug. the Reg. was re-lieved from duty and ordered home; he was ordered forward on Quar-

Master's duty, and was near being captured at Dalton, Ga., when it was taken by the rebel Gen Wheeler. He was discharged at St. Louis at the date above mentioned. He m. Sarah Curtis, Feb. 13, 1853, at St. Joseph's, Mo., and had,

    (1.) Francis-L., born at Cincinnati, O., Dec. 19, 1853.
    (2.) Alice-M., b. at Warsaw, Ill., Aug. 13, 1855.
    (3.) Henrietta-G., b. at Hamilton, Ill., April 15, 1858.
    (4.) Vincent, b. at Hamilton, Ill., Nov. 20, 1860.
                               South Manchester, Conn.

292. ABNER,[4][122] (*Joseph,*[3] *Joseph,*[2] *John,*[1]) b. Feb. 28, 1743–4; m. Sarah Russell, probably in 1765. She died Aug., 1822, said to be 84 years of age. Their children were as follows:—

293. 1. WILLIAM,[672] b. 1766; d. March 20, 1839; m. Elizabeth Peters.
294. 2. ABNER, b. 1768; d. May 20, 1852; m. Susan, and had: (1.) Hannah,
        (2.) Sarah, (3.) Alonzo, (4.) George, (5.) Samuel, (6.) Juda.
295. 3. DAVID. }
296. 4. JOSHUA. } Of these no information has been obtained.
297. 5. JOSEPH. }
298. 6. ABRAHAM,[677] b. March 29, 1775; d. March 17, 1865; m. Anna Mann.

299. JOSEPH,[4][123] (*Joseph,*[3] *Joseph,*[2] *John,*[1]) b. Oct. 10, 1745; m. Lois King of R. I. He was a soldier in the revolutionary war. Is said to have been in the service most of the time during the war. He declined to receive a pension, saying that his services were freely given, and he was not in need of aid. He was held in great respect and esteem. Resided in Foster, R. I., until about 1778, when he removed to Guilford, Vt., and again removed to Preston, N. Y., about 1814. The first eight of his children were born in Foster, R. I., the rest in Guilford, Vt., where he resided many years. Late in life he removed to Preston, N. Y. Their children were as follows:—

300. 1. ISAAC,[683] b. Jan. 28, 1765; d. Aug. 4, 1847; m. Mary Harrington.
301. 2. KEZIAH[704] b. June 29, 1766; d. July 11, 1815; m. Isaac Stafford.
302. 3. BARBARA, d. young, but was living in 1774.
303. 4. AMY,[695] b. Aug. 11, 1769; d. April 25, 1840; m. Job Stafford.
304. 5. RUTH, m. Stephen, son of Rev. Maturin Ballou of Richmond, N. H., and
        had (a.) Barbara, (b.) Rebecca, (c.) Stephen, (d.) Tryphosa, (e.) Lu-
        cinda.   *Preston, N. Y.*
305. 6. BENJAMIN, d. in his 21st year.
306. 7. MARY, m. John Bennet, and had (a.) Lydia, (b.) Naomi, (c.) Delana,
        (d.) Ruth, (e.) Lois.
307. 8. JONATHAN,[715] b. Jan. 19, 1776; d. April 28, 1841; m. 1st, Abigail
        Holmes; m. 2d, Persis Graves.
308. 9. JOSEPH, b. May 7, 1778; m. Relief Farnsworth.
309. 10. LOIS,[723] b. April 20, 1780; d. Feb. 25, 1844; m. Royal Moses.
310. 11. ISRAEL,[737] b. May 7, 1782; d. Jan. 5, 1865; m. Susannah Gage.
311. 12. NATHAN, b. June 17, 1784; m. Lovina Wilcox; no chil.
312. 13. CHLOE,[731] b. June 17, 1784; d. May 15, 1864, m. Elihu Hayes.
313. 14. MOSES,[746] b. Oct. 8, 1787; d. Aug. 16, 1836; m. Milly Fisher.

314. ABIAL,[4][124] (*Joseph,*[3] *Joseph,*[2] *John,*[1]) b. Sept. 15, 1747; d. 1813; m. Anna, dau. of Ahijah Adams; she died in 1826. Their children were as follows:—   *Foster, R. I.*

315. 1. MOSES, b. before 1774; d. about 1840; unm.   *Foster, R. I.*
316. 2. ANNA, b. after 1774; m. Henry Randall, and had (1.) Eliza, (2.) Hannah,
        (3.) Prudence, (4.) Henry, (5.) Silas, (6.) Aaron. Removed to Cayuga
        Co., N. Y.
317. 3. PRUDENCE,[763] b. April 8, 1781; m. Samuel Brown.
318. 4. SILAS,[750] b. Aug. 25, 1783; d. May 10, 1855; m. 1st, Mary Randall;
        m. 2d, Alice Harrington.
319. 5. ABIAL, unmarried; died, 1829.   *Foster, R. I.*

320. SILAS,[4][125] (*Joseph,*[3] *Joseph,*[2] *John,*[1]) b. Nov. 26, 1754; d. Aug. or Sept., 1825; m. 1773, Beulah, dau. of Ahijah Adams of Killingly; m. 2d, Sarah, dau. of Stephen Coomer, widow of —— Whitney. His will was signed Aug. 2, 1825, and was offered for probate, Sept. 19, 1825. He was a Justice of the Peace, and exercised a great influence among his neighbors. Had clear views on many subjects, and facility in expressing them. Their children, the two last by 2d wife, were as follows: *Foster, R. I.*

321. 1. HANNAH,[777] b. Feb. 29, 1775; d. Oct. 21, 1857; m. Joseph Smith.
322. 2. SILAS,[791] b. Nov. 28, 1777; d. April 1, 1865; m. Susan Burgess.
323. 3. STEPHEN,[805] b. Nov. 15, 1779; d. May 20, 1851; m. Sarah Williams.
324. 4. MARY,[815] b. Oct. 4, 1781; m. Brinton Arnold.
325. 5. JOHN,[826] b. Sept. 7, 1784; m. Naomi Rice.
326. 6. BEULAH, b. Sept. 12, 1786; died young.
327. 7. PAUL,[785] b. June 3, 1788; m. Chloe Shippee.
328. 8. ANNA, b. May 6, 1790; died young.
329. 9. PATIENCE,[789] b. Nov. 3, 1791; d. Oct. 18, 1820; m. Whitford Whitney.
330. 10. CHARLOTTE,[771] b. Sept. 29, 1793; d. Sept. 28, 1858; m. William Turner.
331. 11. JOSEPH,[840] b. March 30, 1795; m. Roby Bates.
332. 12. JAMES, b. 1816; d. 1822.
333. 13. SARAH-ANN, b. 1819; d.

334. JOHN,[4][126] (*Joseph,*[3] *Joseph,*[2] *John,*[1]) b. 1756; d. in Guilford, Feb. 14, 1815; m. Lois, dau. of the Hon. Benjamin Carpenter of Guilford, Vt., Lieut. Governor of that State in 1779. On a large marble slab, in the Cemetery in the western part of Guilford, is the following unique inscription:

" SACRED TO THE MEMORY OF THE HON. BENJ. CARPENTER, Esq. Born in Rehoboth, Mass., A. D. 1726. A magistrate in Rhode Island in A. D. 1764. A public teacher of righteousness, An able advocate to his last for Democracy, And the equal rights of man. Removed to this town, A. D. 1770. Was a field officer in the revolutionary war. A founder of the first Constitution and government of Vermont. A Councillor of Censors in A. D. 1783, A member of the Council and Lieut. Governor of the State in A. D. 1779. A firm professor of Christianity in the baptist church 50 years. Left this world and 146 persons of lineal posterity, March 29, 1804. Aged 78 years 10 months and 12 days, with a strong Mind and full faith of a more Glorious state hereafter. Stature about six feet—weight 200. Death had no terror."

Their children were as follows:

335. 1. JOSEPH,[854] b. July 26, 1772; d. Feb. 26, 1861; m. Hannah Spaulding.
336. 2. HANNAH,[870] b. Sept. 4, 1774; d. March 14, 1835; m. Ezra-Gleason Ayers.
337. 3. RHODA,[876] b. May 23, 1778; d. Feb. 14, 1862; m. Alanson Hayes.
338. 4. HULDA,[864] b. Nov. 1, 1780; d. Jan. 24, 1866.
339. 5. PRUDENCE,[886] b. Feb. 5, 1783; d. May 30, 1852; m. John Hammond.
340. 6. JOHN,[902] b. Aug. 27, 1786; d. Dec. 16, 1853; m. Sarah Gove.
341. 7. LOIS,[897] b. April 10, 1788; d. Oct. 5, 1860; m. Leverett Mallory.
342. 8. IRA,[919] b. Nov. 15, 1790; m. Sally Liscom.
343. 9. FANNY,[908] b. Feb. 21, 1796; d. Sept. 1, 1868; m. Luther Fuller.

344. SARAH,[4][128] (*Joseph,*[3] *Joseph,*[2] *John,*[1]) d. Aug. 1808; m. William, son of Thomas Taylor; he was seven years a soldier in the revolutionary war; was at the battle of Bunker Hill; removed from

Rhode Island to Burlington, N. Y., where he died, March 20, 1802.
Their children were as follows :

345.   1. JOSEPH, m. Lois Booth, and had :
        (1.) Joseph, who, in war of rebellion, was in Comp. I, Indiana Vol.
        (2.) George-Silas.
        (3) Lois-Mariah
346.   2. THOMAS, m. Nancy Gorham, and had : (1.) William ; (2.) Margaret ;
        (3.) Hiram ; (4.) Anna ; (5.) George ; (6.) Israel.
347.   3. STEPHEN, m. Prudence Fox.
348.   4. ESTHER, m. Cornelius Bulson.
349.   5. WARREN, resided at Spring Valley, Rock Co., Wisconsin ; m. Hannah
      Osgood, and had :
        (1.) Hiram-Moses, who, in war of rebellion, was in Comp. G, 13th
          Mich. Vol.
        (2.) Warren, who was in Comp. G, 13th Mich. Vol.
        (3.) William-James.
350.   6. GEORGE, m, Lydia Markham, and had : (1.) John-Amasa ; (2) Clarinda ;
        (3.) Horatio-Theodore ; (4.) Jennette ; (5.) Lucinda ; (6.) Caroline.
351.   7. SILAS.
352.   8. AMASA, b. June 24, 1797 ; m. Mary-Ann Goodwin, and had :
        (1.) Sarah ; (2.) Ezekiel-Valarous, who, in war of rebellion, was in
          Comp. K, 7th Mich. Cavalry ; died in service, Dec. 28, 1864.
353.   9. SUSANNAH, b. Feb. 27, 1800 ; m. Arnold Dyer, June 26, 1820.
354. 10. SARAH, b. —— ; d. 1811.

355. RHODA,[4][146] (*John,[3] Joseph,[2] John,[1]*) b. Feb. 24, 1771 ; d.
March 5, 1859 ; m. Willard, son of Job Shippee, April 10, 1794. He
was b. May 9, 1761 ; d. March 6, 1844. His children were as follows :
                                   Foster, R. I.

356.   1. ROBERT, b. Dec. 22, 1794 ; m. 1st, Anna, daughter of Thomas Shippee ;
      2d, Mary Place ; and by 1st wife had (1.) Willis-Hubbard, (2.) Diana,
      (3) Hannah-Mahala, (4.) Emily-Ann, (5.) John-Washington, (6.) Ra-
      chel-Matilda ; by 2d wife, (7.) William, (8.) Catharine-Melissa, (9.)
      Harriet-Adaline.   *North Foster, R. I.*
357.   2. ELIJAH, b. March 22, 1799, married Levila Simons, widow, dau. of King
      Easton of Foster, R. I., April, 1833, and had, (1.) Olney, (2.) James-
      Lewis, (3.) Albert-Henry.   *North Foster, R. I.*
358.   3. CELIA, b. June 24, 1805.   *North Foster, R. I.*
359.   4. ESEK, b. Dec. 16, 1808 ; married Catharine-Matilda, dau. of Cyrus
      Collins of Scituate. She d. Sept. 2, 1848. They had, (1.) Andrew-
      Lewis, (2.) Lorenzo-Munroe, (3.) Waterman-Allen-Francis.
                                   North Foster, R. I.
360.   5. MARY-ANN, b. Aug. 1, 1816.   *North Foster, R. I.*

361. SARAH,[4][141] (*John,[3] Joseph,[2] John,[1]*) b. 1760 ; d. Sept., 1828 ;
m. John, son of Constant Maguire of East Greenwich, R. I., 1784. He
was b. 1755 ; d. Aug. 9, 1827 : was in U. S. service in revolutionary
war. Their children were as follows :   *Exeter, R. I.*

362.   1. RUTH, b. Oct. 6, 1784 ; m. George, son of Samuel Money, Nov., 1815,
      and had :
        (1.) Sarah, b. Feb. 17, 1817, who m. William-Armstrong Hendrick.
          He was in Com. C, 3d Rhode Island Vols. ; in war of rebellion
          served as "fifer" three years. Their son, Albert-Everton Hen-
          drick, enlisted, Oct., 1861, in Battery B, 1st Rhode Island Light
          Artillery, and was in battles of Fair Oaks, Antietam, and
          Fredericksburg, where he received a wound of which he died,
          Dec. 23, 1862.
        (2) Priscilla, b. Aug. 22, 1818 ; d. July 9, 1840.
        (3) Samuel, b. Sept. 10, 1820 ; d. July 1, 1856.   *Pine Hill, R. I.*
363.   2. CONSTANT, b. July 4, 1786 ; d. Aug. 11, 1854 ; m. Christina Darling,
      and removed to Royalton, N. Y.
364.   3. PHEBE, b. July 13, 1790 ; m. July, 1809, Daniel Lewis, and had (1.)
      Daniel.

365.   4. SOPHIA, b. Sept. 7, 1799; m. Joshua Davis, and had, (1) Sibel, (2.) James,
(3.) Elizabeth.   *Royalton, N. Y.*

366. BENJAMIN,[4][140] (*John*,[3] *Joseph*,[2] *John*,[1]) b. Aug. 28, 1758; d.
in Seneca, N. Y., 1812; m. Waitie, dau. of Nicholas Hopkins of Foster, R. I., and widow of Zebulon Bennet, who fell at the battle of Bennington; she was b. Jan., 1751; d. in Richland, N. Y., Dec., 1834; she
had four sons by her first husband, Asa, David and Zebulon, who, with
a fourth, died young. The subject of this notice was a soldier in the
revolutionary war, having served four years, and related with pride
to his grandchildren how he had guarded the tent of Washington. He
resided first, after his marriage, in Preston, Ct., where the eldest two of
his children were born; afterward in Ashford, Ct., where the rest of his
children were born, and where he owned a landed estate, which he sold,
and removed to Eaton, N. Y., in 1804. The following were his children:

367.   1. BENJAMIN,[931] b. Jan. 7, 1780; d. Aug. 1, 1848; m. Mary Burdick.
368.   2. DANIEL,[943] b. Aug. 17, 1781; d. Jan. 13, 1842; m. Rhoda Hopkins.
369.   3. NATHAN,[952] b. April 9, 1784; m. Freelove Crossman.
370.   4. LEVI, b. 1790; d. at the age of nine months.
371.   5. ELISHA,[958] b. Jan. 3, 1795; d. May 24, 1832; m. Hannah Merithew.

372. SAMUEL,[4][134] (*Abraham*,[3] *Joseph*,[2] *John*,[1]) m. Delana, daughter of Andrew Moffit of Salisbury, Conn. He d. about 1822. She
was born about 1769, and died, 1851. Their children were as follows:
Salisbury, Ct.

373.   1. ELIZABETH,[1049] b. May 6, 1793; d. Oct. 9, 1861; m. 1st, Ebenezer
Foot; 2d, Alexander Jackson.
374.   2. ABRAHAM, b. 1795; m. Jane Worden, and had children.
375.   3. HANNAH, b. about 1797; died young.
376.   4. AMY, b. 1799; died young.
377.   5. ASENATH,[1009] b. Aug. 28, 1802; m. William Waters.
378.   6. PHILENA, b. about 1804; m. Freeman Worden.
379.   7. SAMUEL,[1001] b. Sept. 5, 1806; m. Olive Dibell.
380.   8. JOHN,[1028] b. Jan. 1, 1809; m. Eliza Carl.
381.   9. PERRY-PRATT,[1038] b. April 12, 1812; m. Lucinda More.
382. 10. FANNY; m. Caleb Spade.
382½. 11. LUTHER,[1019] b. Dec. 18, 1818; m. Emma Jones.

383. STEPHEN,[4][131] (*Abraham*,[3] *Joseph*,[2] *John*,[1]) b. Aug. 1, 1752;
d. Sept., 1821; m. his cousin Hannah, daughter of his uncle Joseph, 1776,
(see No. 127); resided in Halifax, Vt., Plymouth, Vt., and removed
to Western New York. Their children were:
Brownsville, Jeff. Co., N. Y.

384.   1. SILAS, b. 1777; d. July 10, 1864; m. 1st, Bethia Thomas; m. 2d, Ap-
pelone Morton.
385.   2. HANNAH, b. 1779; d. Aug., 1859; m. Joseph Boynton.
386.   3 PHEBE, b. 1781; m. —— Sawyer.
387.   4. STEPHEN,[962] b. Jan. 9, 1783; d. Dec. 16, 1855; m. Eunice Temple.
388.   5. SARAH, d. in infancy.
389.   6. ABIAL,[974] b. May 25, 1789; d. May 5, 1853.
390.   7. SARAH, b. 1793; d. 1810.
391.   8. BELINDA, b. 1794; d. 1847; m. Daniel Whipple.
392.   9. LOIS, b. 1795; d. 1844; m. Joseph Jeffers.
393. 10. JOSEPH,[982] b. Aug. 18, 1798; m. 1st, Zylpha Morgan; 2d, Sarah
Smith.

394. EXPERIENCE,[4][151] (*Anthony*,[3] *Moses*,[2] *John*,[1]) b. Jan. 4, 1773 ;
d. 1844, m. Noah Paulk, Jan., 1793 ; he died July 18, 1795 ; he was son
of Noah, and a grandson of Samuel and Sarah (Slafter) Paulk, see No.
45. They had but one child.   *Springfield, Mass.*

395. 1. NOAH, b. June 3, 1795 ; d. March 25, 1861 ; m. Roxana Bolton, widow of
—— Webster, and had :
(a.) Roxana-Matilda, b. Oct. 9, 1827.
(b.) Noah-Webster, b. May 20, 1830. In war of rebellion was in
Com. I, 122d New York Vol., and in Invalid Corps.
(c.) Elizabeth-Elvira, b. June 23, 1833.
(d.) Arthur-Monteith, b. May 28, 1836.
(e.) John-Lovin, born March 20, 1840. In war of rebellion in Comp.
H, 12th New York Vol., two years, and afterward in 15th N.
Y. Cavalry.
(f.) Ettie-Ruth, b. April 12, 1843.
                                   Plank Road, Onondaga Co., N. Y.

396. ANTHONY,[4][153] (*Anthony*,[3] *Moses*,[2] *John*,[1]) b. about 1779; d.
Feb. 16, 1850; m. Lovina Carpenter. She was b. about 1785 ; d. June
14, 1849. They had the following children :   *Ludlow, Mass.*

397. 1. ANTHONY, m. 1st, Maria Fuller ; 2d, Paulina Pollard, and had : (a.)
Paulina ; (b.) Edwin ; (c.) Sarah ; (d.) Dexter ; (e.) Benjamin ; (f.)
Rhoda ; (g.) Mary-Jane, b. March 9, 1845.
398. 2. HORATIO,[1171] b. Feb. 1, 1807 ; m. 1st, Lucinda Fuller ; 2d, Julia Butler.
399. 3. MARY, b. Sept. 4, 1808 ; d. March, 1836 ; m. Joseph Brown, and had
Frances and Charles.
400. 4. AMELIA,[1180] b. Sept. 12, 1810 ; d. Sept. 24, 1863 ; m. Orrin Bramble.
401. 5. ALMIRA ; d. young.
402. 6. IRENE, m. 1st, Hiram Ferry, and had : 1. Hiram ; 2. Filena ; she m. 2d,
Francis Bliss.   *Palmer Depot, Mass.*
403. 7. SARAH-FROST,[1193] b. April 4, 1817 ; m. Alfred Trumball.
404. 8. EDMUND, d. young.
405. 9. SALMON, d. young.
406. 10. SOPHIA-DWIGHT ; m. —— Packard.
407. 11. JULIA, d. young.
408. 12. SALMON, b. Sept. 27, 1829 ; m. Mary-Eliza Warriner, Aug. 13, 1849 ;
she d. April 4, 1852 ; m. 2d, Caroline Lyons, Feb. 13, 1853. Children
by first wife : 1, Mary-Ann, b. Nov. 13, 1850 ; 2, Jane, b. March 8,
1852.   *Palmer Depot, Mass.*

409. SARAH,[4][154] (*Anthony*,[3] *Moses*,[2] *John*,[1]) b. Jan. 21, 1783; m.
Alpha, son of Aaron Frost of East Winsor, Ct., 1805. He was b.
July 30, 1782; d. Nov. 8, 1863 ; he removed to Western New York.
Their children were as follows :   *Leonardsville, N. Y.*

410. 1. SALMON, b. March 16, 1806; d. Feb. 10, 1852 ; m. Mary-Ann Davis,
and had : (a.) Henry ; (b.) Sarah ; (c.) Amos ; (d.) Adeline ; (e.)
Maria.   *West Edmeston, N. Y.*
411. 2. EXPERIENCE, b. June 29, 1807, m. Oliver Hooker, and had : (a.) Ed-
win-Smith ; (b.) Pallas-Henrietta ; (c.) Hiram-Clark ; (d.) Alonzo- Leroy ; (e.) Frank-Horace.   *Leonardsville, N. Y.*
412. 3. CLARISSA-HARLOW, b. Jan. 21, 1810; m. —— Lattin, and had : (a.)
Athalinda-Adaline ; (b.) Lucinda ; (c.) Ansel ; (d.) Edmund.
                                            Hartwick, N. Y.
413. 4. ZEBULON-SLAFTER, b. Nov. 17, 1811 ; d. April 12, 1821.
414. 5. DIMMIS-ADALINE, b. Oct. 24, 1813 ; m. Amos Fitch, and had : (a.) Melissa ; (b.) George ; (c.) Emma-Mary ; (d.) Franklin ; (e.) Romina.
415. 6. DAVID, b May 23, 1823 ; d. Nov., 1823.

416. DAVID-FROST,[4][155] (*Anthony*,[3] *Moses*,[2] *John*,[1]) b. March 1,
1784; d. May 31, 1866; m. 1st, Dimmis, dau. of Elijah Baldwin of
Norwich, Vt., Feb. 10, 1811. She was born Dec. 18, 1791 ; d. Aug. 15,
1819. He m. 2d, Emelia, dau. of Rev. Timothy and Phalle (Richard-

son) Grow of Hartland, Vt., Jan. 18, 1820. He resided in Ludlow, Ms., in Chelsea, Norwich, Royalton, and Cabot, Vt. His children by his last wife were born in Norwich. *Cabot, Vt.*

417. 1. DIMMIS-EVELINE, b. Dec. 15, 1812; d. April 28, 1830.
418. 2. EDMUND-BALDWIN, b. 1815; d. Aug. 27, 1821.
419. 3. CHASTINA, b. Aug. 15, 1817; d. Aug. 28, 1821.
420. 4. RACHEL,[1198] b. Oct. 5, 1820; m. George Lyman.
421. 5. JAMES-GROW,[1201] b. Jan. 11, 1822; m. 1st, Lucy-Melinda Wheeler; 2d, Mrs Julia-Augusta Lamkin.
422. 6. CHARLOTTE-ELIZABETH,[1203] b. Jan. 23, 1826; m. John Wilde.
423. 7. CLARISSA, b. Oct. 9, 1827.
424. 8. CLARINDA-LAMSON, b. Oct. 25, 1829; d. Dec. 22, 1855.

425. ZEBULON-WEST,[4][156] (*Anthony,[3] Moses,[2] John,[1]*) b. Aug. 26, 1785; d. in New Haven, Ct., March 22, 1862; m. 1st, Hannah, daughter of Reuben Frost of Ludlow, Mass., Nov. 5, 1807; m. 2d, Mrs. Sarah Foster, Dec. 24, 1844. Their children were as follows:
New Haven, Conn.

426. 1. EUNICE,[1207] b. July 13, 1809; m. 1st, Parsons-Gates Willey; m. 2d, Edwin-McRea Billings.
427. 2. DWIGHT, b. Jan. 7, 1811; d. May 7, 1823.
428. 3. LOVICE,[1218] b. March 22, 1813; m. 1st, Samuel Eley; m. 2d, Samuel Philips.
429. 4. ANGELINA,[1223] b. April 23, 1815; m. William Ballou.
430. 5. HENRY, b. Aug. 10, 1817; d. May 8, 1823.
431. 6. JESSE-FARNUM,[1233] b. Sept. 3, 1820; m. 1st, Fidelia Burnet; m. 2d, Anngenett Loomis.
432. 7. ELIZABETH-BULLARD,[1238] b. April 22, 1822; m. Benjamin-Daniel Tilden.

433. JEHIEL,[4][159] (*Moses,[3] Moses,[2] John,[1]*) b. Nov. 15, 1778; d. June 23, 1860; m. 1st, Mary Weaver; m. 2d, Lydia Avery, Oct. 16, 1808—she was b. Dec. 25, 1784, d. July 12, 1854; m. 3d, Susan Payne, July 23, 1855. He resided in Potsdam, N. Y., and afterward removed to Ohio. Their children were as follows:
Norwalk, Huron Co., Ohio.

434. 1. AVICE; d. in infancy.
435. 2. ROYAL-GAY, b. in Tolland, Ct., May 7, 1803; in war of rebellion he was in Comp. F, 43d Ohio Vol., from Dec. 20, 1861, to Aug. 1, 1862; discharged for disability; m. Cynthia, daughter of Calvin Munsell of Winsor, Ct., and had Mary-Jane, b. Dec. 19, 1828; d. about 1848, in Thomsonville, Ct. *Elyria, Lorain Co., Ohio.*
436. 3. CORDELIA, b. in Potsdam, N. Y., Sept. 4, 1810; d. Nov. 7, 1810.
437. 4. CHARLES-AVERY,[1060] b. in Potsdam, Sept. 12, 1811; m. 1st, Sarah Williams; 2d, Emeline Slater.
438. 5. JEHIEL, b. in Potsdam, Dec. 22, 1813; d Sept. 27, 1815.
439. 6. CHARLOTTE,[1067] b. in Potsdam, June 6, 1816; m. 1st, Daniel Crandall; 2d, William Bridges; 3d, Asaph-Dickinson Leonard.
440. 7. CATHARINE,[1074] b. in Potsdam, April 10, 1818; d. June 17, 1857; m. 1st, John Fox Van Eman; 2d, Isaac-Thomas Gaylord.
441. 8. MARIA,[1080] b. in Potsdam, April 24, 1820; m. William-Henry Phillips.
442. 9. IRA, b. in Potsdam, Nov. 15, 1822; d. May 11, 1844.
443. 10. BENJAMIN-FRANKLIN, b. in Hanover, N. Y., March 31, 1825; m. Corde Burroughs, May 15, 1855. She was b. Nov. 6, 1828.
Brighton, Sacramento Co., California.
444. 11. MARY-ELECTA,[1087] b. in Hanover, N. Y., June 17, 1830; m. Henry Reddington.

445. MOSES,[4][161] (*Moses,[3] Moses,[2] John,[1]*) b. Sept. 30, 1782; d. Feb. 21, 1863; m. Mary, daughter of Robert-Barker Gray of Brid-

port, Vermont, Aug. 8, 1810. She was born May 22, 1790; d. May
11, 1867. Their children were born in Potsdam, N. Y., where he resided many years; late in life he removed to Wisconsin. Their
children were: *Monticello, Wisconsin.*

446. 1. EMELINE,[1060] b. Dec. 15, 1813; m. Rev. Charles-Avery Slater.
447. 2. MARY-ELMIRA,[1092] b. May 2, 1815; d. Sept. 8, 1856; m. Newman
      Dutcher.
448   3. WILLIAM-GRAY,[1099] b. Sept. 7, 1819; m. Catharine Stoddard.
449. 4. ELIZA-ANN,[1104] b. Aug. 8, 1822; d. Dec. 12, 1854; m. Harvey Rich-
      ardson.

450. PHEBE,[4][162] (*Moses,*[3] *Moses,*[2] *John,*[1]) b. March 1, 1784; d.
Nov., 1850; m. Nov. 30, 1805, Asa Lewis of Glastonbury, Ct. Their
children were: *Ellington, Ct.*

451. 1. NELSON, b. March 9, 1806; d. March, 1856; m. 1st, Mary Maynard; 2d,
      Sarah Weaver.   *Stafford, Ct.*
452. 2. PHEBE, b. April 7, 1809; d. Nov. 5, 1851; m. Norton Braman.
453. 3. ASA, b. Nov. 20, 1810; m. Louisa Lyon. *Hazardsville, Conn.*
454. 4. IRA, b. March 11, 1813; m. Elsie-Ann Foster. *Square Pond, Conn.*
455. 5. LYDIA-LOUISA, b. June 14, 1815; m. Selden Hare.
                                                 Square Pond, Conn.
456. 6. MARY-MARANDA, b. Oct. 19, 1817; m. 1st, Henry Sweet; 2d, Hiram
      Smith.   *Square Pond, Conn.*
457. 7. PHILURA-MINERVA, b. May 26, 1819; d. young.
458. 8. ARIEL-MUNROE, b. July 16, 1827; d. young.

459. ADONIJAH,[4][163] (*Moses,*[3] *Moses,*[2] *John,*[1]) b. Jan. 31, 1787;
d. Feb. 12, 1865; m. 1st, Lura, daughter of Nathaniel Pond of Hartland, N. Y., May, 1810. She d. Jan. 1819; m. 2d, Mrs. Rebecca
Dagget, daughter of Ezra Mansfield of Charlotte, Vt., May 5, 1819.
His children, all born in Potsdam, N. Y., were as follows:
                                                 Madrid, N. Y.

460. 1. ADONIJAH, b. Dec. 20, 1813.
461. 2. JEROME-POND,[1109] b. Oct. 8, 1817; d. June 11, 1867; m. Margaret
      Axe.
462. 3. FRANCIS-MANSFIELD,[1115] b. Jan. 6, 1821; m. Betsey-Azubah Wright.
463. 4. FRANKLIN-AURELIUS,[1117] b. Feb. 11, 1823; m. Sophronia-Eunice
      Hovey.
464. 5. ALMEDA-MALVINA,[1122] b. Feb. 5, 1825; d.; m. George-Washington
      Bullard.
465. 6. MYRON-ROCKWOOD, b. March, 1827; d. Oct. 29, 1854.
466. 7. ORRIN-REXFORD,[1124] b. Nov. 7, 1830; m. Emily Rexford.
467. 8. LURA-LOUISA,[1126] b. Aug. 23, 1833; m. John-Chubb Streeter.

468. MARY,[4][164] (*Moses,*[3] *Moses,*[2] *John,*[1]) b. March 3, 1789; m. Ira
Hodges of Glastonbury, Conn., Sept. 11, 1808. He was b. June 27,
1787. They resided in Enfield, Ct., and removed to Illinois. Their
children were as follows: *Big-Rock, Kane Co., Illinois.*

469. 1. CYRUS, b. July 25, 1809; m. Ruey-C. Bartlett, and had: (1.) Mary
      Meacham, b. Dec. 5, 1832; (2.) Ira-Bertram; (3) Henry-Dexter; (4.)
      Francisco-Leroy.   *Monona, Clayton Co., Iowa.*
470. 2. MIRANDA, b. Aug. 11, 1814; d. Jan. 28, 1815.
471. 3. HORATIO-FRANKLIN, b. Oct. 14, 1822; m. Louisa-Relief Kent, Aug. 15,
      1841, and had: (1.) Alice-Adelaide, b. Aug. 19, 1842, who m. Rev.
      Geo. L. Shepherdson of Burlington, Illinois, Jan. 23, 1862; (2.) Anna-
      Relief, b. Aug. 9, 1846; (3.) Erastus-McCloud.
                                      Big-Rock, Kane Co., Illinois.

472. RHODA,[4][165] (*Moses*,[3] *Moses*,[2] *John*,[1]) b. July 18, 1791; m. Roswell, son of Jabez Green, June 11, 1811. He d. April 5, 1867. They had the following children : *Ellington, Conn.*

473. 1. SETH-WHITMORE, b. Feb. 8, 1812 ; m. Theodacia Edwards.
474. 2. BENJAMIN, b. May 7, 1813 ; d. Feb. 1862.
475. 3. SAMUEL, d. in infancy.
476. 4. MARY, d. in infancy.
477. 5. MARY-ANN, b. Feb. 18, 1816 ; m. Otis Rider.   *East Windsor, Ct.*
478. 6. GILBERT-GREENLEAF, b. June 26, 1818 ; d. about 1851 ; m. Eunice Starkweather, and had children.
479. 7. ORECTOR, b. Feb. 20, 1820 ; m. 1st, Mary Gates ; 2d, Lucy Skinner.
                                                              Wales, Mass.
480. 8. LAURA-ANN, b. April 18, 1827 ; d. 1858 ; m. Loren Trask.
481. 9. LYDIA-CORDELIA, b. June 20, 1828 ; m. Freeman Marcey.
482. 10. PHEBE, b. Jan. 31, 1830 ; d. July 12, 1866 ; m. Calvin Smith.
483. 11. LUCIA-JANE, d. about 1852.
484. 12. ROSWELL, b. about 1835 ; d. about 1856.
485. 13. AURELIA, b. about 1837 ; d. Oct., 1860.
486. 14. HENRIETTA, b. about 1839 ; d. about 1859.

487. ESTHER,[4][167] (*Moses*,[3] *Moses*,[2] *John*,[1]) b. May 14, 1793 ; m. Park, son of Benjamin and Eunice (Lillibridge) Rockwell of Stafford, Conn., April 12, 1814. He was born Sept. 16, 1790. He owns, and resides on his paternal estate, where their children all were born, in Stafford, Ct.

488. 1. MARIA-HOWARD, b. Feb. 4, 1815 ; d. July 10, 1838 ; m. Ezekiel Hosford, Oct. 16, 1834, and had : (1.) Ellen-Maria, b. Dec. 24, 1835, Brooklyn, N. Y.; (2.) Henry-Ezekiel, b. June 30, 1837, who m. Kate Hunting, and had Alice, and resides in New York.
489. 2. MIRANDA-HODGES, b. Aug. 11, 1817 ; m. Danford, son of Daniel and Hannah (Knowlton) Knowlton of Ashford, Conn., Sept. 26, 1837. He was born in Ashford, Ct., May 5, 1811. He was for some years in business in Hartford, Ct , but removed to New York in Dec., 1843, and is now a merchant in that city. To the firm of " Danford Knowlton & Co., Commission Merchants, 94 Front Street, New York," belong also his two sons. Their children were born, the eldest in Hartford, Ct., the others in New York, and are as follows :
       (1.) Maria-Rockwell, b. July 15, 1842 ; d. April 27, 1845.
       (2.) Danford-Henry, b. April 15, 1846. He was educated at the New York Free Academy.
       (3.) Miner-Rockwell, b. June 6, 1847; educated at the New York Free Academy ; m. Sept. 17, 1868 ; Harriet, dau. of Edmund B. and Mary-Emeline (Dean) Hull of Boston.
       (4.) Gertrude-Miranda, b. July 14, 1858.   *New York.*
490. 3. BENJAMIN, b. Oct. 24, 1819 ; d. June 30, 1822.
491. 4. EMELINE-DEAN, b. May 14, 1827 ; m. Austin-Graves Kibbee, May 6, 1846, and had: (1.) Walter-Rockwell, b. July 15, 1850 ; (2.) Arthur-Park, b. July 16, 1861.   *Spring Grove, Iowa.*

492. LYDIA,[4][168] (*Moses*,[3] *Moses*,[2] *John*,[1]) b. Oct. 26, 1795; m. Jesse, son of James Willes of Tolland, Conn., and had the following children :   *Stafford, Conn.*

493. 1. SYLVESTER, b. about April, 1820.
494. 2. MATTISON, b. about 1825 ; d. in the U. S. service, in war of rebellion.
495. 3. ORRIN-ISHAM, b. May 15, 1835.   *Illinois.*

496. SAMUEL,[4][169] (*Moses*,[3] *Moses*,[2] *John*,[1]) b. June 10, 1797 ; m. Sarah, daughter of Benjamin Norris of Tolland, Conn., Jan. 29, 1821. She was born in Tolland, Oct. 25, 1799. Their children were as follows :   *Tolland, Conn.*

497. 1. SARAH-ANGELINE, b. in Ellington, Feb. 10, 1822 ; d. Sept. 16, 1843.

498. 2. Julia-Esther, b. in Ellington, Sept. 24, 1823; d. Oct. 24, 1843.
499. 3. Emily-Alzina, b. in Ellington, March 8, 1825; m. Henry, son of Jesse Meacham of Ellington, Conn., Jan. 4, 1847. He was b. in Somers, Dec. 8, 1824. They have adopted a daughter, Amelia-Elizabeth, b. March 8, 1860, at Flag Staff, Me. Her parents were Austin-Henry and Amelia-Sarah (Savage) Dawes. He is President of the Young Men's Christian Association, and holds some other offices. *Somers, Conn.*
500. 4. Samuel Benjamin, [1127] b. in Tolland, Jan. 18, 1827; m. Maria-Olive Pease.
501. 5. Lemuel, [1130] b. in Tolland, Feb. 10, 1829; m. Mary-Jane Cushman.
502. 6. William-Albert, [1132] b. in Tolland, Feb. 3, 1831; m. Elizabeth Wakefield.
503. 7. Maria-Antoinette, b. in Tolland, Dec. 11, 1832; d. Sept. 20, 1843.
504. 8. Jane-Philenda, [1137] b. in Tolland, Jan. 10, 1835; m. Rev. Charles-Frederick Newell.
505. 9. John-Greenleaf, [1142] b. in Tolland, June 23, 1837; m Emily-Jane Harwood.
506. 10. Mary-Elizabeth, b. in Tolland, Dec. 23, 1838; d. June 13, 1840.
507. 11. Charles-Henry, b. in Tolland, Dec. 31, 1840; d. Feb. 11, 1843.
508. 12. Silas-Henry, b. in Manchester, Ct., Oct. 19, 1842; m. Mary-Ann Wright of Coventry, Dec. 4, 1865. *Square Pond, Ct.*
509. 13. Norris-Manning, b. in Ellington, July 26, 1848; d. Sept. 28, 1848.

510. William,[4][170] (*Moses,[3] Moses,[2] John,[1]*) b. June 5, 1799; m. Fanny, daughter of Medad Kellogg of Tolland, Conn., Oct. 23, 1823. She died Sept. 26, 1861. Their children, b. in Ellington, were as follows: *Square Pond, Ct.*

511. 1. Fanny-Charlotte, [1145] b. Dec. 16, 1824; m. Henry-Curtis Aborn.
512. 2. Henrietta-Ann, [1147] b. July 21, 1826; m. Ephraim-Harlem Dimmick.
513. 3. William-Dwight, [1150] b. March 16, 1828; m. Emeline-Catharine Thompson.
514. 4. Juliana-Lucretia, b. Aug. 4, 1831; d. May 6, 1832.
515. 5. Benjamin-Franklin, [1155] b. May 30, 1833; m. Marietta-Lura Richardson.
516. 6. George-Washington, [1157] b. July 27, 1836; m. Lora-Selenda Aborn.

517. Ariel,[4][171] (*Moses,[3] Moses,[2] John,[1]*) b. June 15, 1803; m. Mary, daughter of Thomas Fox of Tolland, Conn., April 15, 1829. She was b. Sept. 19, 1803. He was a Justice of the Peace many years in Ellington, Conn., before his removal to Iowa. His children, all born in Ellington, Ct., were as follows: *Grove City, Iowa.*

518. 1. Chauncy-Fox, [1160] b. March 19, 1830; m. Abby-Elizabeth Read.
519. 2. Clarinda, [1162] b. May 31, 1832; m. 1st, Jonathan-Park Clark; 2d, William-Henry Conover.
520. 3. Mary, [1165] b. April 5, 1834; m. John-Sanford Cromwell.
521. 4. Harriet-Eliza, [1167] b. June 3, 1836; m. Charles-Hiram Aborn.
522. 5. Paulina, [1169] b. Nov. 26, 1839; m. John-Quincy Greenleaf.
523. 6. William-Bradley, b. July 10, 1842; d. July 28, 1868.

524. Emeline,[5][218] (*Edmund-Farwell,[4] John,[3] Samuel,[2] John,[1]*) b. Sept. 20, 1799; m. James, son of Daniel and Susannah (Durgin) Brown of Corinth, Vt., June 17, 1819. He was b. in Thornton, N. H., May 20, 1791; d. April 24, 1866. He removed from Corinth to Ohio in 1837. Their children were born in Vermont, excepting the last two. *Johnstown, Licking Co., Ohio.*

525. 1. Emeline-Christiana, b. Feb. 27, 1820; m. John-Compton Johnston *Liberty, Ohio.*
526. 2. Clarissa-Susan, b. April 26, 1822; d. Oct. 29, 1853.

527. 3. HARRIET-MIRANDA, b. Jan. 7, 1824 ; m. George-Alvin Derby of Licking Co., Ohio, March 1, 1843. They removed from Ohio in 1854 to
Union City, Ind., and to their present residence in Iowa in 1856. He
was sheriff of Wapello Co., Iowa, from 1863 to 1867. Their children
are :
> (1.) Orin-Alvin, b. Nov. 15, 1843 ; he enlisted in the war of rebellion
> in Comp. B, 36th Iowa Vol., Aug. 8, 1862, and was dis-
> charged Sept. 7, 1865 ; served three years and one month ; par-
> ticipated in nine battles and many skirmishes.
> (2.) Emily-Esther, b. March 28, 1845 ; d. April 17, 1863.
> (3.) Nancy-Marilla, b. Oct. 6, 1846.
> (4.) Alonzo-Farwell, b. Feb. 6, 1848 ; in war of rebellion he was in
> Comp. R, 47th Iowa Vol. ; service about five months.
> (5) Clarissa-Emeline, b. Oct. 8, 1849.
> (6.) Mercy-Ann-Maria, b. March 25, 1851.
> (7.) George-Jerome, b. Sept. 19, 1853.
> (8.) Frank-Nelson, b. Oct. 11, 1859.
> (9.) Scott-Brown, b. Oct. 31, 1857.
> (10.) Edward-Lincoln, b. March 7, 1860 ; d. June 11, 1863.
> (11.) Ermine-Mastick, b. May 9, 1862 ; d. Nov. 9, 1864.
> (12.) Willie-Sherman, b. Feb. 4, 1865.
> (13.) Emma-Miranda, b. Aug. 29, 1867.
>
> *Ottumwa, Wapello Co., Iowa.*

528. 4. BLOOMY-FAIR, b. Oct. 13, 1826 ; m. Simon-Wellington Converse, and
had : (1.) Franklin ; (2.) Franklin ; (3.) Rosa-Alice ; (4.) James ; (5.)
Nelson ; (6) Emeline. *Spencerville, Allen Co., Ohio.*

529. 5. MARY-ANNE, b. Jan. 8, 1829 ; m. Horace Elkins, Oct. 4, 1847.
Liberty, Licking Co., Ohio.

530. 6. JAMES-FRANKLIN, b. June 16, 1831 ; m. Hannah Anderson, and had :
(1.) Ida-Delphine ; (2.) Dennis-Calvin ; (3.) John-Henry.
Liberty, Licking Co., Ohio.

531. 7. ALONZO-FARWELL, b Jan. 6, 1834 ; d. March 9, 1861 ; m. Mary Hillery,
and had : (1.) Alonzine-Estella. *Johnstown, Licking Co., Ohio.*

532. 8. JOHN, b. April 5, 1836 ; in war of great rebellion served two years and
eight months in Comp. M, 3d Ohio Cavalry. He called himself John
A. Brown in the army for the sake of distinction. *Fairfield, Iowa.*

533. 9. RODNEY-SLAFTER, b. March 23, 1839 ; served one year and twenty days
in Com. F, U. S. Engineers, in war of rebellion ; m. Dec. 24, 1866,
Mary-Philomela Peck, and had : Esther, b. Oct. 1, 1867. *Alton, Iowa.*

534. 10. George-Washington, b. Aug. 9, 1843 ; served eight months in Comp. H,
76th Reg., Ohio Vol. ; discharged for ill health ; died by a " stroke of
lightning," July 31, 1863.

535. BLOOMY-FAIR,[5][221] (*Edmund   Farwell,*[4] *John,*[3] *Samuel,*[2]
John,[1]) b. Nov. 28, 1803 ; m. Joseph-Stephens, son of Reuben and
Mary (Stephens) Crooke of Cornish, Vt., March 31, 1824. He was b.
June 4, 1796 ; d. Oct. 19, 1867. Their children were born in
Bradford, Vt.

536. 1. REUBEN, born March 2, 1825 ; m. Flora-Mary, dau. of Daniel-Sutherland Grant of Brora, Sutherlandshire, Scotland, now of Boston, Jan. 8,
1853. She was b. in Lunenburg, Nova Scotia, July 24, 1831. He has
edited the Boston Daily Evening Traveller for several years. Their
children, born in Boston, are :
> (1.) Daniel-Joseph, b. Feb. 5, 1854 ; d. April 18, 1855.
> (2.) Flora-Irene, b. Feb. 28, 1856.
> (3.) Reuben-Francis, b. Feb. 5, 1861.
> (4.) Jessie-Mary, b. Feb. 28, 1863. *Boston, Mass.*

537. 2. RODNEY-RICHARDSON, b. Sept. 19, 1829 ; m. Matilda-Catharine, dau. of
Daniel-Sutherland Grant, sister of his brother's wife, April 11, 1857.
She was b. April 9, 1804. They have had : (1.) Arthur-Bradford, b.
April 6, 1858 ; (2.) Bloomy-Fair, b. Feb. 28, 1869. *Bradford, Vt.*

538. PHALLE-RICHARDSON,[5][225] (*John*,[4] *John*,[3] *Samuel*,[2] *John*,[1]) b. Jan. 1, 1806; d. Aug. 12, 1863; m. Naham-Newton, son of John Wilson of Barre, Vt., March 17, 1828. He was b. in Newport, N. H., Jan. 10, 1805.   He is a Justice of the Peace, and has held other local offices; he m. 2d, Mary Woodward of Barre, Vt., Oct. 31, 1867; she was born in Hartford, Vt., July 12, 1819.   *Whitesburg, Mich.*

539.   1. MERCY-EMELIA, b. in Bolton, L. C., July 26, 1836; m. Martin-Luther Miller, Feb. 25, 1849, and had: (1.) William-Newton, b. Jan. 22, 1850; (2.) Galen-Carlos, b. Feb. 3, 1852; (3.) Martin-Luther, b. Dec. 16, 1853; (4.) James-Edgar, b. April 13, 1855; (5.) Leanthie-Rose, b. July 13, 1858; (6.) Mary-Amelia.   *Worth, Mich.*

540.   2. CARLOS, b. in Bolton, L. C., March 9, 1833; m. Esther White, Nov. 1, 1857, and had: (1.) Ella-Jeanette, b. Feb. 15, 1861; (2.) Cecelia-Almina, b. Sept. 13, 1863; (3.) Phalle-Lucy, b. Nov. 8, 1866.
                           Frankenmuth, Saginaw Co., Mich.

541.   3. WILLIAM-HOTCHKISS, b. in Vienna, Mich., Aug. 8, 1839; m. Amelia-Elizabeth Root, Dec. 1, 1861, and had: (1) Emma-Theresa, b. Feb. 3, 1863; (2.) Samuel-Averill.   *Otisville, Genesee Co., Mich.*

542.   4. FARWELL-ALONZO, b. in Vienna, Mich., July 18, 1841; m. Ann Hoover, March 30, 1865, and had: Phalle-Mary, b. Sept. 13, 1866.
                           Otisville, Genesee Co., Mich.

543.   5. JOHN-NEWTON, b. in Thetford, Mich., Nov. 19, 1843; he enlisted in the war of the rebellion, Sept. 1862, in 7th Mich. Cavalry, and was in service one year; m. Eliza-Ann Farnham, Oct. 3, 1862, and had: (1.) Alfred-Newton, b. Dec. 28, 1864.   *Whitesburg, Mich.*

544.   6. PERSIS-AUGUSTA, b. in Thetford, Mich., March 1, 1846; m. William-Henry Long, June 20, 1867.   *Whitesburg, Mich.*

545.   7. SAMUEL-JUDSON, b. in Thetford, Mich., Sept. 3, 1849.
546.   8. NAHAM-THOMAS, b. in Thetford, Mich., Feb. 22, 1852.

547. WILLIAM,[5][226] (*John*,[4] *John*,[3] *Samuel*,[2] *John*,[1]) b. Oct. 1, 1807; m. 1st, Roisa-Hovey, daughter of Samuel and Elizabeth (Hovey) Johnson of Norwich, Vt., Feb. 4, 1830.   She was born March 17, 1809; d. Oct. 31, 1849.   She was grand daughter of Calvin Johnson; see foot note at No. 234.   He m. 2d, Mary-Pierson Sutherland, widow of Martin Waters, Nov. 23, 1861.   She died Dec. 4, 1865. His eldest daughter and eldest son were born in Bolton, Lower Canada; the others were born in Norwich, Vermont.   *Worth, Mich.*

548.   1. FLORA-ELIZABETH,[1245] b. March 26, 1832; m. Gilbert Baldwin.
549.   2. ALBERT,[1251] b. Sept. 15, 1833; d. July 2, 1863; m. Ruth Smith.
550.   3. PERSIS-AUGUSTA, b. April 30, 1838; d. Sept. 4, 1864; m. Harvey, son of Daniel Fellows of Cambria, N. Y.   *Lockport, N. Y.*
551.   4. MARY, b. Dec. 16, 1840; d. Feb. 3, 1841.
552.   5. ALONZO, b. Dec. 27, 1842; in war of rebellion was in Comp. I, 30th Mich., from Dec. 14, 1864, to June 23, 1865, at Detroit, on frontier service.
553.   6. MARY, b. June 23, 1846; d. Oct. 19, 1849.
554.   7. ANN-ROISA, b. Sept. 11, 1848.

555. DAVID GROW,[5][230] (*John*,[4] *John*,[3] *Samuel*,[2] *John*,[1]) b. Jan. 1, 1817; m. Ann-Calista, daughter of John Lucas of Pierpont, N. Y., Feb. 11, 1843.   She was b. Dec. 6, 1825.   He was a Justice of the Peace in Norwich, Vt., from 1846 to 1850, and also in Tuscola Co., Mich., from 1852 to the time of this writing (1867), with the exception of one year; Judge of Probate four years, from 1856 to 1860.   Notary for term of four years, beginning 1865.   Enrolling officer for his county, appointed June 3, 1863.   Deputy Provost Marshal for the 6th District, Mich., from July 8, 1863, to end of the war of the rebellion; was a representative in Legislature of Michigan in 1863, and at the

extra session of 1864. He has had no children. He has, however, adopted an orphan, son of James Morgan and Antoinette (Fry) Baldwin, who by act of Legislature has taken the name of Morgan-Baldwin Slafter; b. May 26, 1855. *Worth, Tuscola Co., Mich.*

556. ALMINA-LOUISA,[5][231] (*John,*[4] *John,*[3] *Samuel,*[2] *John,*[1]) b. July 25, 1819; m. Paschal, son of Harper Richardson of Randolph, Vt., Sept. 6, 1843. He was born Dec. 29, 1803; he was representative in Legislature of Michigan in 1853 and 1857. *Worth, Mich.*

557. 1. AUSTIN-PASCHAL, b. in Thetford, Mich., Oct. 29, 1844; d. Sept. 4, 1863.
558. 2. CHARLES-JUDSON, b. in Tuscola, Mich., June 5, 1848.
559. 3. IDA-ALMIRA, b. in Tuscola, Mich., Dec. 3, 1854.

560. JUDSON,[5][232] (*John,*[4] *John,*[3] *Samuel,*[2] *John,*[1]) b. Jan. 3, 1822; d. Dec. 31, 1863; m. Fanny, daughter of Silas-Beebe Rogers, and widow of William Tice, Nov. 4, 1852. She was born Nov. 20, 1825. He enlisted in war of rebellion, Aug. 12, 1862; was sergeant in Comp. D, 23d Mich. Vol.; he was wounded at Cambell's Station, Tenn., on 16th Nov., and died in hospital at Knoxville. His children, all b. in Tuscola, Mich., are as follows: *Worth, Mich.*

561. 1. LOIS-ISABEL, b. Aug. 10, 1855.
562. 2. PERSIS-ELIZABETH, b. May 10, 1858.
563. 3. ALVINA-AMERICA, b. April 12, 1863.

564. AUGUSTA-MALVINA,[5][233] (*John,*[4] *John,*[3] *Samuel,*[2] *John,*[1]) b. July 11, 1826; m. Oliver-Paul, son of Samuel Tobey of Eliot, Me., Nov. 18, 1851. He was b. Feb. 14, 1826. Their children, all born in Tuscola, Mich., are as follows: *Worth, Mich.*

565. 1. EDGAR-OLIVER, b. Dec. 31, 1852.
566. 2. FREDERICK-WAYLAND, b. Feb. 21, 1855.
567. 3. WILLIAM-LINCOLN, b. July 18, 1860.
567½. 4. MARY-ALICE, b. June 11, 1868.

568. THOMAS-JEFFERSON,[5][235] (*Sylvester,*[4] *John,*[3] *Samuel,*[2] *John,*[1]) b. Aug. 19, 1803; m. Rebecca, daughter of Peter-Whitcomb and Eunice (Leffingwell) Seaver of Montpelier, Vt., Dec. 31, 1827. She was b. Nov. 4, 1802. Her grandfather was Josiah-Willis Seaver, b. July 18, 1742. (See note at No. 210.) He resided first in Thetford, Vt., where his eldest son was born, but removed in 1831 to Amity, Alleghany Co., N. Y., where his other children were born, and where he continues to reside. He has a natural gift for mechanics, and has tried several departments, both as artist and artisan. *Belmont, N. Y.*

569. 1. OROMEL-WILLIS,[1254] b. Oct. 7, 1828; m. Caroline-Eliza Cox.
570. 2. CARLOS-LEWIS,[1258] b. March 16, 1832; m. Lucy-Chamberlin Tracy.
571. 3. Mary-Jane, b. April 12, 1834; m. Harvey-Austin, son of Oliver and Lydia (Austin) Wright of Brattleboro', Vt., June 13, 1858. He was b. Jan. 24, 1835; was in war of rebellion in an Engineer Corps; in service about two years. *Belmont, N. Y.*

572. SYLVESTER,[5][239] (*Sylvester,*[4] *John,*[3] *Samuel,*[2] *John,*[1]) b. Aug. 16, 1812; d. in Lindenwood, Ill., Aug. 23, 1854; m. Eliza, daughter of Rufus and Lydia (Wallace) Read of Thetford, Vt., Jan. 15, 1837. She was b. Aug. 8, 1815. He resided in Fairlee, Vt., where he was a

Justice of the Peace, and held various town offices. He removed, in the spring of 1854, to Lindenwood, Ogle Co., Illinois.

Lindenwood, Ill.

573. 1. EDMUND-FARWELL,[1259] b. in Thetford, Vt., Sept. 21, 1838; d. April 27, 1859; m. Lucy-Emily Bulkley.

574. 2. ABBIE-ANN, b. in Fairlee, Dec. 27, 1845; m. Dec. 23, 1868, Calvin, son of Daniel Countryman of Lynnville, Ogle Co., Illinois. He was b. March 11, 1844, and resides at Lynnville.

575. 3. ESTHER-ARDELL, b. in Lindenwood, Nov. 23, 1854; d. Feb. 1, 1856.

576. EDMUND-FARWELL,[5][241] (*Sylvester,[4] John,[3] Samuel,[2] John,[1]*) b. May 30, 1816; m. Mary-Anne, daughter of Charles and Elizabeth (Brown) Hazen* of Boston, Aug. 16, 1849. She was b. in Boston,

---

* 1. *Edward Hazen*, the emigrant ancestor, settled in Rowley as early as 1648. His first wife's name was Elizabeth, who died without children, 1649. In March, 1650, he m. 2d, Hannah, by whom he had eleven children: (1.) Elizabeth, b. March 8, 1650–1; (2.) Hannah; (3.) John; (4.) Thomas; (5.) Edward; (6.) Isabella; (7.) Priscilla; (8.) Edna; (9.) *Richard*, b. Aug. 6, 1669; (10.) Hepsabah; (11.) Sarah.

2. *Richard*, b. Aug. 6, 1669; m. Dec. 5, 1694, Mary, daughter of Capt. John and Hannah (Andrews) Peabody of Boxford. Hannah Andrews was the daughter of Robert Andrews, the emigrant ancestor of the late Governor John A. Andrew, LL.D. Mary Peabody was the granddaughter of Lieut. Francis Peabody, from whom is descended Mr. George Peabody, the London banker. Richard Hazen resided in Haverhill, Mass. Their children were: (1.) Richard; (2.) Richard; (3.) Priscilla; (4.) Moses, b. May 17, 1701; (5.) George; (6) Mary; (7.) Sarah; (8.) Hannah; (9.) Elizabeth; (10.) John; (11.) Ann. His wife, Mary, died Sept. 13, 1731; he m. 2d, Grace Kimball, April 3, 1773, but by her had no children; he d. Sept. 25, 1733. He was a large landholder, and Lieut. in the militia.

3. *Moses*, b. May 17, 1701; m. March 5, 1727–8, Abigail, dau. of John and Lydia (Gilman) White of Haverhill, Mass. Her great grandfather was the Worshipful William White of Haverhill, the emigrant ancestor. The children of Moses Hazen were: (1.) Abigail, b. Jan. 7, 1729; m. Moses Moors, Nov. 16, 1749. She was the mother of Gen. Benjamin Moors of Plattsburg. (2.) John, b. Aug. 11, 1731; m. Anne Swett, Nov. 30, 1752. He was an officer in the old French war; he was active in the settlement of Haverhill, N. H., which through his influence was named *Haverhill*, after the place of his nativity in Mass. He had a son John, who settled in the province of New Brunswick. (3.) Moses, b. June 1, 1733; m. Charlotte La Saussee, a French lady of Canada. He was in the Provincial service in the war of 1756, and distinguished himself under Gen. Wolfe on the Plains of Abraham, where he was severely wounded. Capt. Hazen retired after the war on half pay for life, and settled at St. Johns on the Sorelle in Canada. On the breaking out of the Revolutionary war he was made Colonel of the Canada, or "Hazen's" regiment; he served with credit and distinction to the end of the war, having been made a Brigadier Gen. He died in Troy, N. Y., Feb. 4, 1803. His wife died in 1827. (4.) Ann, b. July 30, 1735. (5.) *William*, b. July 17, 1738.

4. *William*, b. July 17, 1738; d. March 23, 1814; m. Sarah, dau. of Dr. Joseph and Sarah (Leonard) Le Baron of Plymouth, Mass., July 17, 1764; she was b. Feb. 22, 1748–9; d. April 3, 1823. Dr. Le Baron was the son of Dr. Lazarus Le Baron of Plymouth, and grandson of Dr. Francis Le Baron, who was surgeon of a French privateer captured in Buzzard's Bay; he afterward settled at Plymouth; she was also descended from Richard Warren of "The Mayflower," from James Leonard of Taunton, from the Rev. Nathaniel Rogers, first minister of Ipswich, and from Samuel Appleton, who came to Ipswich in 1635 The Hon. Wm. Hazen had removed to St. John, N. B., before the Revolution. He took the English side in politics; after the war he became a member of the Governor's Council, on the establishment of the Province of New Brunswick, and so continued till his death. He left a large landed estate. He had sixteen children as follows: (1.) Elizabeth, b. in Newburyport, Mass.,

F.T.Stuart Boston.

Edmund F. Slafter

April 27, 1819. He was b. in Norwich, Vt., baptized in Thetford, Vt., by the Rev. Asa Burton, D.D., June 22, 1817. He was fitted for College at Thetford Academy ; entered Dartmouth College in 1836 ; graduated Bachelor of Arts in 1840 ; A. M. from same college, 1865. Entered the Theological Seminary at Andover, autumn of 1840. He was Principal of Topsfield Academy one year, from Dec. 1, 1841. He became a communicant in the Protestant Episcopal Church, and was confirmed by the Rt. Rev. Bishop Griswold, D. D., at Andover, June 1, 1842, and became a candidate for Holy Orders. He returned to the Theological Seminary at Andover, Nov. 27, 1842 ; took up his connection with the Seminary, April, 1844. He was examined for Deacon's Orders, by the Rev. C. M. Butler, D. D., Rector of Grace Church, Boston, and the Rev. P. H. Greenleaf, D. D., Rector St. John's Church, Charlestown, on the 1st, 2nd and 3rd of July, 1844, and was ordained Deacon in Trinity Church, Boston, July 12, 1844, by the Rt. Rev. Manton Eastburn, D. D. He preached his first sermon in St. John's Church, Charlestown, July 14, 1844 ; entered upon the Rectorship of St. Peter's

June 2, 1766 ; m. the Hon. Ward Chipman (Har. Coll. 1770), Judge of the Supreme Court of New Brunswick, and acting Governor at the time of his death. Their only son was the Hon. Ward Chipman, LL.D., (Har. Coll. 1805), the late Chief-Justice of that Province (2.) William, b. June 28, 1768 ; m. Miss Murray, dau. of Col. John Murray ; their son, the Hon. Robert L. Hazen is the Recorder of St. John, and a Senator of Canada (1869). (3.) *Charles*, b. Jan. 10, 1771, in Newburyport. (4) Robert, b. Sept. 7, 1773 ; an officer in Eng. Army ; m. Miss Jarvis, and left a son, Robert F. Hazen, Esq., who m. a granddaughter of Col. Beverly Robinson and resides in St. John. (5.) Sarah-Lowell, b. Oct. 12, 1775, at Portland, N. B. ; m. 1st, Thomas Murray, 2d, Wm. Botsford, late Judge of the Supreme Court of N. B. The Hon. Amos E. Botsford, a Senator of Canada, the Hon. Geo. Botsford of Fredericton and Dr. Le Baron Botsford of St. John, are her sons. (6.) Charlotte, b. May 12, 1778 ; d. July, 1831 ; m. Gen. Sir John-Forster Fitz Gerald, Dec. 27, 1805 ; resides in England ; member of the House of Commons, &c. She had two daughters, (a.) Charlotte, b. Nov. 1, 1806 ; d. Oct. 26, 1853 ; m. Otto Leopold, Baron Von Ende, chamberlain to the king of Saxony ; she left children. (b.) Anne, m. Sir Robert-Keith Arbuthnot, Baronet, and has children ; resides in Scotland. (7.) George, b. Sept, 22, 1779 ; d. Dec. 24, 1783. (8.) Henry, b. Jan. 5, 1781 ; d. Jan. 16, 1781. (9.) Le Baron, b. April 17, 1782 ; d. Nov. 2, 1810. (10.) Edwin, b. Aug. 5, 1783 ; d. Sept. 14, 1818. (11.) George-Henry, b. Dec. 27, 1784 ; d. Dec. 4, 1836. (12.) A daughter, b. March 17, 1786 ; d. same day. (13.) Frances-Amelia, b. July 17, 1787 ; m. Dec. 27, 1805, Col. Charles Drury of English Army ; Gen. Charles Drury and Ward-Chipman Drury, Esq., of St. John, are her sons. (14.) Frederick-Edward, b. Sept. 22, 1788 ; d. June 24, 1790. (15.) Frederick, b. Dec. 25, 1792 ; d. Jan. 8, 1825. (16.) Sophia-Ann, b. April 5, 1796 ; d. July 21, 1812.

5. *Charles*, b. Jan. 10, 1771 ; d. in Boston, Feb. 23, 1849 ; he m. 1st, Elizabeth, b. July 6, 1781, d. Dec. 13, 1822 ; m. 2d, Nancy, b. Aug. 17, 1783, d. Sept. 13, 1863, daughters of Joseph-Lasinby and Susannah (Adams) Brown of Boston. His first marriage took place Sept. 30, 1811 ; his second, Jan. 20, 1824. Mr. Hazen resided in Boston. His children were all by his first wife, and were as follows : (1.) Sophia-Ann, d. at the age of four years. (2.) Charles-Drury, b. March 11, 1814 ; m. Charlotte, dau. of the Right Hon. Baron Richards, of Ireland. Mr. Hazen resides in Germany. (3.) Elizabeth-Chipman, b. Nov. 22, 1816 ; d. April 23, 1865 ; m. Samuel-Fox Dorr, a merchant of New York. Samuel Dorr, Esq., Harvard College, 1857, is her son. (4.) *Mary-Anne*, b. April 27, 1819. (5.) John-Prince, b. Oct. 16, 1821 ; d. May 9, 1852 ; m. Emily-Eugenie Rosseter. An only child, Sarah-Rosseter Hazen, survives him.

6. *Mary-Anne*, b. April 27, 1819 ; m. the Rev. Edmund F. Slafter.

Church, Cambridgeport, July 21, 1844. He was ordained Priest by Bishop Eastburn in St. Peter's Church, Salem, July 30, 1845, presented by the Rev. Charles Mason, D. D. Resigned the Rectorship of St. Peter's Church, Cambridgeport, Sept. 20, 1846; was instituted Rector of St. John's Church, Jamaica Plain, by the Rt. Rev. Bishop Eastburn, Sept. 27, 1846. His health failing, he resigned the Rectorship of St. John's Church, Jamaica Plain, Nov. 15, 1853 ; became Assistant to the Rector of St. Paul's Church, Boston, Dec., 1853, with nominal duty ; resigned, and became financial agent of American Bible Society, for the Protestant Episcopal Church, in the New England and Middle States, March, 1857, and so continues. He is Vice-President of the Prince Society, Boston, and member of its Council ; member of the New England Historic-Genealogical Society, and Corresponding Secretary since Jan., 1867 ; member of the Boston Numismatic Society ; corresponding member of the Vermont Historical Society ; corresponding member of the State Historical Society of Wisconsin ; was five years a member of the School Committee in Roxbury, and chairman of the Board in West Roxbury in 1853 ; he published a sermon " on the occasion of the death of General Zachary Taylor, President of the United States," delivered in St. John's Church, Jamaica Plain, July 28, 1850 ; also, a sermon on "The planting and growth of the Protestant Episcopal Church in the United States," delivered at Norwich University, July 19, 1863. He has been a contributor to the periodical press for many years. A few articles have been reprinted in pamphlet form, as, " Notes on the Charter of Norwich, Vt.," and " The Assassination Plot in New York in 1776, a letter of William Eustis, a surgeon in the American Army and late Governor of Massachusetts, with Notes." He is the author of this work.   *Boston, Mass.*

577. CHRISTIANA-SEAVER,[5][242] *(Sylvester,[4] John,[3] Samuel,[2] John,[1])* b. Feb. 1, 1819 ; m. Reuben-Chamberlain, son of Timothy and Sophia (Frarey) Tilden of Norwich Vt., Dec. 5, 1844. He was b. in Norwich, May 1, 1817. Their children were born in Norwich. *Norwich, Vt.*

578. 1. REUBEN-APPLETON, b. Dec. 16, 1845; m. Aug. 31, 1867, Julia-Alice, dau. of William and Marietta-Jane (Wright) Fullington of Hanover, N. H. She was b. in Stowe, Vt., May 19, 1850.   *Norwich, Vt.*
579. 2. MARY-SOPHIA, b. April 23, 1848 ; m. Josiah, son of Jeduthan and Abigail (Currier) Taylor of Thetford, Jan. 1, 1868. He was born June 13, 1846.   *Thetford, Vermont.*
580. 3. ALICE-CHRISTIANA, b. May 30, 1849 ; d. Nov. 10, 1858.
581. 4. EMMA-JANE, b. Feb. 19, 1853 ; d. Aug. 19, 1852.

582. LYMAN,[5][243] *(Sylvester,[4] John,[3] Samuel,[2] John,[1])* b. Jan. 22, 1822 ; m. 1st, Mary, daughter of Josiah and Lydia (Cummings) Taylor of Thetford, Sept. 28, 1845 ; she was b. Jan. 3, 1821, d. April 15, 1855 ; m. 2d, Mrs. Mary-Ann, widow of Henry Green, and daughter of Leonard and Matilda (Cook) Perkins of Parishville, N. Y., Oct. 15, 1856. She was b. Dec. 13, 1825. He occupies the paternal estate known as the Old Parsonage, where his children were born.
                                                    Thetford Vt.

583. 1. CHARLES-SYLVESTER, b. Feb. 12, 1847.
584. 2. CARLOS, b. July 5, 1850.

585. CARLOS,[5][244] *(Sylvester,[4] John,[3] Samuel,[2] John,[1])* b. July 21, 1825 ; m. Rebecca, daughter of William and Rebecca (Daggett)

Bullard* of Dedham, Aug. 4, 1853. She was b. Sept. 4, 1827. He was fitted at Thetford Academy, and entered Dartmouth College, 1845; graduated as Batchelor of Arts in 1849. He was elected a member of the Phi Beta Kappa Society at Dartmouth; received the degree of Master of Arts from Trinity College, Hartford, Ct., 1867. He taught in the Autumn of 1849 a select school at Lyme, N. H., and afterward a Grammar School in Dedham, Mass., six months; studied law in the same town six months; resumed teaching in Dedham, and continued from Nov., 1850, to July, 1851; became Principal of Framingham Academy, Sept., 1851, where he continued one year. He was appointed Principal of the Latin High School in Dedham in 1852, which office he now (1869) holds. He became a candidate for Holy Orders in the Protestant Episcopal Church in 1862; was ordained Deacon in Trinity Church, Boston, at the Annual Convention, May, 1865, by the Rt. Rev. Manton Eastburn, D. D. He has officiated from time to time, so far as his other official duties would permit. He has been Chaplain of the " County House of Correction " in Dedham since Dec., 1867. He has been a frequent contributor to the periodical press, and has been president for some years of the " Library Association " in Dedham, an institution established at his suggestion. His children, born in Dedham, are as follows: *Dedham, Mass.*

586. 1. THEODORE-SHOREY, b. April 25, 1854. He is preparing for college under the instruction of his father. In the summer of 1867, at the age of 13 years, he made the very accurate pencil sketches of "the residence of Dea. John Slafter of Norwich, Vt., 1786," and of " the Old Parsonage, the residence of Sylvester Slafter, Thetford, Vt.," engravings of which accompany this volume.

587. 2. ANNA-REBECCA, b. Jan. 20, 1863.

---

* 1. *William Bullard* came to this country, probably, in 1635; abode first at Watertown; at Dedham, probably in 1637, among the first settlers; removed to Cambridge, 1653; m. there, 2d wife, Mary, widow of Francis Griswold. He died in Dedham, Dec. 23, 1686. His children were: 1, *Isaac*; 2, Nathaniel; 3, Elizabeth; 4, Mary.

2. *Isaac*, son of above, b. probably in England, perhaps as early as 1630; m. Ann Wight, 1655; resided in Dedham; had, 1, Hannah; 2, Sarah; 3, Samuel; 4, Judah; 5, Ephraim; 6, Ann; 7, John; 8, Mary; 9, *William*, b. May 19, 1673.

3. *William*, b. May 19, 1673; d. Feb. 9, 1746; a large landholder, and a preserver of ancient family papers; m. Elizabeth Avery, Aug. 6, 1697, and had, 1, William; 2, Elizabeth; 3, Jemima; 4, Anna; 5, *Isaac*, b. April 4, 1709.

4. *Isaac*, b. April 4, 1709; ensign and coroner; inherited homestead in Dedham; m. Mary Deane, 1731-2; she died, 1745; m. 2d, Wid. Grace Deane, 1747; had, 1, Mary; 2, Mary; 3, Catharine; 4, Catharine; 5, *Isaac*, b. July 10, 1744.

5. *Isaac*, b. July 10, 1744; d. July 18, 1808; inherited homestead; deacon; representative in Gen. Court many years; Treas. of Norfolk Co., from 1793 to 1808; m. 1766, Patience Baker, and had, 1, Mary; 2, *William*, b. July 19, 1769; 3, Isaac; 4, John.

6. *William*, b. July 19, 1769; d. March 15, 1803; m. Lydia Whiting, and had, 1, Charles, b. Aug. 13, 1794, unmarried; 2, *William*, b. April 27, 1796; 3, Isaac, b. Oct. 10, 1799, m. Penelope, daughter of Cornelius Doremus of New York city, and had no children.

7. *William*, b. April 27, 1796; m. Dec. 11, 1822, Rebecca Daggett, and had, 1, Lydia, b. Oct. 20, 1823; 2, William-Augustus, b. Oct. 3, 1826; 3, *Rebecca*, b. Sept. 4, 1828; 4, Mary-Ann, b. Aug. 20, 1833; 5, Isaac, b. March 12, 1837.

8. *Rebecca*, m. the Rev. Carlos Slafter.

588. HERMONA,[5][246] (*Elijah,*[4] *John,*[3] *Samuel,*[2] *John,*[1]) b. Nov. 14, 1809; m. Clark, son of Stephen Chandler of Potsdam, N. Y., Sept. 18, 1837. He was b. Feb. 2, 1807.   *Granby, N. Y.*

589.   1. CORODEN-SLAFTER, b. Dec. 2, 1839, in Tekousha, Mich. He resides in Granby, N. Y.
590.   2. STEPHEN-EDWIN, b. Nov. 20, 1841, in Convis, Mich. He enlisted on the breaking out of the rebellion in Comp. E, 24th N. Y. Vol., May 4, 1861. He was stationed, after the first battle of Bull Run, at Bailey's Cross Roads and Arlington Heights, and at Fredericksburg, Va., where he was engaged in the attack on the rebels near Falmouth, April 18, 1862. He was detached, on the 8th of May, 1862, to join an Engineer Corps, with which he remained till the 21st of the Sept. following, participating in the battles of "Cedar Mountain," "Rappahannock Station," "Rappahannock Crossing," "Second Bull Run," "Chantilla," "South Mountain " and "Antietam." On the 2d of Dec. of the same year, he again joined an engineer corps in the Division under Gen. Wadsworth, and was in the battle of Fredericksburg under Gen. Burnside, and of Chancellorsville under Gen. Hooker, and on the 29th of May, 1863, his regiment was mustered out at Elmira, N. Y., having completed its two years' service. He re-enlisted as a veteran, Oct. 5, 1863, for three years, in Comp. A, 24th N. Y. Cavalry. He was appointed Quarter-Master Sergeant, and remained such to the end of his service. His regiment was assigned to the 9th Corps. He was in the battles of the Wilderness, Spottsylvania, North Anne, Bethesda Church, Cole Harbor, Petersburg, and was in the works before that place until the battle of Cemetery Hill, when the rebel fort was blown up, on the 31st of July, 1864. He was wounded on the 16th of August, 1864, a Minié ball passing through his left side near the heart. He was in hospital three months and ten days. He again joined his Reg., and was in battles of Hatcher's Run, Five Forks, Harper's Farm, Painville, Getersville, Farmersville, and was with the Army of the Potomac at Lee's surrender, April 9, 1865. He had a horse shot under him on the 5th, and another on the 6th of April, just before the surrender. He received his discharge from the U. S. service, Aug. 4, 1865. His whole service was three years and nine months. He m. Mary-Amelia-Valentine, dau. of Franklin Gill of Canton, N. Y., January 16th, 1868. She was b. Feb. 14, 1847.   *Dayton, Ohio.*
591.   3. MARIA-SALOME, b. Aug. 9, 1844 ; d. Sept. 13, 1845.
592.   4. ROBINSON-EGBERT, b. Dec. 29, 1845 ; d. Sept. 15, 1847.
593.   5. HARRIET-AMELIA, b. May 28, 1853, in Westbury, N. Y.

594. CORODEN-HOVEY,[5][247] (*Elijah,*[4] *John,*[3] *Samuel,*[2] *John,*[1]) b. Jan. 31, 1811 ; d. in Bangkok, Siam, April 7, 1841 ; m. Maria Maine of Oxford, N. Y., August 19, 1838. He was educated at the "Hamilton Literary and Theological Institution," afterward incorporated and now known as "Madison University," at Hamilton, N. Y., and was ordained to the Baptist ministry and sailed for Siam in 1838. After his arrival at Bangkok, he entered upon his mission with great energy, and continued to labor with unflagging zeal till prostrated by disease. He made several tours into the interior, penetrating beyond where any protestant missionary had before gone, and distributed many thousands of religious tracts and portions of the Holy Scriptures. But his career was destined to be short; he contracted a disease on a missionary tour into the interior, of which, after lingering a few months, he died on the date above mentioned. The Baptist Register (Utica, Nov. 5, 1841), says he was a man of no ordinary powers or common piety, but in every respect of great promise. Few have left the institution at Hamilton of whom higher hopes were indulged. The President of Madison University, in a note to the writer, Dec. 21, 1867, says, "Mr. Slaf-

ter was a man of ability, and one of the most devoted and fervent and consistent Christians we ever had among us." And again he adds, he was "one of the truest, most conscientious, consecrated and devout men of God I ever knew."

595. LEVINA,[5][250] (*Elijah,[4] John,[3] Samuel,[2] John,[1]*) b. June 2, 1817; m. Jacob, son of Amos-Melvin Smith of Canton, N. Y., Sept. 10, 1844. He was b. Feb. 1, 1811. Their children were born in the same town. *Canton, N. Y.*

596. 1. ELLEN-CHRISTIANA, b. July 16, 1846; m. Ira-Smith Spalding, Feb. 21, 1867. *Herman, St. Lawrence Co., N. Y.*
597. 2. ALVARO-EDWIN, b. Feb. 15, 1847.
598. 3. ALICE-EVELO, b. May 20, 1850.
599. 4. LILLIE-LUCELIA, b. May 14, 1855.
600. 5. CAROLINE-MATILDA, b. June 16, 1858.
601. 6. GEORGE-VERNON, b. Oct. 8, 1860.

602. OLIVE-SALOME,[5][251] (*Elijah,[4] John,[3] Samuel,[2] John,[1]*) b. May 4, 1819; m. Amos-Emerson, son of Amos-Melvin Smith of Canton, N. Y., Oct. 8, 1846. He was b. Feb. 21, 1820. Their eldest child was b. in Lawrence; the others in Canton, N. Y. *Canton, N. Y.*

603. 1. MELVIN-WRIGHT, b. July 9, 1847; d. Jan. 28, 1863.
604. 2. OLIVE-ISSORA, b. April 29, 1855.
605. 3. JACOB-ALBERTO, b. Jan. 5, 1861; d. Oct. 31, 1865.

606. TOLMAN-TENNY,[5][252] (*Elijah,[4] John,[3] Samuel,[2] John,[1]*) b. Sept. 12, 1821; m. Eliza, daughter of James Waters of England, Jan. 4, 1849; she was b. July 13, 1825; d. Feb. 18, 1867; m. 2d, Mary-Elizabeth Chittenden, April 1, 1868; she was b. Oct. 26, 1838, and was the dau. of Noah and Sarah (Miller) Chittenden of Genesee, Mich.; granddaughter of Giles and Mary (Hawley) Chittenden of Williston, Vt.; great granddaughter of Thomas and Elizabeth (Meigs) Chittenden of Arlington, Vt.; the latter was elected the first Governor of Vermont in 1778, and was re-elected, holding the office in all 18 years. (See Vermont Historical Magazine, p. 906.) He has been a Justice of the Peace, and Deacon of the Baptist Church, of which he is a member, town clerk, Treasurer of Flint River Baptist Association since 1859, and so continues, (1869). *Genesee, Mich.*

607. 1. CORODEN-JAMES, b. Nov. 22, 1849, in Medina, Ohio.
608. 2. ONCKEN-DELOS, b. Oct. 27, 1854, Lawrence, N. Y.
609. 3. LECCA-OLIVE, b. Jan. 30, 1860, Genesee, Mich.

610. EDWIN-MAROW,[5][255] (*Elijah,[4] John,[3] Samuel,[2] John,[1]*) b. Jan. 7, 1830; m. Lominda, daughter of Leonidas Palmer of Lawrence, N. Y., Jan. 11, 1857. She was b. Jan. 28, 1834. He has held the office of school inspector for several years. They have one child. *Worth, Mich.*

611. 1. OCEL HARWET, b. July 30, 1861, in Tuscola, Mich.

612. ARTEMAS,[5][257] (*Eleazer,[4] Eleazer,[3] Samuel,[2] John,[1]*) b. Nov. 18, 1796; m. Hannah, daughter of Eleazer Baker of Mansfield, Dec. 11, 1822; she was b. Oct. 5, 1797, d. Sept. 20, 1864; m. 2d, Esther, daughter of Elijah Eldridge of Willington, and widow of David Buffington of Willington, March 21, 1865. She was born May 5, 1809.

He resides on a part of the estate purchased by his great grandfather, Samuel Slafter, of Robert Fenton, June 13, 1723.   *Mansfield, Ct.*

613.   1. OLIVE-NORTON, b. June 9, 1823; d. Nov. 27, 1859; m. Theodore-Obookiah, son of Theodore Stearns of Southampton, Mass., July 2, 1849; he was b. May 13, 1823. They had, Ellen-Almira, b. May 2, 1856; d. Sept. 22, 1859.   *Mansfield, Ct.*

614. ALMIRA,⁵[259] (*Eleazer,⁴ Eleazer,³ Samuel,² John,¹*) b. Dec. 29, 1804; m. Royal-Chapman, son of Elijah Eldridge of Willington, March 26, 1829.   He was b. March 20, 1806; d. March 19, 1861. He was Deacon in Cong. Church in Willington, Ct., and representative to the State Legislature from that town.   They had no children.
Willington, Ct.

615. ZEMIRA-MAHALA,⁵[261] (*Ira,⁴ Eleazer,³ Samuel,² John,¹*) b. Sept. 11, 1802; m. Joel, son of Joel Bishop of Rose, N. Y., July 4, 1826.   He was b. Feb. 15, 1800.   The first six of their children were born in Rose, and the last four in Butler, N. Y.
South Butler, N. Y.

616.   1. MALINDA-ELIZABETH, b. May 4, 1827; m. 1st, Patrick Fanning, June 3, 1851; he d. Feb. 8, 1865; m. 2d, William Taylor, Feb. 14, 1867. In war of rebellion he was in Comp. C, 185th New York Vol., length of service eleven months, and in several engagements. Her children by 1st husband were, (1.) George-William, b. Aug. 24, 1853; (2.) Joel-Jerome, b. June 18, 1855; (3.) Mary, b. April 7, 1857, d. Sept. 10, 1861.
South Butler, N. Y.

617.   2. BENJAMIN, b. Dec. 15, 1829; m. Lucy Hall, Jan. 5, 1854, and had, (1.) Josephine, b. Dec. 9, 1854; (2.) Joel-Hall, b. July 19, 1857; (3.) Frances-Eveline, b. Feb. 11, 1860; (4.) Rose-Ellen, b. April 30, 1862; (5.) Stella, b. March 30, 1865, d. Aug. 26, 1865; (6.) John-Elias, b. Oct. 7, 1868.   *South Butler, N. Y.*

618.   3. CHARLOTTE-GRACE, b. March 7, 1832; m. Addison Harwood, and had, Laura-Maranda, b. Aug. 3, 1863.   *South Butler, N. Y.*

619.   4. ERON-DORSON, b. Sept. 21, 1834; d. Jan. 25, 1854.

620.   5. MARTHA-FREELOVE, b. March 27, 1837; m. Elias Taylor, Feb. 18, 1857, and had, (1.) Vesta-Elnora, b. Sept. 20, 1859; (2.) Lucia-Ethimer, b. Sept. 9, 1861, d. July 24, 1863; (3.) Eliza, b. Jan. 9, 1867.
South Butler, N. Y.

621.   6. MARY-JOANNA, b. May 12, 1839; m. Porter Van Deusen, Dec. 3, 1858, and had, (1.) Parker-Boynton, b. Nov. 22, 1859; (2.) Horatio-Eugene, b. Sept. 13, 1861; (3.) Martha-Zemira, b. March 27, 1864; (4.) Edwin, b. Feb. 5, 1867.   *Port Byron, Pineville-Box, N. Y.*

622.   7. SARAH-SUBMIT, b. Nov. 3, 1841; m. George Harwood, and had, Anna-Maria, b. Sept. 19, 1866.   *South Butler, N. Y.*

°623.   8. HARRIET-ZEMIRA, b. May 30, 1844; m. Sylvanus Campbell, March 19, 1867, and had, —— ——, b. June 24, 1868.   *Pompey, N. Y.*

624.   9. EMMA, b. Oct. 4, 1847; d. June 3, 1848.

625.   10. ANTHA, b. July 5, 1849; d. Aug. 12, 1849.

626. MARILDA,⁵[262] (*Ira,⁴ Eleazer,³ Samuel,² John,¹*) b. July 1, 1805; d. in Solon, N. Y., Dec. 10, 1849; m. Simmons, son of Russell and Lois (Pierce) Warren, Jan. 8, 1831; he d. Nov. 27, 1867.   Her children were born in Solon, N. Y.   *McGrawville, N. Y.*

627.   1. ELON-GALUSHA, m. Eveline Hicks, and had, Eugene, b. Oct. 14, 1854. He was in war of rebellion in Comp. F, 76th New York Vol.; was taken prisoner in battle of Wilderness, and died of starvation at Andersonville, Aug., 1864.   *Homer, N. Y.*

628.   2. ELIZABETH-PENELOPE, m. Sylvanus Campbell; she died Dec. 19, 1864. Their children were: (1) Francis H., b. Jan. 7, 1856; (2) Flora F., b. Jan. 10, 1858; (3) Minna-Bertha, Feb. 29, 1860.   *Solon, N. Y.*

629. SANDFORD,[5][263] (*Ira*,[4] *Eleazer*,[3] *Samuel*,[2] *John*,[1]) b. Jan. 24, 1808; d. Dec. 10, 1842; m. Elmina, daughter of Orin Wood of Adams Centre, N. Y., Sept. 20, 1836. She was born March 29, 1813.
Watervale, N. Y.

630.   1. WILLIAM-BUNCE, b. in Adams, N. Y., July 20, 1838; m. Francenia-Josephine, daughter of John Boom of Salmon River, N. Y., Aug. 14, 1860. She was b. Sept. 12, 1841, and had, Ada-May, b. Feb. 24, 1866. He was in war of rebellion three years and nine months; was five or six months in the 3d N. Y. Cavalry, in Comp. C, and in Comp. M, 11th N. Y. Cavalary, the remainder of his service.
Sand Bank, Oswego Co., N. Y.

631. JESSE-BENNET,[5][266] (*Ira*,[4] *Eleazer*,[3] *Samuel*,[2] *John*,[1]) b. March 25, 1815; m. Ophelia-Brunette, daughter of William Gage of Kirkland, N. Y., Sept. 5, 1840; she was born Oct. 9, 1815, d. Sept. 1, 1852; m. 2d, Henrietta-Maria, daughter of David Holman of Lawrence, N. Y., Sept. 29, 1853. She was b. Feb. 12, 1827. Their children were as follows:
Woolcotville, N. Y.

632.   1. MARY-JANE, b. in Clinton, N. Y., Oct. 3, 1842; m. Rufus Yarrington.
Bennett's Corners, N. Y.
633.   2. FLORA-MATILDA, b. in Carlton, N. Y., July 18, 1858.
634.   3. NETTIE-PHILENA, b. in Carlton, N. Y., Sept. 13, 1861.
635.   4. CHARLES-EMMET, b. Jan. 22, 1862; d. Sept. 28, 1862.

636. MARY-FREEMAN,[5][267] (*Ira*,[4] *Eleazer*,[3] *Samuel*,[2] *John*,[1]) b. July 24, 1817; m. Luther-James, son of Gurshom-Blashfield Wheelock of Pompey, N. Y., Jan. 12, 1843. He was b. Aug. 17, 1808. Their children, born in Pompey, were as follows:
Watervale, N. Y.

637.   1. RALPH-RODOLPHUS, b. Oct. 2, 1843; m. Dec. 19, 1866, Ada Sloan of Pompey, N. Y.
638.   2. DOLLIE-AMELIA, b. July 22, 1846.
639.   3. ANN-MARIA, b. July 30, 1850.
640.   4. MARY-ELLEN, b. Oct. 7, 1852.
641.   5. ALMA-ELIZA, b. Aug. 25, 1856.
642.   6. DORA, b. June 21, 1859.
642½. 7. AVERY-GRANT, b. Dec. 28, 1865.

643. WILLIAM-PURLEE,[5][279] (*Samuel*,[4] *Eleazer*,[3] *Samuel*,[2] *John*,[1]) b. Oct. 11, 1817; m. Mary, daughter of John Campbell of Bath, N. Y., Aug. 31, 1843. She was b. March 15, 1818. Their children are as follows:
Wautoma, Waushara Co., Wis.

644.   1. MARY-FRANCES, b. in Bath, N. Y., July 14, 1844; m. Aug. 1, 1866, Charles-Edward Storm, hardware merchant, at   *Wautoma, Wis.*
645.   2. CLARENCE-EUGENE, b. in Virgil, N. Y., Aug. 23, 1846.

646. EDWIN-PHILANDER,[5][281] (*Samuel*,[4] *Eleazer*,[3] *Samuel*,[2] *John*,[1]) b. Sept. 26, 1821; m. Sarah-Miranda, daughter of Clark-Munson Johnson of Cortlandville, N. Y., March 6, 1845. She was b. March 11, 1824; d. May 29, 1864; no children. He has been Postmaster at Virgil, N. Y., and Cashier of the " First National Bank of Cortland," and is now a Director of the same. He m. 2d, Helen-Maria, dau. of Ephraim-Peabody and Lydia-Maria (Bennet) Sumner* of Homer,

---

*1. William Sumner, the emigrant ancestor, was born in England about 1605. He is said to have been of Burchester, Oxfordshire. He, with his wife Mary, settled in Dorchester, Mass. Bay, and was made a freeman in 1637; admitted

N. Y., June 6, 1865. She was born July 27, 1840. They have
adopted a daughter of Edward and Mary Bridgeman, whose name is
Julia-Maria, born Feb. 3, 1859. *Cortland, N. Y.*

647. ASAHEL,[5][269] (*Calvin,*[4] *Eleazer,*[3] *Samuel,*[2] *John,*[1]) b. Feb. 28,
1810; m. Electa, daughter of Luke Pierce of Cuba, N. Y., Oct. 24,
1833. She was b. April 19, 1815. The eldest three of his children
were born in Portville, N. Y., and the others were born in Bonus, Ill.
Belvidere, Ill.

648. 1. EMILY-DIANTHA,[1261] b. Oct. 25, 1834; m. Henry-Jacob Tripp.

---

to church, 1652; was 12 years deputy to General Court; selectman 23 years;
his wife died June 7, 1676. His will was proved 24th March, 1691-2. Children were: 1, William, b. in England; 2, Roger, b. in England; 3, *George*,
b. in England, Feb. 14, 1634; 4, Samuel, b. in Dorchester; 5, Increase; 6,
Joan; 7, Abigail.

2. *George*, b. in England, Feb. 14, 1634; d. Dec. 11, 1715; m. Mary, dau. of Edward Baker, Nov. 7, 1662. She was b. April 1, 1642; d. Dec. 1, 1719. He
lived on Brush Hill in Milton, and was a deacon of the church. Children:
1, Mary, b. Feb. 11, 1663-4; 2, George, b. Feb. 9, 1666; 3, Samuel, b. Oct.
19, 1669; 4, William, b April 7, 1671; 5, Ebenezer, b. Dec. 9, 1673; 6,
Edward, b. Aug. 29, 1675; 7, Joseph, b. Aug. 26, 1677; 8, Benjamin, b.
Dec. 15, 1683.

3. *Edward*, b. Aug. 29, 1675; d. 1763; m. Elizabeth, dau. of Elder Samuel
Clap of Dorchester, Sept. 25, 1701. He was a fellmonger and glover; re-
sided in Roxbury, Mass. Children were: 1, Edward, b. July 16, 1702; 2,
Elizabeth, b. April 30, 1704; 3, John, b. Aug. 1, 1705; 4, Elizabeth, b.
April 7, 1708; 5, Samuel, b. Oct. 21, 1710; 6, Increase, b. June 9, 1713; 7,
Hannah, b. May 8, 1715; 8, Mary, b. Oct. 9, 1717; 9, Nathaniel, b. 1718;
10, Ebenezer, b. June 10, 1722; 11, *Benjamin*, b. Dec. 29, 1724.

4. *Benjamin*, b. Dec. 29, 1724; d. Jan. 27, 1803; m. Bridget Perry, Oct. 3,
1748; she died Dec. 6, 1803, aged 75; resided in Ashford, Ct., and represented that town in the General Court in 1775; he was styled Capt.; the late
Governor Increase Sumner of Massachusetts was his nephew. The Hon.
Charles Sumner, U. S. Senator, is descended from Roger Sumner, the 2d
son of the emigrant ancestor. His children were: 1, James-Fitch, b. July
29, 1749; 2, Sibil, b. Sept. 10, 1751; 3, *Samuel*, b. Jan. 5, 1754; 4, Lucy,
b. Aug. 25, 1761; 5, John-Newman; 6, Increase; 7, Irena, b. April 29,
1767, d. Feb. 10, 1850.

5. *Samuel*, b. Jan. 5, 1754; m. Abigail Peabody, April 10, 1777; she was b. June 10,
1755, d. March 3, 1778; (she was the dau. of Ephraim and Abigail (Bosworth)
Peabody, who removed from Boxford, Mass., to Ashford, Ct.; granddaughter of Ephraim and Hannah (Reddington) Peabody of Boxford, Mass.;
great granddaughter of William and Hannah (Hale) Peabody of Boxford;
great-great granddaughter of Francis and Mary (Foster) Peabody. Francis
was the emigrant ancestor, born 1614; came from the parish of St. Albans,
Hertfordshire, Eng., in the ship Planter,.1635; resided in Ipswich, Hamp-
ton, N. H., and finally in Topsfield, Mass., where he died, Feb. 19, 1697-8.
Samuel Sumner m. 2d, Lydia Utley, Jan. 3, 1782. His children were: 1,
Ephraim Peabody, b. March 3, 1778—the mother died, as above noted, the
same day on which her son was born; 2, Olive, b. April 4, 1783; 3, Oliver, b.
Sept. 27, 1784; 4, Abigail-Peabody, b. Sept 13, 1786; 5, Azeb, b. Jan. 19,
1789; 6, Lydia, b. Feb. 28, 1791; 7, Samuel, b. March 30, 1794; 8, Increase, b. June 20, 1796. They resided in Ashford, Ct.; he was a deacon in
the church. The above children were born in Ashford.

6. *Ephraim-Peabody*, b. March 3, 1778; m. Alathea Stoddard of Woodstock, Ct.,
and had, 1, Abigail; 2, Alathea; 3, Samuel; 4, Otis-Stoddard; 5, Sophia;
6, Pamela; 7, *Ephraim-Peabody*, b. Jan. 24, 1814; 8, Lurilla; 9, Increase;
10, Marrett.

7. *Ephraim-Peabody*, b. Jan. 24, 1814; m. Lydia-Maria Bennet, and had, 1, Helen-
Maria, b. July 27, 1840; 2, William-Peabody, b. Oct. 18, 1848.

8. *Helen-Maria*, b. July 27, 1840; m. Edwin-Philander Slafter.

649. 2. Melvin-Clarkson,[1265] b. Nov. 25, 1835 ; m. Sarah-Maria Roscrans.
650. 3. Euretta-Olive,[1266] b. Feb. 23, 1837 ; m. Thomas-Sir Rogers.
651. 4. Julia-Ann, b. Aug. 14, 1839.
652. 5. Albert-Alphonzo, b. Sept. 21, 1846. He was, by enlistment in the Elgin Battery, 5th Illinois Light Artillery, in war of rebellion, from Aug., 1864, to July 1st, 1865. *Belvidere, Ill.*

653. Elijah-Dexter,[5][271] (*Calvin*,[4] *Eleazer*,[3] *Samuel*,[2] *John*,[1]) b. Dec. 14, 1814 ; m. Maria-Lucretia Lilly, March, 1846. She was b. June 16, 1826. *McHenry, Ill.*

654. 1. Orin-Augustine, b. in Greenwood, Ill., Jan. 11, 1849.
655. 2. Emily-Diana, b. in Greenwood, Ill., Sept. 19, 1852.
656. 3. Reuben, b. in Rock Co., Wis., March 9, 1855.
657. 4. Sylvester, b. in McHenry, Ill., Aug. 8, 1858 ; d. Jan. 8, 1859.
658. 5. Charles-William, b. in McHenry, Ill., Nov. 4, 1862.

659. Orin,[5][272] (*Calvin*,[4] *Eleazer*,[3] *Samuel*,[2] *John*,[1]) b. Feb. 16, 1818 ; m. Dorcas-Reinshaw, daughter of George-Washington Collins of McMinnville, Warren Co., Tenn., Nov. 15, 1863.

660. Tryphena,[5][273] (*Calvin*,[4] *Eleazer*,[3] *Samuel*,[2] *John*,[1]) b. Feb. 25, 1820 ; m. Henry-Wallace, son of Royal Bruce of Shopiere, Wis., Jan. 30, 1844. He was b. April 25, 1813 ; d. Feb. 5, 1853. He was a Justice of the Peace, Supervisor, &c. Her eldest child was b. in Bonus, Ill., the others where she now resides. *Fond du Lac, Wis.*

661. 1. Emily-Melvina, b. March 2, 1845; m. Charles-Theodore Stringham, Aug. 31, 1863.
662. 2. Amanda-Rosina, b. April 18, 1847.
663. 3. Phebe-Miranda, b. June 23, 1851.

664. Cynthia,[5][275] (*Calvin*,[4] *Eleazer*,[3] *Samuel*,[2] *John*,[1]) b. May 25, 1824 ; d. Aug. 14, 1845 ; m. John-Michael, son of John-Michael Kull of Wurtemberg, Germany, Jan. 8, 1841. He was b. in Wurtemberg, Nov. 15, 1814. Her children were b. at Bloomfield. *Bloomfield, Wis.*

665. 1. Margaret-Elizabeth, b. Nov. 16, 1842 ; m. Edwin-Rose Frisbie, son of the Rev. Ichabod-Andrus Hart of Bloomfield, Wis. In war of rebellion, he was in Comp C, 22d Wis. Vol. ; was in Sherman's march through Georgia and South Carolina. *Geneva, Walworth Co., Wis.*
666. 2. Andrew, b. April 29, 1845 ; m. Ann Reitbrock, and had, (1.) Franciska-Carolina-Christina, b. May 23, 1863 ; (2.) Helen-Margaret, b. April 30, 1866 ; (3) Henry-Andrew, b. Jan. 25, 1868. *Geneva, Wis.*

667. Marilda,[5][276] (*Calvin*,[4] *Eleazer*,[3] *Samuel*,[2] *John*,[1]) b. Oct. 23, 1826 ; d. Jan. 28, 1859 ; m. Edwin-Ruthvin, son of Charles Roberts of Amherst, Mass., Aug. 24, 1850. He was b. March 15, 1823. *Fond du Lac, Wis.*

668. 1. Julius-Sylvester, b. in Fond du Lac, Aug. 26, 1851.
669. 2. William-Warren, b. in North Amherst, Mass., Aug. 20, 1853.
670. 3. John-Justin, b. in Fond du Lac, Sept. 25, 1856.

671. William,[5][293] (*Abner*,[4] *Joseph*,[3] *Joseph*,[2] *John*,[1]) b. ——— ; d. March 24, 1832 ; m. Elizabeth, daughter of Israel Peters of Westport, N. Y. *Westport, Essex Co., N. Y.*

672. 1. William, m. Mary Knickabocker, and had children. *Sacketts Harbor, N. Y.*
673. 2. Abner, b. Sept. 13, 1807, unmarried. *Grove City, Iowa.*

674. 3. SARAH, b. Jan. 1, 1809 ; m. 1st, Seth Barber, 1827 ; he died 1838. She
      m. 2d, Horace Atwood, 1843. She had five children by her first
      husband and three by her second, as follows :—
      (1.) Silvia, b April 13, 1827 ; (2.) Sylvester, b. Nov. 24, 1829; (3.)
      Matilda, b. May 24, 1832 ; (4.) Lucinda, b. April 26, 1834 ; (5.) Rebecca,
      b. April 11, 1836 ; (6.) Mary, b. April 13, 1844 ; (7.) Esther, b. Dec. 3,
      1846 ; (8.) William, b. April 3, 1848.   *Grant, Cass Co., Iowa.*
675. 4. EUNICE, b. 1811 ; m. Dependence Nichols, and has, (1.) Clarissa, b. 1832 ;
      (2.) Benjamin, b. 1834 ; (3.) Elizabeth, b. 1836.   *Clayton Co., Iowa.*
676. 5. ISRAEL ; died young.

677. ABRAHAM,[5][298] *(Abner,[4] Joseph,[3] Joseph,[2] John,[1])* b. March
29, 1775 ; d. March 17, 1865 ; m. Anna Mann.   *Westport, N. Y.*

678. 1. ABNER, resides in Westport ; m. Lois, dau. of Aaron Palmer, and had,
      (1.) Jacob ; (2.) Mary-Ann ; (3.) Julia-Ann ; (4.) Robert ; (5.) Elizabeth ;
      (6.) John.
679. 2. THERON,[1277] b. Sept. 7, 1805 ; m. Julia Lobdell.
680. 3. JOSHUA,[1286] b. Feb. 11, 1806 ; d. June 12, 1864 ; m. 1st, Salome Bur-
      roughs ; 2d, Sarah Benedict.
681. 4. LUCINDA, m. Marcus Storrs ; she died, 1861, at Elizabethtown, N. Y.
682. 5. NATHAN,[1294] b. Aug. 29, 1814 ; m. Roxana Goodale.

683. ISAAC,[5][300] *(Joseph,[4] Joseph,[3] Joseph,[2] John,[1])* b. Jan. 28,
1765 ; d. Aug. 4, 1847 ; m. Mary Harrington, March 18, 1785. She
was b. Feb. 15, 1764 ; d. Jan. 4, 1849.

                              Preston, Chenango Co., N. Y.

684. 1. ISAAC, b. Aug. 27, 1785, d. Dec. 3, 1849 ; m. Tryphena Chapel.
685. 2. JOB,[1359] b. April 24, 1787 ; d. Sept. 19, 1862 ; m. Phila Beckwith.
686. 3. BENJAMIN,[1336] b. March 26, 1789 ; m. Maria Johnson.
687. 4. JONATHAN,[1298] b. May 7, 1793 ; m. Elizabeth-Dickson Wheaton.
688. 5. MARY, b. June 10, 1795 ; d. Sept. 3, 1841 ; m. Amos Chapel.
689. 6. SARAH, b. April 7, 1797 ; m. David Strong, and had Ephraim and Isaac.
690. 7. AARON,[1316] b. Aug. 31, 1799 ; m. Sarah Scranton.
691. 8. LOIS,[1306] b. July 8, 1801 ; d. Jan. 9, 1844 ; m. Augustus Ross.
692. 9. DANIEL,[1371] b. May 17, 1803 ; m. Sarah Fletcher.
693. 10. JOSEPH,[1354] b. Jan. 8, 1805 ; d. Sept. 23, 1857 ; m. Lura Webster.
694. 11. ELIZA,[1326] b. June 24, 1807 ; m. Alfred Goodrich.

695. AMY,[3][303] *(Joseph,[4] Joseph,[3] Joseph,[2] John,[1])* b. Aug. 11,
1769 ; d. April 25, 1840 ; m. Job, son of John Stafford of Rhode Island,
Nov. 7, 1790. He was b. Feb. 11, 1767 ; d. July 30, 1846.

                              Preston, Chenango Co., N. Y.

696. 1. ELIZABETH, b. Oct. 11, 1791 ; she m. Whitman Wilcox, and had, (1.)
      Bradford ; (2.) Minerva ; (3.) Hannah-Elizabeth ; (4.) Lydia.
                              Norwich, Chenango Co., N. Y.
697. 2. MARY, b. June 1, 1793 ; d. July 3, 1849 ; m. John Skinner, and had,
      (1.) Julia ; (2.) John ; (3.) Luke ; (4.) Phœbe ; (5.) Levi ; (6.) Amy-
      Elizabeth ; (7.) Daniel-Perry ; (8.) Mary-Almira.
                              Norwich, Chenango Co., N. Y.
698. 3. LOIS, b. Aug. 27, 1796 ; d. Aug. 10, 1858 ; m. John Tracy, and had,
      (1.) Harriet ; (2.) George ; (3.) Willard ; (4.) Henry-Austin ; (5,) Amy-
      Elizabeth ; (6.) Joseph-Slater (of Norwich, N. Y.)
                              Preston, Chenango Co., N. Y.
699. 4. AMY, b. May 17, 1798 ; d. March 6, 1860 ; m. Reuben Aldrich, and had,
      (1.) Amy-Frances ; (2.) Reuben ; (3.) Reuben-Stafford ; (4.) Abraham-
      Slater.   *Norwich, Chenango Co., N. Y.*
700. 5. CHLOE, b. April 3, 1800 ; m. Amaziah Tracy, and had, (1.) Job-Staf-
      ford ; (2.) Peter-Alexander ; (3.) Amaziah ; (4.) Chloe-Ann.
                              Norwich, Chenango Co., N. Y.
701. 6. ESTHER, b. July 10, 1803 ; m. John Skinner.
                              Norwich, Chenango Co , N. Y.

702. 7. MERCY, b. May 20, 1809; d. Dec. 19, 1838; m. Joseph-Hurlburt Scott.
Coventry, Chenango Co., N. Y.
703. 8. GEORGE-WASHINGTON, b. Feb. 22, 1815; d. Nov. 3, 1836.

704. KEZIAH,[301] *(Joseph,[4] Joseph,[3] Joseph,[2] John,[1])* b. June 29,
1766; d. July 11, 1815; m. Isaac, son of John Stafford of Guilford, Vt.,
June 11, 1786. He was b. Sept. 2, 1763; d. Jan. 13, 1831. Their
children were born in Guilford, Vt

Ellington, Chatauque Co., N. Y.

705. 1. RUTH, b. Dec. 22, 1786; d. Aug. 20, 1866; m. Thomas-Washington
Randall in 1808; he was b. Aug. 27, 1780; d. April 7, 1867. Their
children were :
(1.) Edwin, b. Dec. 23, 1808; m. Lydia Holcomb, Jan. 10, 1844;
Children,— *Waymart, Wayne Co., Pa.*
(a.) George-Emery, b. Dec. 31, 1846.
(b.) Ralph-Emerson b. March 26, 1850.
(2.) Mary, b. Dec. 27, 1809; d. Sept. 5, 1854; m. Burlin-Nelson Gold-
smith, June 5, 1834, and had :
(a.) Ruth-Elizabeth, b. Jan. 4, 1836.
(b.) Oliver, b. Aug. 26, 1844.
(3.) Pamela, b. Feb. 19, 1811. *Masonville, Delaware Co., N. Y.*
(4.) Barbara, b. March 3, 1813; d. Dec. 27, 1841; m. Peter-Winchel
Connelly, Oct. 12, 1830, and had :
(a.) Samuel-Lucien, b. Nov. 1, 1832; d. Dec. 5, 1832.
(b.) Charles-Merrihue, b. April 2, 1834.
(c.) Thomas, b. April 12, 1836.
(d.) Mary-Jane, b. Aug. 24, 1837.
(e.) Barbara-Matilda, b. Dec. 12, 1841; d. Feb. 19, 1842.
(5.) Isaac, b. June 10, 1814; m. Sally May, Sept. 24, 1843.
Children,— *Masonville, N. Y.*
(a.) Lucy-Elizabeth, b. Feb. 14, 1845.
(b.) Edward-Payson, b. Jan. 8, 1849.
(c.) Bertha, b. Jan. 26, 1862; d. March 8, 1862.
(6.) Kezia, b. Nov. 27, 1815; d. March 10, 1842.
(7.) Robert-Shaw, b. July 31, 1817; m. Abigail-Augusta Brainard,
Nov. 16, 1843. Children,— *Masonville, N. Y.*
(a.) David-Brainard, b. and d. Sept. 9, 1844.
(b.) Mary-Emma, b. Aug. 11, 1845.
(c.) Phebe, b. March 12, 1847.
(d.) Marcus, b. May 27, 1849.
(e.) Fanny-Emily, b. Jan. 8, 1851.
(f.) Cynthia-Eliza, b. June 24, 1853; d. Feb. 27, 1863.
(g.) Rufus, b. June 27, 1855.
(h.) Sarah-Elizabeth, b. July 24, 1859.
(8.) Lucia, b. March 14, 1819; d. July 21, 1844; m. Lawson Blackman, and had,—
Sarah Matilda, b. Aug. 20, 1843; d. Aug. 17, 1866.
(9.) Daniel, b. Oct. 10, 1820; d. April 10, 1832.
(10.) Enoch, b. March 8, 1822; d. Feb. 3, 1864; m. Harriet-Matilda
Northrup, Feb. 23, 1851. Children,—
(a.) Olive-Marcella, b. Jan. 14, 1853.
(b.) Clark-Morris, b. March 26, 1856; d. June 29, 1862.
(c.) Charles-Howard, b. March 22, 1860.
(11.) Sarah-Esther, b. Nov. 14, 1823; d. Nov. 3, 1844.
(12.) Elizabeth, b. March 18, 1826; m. Charles-Howard Stebbins, Dec.
7, 1848. He d. Sept. 2, 1862. Children,— *Masonville, N. Y.*
(a.) William, b. Jan. 11, 1850; d. March 5, 1864.
(b.) Chrissie, b. Oct. 6, 1852.
(c.) Charles-Howard, b. Oct. 9, 1862.
(13.) Nancy-Matilda, b. Dec. 12, 1827; d. Jan. 29, 1858; m. John-
Hunt Stebbins, April 7, 1853.

(14.) Laban, b. June 28, 1830; m. Sarah-Emily Rounds, June 25, 1856.
Children,—   *Wharton, Potter Co., Pa.*
  (a.) Mary-Ida, b. Oct. 13, 1857.
  (b.) Winnie-Gertrude, b. Feb. 12, 1860.
  (c.) John-Emmet, b. April 1, 1863.
  (d.) Ruth-Pamela, b. Dec. 2, 1867.

706. 2. ABEL, b. Dec. 5, 1788; m. Rachel Chappel, and had, (1.) Betsey-Ma-
tilda; (2.) Job-Nelson; (3.) Alma-Athalia; (4.) Sophia-Lucelia.
                                             Preston, N. Y.

707. 3. BARBARA, b. Oct. 21, 1790; m. Peter Worden, and had, (1.) Diadema;
(2.) Marcus; (3.) Allen; (4.) Emily; (5.) Hayden; (6.) Mary; (7.)
Belinda; (8.) Alcena; (9.) Rowena; (10.) Ephraim.
                                      Green River, Vt.

708. 4. JOHN, b. May 13, 1792; d. 1855; m. Sophia Randall, and had, (1)
John-Austin; (2.) Abel; (3.) Sophia-Cornelia; (4) Electa; (5.)
Russel; (6.) Orinda; (7.) Martin-Van Buren.   *Ellington, N. Y.*

709. 5. HANNAH, b. Nov. 10, 1794; d. Oct. 14, 1861; m. Israel Chapin, and
had, (1.) Seth-Eli.   *Norwich, N. Y.*

710. 6. ISAAC, b. Oct. 31, 1796; m. Lucy Seymour, and had, (1.) Diadema;
(2.) Hannah; (3.) Saxa-Seymour; (4.) Isaac-Samuel; (5.) George-
Edgar; (6.) Lucy-Elizabeth.   *Courtland Station, Ill.*

711. 7. KEZIAH, b. Dec. 10, 1799; m. Miner Tracy, and had, (1.) Hannah;
(2.) John; (3.) Miner.   *Coventry, Chenango Co., N. Y.*

712. 8. JOSEPH, b. Oct. 30, 1801; m. Oct. 9, 1823, Sally, dau. of Uzziel Taylor
of South Hadley, Mass. They had :   *Howell, Mich.*
  (1.) Philena, b. in Butternuts, N. Y., Sept. 23, 1824. *Howell, Mich.*
  (2.) Polly, b. in Ellington, N. Y., Nov. 4, 1825; m. William H. Kel-
     logg of Spring Brook, Gratiot Co., Mich., Sept. 25, 1851, and
     had (a.) Joseph-Philander, (b.) Minerva-Louisa, (c.) George-A.
  (3.) Lucinda, b. in Ellicott, N. Y., Jan. 2, 1828; m. Cornelius-Harlow
     Persons of Howell, Mich.
  (4.) Minerva, b. in New Lisbon, N. Y., March 8, 1832; d. Oct. 19,
     1852; m. John Carl, Aug. 14, 1851.   *Howell, Mich.*
  (5.) Helen, b. in Lawrence, Penn., Dec. 26, 1833; m. 1st, George-
     Washington Andrews, Aug. 5, 1852; he died Nov. 7, 1855; she
     m. 2d, Ira Cronk, Jr., of Sturgis, Mich., Sept. 4, 1856, and by
     last husband had (a.) Lurissa, (b.) Nora.
  (6.) Nancy, b. in Lawrenceville, Penn., Oct. 23, 1836; m. Lewis Ro-
     land of Howell, Mich., Sept. 1863.
  (7.) George, b. in Addison, N. Y., Dec. 21, 1838; d. Oct. 28, 1868; m.
     Orvilla Carson, June 19, 1866. He was in Comp. K, 9th Mich.
     Vol., in war of rebellion, and served over four years; he was
     never well after he left the army; he died at   *Howell, Mich.*

713. 9. SARAH, b. July 14, 1803; d. Feb. 19, 1839; m. Hiram Snow, and had,
(1.) Roxa-Sarah, (2.) Alanson-Hubbard, (3.) Isaac, (4.) Francis-Ray,
(5.) Catharine.   *Willet, N. Y.*

714. 10. ESTHER, b. June 15, 1805; d. March 6, 1864; m. Orrin Randall, and
had (1.) Ruth-Catharine, (2.) Roxa-Louisa, (3.) Hannah-Stafford, (4.)
Orrin-Hubbard, (5.) Isaac-Samuel, (6.) Clarinda, (7.) Joseph-Wallace,
(8.) Mary-Esther, (9.) Abel-Howard, (10.) William-Luther, (11.) Zina-
Case, (12.) Jabez-Delawn.   *Licking, Mo.*

715. JONATHAN,[5][307] (*Joseph,[4] Joseph,[3] Joseph,[2] John,[1]*) b. Jan. 19,
1776; d. April 28, 1841, near Aurora, Ill.; m. Abigail, daughter of
Joseph Holmes of Chesterfield, N. H., Jan. 17, 1804; she was b. Jan.
5, 1784; she d. at Champlain, N. Y., April 15, 1828;—m. 2d, Persis
Graves, widow, daughter of John Squires, North Hero, Vt., June 10,
1830. She was b. Sept. 12, 1789; d. Oct. 15, 1846, at Racine, Wis.
He was a Lieut. in the war of 1812, and Captain in the Militia many
years. His children were by his first wife, and all born in Champlain,
near Rouse's Point.   *Champlain, N. Y.*

716. 1. NELSON,[1384] b. Sept. 25, 1805; m. Emily Kitchel.

717. 2. HARVEY, b. Sept. 13, 1807; d. at St. Francisville, La., July 30, 1830, unmarried.
718. 3. JOHN-HOLMES, b. Sept. 22, 1810; d. May 20, 1828.
719. 4. GEORGE-KING,[1393] b. March 16, 1812; m. Mrs. Maria Loomis.
720. 5. BENJAMIN-FRANKLIN, b. Jan. 10, 1815; a dentist at San Francisco, Cal.; m. Emily Duncan.
721. 6. PHILANDER, b. May 6, 1816; m. Mary-Alice, dau. of Thomas Sullivan, Nov. 23, 1862. He is a printer, and has held offices of trust.
Elkhart, Ind.
722. 7. JONATHAN-EDWARDS, b. Aug. 21, 1820; m. Dec. 30, 1849, Caroline F. Powers. *Yuba Co., Cal.*

723. LOIS,⁵ [309] (*Joseph,⁴ Joseph,³ Joseph,² John,¹*) b. April 20, 1780; d. Feb. 25, 1844; m. Royal, son of Samuel Moses of Warwick, Mass., Feb. 23, 1800. He was born Oct. 11, 1774; died Jan. 27, 1856. Their children were as follows:
Newark Valley, Tioga Co., N. Y.
724. 1. GRATIA, b. March 9, 1801; m. Charles Potter, and had Celia Ann.
Berkshire, Tioga Co., N. Y.
725. 2. SAMUEL, b. June 23, 1802; m. Jan. 14, 1822, Thankful Wheeler, and had no children. *Newark Valley, Tioga Co., N. Y.*
726. 3. LAURA, b. Oct. 6, 1808; m. Joel Shaw of Butternuts, N. Y., Nov. 28, 1829, and had Philander-Moses, b. in Butternuts, Sept. 25, 1830. He m. Emily-Mercy Butler, Jan. 29, 1853, and had (gemini) (1.) Laura-Adelia and (2.) Olive-Amelia, b. in Oswego, Feb. 25, 1854; and (3.) George and (4.) Jerome (gemini), b. July 1, 1856, in Newark Valley, and both died Aug. 29, 1858; (5.) Chloe-Bidwell, b. July 1, 1859. Philander-M. Shaw enlisted in Comp. B, 109th New York Vol., Aug. 6, 1862, and served as " Wagon Master of the Reg. " until May 5, 1865. His wife joined him in Oct., 1862, and remained through the whole, doing much for his comfort and that of many a sick soldier.
Newark Valley, Tioga Co., N. Y.
727. 4. LYDIA, b. May 3, 1812; m. Riley Steere, and had Lorinda-Fidelia.
East McDonough, Chenango Co., N.Y.
728. 5. NATHAN-SLATER, b. Jan 30, 1818; m. Freelove Aldrich, and had, (1.) Lucy-Maria, (2.) Ambrose, (3.) LeGrand, (4.) Lucina.
Kirkville, Onondaga Co., N. Y.
729. 6. PHILO-FERRY, b. May 28, 1823; m. Cynthia Close, and had (1.) Edson-Hartwell, (2.) Alice-Carrie. *McGrawville, Cortland Co., N. Y.*
730. 7. PHILANDER-PERRY, b. May 28, 1823; m. Mary Seymour.
Cortland Valley, Cortland Co., N. Y.

731. CHLOE,⁵[312] (*Joseph,⁴ Joseph,³ Joseph,² John,¹*) b. June 17, 1784; d. May 15, 1864; m. Elihu, son of Jeremiah Hayes of Brattleborough, Vt., Jan. 12, 1806. He was b. Oct. 5, 1783; d. Aug. 7, 1853. Their children are as follows: *Keesville, N. Y.*
732. 1. HARTWELL-SLATER, b. Aug. 4, 1807; d. Oct. 15, 1859; m. 1st, Mary Vanderwakes; m. 2d, Charlotte Elizabeth, dau. of Samuel Weston of Chesterfield, N. Y., and had (1.) DeByron, (2.) Mary-Bell, (3.) Napoleon-Bonaparte, (4.) Napoleon-Bonaparte, who was in 44th Ohio Vol., in war of rebellion.
733. 2. SYLVESTER, b. Sept. 12, 1810; d. Feb. 4, 1813.
734. 3. THOMAS-MCDONOUGH, b. Sept. 7, 1814; d. May 27, 1839. He was a physician, died in Smithland, Ky.
735. 4. ELIHU, b. Jan. 24, 1816; d. Feb. 24, 1855; m. Paulina, dau. of Elias Sheldon of Lewis N. Y., and had (1.) Thomas-McDonough, (2) Rosaltha, (3.) Wilbur-Fisk, (4.) Rozina-Chloe, (5.) Arabella-Senelda.
736. 5. SIMON-BOLIVAR, b. Oct. 26, 1828; m. Eleanora-Fidelia, dau. of Nathan Jackson of Whitehall, N. Y. *Keesville, N. Y.*

737. ISRAEL,⁵[310] (*Joseph,⁴ Joseph,³ Joseph,² John,¹*) b. May 7, 1782; d. Jan. 5, 1865; m. Susannah, daughter of Jabez Gage of

Greenwich, Washington Co., N. Y., Feb. 2, 1808. She was b. Nov. 21, 1785; d. Sept. 5, 1854. He studied with Dr. Richardson, and practised medicine a short time in Guilford, Vt., and in Washington Co., N. Y., but soon gave up the profession. Their children are as follows:

Bainbridge, Chenango Co., N. Y.

738. 1. Marcus-Tullius-Cicero,[1396] b. July 28, 1809; m. Maria Mickel.
739. 2. Joseph,[1422] b. Aug. 14, 1811; d. April 22, 1847; m. Sarah Sylvius.
740. 3. Nathan,[1407] b. Nov. 27, 1813; m. Eve McFarland.
741. 4. Caroline, b. Nov. 2, 1816.
742. 5. Benjamin-Milton, b. Jan. 10, 1819; d. Aug. 12, 1846.
743. 6. Albert,[1417] b. Sept. 9, 1821; d. May 14, 1864; m. Rhoda-Jane Richardson.
744. 7. Adelia, b. July 3, 1824; d. Feb. 23, 1844.
745. 8. Charlotte,[1419] b. Nov. 27, 1827; m. Herman-Birdsall Fuller.

746. Moses,[313] (*Joseph,⁴ Joseph,³ Joseph,² John,¹*) b. Oct. 8, 1787; d. Aug. 16, 1836; m. Pamela Fisher, Feb. 14, 1805. She was b. Sept. 30, 1787; d. Sept. 18, 1855. The following are their children:—

Preston, N. Y.

747. 1. Lois, b. May 17, 1806; m. Abraham Cummings, Sept. 1824; and had (1.) Moses, (2.) DeWitt-Clinton, (3.) Louisa-Priscilla, (4.) Rhoda-Amelia, (5.) Stephen-Maxon, (6.) Winfield-Scott.
East McDonough, N. Y.
748. 2. Delana, b. Jan. 26, 1808; m. Daniel Nicholson, and had (1.) Almeda-Ann, (2.) Nelson. *Fremont, Ohio.*
749. 3. Nelson-Moses, b. Dec. 17, 1810; m. Mary-Ann Kelsey, Oct. 18, 1827; and had (1.) Hartwell-Nelson, (2.) Augustus-William.
East McDonough, Chenango Co., N. Y.

750. Silas,[318] (*Abial,⁴ Joseph,³ Joseph,² John,¹*) b. Aug. 25, 1783; d. May 10, 1855; m. 1st, Mary Randall of Foster; she was b. Feb. 5, 1787, d. Aug. 29, 1828; m. 2d, Alice Harrington, widow, dau. of Jason White of Scituate, R. I. Their children are as follows:—

751. 1. Susan, b. Dec. 9, 1805; m. Joseph-Wilkinson Smith, Jan. 16, 1826.
South Foster, R. I.
752. 2. Anna, b. Dec. 23, 1807. *Foster, R. I.*
753. 3. Aaron,[1428] b. March 20, 1810; m. Lucy-Carter Bailey.
754. 4. Silas,[1434] b. April 21, 1812; m. Susannah Boswell.
755. 5. Israel, b. Nov. 5, 1814; m. Rebecca Shearer, and had (1.) George-Silas, (2.) Anna-Mary, (3.) Daniel-Peter, (4.) Joseph.
756. 6. Ahijah,[1442] b. Feb. 22, 1817; m. 1st, Eliza Pray, 2d, Lucretia-Ann Tucker.
757. 7. George,[1448] b. April, 11, 1819; m. Chalcedana Shippee.
758. 8. Mary-Celista, b. Aug. 11, 1821. *South Foster, R. I.*
759. 9. Selinda,[1451] b. Nov. 10, 1823; m. Atwell-Anthony Williams.
760. 10. Louisa, b. July 19, died young.
761. 11. David-Olney, b. Nov. 21, 1837.
762. 12. Harriet-Amanda,[1453] b. April 14, 1842; m. Jabez Chase.

763. Prudence,[317] (*Abial,⁴ Joseph,³ Joseph,² John,¹*) b. April 8, 1781; m. Samuel Brown, Feb. 5, 1801. He was b. July 22, 1779; d. Feb. 6, 1853. Their children were as follows:— *Killingly, Ct.*

764. 1. Clara, b. Nov. 28, 1801; d. Sept. 17, 1831.
765. 2. David, b. Nov. 3, 1803; m. Eliza Peterson, and had (1.) Prudence, (2.) John, (3.) Lucinda, (4.) Mary-Jane, (5.) Selenda, (6.) Lysetta, (7.) Lorenzo, (8.) Harvey, (9.) Emily, (10.) Calvin, and others.
Truxton, N. Y.
766. 3. Roba, b. July 7, 1805; died about 1845.
767. 4. Mary, b. Dec. 30, 1808; d. Aug. 1852.

768. 5. LEONARD, b. Nov. 6, 1810; m. Reba Griffis, and had Samuel Milton.
    South Killingly, Ct.
769. 6. LUCINDA, b. Oct. 16, 1817; m. Caleb Harrington and had (1.) Almira,
    (2.) Mary-Jane, (3.) Albert-Erastus, (4) Arminda, (5.) Louisa-Frances,
    (6.) James Henry.   *Providence, R. 1.*
770. 7. Almon, b. June 30, 1824; m. Harriet-Almira Wilcox, and had (1.)
    Charles-Ira, (2.) Fanny-Maria.

771. CHARLOTTE,[5][330] (*Silas,*[4] *Joseph,*[3] *Joseph,*[2] *John,*[1]) b. Sept.
29, 1793; d. Sept. 28, 1858; m. William, son of William Turner of
Gloucester, R. I., Aug. 1, 1813. He was b. Jan. 18, 1793; d. Nov.
21, 1850. He was a Justice of the Peace in 1840. He removed from
Rhode Island and resided in several towns in New York, but lastly in
Ohio. They had the following children: *North Fairfield, Ohio.*

772. 1. OTIS-HARRIS, b. April 24, 1814; d. May 13, 1816.
773. 2. JANE-AUGUSTA, b. at Glens Falls, N. Y., March 3, 1816; m. Zalmon-
    Bailey Stilson, July 29, 1835, and had,—
    (1.) Mary-Augusta, b. Nov. 21, 1844; d. Nov. 13, 1849.
    (2.) Lucy-Levantia, b. Feb. 28, 1847.   *Reading, Hillsdale Co., Mich.*
774. 3. NELSON-MARMADUKE WOOD, b. in Winfield, N. Y., Dec. 15, 1817; m.
    Harriet-Newell Sutton, Jan. 13, 1838, and resides in Staunton, Mich.
    They have had,—
    (1.) Louisa-Marian, b. April 22, 1840; drowned July 4, 1859.
    (2.) Verona, b. May 15, 1842; d. March 10, 1843.
    (3.) Santley-William, b. July 15, 1843; was 2d Lieut. in Comp. F, 18th
       Mich. Vol., in war of rebellion eight months; again, Comp. C,
       1st Mich. Sharp-Shooters, and was seven months in Dansville
       prison; now (1868) clerk of Ingham County, Mich.
    (4.) Josephine, b. March 15, 1846.
    (5.) Mary-Ambrosia, b. Feb. 25, 1848.
    (6.) Olin-Sutton, b. July 23, 1851; drowned July 4, 1859.
    (7.) Emma, b. June 23, 1854.   *Mason, Ingham Co., Mich.*
775. 4. WILLIAM-FENNER, b. in Scott, N. Y., Dec. 10, 1822; m. 1st, Salome Tut-
    tle, March 10, 1849; she was drowned July 4, 1859; he m. 2d, Adelaide
    Campbell, Nov. 12, 1862. He was appointed Postmaster at Reading,
    Mich., 1861, which office he held several years.   *Staunton, Mich.*
776. 5. MARY-AMBROSIA, b. in Homer, N. Y., Aug. 22, 1828; m. Jensou Beers,
    April 4, 1855, and had,—
    (1.) William-Turner-Clyde, b. Jan. 24, 1858 in Goshen, Ind.; d. Oct.
       18, 1862.
    (2.) Jennie-Augusta, b. in Waterloo, Ind., Feb. 5, 1860.
    (3.) Edward-Carlton, b. in Staunton, Mich., Sept. 17, 1865; d. July 4,
       1866. Mr. Beers was an undergraduate of "Lima College," N.Y.
       He was admitted to the bar in Indiana, 1857; he has been in prac-
       tice in Staunton, Mich., since 1864; has been Register of Deeds in
       Montcalm County, and has just been re-elected, 1868.
       Staunton, Mich.

777. HANNAH,[5][321] (*Silas,*[4] *Joseph,*[3] *Joseph,*[2] *John,*[1]) b. Feb. 29,
1775; d. Oct. 21, 1857; m. Joseph, son of Elijah Smith of Killingly,
Ct., Jan. 5, 1794, in Foster, R. I. He was born Jan. 19, 1773; d. July
30, 1845. He resided in Killingly, Ct.; removed in 1805 to Sempronius, N. Y., and afterward to Ohio.
    North Fairfield, Huron Co., Ohio.

778. 1. ROXANA, b. April 11, 1795; d. Aug. 28, 1858; m. Vincent-Whitman
    Rathbun; he resides at Fremont, Steuben County, Ind. They had,—
    Nancy-Lovinia, b. June 8, 1820; m. May 1, 1842, Capt. Solomon-
    Smith Phillips (who was b. Jan. 11, 1816), and had,—
6

   (1.) Alice-Amelia, b. Feb. 15, 1843.
   (2.) Lesbia-Lavantia, b. Sept. 6, 1853 ; d. April 24, 1856.
          Berlin Heights, Erie Co., Ohio.
779. 2. HAVILLA, b. Jan. 9, 1798 ; m. Sarah, daughter of Asa Harwood of
   Sempronius, N. Y., Aug. 30, 1821 ; she was b. April 28, 1804, Plymouth, Ohio. They had,—
    (1.) Joseph, b. Sept. 5, 1829 ; m. Rebecca Trunell, Feb. 17, 1860,
     and had, (a.) Louis-Jay ; (b.) Lola-Matilda.
    (2.) Harriet, b. Sept. 15, 1831 ; m. Wiles Harvey, and had, (a.) Al-
     bert-Smith ; (b.) Carlton ; (c.) Amanda ; (d.) Isabella ; (e)
     Clement.   *Mantonville, Minn.*
    (3.) Walter-Augustus, b. March 14, 1839 ; photographer ; m. Lora-
     Melinda Harris, Jan. 18, 1863, and had, Calvin-Day, b. May 4,
     1866.   *Plymouth, Ohio.*
    (4.) Lucy-Maria, b. July 3, 1841 ; m. Chester Carpenter, Dec. 7, 1865 ;
     he d. Sept. 25, 1866 ; she had, Chester, b. Jan. 9, 1866.
              Plymouth, Ohio.
    (5.) Sarah-Matilda, b. Dec. 18, 1849.
780. 3. SCHUYLER, b. Jan. 20, 1800 ; d. June 19, 1819. *North Fairfield, Ohio.*
781. 4. SOPHIA, b. June 8, 1802.   *North Fairfield, Ohio.*
782. 5. ELISHA, b. March 6, 1812.   *North Fairfield, Ohio.*
783. 6. WALTER-BRANCH, b. Aug. 1, 1814, in Sempronius, N. Y.; m. Oct. 31,
   1841, Cynthia Coborn ; she was b. Aug. 17, 1825 ; res. North Fairfield,
   Ohio, where their children were born.
    (1.) Dorr-Walter, b. March 6, 1843 ; m. Dec. 12, 1865, Madessa-
     Catharine Jennings ; she was b. at North Fairfield, Feb. 18,
     1846 ; and had, Lola-Ina, b. Nov. 26, 1867.
             North Fairfield, Ohio.
    (2.) Dwight-Kellogg, b. April 11, 1846. In war of rebellion, he
     served in Comp. B, 25th Ohio Vols., by enlistment, from Feb.
     22, 1864, till discharged, June 18, 1866, two years and four
     months.   *North Fairfield, Ohio.*
    (3.) Delphene-Augusta, b. July 23, 1848 ; m. Sept. 24, 1868, Henry-
     William Butler ; he was b. in Fitchville, O., July 26, 1846.
             North Fairfield, Ohio.
    (4.) Dorlesca-Jane, b. Aug. 30, 1851.
    (5.) Hannah-Athalia, b. March 9, 1854.
    (6.) Day-Orin, b. Sept. 3, 1858 ; d. Dec. 9, 1865.
    (7.) Douglas, b. Jan. 27, 1861 ; d. Oct. 10, 1865.
784. 7. ELEANOR, b. July 25, 1808 ; d. 1845.
784½. 8. POLLY-JANE, b. in Sempronius, N. Y., April 4, 1824 ; m. 1st, Sylvester
   Rairdon, May, 1844, who was b. Jan. 1820 ; d. Sept. 19, 1848 ; m. 2d,
   April 4, 1853, Solomon-Ezra Watros ; he was b. Aug. 29, 1824 ; d. July
   30, 1862, in hospital at Keokuk, Iowa, having enlisted Nov. 18, 1861, in
   Comp. K, 4th Indiana Vol. ; service eight months and twelve days.
   She m. 3d, Dec. 10, 1865, Jeremiah White ; he was b. Oct. 31, 1812 ;
   res. Three Rivers, St. Joseph's Co., Mich. Her children by Solomon-
   Ezra Watros, all born in York, Ind., were—
    (a.) Wealthy-Loraine, b. March 14, 1855.
    (b.) Elizabeth-Ann, b. June 24, 1856.
    (c.) Hannah-Delight, b. Feb. 3, 1858 ; d. March 24, 1858.
    (d.) Ida-Florence, b. March 19, 1860 ; d. June 6, 1862.

 785. PAUL,[5][327] (*Silas,*[4] *Joseph,*[3] *Joseph,*[2] *John,*[1]) b. June 3, 1788, d.
Feb. 27, 1868 ; m. Chloe, dau. of John Shippee of Smithfield, R. I. ;
removed to Norwalk, Ohio, where he died as above. Their children
were as follows :

786. 1. MILTON,[1455] b. March 1, 1813, m. Elizabeth Bathrick.
786½. 2. ANNAH, b. March 13, 1815.   *Milton, Wood Co., Ohio.*
787. 3. SARAH,[1458] b. Aug. 30, 1817, m. Gilkey Morton.
787¼. 4. MARIA, b. Feb. 22, 1823, d. Jan. 30, 1853 ; m. John-Nelson Butt, and had

(1.) Lucy-Maria, who m. George-Henry Bailey, Feb. 15, 1864, and has
two children, Frederick-Nelson, b. May 14, 1866, and John-
Henry, b. Aug. 20, 1868. Mr. Bailey enlisted in 1861 in Comp.
D, 55th Ohio, in war of rebellion, and was discharged in 1865.
(2.) Ludencia, who m. Nov. 20, 1864, Charles Adams, and has Charles-
Henry, b. Jan. 10, 1866, and Ludencia, b. Dec. 6, 1868.
(3.) Henry-Ovington.
(4.) John-Hamilton. *Norwalk, Ohio.*
787½. 5. ASHER-WASHINGTON, b. July 12, 1819. *Logansport, Ind.*
788. 6. CHLOE-ANN, b. July 9, 1825, m. Hamilton-Lafayette Williams, Feb. 22,
1848, and had Hamilton- Francis, b. Nov. 17, 1863. *Rochester, Minn.*
788½. 7. PHEBE, b. Oct. 10, 1831, m. Philip Fishburn. *Milton, Wood Co., Ohio.*

789. PATIENCE,[5][329] (*Silas*,[4] *Joseph*,[3] *Joseph*,[2] *John*,[1]) b. Nov. 3,
1791, d. Oct. 18, 1820; m. Whitford, son of Asa Whitney of Killingly,
Nov. 10, 1817. He was b. May 6, 1796. He was in service in war
of 1812. *Abington, Ct.*

790. 1. CALISTA, b. Jan. 12, 1819; m. Horace Cornell, May 6, 1838, and had,
• (1.) Clark-Brown, (2.) Ellen-Eunice, (3.) Albert-Olney, (4.) John-
Henry, (5.) Cora-Lee, (6.) Mary-Marcelia.

791. SILAS,[5][322] (*Silas*,[4] *Joseph*,[3] *Joseph*,[2] *John*,[1]) b. Nov. 28,
1777, d. April 1, 1865; m. Susan, dau. of Thomas Burgess of Killingly,
Ct., April, 1799. She was b. Sept. 14, 1781, d. Oct. 7, 1861. She
was descended through Thomas,[5] Thomas,[4] Thomas,[3] Thomas,[2] from
Thomas,[1] the emigrant ancestor, [see Burgess Genealogy.] He was
deacon in the Baptist Church in East Killingly, Ct., 22 years, and was
also a selectman of the town in 1830, 1842, '3. *East Killingly, Ct.*

792. 1. BEULAH,[1466] b. July 6, 1800, m. Hosea Martin.
793. 2. SUSAN,[1478] b. Aug. 30, 1802, m. Otis Bastow.
794. 3. THOMAS,[1488] b. May 15, 1804, d. May 2, 1866; m. 1st, Polly
Stowell, 2d, Sarah-Ann Chase.
795. 4. ALMEDA-GREENLEAF,[1492] b. March 17, 1806, m. James Babson.
796. 5. BRAYTON,[1505] b. July 10, 1808, m. Patience Millard.
797. 6. HAZAEL-BURGESS,[1513] b. May 6, 1810; m. 1st, Phebe Howe, 2d,
Esther-Wallace Paine, 3d, Mary-Miller Haywood.
798. 7. MARY-ELIZA,[1519] b. Jan. 26, 1812, m. Asa-King Howes.
799. 8. OTIS,[1523] b. April 11, 1814, m. Alfreda Bowen.
800. 9. PHEBE-ANN,[1524] b. Nov. 14, 1817, m. Joseph Clark.
801. 10. CHARLOTTE-TIFFANY,[1532] b. May 12, 1819, m. James Hyde.
802. 11. ALMARIA,[1540] b. Sept. 3, 1821, d. Feb. 23, 1848, m. John-Colby Steere.
803. 12. ARBA-COVEL,[1544] b. April 19, 1824, m. Lucy-Clark Avery.
804. 13. JULIET, b. Sept. 5, 1827, d. Jan. 5, 1828.

805. STEPHEN,[5][323] (*Silas*,[4] *Joseph*,[3] *Joseph*,[2] *John*,[1]) b. Nov. 15,
1779, d. May 20, 1851; m. Sarah, dau. of Peleg Williams of Foster,
R. I., 1804. She was b. Jan. 29, 1787, d. April 30, 1832. He was
a Justice of the Peace, &c., &c. His eldest three children were born
in Killingly, Ct., the others in Foster, R. I., and are as follows:
Slatersville, R. I.

806. 1. ELIZA-WILLIAMS, b. Nov. 29, 1805, d. Dec. 5, 1806.
807. 2. OLNEY-WINSOR, b. Aug. 20, 1807, d. Feb. 25, 1811.
808. 3. OTIS-SHELDON, b. Sept. 18, 1810, d. March 28, 1811.
809. 4. MARY-ELIZA,[1545] b. May 21, 1812, m. Daniel-Franklin Rawson.
810. 5. ESTHER-ANN,[1551] b. Dec. 14, 1813, m. George-Washington Smith.
811. 6. STEPHEN,[1556] b. Aug 17, 1817, m. Sally-Blake Carroll.
812. 7. SARAH-FANNY,[1560] b. Sept. 2, 1820, d. May 24, 1860, m. George Dirk.
813. 8. HENRY-PELEG,[1563] b. Dec. 26, 1822, m. Emily Carpenter.
814. 9. RHODA-ANN-WINSOR,[1566] b. April 18, 1825, m. John-Learned Stimp
son.

815. MARY,[5][324] (*Silas*,[4] *Joseph*,[3] *Joseph*,[2] *John*,[1]) b. Oct, 4, 1781; m. Brinton, son of Josiah Arnold of Killingly, Ct., Nov. 1803. He was b. May 2, 1781. *Sterling, Ct.*

816. 1. NATHAN, b. Dec. 15, 1804, d. March 3, 1827.
817. 2. HARRIET, b. Aug. 16, 1806, d. March 9, 1849.
818. 3 LESTER-NELSON, b. Jan. 16, 1808. *Sterling, Ct.*
819. 4. MARTHA-MARIA, b. Dec. 6, 1809, d. Feb. 14, 1863; m. Horace Dickson of Sterling Co., and had (1.) Sarah-Jane, (2.) Horace-Arnold, (3.) Charles-Elwell.
820. 5. CHARLOTTE, b. Jan. 15, 1812; m. Asa, son of Asa Potter of Baltic, Ct., June, 1831, and had (1.) Sarah, (2.) Samantha, (3.) Maria-Eliza, (4.) Munroe, (5.) Zeriah, (6.) Rebecca, (7.) Ursula, (8.) Welcome-Francis, (9.) Amy, (10.) Noble, (11.) Emma-Jane.
821. 6. PATIENCE-ANN, b. March 3, 1814; m. James Henry, son of Shelden Collins of Plainfield, Ct., and had (1.) Cynthia-Jane, (2.) Mary-Anna.
822. 7. JOSIAH, b. April 7, 1816; m. Ann-Eliza King and had (1.) Maria-Amanda, (2.) Alonzo-Burnham, (3.) Mary, (4.) Harriet, (5.) Rebecca-Jane.
                                                                  Plainfield, Ct.
823. 8. PELEG-ELLIS, b. Oct. 18, 1818; m. Sarah Hopkins of Foster, and had (1.) Mary, (2.) Henry.   *Somersfield, Mich.*
824. 9. WILLIAM-ALEXANDER, b. Jan. 16, 1821; m. Lovina King; had (1.) George-Westcot.   *Sterling, Ct.*
825. 10. BENJAMIN-MORSE, b. Nov. 13, 1825; m. Mary Kettle, and had (1.) Melissa-Caroline, (2.) Mary-Jane, (3.) Ruth, (4.) Charles-Benjamin, (5.) Ida-Harriet, (6.) William.   *Plainfield, Ct.*

826. JOHN,[5][325] (*Silas*,[4] *Joseph*,[3] *Joseph*,[2] *John*,[1]) b. Sept. 7, 1784; m. Naomi, dau. of Abraham Rice of Killingly, Ct., Nov. 25, 1805. She was b. Dec. 1, 1789.   Their children were as follows:
                                                         North Fairfield, Ohio.

827. 1. ALMIRA,[1583] b. Dec. 3, 1806, m. James Murry.
828. 2. ALZADA,[1623] b. Jan. 25, 1808, m. Richard Commins.
829. 3. JOHN,[1615] b. Feb. 9, 1810, m. Harriet Butler.
830. 4. ELEAZER-ARNOLD, b. Aug. 12, 1811, d. Oct. 12, 1831.
831. 5. ABIGAIL-CAROLINE,[1624] b. Feb. 13, 1814, m. Hosea Shippee.
832. 6. WAKEMAN-RICE,[1569] b. Feb 21, 1815, m. Sarah-Ann Probasco.
833. 7. CYNTHIA,[1573] b. March 21, 1819, m. Ira Wood.
834. 8. DAVID-AMES,[1608] b. Aug. 21, 1818, m. Adaline Shippee.
835. 9. JANE-LUCRETIA,[1589] b. Dec. 25, 1821, m. Otis Shippee.
836. 10. ABRAHAM,[1597] b. Aug. 28, 1824, m. Esther-Ann Turwellager.
837. 11. BEULAH,[1581] m. James-Gardiner Mead.
838. 12. SILAS,[1602] b. Oct. 20, 1827, m. Julia-Minerva St. John.
839. 13. GEORGE-WASHINGTON,[1606] b. Dec. 28, 1829, m. Harriet-Ann Turwellager.

840. JOSEPH,[5][331] (*Silas*,[4] *Joseph*,[3] *Joseph*,[2] *John*[1],) b. March 30, 1795; m. Roby, dau. of Thomas Bates of Smithfield, R. I., 1822.   She was b. Oct. 10, 1803, d. Sept. 20, 1861.   He was in war of 1812.
                                                   Hadley, Lapeer Co., Mich.

841. 1. ALVIRA,[1625] b. March 9, 1823, d. Sept. 19, 1862, m. Alvin Bates.
842. 2. PATIENCE, b. July 27, 1824, m. Matherson Thomas.   *Barkerville, N. Y.*
843. 3. JOSEPH-WILLIAMS,[1622] b. Feb. 11, 1825, m. Mary-Ann Fedder.
844. 4. PHEBE, b. Feb. 20, 1827, m. Seely Platt.   *Lapeer, Mich.*
845. 5. CALVIN-GREEN, b. Dec. 22, 1828; m. Barbara White; served three years in 10th Wisconsin, was wounded twice; resides near Wolf River, Wisconsin.
846. 6. SILAS,[1641] b. May 30, 1831, m. Amanda Terry.
847. 7. SIMON, b. June 10, 1833.   *Gentryville, Missouri.*
848. 8. CHARLES, b. Feb. 19, 1835.   *Memphis, Tenn.*
          9. DORCAS, b. Nov. 10, 1838, d. June 20, 1843.
849. 10. HELEN,[1645] b. March 19, 1840, d. Oct. 4, 1866, m. Wm. Henry Duncan.

850. 11. ISAAC, b. April 25, 1842, d. March 3, 1843.
851. 12. REBECCA, b. Nov. 9, 1844, d. Dec. 10, 1845.
852. 13. MARY-CATHARINE, b. May 29, 1847, m. Lyman Garfield.
853. 14. HUMPHREY-MATTISON, b. March 15, 1850.

854. JOSEPH,[5][335] (*John*,[4] *Joseph*,[3] *Joseph*,[2] *John*,[1]) b. July 26, 1772, d. Feb. 26, 1861; m. Hannah, dau. of John Spaulding of Monson, Mass., Dec., 1791. She was b. Feb. 23, 1773, d. 1855. Was in the battle of Plattsburgh in the war of 1812. He bore the title of captain, and held such town offices as assessor, constable, &c. He resided in Guilford, Vt., where the first four of his children were born, the others were b. in Jay, N. Y., where he afterwards resided.

Jay, N. Y.

855. 1. CHAUNCY,[1651] b. May 2, 1795, m. Margaret Kenedy.
856. 2. ABIGAIL,[1661] b. June 10, 1797, m. Eli-Beckwith Hull.
857. 3. CHARLOTTE, b. Dec. 25, 1799; m. Ezra-G. Varney, and had (1.) Ezra, (2.) Charlotte, (3.) Orilla.
858. 4. LYMAN,[1671] b. March 15, 1802; m. 1st, Mary Hamilton; 2d, Sarah Ingals.
859. 5. JOHN, b. July 7, 1804, m. Martha Potter.
860. 6. JOSEPH, b. April 9, 1807, d. Sept. 23, 1857, m. Marcia Trumbull.
861. 7. GEORGE-WASHINGTON,[1684] b. June 15, 1810; m. 1st, Harriet Trumbull; 2d, Candace-Arabella Temple.
862. 8. DE WITT,[1675] b. July 16, 1812, m. Roxa Thomas.
863. 9. ANDREW-JACKSON, b. Aug. 18, 1814, d. March 24, 1854; m. Mary Dudley, and had
(1.) Addison.
(2.) Samuel, who in war of rebellion was in Comp. A, 1st Colorado Cavalry.
(3.) Dillon-Pomroy, in Comp. H, 32d Wisconsin Vols.
(4.) John, in Michigan Vols.
(5.) George-Levi, in United States service, New York Vols.
(6.) Wallace, in United States service, New York Vols.
(7.) Lewis.
(8.) Mary.

864. HULDA,[5][338] (*John*,[4] *Joseph*,[3] *Joseph*,[2] *John*,[1]) b. Nov. 1, 1780, d. Jan. 24, 1866. The date of her several marriages not obtained. Her first child was by William Richardson; her second by Jacob Lombard, who went West to purchase land, and was killed by Indians in 1809. Her other children were by Sylvanus, son of Hezekiah Nelson of Brimfield, Mass. He was born about 1783, and died in Russell, St. Lawrence Co., N. Y., Aug. 10, 1856. Their children were as follows:—

864½. 1. AMANDA, b. in Brattleborough, Vt., about 1800, d. March, 1821; m. Jonathan Hammond, Nov., 1819, and had Amanda, b. Dec. 9, 1820, who m. April 2, 1840, Stephen Murray, and had
(1.) Huldah Georgeanna, b. April 12, 1841; m. Wallace Smith, and had
(a.) Freeman, b. Feb. 18, 1858.
(b.) Wallace, b. Sept. 6, 1862.
(c.) Ormon, and } (gemini) b. March 9, 1866.
(d.) Normon, }
(e.) Ira, b. May 5, 1868.
(2.) Fanny-Louisa, b. April 27, 1843; m. John Miller of Stockholm, and had
(a.) Nettie, b. June 18, 1860.
(b.) Cora, b. April 22, 1864.
(c.) John, b. May 15, 1866.

(3.) Wealthy-Melissa, b. July 26, 1845; m. Ira Graves, and had
  Nellie-Mary.
(4.) Freeman-Blake, b. April 22, 1848 ; m. Ann Cheney.
(5.) Norman-Marshall, b. June 10, 1850.
(6.) Charles-Wesley, b. Aug. 1, 1852.
(7.) Prudence-Alcina, b. June 17, 1855.
(8.) Flora-Amanda, b. June 5, 1865.
                      South Colton, St. Lawrence Co., N. Y.
865. 2. PRUDENCE, b. April 29, 1809, m. James-Roldon Brown, and had
    (1.) Amanda-Prudence, b. Feb. 8, 1828.
    (2.) James-Oscar, b. March 4, 1829.
    (3.) Charles-Norman, b. Aug. 10, 1830; in war of rebellion he served
      three years in Battery D, 1st Ohio Light Artillery ; m. Lucy
      Manning, Oct. 8, 1855.   *Birmingham, Ohio.*
    (4.) Huldah-Esther, b. March 25, 1832 ; m. John M. Root, Jan. 7, 1856,
      and had Irwin Burnham, b. Sept. 1, 1857.
    (5.) Alonzo-Emery, b. Sept. 17, 1834 ; in war of rebellion he was in
      Comp. H, 10th New York Heavy Artillery, one year ; m. July 4,
      1858, Rebecca Hinman.   *Breckenridge, Mo.*
    (6.) Mary-Jane-Ann, b. Sept. 8, 1836 ; m. June 1, 1861, Horace
      Wilkins.   *Wilmington, N. Y.*
    (7.) Cordelia-Rosette, b. Nov. 29, 1838.
    (8.) Franklin-Roldon, b. May 1, 1840; in war of rebellion he was in
      Comp. D, 4th New York Artillery, two and a half years; m.
      Elizabeth Smith, Nov. 25, 1858.
    (9.) Juliette-Imogen, b. July 26, 1842.
    (10.) Martin-Horace, b. Nov. 11, 1844; in war of rebellion he was in
      Comp. K, 142d New York Vols., served three years ; m. Martha
      Snow, April 14, 1865.   *Utica, N. Y.*
    (11.) Ellen-Annette, b. May 3, 1846.
    (12) Hiram-Gilbert, b. Sept. 30, 1849 ; in war of rebellion was in
      Battery D, 1st New York Artillery, 1 year.
    (13.) Florence-Emma, b. July 15, 1850.
    (14.) Reuben-Nathaniel, b. Dec. 6, 1851.
      This family gave an aggregate of ten and a half years, and
      risked five lives to put down the rebellion.
866. 3. EMERY-FITZ ALLEN, b. Feb. 19, 1814 ; m. Jane-Ann Blanchard, and had
    (1.) Charles-Henry,   (2.) Sylvanus,
    (3.) Hulda-Jane,   (4.) Franklin. *Burke, Franklin Co., N. Y.*
867. 4. OSCAR, b. Feb. 20, 1817, d. April 14, 1817.
868. 5. LOUISA, b. Jan. 3, 1819, d. Aug. 10, 1819.
869. 6. AUGUSTUS-PERRY, b. June 6, 1821, d. Aug. 6, 1842.

870. HANNAH,[336] (*John,*[4] *Joseph,*[3] *Joseph,*[2] *John,*[1]) b. Sept. 4,
1774, d. March 14, 1835 ; m. Ezra-Gleason, son of Joseph Ayers of Jay,
N. Y., March 9, 1797. He d. Nov. 8, 1811. *Jay, Essex Co., N. Y.*

871. 1. CLARISSA, b. Nov. 13, 1799 ; m. Israel Jones of Keene, N. Y., Oct. 7,
      1817, and had (1.) Elijah-Brown, (2.) Israel, who in war of rebellion
      was in Comp. K, 77th New York Vols.; (3.) Electa, (4.) Charlotte, (5.)
      Sarah-Minerva, (6.) William-Henry, who in war of rebellion was in
      Comp. K, 4th, Wisconsin Vols.; (7.) John Ezra, (8.) Charles-Wesley,
      (9.) Pierpont-Edwards, who in war of rebellion was in Comp. A, 39th
      Wisconsin Vols.
872. 2. ELECTA, b. Dec. 14, 1802, d. March 28, 1844 ; m. Artemas Wheeler of
      Ausable Forks, N. Y., and had (1.) Francis, (2.) Hannah, (3.) Arte-
      mas, (4.) Electa-Ann, (5.) Angeline.
873. 3. LOUISA, b. Jan. 5, 1804 ; m. Lyman Wheeler, May 8, 1824, and had (1.)
      Hiram, (2.) Ella-Ann, (3.) Sarah, (4.) George.
874. 4. JOHN-SLATER, b. Nov. 23, 1806, d. March 8, 1845 ; m. Rena Sumner,
      Sept. 26, 1829, and had (1.) Lydia, (2.) Ezra-Gleason, (3.) Sarah-
      Emily.

875. 5. SARAH-EMILY, b. Jan. 10, 1812, m. May 7, 1838, Samuel Muzzy, Sara-
nac, Clinton Co., N. Y., and had (1.) James-Samuel, who in war of
rebellion was in Comp. E, 16th New York Vols., (2) John, (3.) Harriet, (4.) Artemas-Wheeler, (5.) Annette, (6.) Orlin.

876. RHODA,⁵[337] (*John,⁴ Joseph,³ Joseph,² John,¹*) b. May 23,
1778, d. Feb. 14, 1862; m. Alanson, son of Jeremiah Hayes of
Granby, Ct., Aug. 31, 1801. He was b. April 17, 1781, d. April 3,
1862. *Marion, Allen Co., Ohio.*

877. 1. RHODA, b. Sept. 14, 1802, d. Oct. 15, 1848; m. Miletus Newcomb, and
had (1.) Luther, (2.) Miletus-Madison, (3.) Alanson-Hayes, (4.) Joseph,
(5.) Samantha, (6.) Mille-Ann, (7.) Rosetta.
878. 2. ALANSON, b. Oct. 25, 1804; m. Fanny Fulton, and had (1.) Margaret,
(2.) Eliza, (3.) Flavilla, (4.) Helen, (5.) Fanny; m. 2d, Mrs. Minerva
Johnson, and had (6.) Sarah Jane, (7.) Harrison, who in the war of the
rebellion was in Comp. I, 34th Ohio Vols. (see No. 1982); m. 3d, Abby-
Catharine Canet, and had (8.) Phebe-Ann, (9.) Freeman-Finn, (10.)
Melissa, (11.) Elihu, (12.) Alice-Minerva, (13.) Nettie-Angelina; m. 4th,
Catharine Long. *Marion, Ohio*
879. 3. FLAVILLA, b. Jan 16, 1806, d. Aug. 22, 1830; m. Joseph Whitman, and
had (1.) Harriet, (2.) Rhoda.
880. 4. NELSON, b. Jan. 12, 1808; m. Sarah Jones, and had (1.) Alexis-Pope,
who in the war of the rebellion was in Comp. B, 15th Ohio Cavalry;
(2.) Juliette-Cordelia, (3.) Eunice-Cordelia, (4.) Isaac-Boyer, (5.) Russell-
Jones, (6.) Hester-Ann, (7.) Enos-Oscar. *Marion, Allen Co., Ohio.*
881. 5. CYNTHIA, b. Nov. 28, 1810; m. George Chappell, and had (1.) Elizabeth-
Ann, (2.) Adelia, (3.) James, (4.) Ermina-Lorinda, (5.) William-Henry,
who in the war of the rebellion was in Comp. B, 99th Ohio Vols ; (6.)
George-Riley, (7.) Samuel-Edwin, (8.) Josephine.
882. 6. ENOS, b. Sept. 4, 1812; m. Amanda Smith, and had (1.) Nelson, who
in the war of the rebellion was in Comp. I, 34th Ohio Vols.; (2.) David-
Smith, who was in Comps. I and C, 84th Ohio Vols.; (3.) Levi, (4.)
Lovisa, (5.) Emily, (6.) Rhoda-Tryphena, (7.) Ira-Slater, (8.) Eliza-
Matilda, (9.) Mary-Alice, (10.) Reuben-William, (11.) Sarah-Elma.
883. 7. DAVID, b. Feb. 4, 1814, d. March 3, 1832.
884. 8. MILLE, b. Dec. 18, 1816, d. Dec. 18, 1855; m. Samuel Coleman, and
had (1.) Theodore-Alfred, who in war of rebellion was in Comp. I, 34th
Ohio Vols.; (2.) George-Henry, who was in Comp. A, 71st Ohio Vols.;
(3.) Harvey, (4.) Orman, (5.) Alanson.
885. 9. AMANDA-ANN, b. March 6, 1819; m. Orman Kephat, and had (1.) Cath-
arine-Cordelia, (2.) George-Henry, (3.) Oscar, (4.) Alexis, (5.) Orman.

886. PRUDENCE,⁵[339] (*John,⁴ Joseph,³ Joseph,² John,¹*) b. Feb. 5,
1783, d. May 30, 1852; m. Jonathan, son of John Hammond of Guilford, Vt., Nov. 18, 1801. He was b. Nov. 14, 1780, d. May 10, 1861.
Their children are as follows: *Hume, Alleghany Co., N. Y.*

887. 1. LUCY, b. Feb. 4, 1802, d. Feb. 18, 1805.
888. 2. SOPHIA, b. Sept. 9, 1803; m. Hiram Landers, and had, 1. Mary-Jane,
2. Emily, 3. Adaline-Augusta, 4. Sophia, 5. William, 6. Hiram-
Wesley. *Afton, Chenango Co., N. Y.*
889. 3. LAURA, b. Nov. 20, 1805; m. Arad-Hitchcock Franklin, and had, 1. Emily,
2. Fayette, 3. Marietta, 4. Jerome, 5. Marion, 6. Hammond, 7.
Prudence, 8. Ashley, 9. De Zeng, 10. Frederick.
Caneadea, Alleghany Co , N. Y.
890. 4. LOIS, b. April 17, 1808; m. Levi Rice, and had, 1, Edward-Augustus,
2. Henrietta. *Hume, Alleghany Co., N. Y.*
891. 5. JOHN-MADISON, b. Jan 23, 1811 ; Justice of the Peace, Member of the
State Legislature, Chairman of the Supervisors of the town of Hume,
Superintendent of the Genesee Valley Canal, Commissioner of Excise
for the County; m. Eliza A. Gillett, and had, 1. Sarah-Jane, 2. Ma-

rietta, 3. Jonas-Devillo, 4. John-Madison, who was in 44th Reg. New
York Vols., Elsworth's Zouaves, Comp. B., fell in a charge at Malvern
Hill; 5. Isadore-Susan, 6, Charles-Henry.   *Filmore, N. Y.*

892. 6. EDSON, b. Aug. 17, 1813; m. 1st, Jerusha Dean, 2d, Mary-A. Meacham,
and had, 1. Adaline-Augusta, 2. George-Washington, 3. Theodore-
M., 4. Edson, 5. Frederick, 6. Hiram-Wesley, 7. Mary-Elizabeth,
8. Mabel-Ellen.   *Hume, Alleghany Co., N. Y.*

893. 7. MARIETTA, b. Aug. 17, 1816, d. Aug. 27, 1833.

894. 8. AUGUSTUS, b. Feb. 22, 1819; m. Susan Grow, and had, 1. Frances-
Sophia, 2. Theodora-Ellen, 3. Dwight-Charles, 4. Burton-Augustus.
                                           Hume, Alleghany Co., N. Y.

895. 9. ORVILLE, b. Oct. 23, 1821; m. Mary-J. Kelly, and had, 1. Adelaide-
Augusta, 2. Oscar-Devillo.   *Hume, Alleghany Co., N. Y.*

896. 10. ADALINE-AUGUSTA, b. Dec. 12, 1824, d. Feb. 13, 1828.

897. LOIS,[5][341] (*John,[4] Joseph,[3] Joseph,[2] John,[1]*) b. April 10,
1788, d. Oct. 5, 1860; m. Leverett, son of James Mallory of Jay,
N. Y., Feb. 18, 1817.   *Jersey, Licking Co., Ohio.*

898. 1. ADALINE-EMILY, b. July 20, 1822; m. Oliver-Perry, son of Solomon
Freeman of Alexandria, Ohio, and had, 1. Clement-Oliver, who in war
of rebellion was in Comp. I., 32d Reg., Ohio Vols.; 2. Clifford-
Dwight.   *Marysville, Union Co., Ohio.*

899. 2. MARY-AMANDA, b. May 26, 1825; m. William-Green, son of Michael
Beem of Jersey, Ohio, and had, 1, Herbert-Leroy-Rodney, 2. Edson-
Florian-Mallory, 3. Oscar-Dudley-Slater. *Beech, Licking Co., Ohio.*

900. 3. ELIZABETH-EURETTA, b. Dec. 29, 1827, d. May 15, 1852.

901. 4. ADELIA-LOIS, b. March 21, 1831; m. Adam, son of Jeremiah Hildreth
of Alexandria, Ohio, and had, 1. Frank-Elmer, 2. Emma Euretta.

902. JOHN,[5][340] (*John,[4] Joseph,[3] Joseph,[2] John,[1]*) b. Aug. 27,
1786, d. Dec. 16, 1853; m. Sarah, dau. of Elijah Gove of Guilford,
Vt., Aug. 5, 1810. She was b. Aug. 12, 1789, d. Sept. 19, 1858. He
removed from Vermont in 1817 to Bainbridge, N. Y., and to Ohio in
1832.   *Chardon, Ohio.*

903. 1. JOHN-MADISON,[1690], b. April 22, 1811, m. Wealthy Wilder.

904. 2. HARRIET-CAROLINE,[1695], b. Dec. 22, 1812, m. Admiral-Nelson Webb.

905. 3. SARAH-ANN, b. Jan. 13, 1815, d. June 17, 1816.

906. 4. SARAH-JANE, b. Dec. 3, 1822; m. Edward-Root Judd, July 11, 1850.
He was b. June 5, 1820.   *Chardon, Ohio.*

907. 5. MARY-MARIA,[1693], b. April 23, 1824, d. May 30, 1851, m. John
Murphy.

908. FANNY,[5][343] (*John,[4] Joseph,[3] Joseph,[2] John,[1]*) b. Feb. 21,
1796, d. Sept. 1, 1868; m. Luther Fuller of Whittingham, Vt., Feb.
12, 1815. He was b. Aug. 29, 1796. They reside at North Adams,
Mass. Their children are as follows:

909. 1. MARY-ALMIRA, b. April 6, 1816, d. Sept. 25, 1824.

910. 2. CALVIN-LEVERETT, b. July 8, 1817; m. Aug. 15, 1841, Eunice, dau. of
Absalom Pike, and had (1.) Maria-Eunice, (2.) Fanny-Jane.
                                                   Florida, Mass.

911. 3. EDSON-LUTHER, b. Sept. 6, 1820; m. Aug. 20, 1842, Sarah-Maria
Brown, and had
(1.) Merritt-Edgar.
(2.) Hiland-Hall, who in war of rebellion was in Comp. B, 10th Mass.
Vols., and served three years and was in 28 battles.
(3.) Elliot-Leverett, who was in Comp. I, 16th Vermont Vols., in war
of rebellion, and served nine months; was in the battle of
Gettysburg.
(4.) Elvira-Maria.   *Heartwellville, Vt.*

912. 4. REXAVILLE-JANE, b. Oct. 1, 1823; m. Jan. 1, 1837, Ransford-Otis, son of
Thomas Canedy, and had
    (1.) Mary-Jane, who m. Joseph-Sanders, and had Agnes-Ella, Mary-
Ada and Joseph-Monroe.   *Williamstown, Mass.*
    (2.) James-Monroe, who m. Lettice-Lodema Northup, Nov. 5, 1861.
    (3.) Thomas-Jefferson, who m. Hattie Allen, May 29, 1867, and had
Charles-Allen, b. May, 1868.
    (4.) Ernest-Edward.   *North Adams, Mass.*
913. 5. MARY, b. Oct. 9, 1825, d. June 15, 1826.
914. 6. ELIOTT-BROWN, b. March 15, 1829; m. April 21, 1861, Ellen, dau. of
N. W. Halladay, and had (1.) George.   Mr. E. B. Fuller has been
deputy sheriff and enrolling officer in Bennington County, Vt.
                                           Heartwellville, Vt.
915. 7. EDWARD-PERRY, b. Aug. 5, 1831; m. Oct. 15, 1849, Elizabeth-Freelove,
dau. of Isaac Kimball, and had George-Edward, Heartwellville, Vt.
In war of rebellion he served two years in 2d Wisconsin Volunteers.
916. 8. CAROLINE-MELISSA, b. May 4, 1833; m. April 23, 1853, Marshall, son
of Levi Sprague, and had Herbert-M.   *Heartwellville, Vt.*
917. 9. EDNA-MAHALA, b. March 29, 1837; m. June 1, 1858, Amos, son of
Thomas Preo, and had Fanny-Bell.   *North Adams, Mass.*
918. 10. ALBERT-DELBERT, b. March 11, 1839; m. Feb. 23, 1858, Mary Dunn,
and had Carrie-Bell.   *North Adams, Mass.*

919. IRA,[5][342] (*John*,[4] *Joseph*,[3] *Joseph*,[2] *John*,[1]) b. Nov. 15, 1790;
m. Sally, dau. of Samuel Liscom of Halifax, Vt., Sept. 19, 1809. She
was b. Sept. 22, 1789. They resided in Guilford, Vt., Jay, N. Y., and
lastly in Ohio. He has held the office of deacon several years in the
Congregational Church in Pierpont.   *Pierpont, Ohio.*

920. 1. DELIA-LISCOM,[1702] b. Jan. 23, 1811, d. Oct. 15, 1842, m. the Rev.
Shermau-Bond Canfield, D. D.
921. 2. SARAH-ANN,[1704] b. Nov. 12, 1812; m. John McArthur; 2d, Robertson
Huff.
922. 3. MELISSA,[1710] b. April 16, 1814, d. Feb. 4, 1858, m. William Aldrich.
923. 4. CYPRIAN,[1717] b. Sept. 21, 1816, m. Elizabeth Brown.
924. 5. EUNICE-THOMAS, b. Jan. 20, 1818, d. April 23, 1818.
925. 6. CAROLINE-FISK, b. Sept. 19, 1820, d. Aug. 19, 1820.
926. 7. IRA,[1719] b. Aug. 16, 1822, m. Redamtha Segur.
927. 8. HENRY,[1725] b. Nov. 18, 1825, m. Mrs. Phebe Burnham.
928. 9. CYNTHIA-PAMELA, b. May 2, 1827, d. Nov. 19, 1846; m. William-Reed
Allen, May 5, 1846. He was in war of rebellion, Capt. of Comp. C, 3d
Kansas Vols.   *Jefferson, Ohio.*
929. 10. JANE-ANN,[1729] b. June 7, 1829, m. Andrew Curtice.
930. 11. STEPHEN-WILLIAM, b. Aug. 1, 1833, d. May 28, 1840.

931. BENJAMIN,[5][367] (*Benjamin*,[4] *John*,[3] *Joseph*,[2] *John*,[1]) b. Jan. 7,
1780, d. Aug. 1, 1848; m. Mary, dau. of Perry Burdick of Scituate,
R. I., Oct. 27, 1803; she was b. Feb. 24, 1784, d. June 20, 1854.
Was in the war of 1812. He was much engaged in teaching, survey-
ing lands, and in agricultural pursuits. He resided first in Eaton,
N. Y., where his children were born, except the eldest, who was born in
Rhode Island. He afterward removed to Girard, Pa.
                                     Girard, Erie Co., Pa.

932. 1. BENJAMIN-PERRY,[1733] b. June 25, 1805; m. 1st, Philantha Moore,
2d, Martha Gillett.
933. 2. LEVI,[1742] b. Oct. 12, 1806, m. Julia Kress.
934. 3. ELIAS,[1749] b. July 2, 1808, m. Emeline Topliff.
935. 4. SHEFFIELD-WELLS, b. June 27, 1810, d. Aug. 19, 1811.
936. 5. HORACE,[1754] b. Jan. 30, 1812, m. Catharine Large.
937. 6. MARY-CAROLINE, b. Aug. 19, 1814.
938. 7. SANFORD,[1765] b. July 19, 1816, m. Catharine Porter.

939.   8. FANNY-WELLS,[1768] b. July 14, 1818, m. Jotham-I. Barnes.
940.   9. ERASTUS,[1770] b. Aug. 13, 1820, m. Adelia-Maria Richey.
941.   10. DENNISON,[1771] b. Sept. 9, 1822, m. Lydia-Jane Badger.
942.   11. AMY-ANN, b. Feb. 11, 1828, d. Sept. 5, 1830.

943. DANIEL,[5][368] (*Benjamin,*[4] *John,*[3] *Joseph,*[2] *John,*[1]) b. Aug. 17,
1781, d. Jan. 13, 1842; m. Rhoda, dau. of Dea. Daniel Hopkins of
Foster, R. I., Oct. 30, 1803. She was b. Nov. 23, 1783, d. May 1, 1864.
He studied medicine with Dr. Collins, and practiced some time in
Rhode Island, afterward in Eaton, N. Y., but abandoned practice in
1815. Of his children, the first, third, sixth and seventh were born in
Foster, R. I.; the second in Exeter, R. I.; the fourth, fifth and
eighth, in Eaton, N. Y. He resided some time in Richland, N. Y.,
but latterly in Girard, Pa.

944.   1. DANIEL-HOPKINS,[1775] b. Aug. 19, 1804, d. Sept. 28, 1855, m.
     Joannah Hopkins.
945.   2. HANNAH-SELINDA,[1786] b. Jan. 5, 1806, d. June 1, 1844, m. Wm.
     Vincent Hubbard.
946.   3. BRAYTON,[1790] b. June 12, 1807, m. Philena Westcott.
947.   4. SUSANNAH,[1801] b. Feb. 26, 1810; m. William Easton.
948.   5. RHODA-LUCINDA,[1788] b. Dec. 28, 1812, d. Sept. 5, 1844, m. Daniel-
     Joseph Burdick
949.   6. DARIUS-MASON, b. May 1, 1815, d. Sept. 16, 1830.
950.   7. ALMIRA,[1802] b. Oct. 25, 1818, d. Feb. 23, 1849, m. Lewis Russell.
951.   8. ALLEN-JOHNSON,[1804] b. Sept. 9, 1825, m. Minerva-Elizabeth Luther.

952. NATHAN,[5][369] (*Benjamin,*[4] *John,*[3] *Joseph,*[2] *John,*[1]) b. in Foster, R. I., April 9, 1784; m. Freelove, daughter of Daniel Crossman
of Eaton, N. Y., Oct. 6, 1808. He was in the army in the war of 1812,
about three months. Their children are as follows: *Eaton, N. Y.*

953.   1. SARAH-MORSE, b. in Eaton, N. Y., Aug. 24, 1809; m. Feb. 13, 1840, Na-
     thaniel, son of Louis Walker of Cranberry, Penn., where he was born,
     June 12, 1810. Mr. Walker m. 1st, Grissel Cran, Aug., 1833, and had,
     Samuel, b. Jan 19, 1835, and John, b. March 17, 1836. Samuel enlisted
     April, 1861, in Comp. H, 13th Penn. Vols., and served three months. He
     again enlisted for three years in Comp. F, 155th Penn. Vols., and
     served till he was wounded, losing a leg in the battle of Chancellors-
     ville, May 3, 1863; he was commissioned 1st Lieut., but could not be
     mustered in on account of physical inability. He was appointed by
     President Lincoln a Lieut. in the Invalid Corps, Feb. 20, 1864, and was
     assigned to Comp. H, 22d Reg., and was mustered out Aug. 27, 1868.
     He was breveted Capt., March 13, 1865; was appointed 2d Lieut. of
     45th U. S. Infantry, Sept. 16, 1868, and is stationed at Knoxville, Tenn.
     John enlisted Aug. 9, 1862; was first Sergeant in Comp. G, 137th
     Penn. Vols., and served till June 6, 1863; was several times under fire,
     but in no great battles. Mr. Nathaniel Walker was some time Trea-
     surer of Butler Co., Penn. The family record was not received in time
     to give the children the consecutive numbers in this and the four follow-
     ing families. The children of Nathaniel and Sarah-Morse Walker, are
     as follows :   *Butler, Pa.*
     (1.) Leonidas, b. May 2, 1842; he was educated at Witherspoon Insti-
         tute, Pa.; studied Law with John McElvain, Esq., McLeansbo-
         rough, Ill.; admitted to the bar May, 1863; was Superintendent
         of schools for Hamilton Co., Ill., from Nov. 20, '1863, to Nov.
         20, 1865. He is now in the practice of Law in McLeansbo-
         borough, Hamilton Co., Ill., in the firm of " Townsend &
         Walker.
     (2.) Carrie, b. April 13, 1844. Educated at Bethlehem, Pa.
     (3.) Addison, b. Oct. 22, 1845, d. Aug. 17, 1861.
     (4.) Clarence, b. March 24, 1848.

(5.) Clara, b. March 14, 1850, d. April 15, 1850.
(6.) Leverett-Hull, b. March 26, 1851 ; a cadet in U. S. Military Academy at West Point ; entered June, 1867.
(7.) Laura, b. Sept. 29, 1853.   *Butler, Pa.*

954   2. AMITY-MATILDA, b. in Eaton, N. Y., Nov. 30, 1810, d. Oct. 2, 1867 ;
m. William-Wilson Bell, and removed to Texas. Their children were,
1. Daniel-Palmer, d. young ; 2. Frances ; 3. Wilson, m. Mary Painter,
and had Mehitable, New York ; 4. Elisha-Sheldon, m. Harriet-Tucker
of Meadville, Pa., and had, William ; 5. Sarah, m. Thomas Campbell,
and had a son, Texas ; 6. John-Henry, in the rebel service; killed at
Manassas, Va. ;   7. Milton, d. in Texas, 1868 ;   8. Walter-Lawrie.
                                            Lynchburg, Harris Co., Texas.

955. 3. HENRY-HARRISON, b. in Eaton, N. Y., Sept. 8, 1813 ; m. Nancy Critchlow, 1835 ; resides at Mt. Blanco, Meigs Co., Ohio.   Their children are
as follows :
(1.) Levi, b. Oct. 23, 1835.
(2.) Sarah-Ann, b. June 15, 1837.
(3.) Amanda, b. March 27, 1839.
(4.) John, b. Jan. 12, 1841.   Entered the service in war of rebellion in
a Cavalry Regiment, and died of typhoid fever at Nashville,
Tenn.
(5.) Mary, b. Jan. 11, 1841 ; died in childhood.
(6.) Matilda, b. Nov. 27, 1845.
(7.) Lucinda, b. April 19, 1847.
(8.) Nancy, b. July 3, 1849 ; d. in childhood.
(9.) Mary, b. Aug. 2, 1851 ; d. in childhood.
(10.) Lovina, b. Jan. 19, 1855.

956. 4. CALISTA-FREELOVE, b. in Eaton, N. Y., Aug. 20, 1816 ; m. Robert
Luse, Jan. 11, 1838.   They had, b. in Middlesex, Pa.,
(1.) Henry-Humphries, b. June 10, 1840 ; he enlisted in Comp. C, 57th
Penn. Vols., Oct. 3, 1861, and died in service in Georgetown,
D. C., Feb. 14, 1862.
(2.) Alice-Virginia, b. March 16, 1849 ; grad. Young Ladies' Inst.,
Granville, Ohio, June 16, 1866.
(3.) Robert-Addison, b. Oct. 29, 1844 ; grad. Iowa City Com. Coll.,
Feb. 28, 1868.
(4.) Judson-Wade, b. in Pymatuning, Jan. 1, 1858, d. April 5, 1862 ;
res. Pymatuning, Penn.   *p. o. Orangeville, Ohio.*

957. 5. NATHAN-MONROE, b. in Cranberry, Pa., Dec. 1, 1822 ; m. Sarah-Ann
McCandless, 1848, and had
(1.) Howard, b. March 28, 1850.
(2.) Daniel-Crossman, b. Jan. 23, 1852.
(3.) James-McCandless, b. April 25, 1854.
(4.) Matilda-Bell, b. Aug. 3, 1856.
(5.) Angelica-C., b. June 21, 1859.
(6.) Liela-Ada, b. Jan. 28, 1862.
(7.) Mary-Lynn, b. March 31, 1865.

958.   ELISHA,[5][371] (*Benjamin,*[4] *John,*[3] *Joseph,*[2] *John,*[1]) b. in Ashford, Ct., Jan. 3, 1795, d. Richland, N. Y., May 24, 1832 ; m. Hannah,
dau. of William Merethew of Foster, R. I., March 7, 1815.   She was b.
Aug. 17, 1795.   He was a soldier in the war of 1812, stationed at
Brownville, N. Y.   *Richland, N. Y.*

959. 1. ELISHA WOOD, b. in Foster, R. I., Nov. 9, 1815 ; m. Rebecca Brown
Jan. 15, 1837.   *Mount Vernon, Linn Co., Iowa.*
960. 2. ALBERT-GREEN, b. in Eaton, N. Y., June 2, 1822.
                                                South Richland, N. Y.
961. 3. WILLIAM-BENJAMIN, b. in Richland, N. Y., July 11, 1828 ; m. Mary
Burke, April 17, 1853.   *South Richland, N. Y.*

962.   STEPHEN,[5][387] (*Stephen,*[4] *Abraham,*[3] *Joseph,*[2] *John,*[1]) b. Jan.
9, 1783, d. Dec. 16, 1855 ; m. Eunice, dau. of Timothy Temple of

Guilford, Vt., Oct. 1, 1809.   She was b. Feb. 25, 1789, d. Feb. 3, 1851. He was in the war of 1812.   *Michigan.*

963.   1. ELIZABETH,[1807] b. May 19, 1811 ; m. Nathaniel Ellis.
964.   2. STEPHEN-MERET,[1816] b. Feb. 25, 1813 ; m. Miriam Ellis.
965.   3. ELLERY-SYLVESTER,[1824], b. Oct. 1, 1815 ; m. Pluma Harding.
966.   4. ANGELINA, b. April 6, 1816 ; d. Aug. 23, 1855 ; m. Isaac Way, and had,
        1. Esther,   2. Timothy.
967.   5. ANSON-BROWN,[1826] b. May 19, 1818 ; m. Diantha Howland.
968.   6. MINERVA,[1835] b. Jan. 21, 1820 ; m. Loren-Daniel Whipple ; 2d,
        Robert-Ambrose McDonald.
969.   7. ALBERT,[1839] b. Feb. 16, 1822 ; m. Arrena Updike.
970.   8. EUNICE,[1848] b. Feb. 16, 1824 ; m. Lorenzo-Dow Evans.
971.   9. MARY-ANN, b. Aug. 23, 1826, d. June 19, 1854 ; m. James Reynolds ;
        no children.
972. 10. AMANDA-MALVINA, b. March 1, 1828, d. June 30, 1837.
973. 11. NATHAN, b. Aug. 1833, d. July 27, 1863.

974.   ABIAL,[389] (*Stephen,[4] Abraham,[3] Joseph,[2] John,[1]*) b. May 25, 1789, d. May 5, 1853 ; m. Mary, dau. of —— ——, July 17, 1814.
                                        Millburgh, Berrien Co., Michigan.

975.   1. ANN, b. July 3, 1815, d. Feb. 26, 1857 ; m. Joseph B. Wood.
976.   2. MARY-ANN, b. Aug. 20, 1817, d. Nov. 10, 1851 ; m. Nelson Delano.
977.   3. JULIET, b. Nov. 23, 1819 ; m. Alanson Day.
978.   4. STEPHEN-AUGUSTUS, b. July 25, 1822, d. Aug. 24, 1847 ; m. Angela
        Spink, and had George, who resides in Millburgh, Berrien Co., Mich.
979.   5. HARRIET-CORDELIA, b. Aug. 2, 1825 ; m. Albert Vincent.
980.   6. JOHN-ABIAL, b. July 24, 1827 ; m. Louisa-Ann Tuttle.
981.   7. JANE, b. June 30, 1829 ; m. Joel Henderson.

982.   JOSEPH,[393] (*Stephen,[4] Abraham,[3] Joseph,[2] John,[1]*) b. Aug. 18, 1798 ; m. 1st, Zylpha, dau. of Richard Morgan of Bloomfield, Prince Edward Co., Canada West, 1820 ; she was b. 1801, d. May 27, 1848 ; m. 2d, Sarah-Jane, dau. of Peter Smith of Canada, 1850 ; she was b. Dec. 5, 1816.   He held the office of constable several years in East Houndsfield, N. Y.   *Brownville, Jeff. Co., N. Y.*

983.   1. VINCENT, b. Sept. 13, 1821 ; m. Emily Glass, and had, 1. Emma-Jane,
        b. April, 1847,   2. Vincent, b. April, 1856, d. Nov. 1861, 3. Frederic,
        b. Aug. 1863.   *Black River, Jefferson Co., N. Y.*
984.   2. CANDACE-LOUISA, b. April 20, 1823, d. April, 1849 ; m. Aaron Clos-
        son, and had Winfield.   *Houndsfield, Jeff. Co., N. Y.*
985.   3. HIRAM, b. May 10, 1826 ; m. March 2, 1848, Lucy Richardson.
                                        Barnes' Corners, Lewis Co., N. Y.
996.   4. STEPHEN-DEANTON,[1852] b. Aug. 20, 1830 ; m. Mary-Ann-Elvira Alex-
        ander.   *Watertown, Jeff. Co., N. Y.*
997.   5. ELIZABETH-ANGELINE, b. Dec. 5, 1832 ; m. Wm. Kirby, and had,
        Frederic, b. Nov. 1861.
998.   6. ALLEN, b. 1836, d. 1838.
999.   7. LYMAN, b. 1841, d. 1841.
1000. 8. HARRIET-ZYLPHA, b. May 16, 1851.

1001.   SAMUEL,[379] (*Samuel,[4] Abraham,[3] Joseph,[2] John,[1]*) b. Sept. 5, 1806 ; m. Olive, dau. of Jeremiah Dibell of Mount Washington, Mass., April 27, 1836 ; she was b. Aug. 22, 1812.   Has been select-man, &c., &c.   *Copake Iron Works, Columbia Co., N. Y.*

1002.   1. OLIVE, b. Aug. 15, 1837 ; m. Dennison Winchell of Copake Iron
        Works, N. Y., March 31, 1862.
1003.   2. SAMUEL, b. Feb. 21, 1839 ; served one year in the war of rebellion, Comp.
        E, 49th Mass. Reg.   *Copake Iron Works, N. Y.*
1004.   3. BETSEY, b. March 29, 1840, d. July 13, 1842.

1005.　4. DELIA, b. July 21, 1842 ; m. Henry-Smith Daken, Kokomo, Howard Co.,
　　　　Indiana, Feb. 26, 1861.
1006.　5. JEREMIAH, b Jan. 23, 1844.
1007.　6. JOHN, b. March 3, 1846.
1008.　7. NATHANIEL, b. March 13, 1850.

1009.　ACENATH,[377] (Samuel,[4] Abraham,[3] Joseph,[2] John,[1]) b.
Aug. 28, 1802 ; m. William, son of Henry Waters of Charlton, Wor-
cestershire, England, Feb. 5, 1821.　He was born Nov. 25, 1796.
　　　　　　　　　　　　　　　　　　　　　　　　　　　Lakeville, Ct.

1010.　1. JAMES-HENRY, b. Nov. 22, 1821 ; m. Nancy Wiley.　　Sharon, Ct.
1011.　2. WILLIAM, b. Nov. 20, 1824 ; Comp. B, 2d Conn. Heavy Artillery ; m.
　　　　Julia Gilbert.　　　　　　　　　　　　　　　　　　　Lakeville, Ct.
1012.　3. MOSES, b. Aug. 14, 1820 ; m. Jane-Sophia Green.　　Spafford, Wis.
1013.　4. LUTHER, b. Feb. 3, 1828 ; m. Eliza-Clary Gault.　　Lakeville, Ct.
1014.　5. EMELINE, b. Aug. 17, 1829 ; m. John Chase.　　　　Painsville, Ohio.
1015.　6. ELISHA, b. July 10, 1831 ; m. Harriet Slater.　　　Lakeville, Ct.
1016.　7. SAMUEL, b. Oct. 18, 1833 ; Comp. D, 98th Illinois Reg., and 1st Lieut.
　　　　in Comp. K, 137th U. S. Reg. ; m. Laura-L. Chariher.　Palestine, Ill.
1017.　8. MARY-ANN, b. Oct. 22, 1835 ; m. Horace-Pinney Frazier.　Dorset, Ohio.
1118.　9. MARCUS-BAXTER, b. Dec. 18, 1845.　　　　　　　　Lakeville, Ct.

1019.　LUTHER,[382½] (Samuel,[4] Abraham,[3] Joseph,[2] John,[1]) b. Dec.
18, 1818 ; m. Emma, dau. of David Jones of Mount Washington,
Mass., Nov. 26, 1840.　She was b. April 22, 1822.
　　　　　　　　　　　　　　　　　　　　　　Copake Iron Works, N. Y.

1020.　1. HARRIET, b. Jan. 9, 1841.
1021.　2. WILLIAM-HENRY, b. Aug. 25, 1842.
1022.　3. ELIZABETH, b. Dec. 18, 1844, d. —— 12, 1845.
1023.　4. MARCUS, b. Feb. 13, 1846, d. June 13, 1846.
1024.　5. BENJAMIN-FRANKLIN, b. Jan. 29, 1849.
1025.　6. ELLEN, b. April 21, 1851, d. May 8, 1855.
1026.　7. ADELINE, b. May 12, 1854.
1027.　8. FREDERICK, b. Jan. 14, 1857.

1028.　JOHN,[380] (Samuel,[4] Abraham,[3] Joseph,[2] John,[1]) b. Jan.
1, 1809 ; m. Eliza, daughter of Thomas Carle of Copake, N. Y., Nov.
7, 1840.　She was born March 4, 1817.　　　　Penn Yan, N. Y.

1029.　1. JAMES, b. Nov. 11, 1841 ; in war of rebellion was in Comp. I, 13th Kan-
　　　　sas, 3 years.
1030.　2. MAHALA, b. April 26, 1843.
1031.　3. TRUMAN, b. April 28, 1845 ; in war of rebellion, Comp. A, 22d N. Y.
　　　　Cavalry, 2 years.
1032.　4. FREEMAN, b. Jan. 7, 1847, d. April 17, 1849.
1033.　5. PHILIP, b. Nov. 27, 1848 ; in war of rebellion was in Comp. A, 22d N. Y.
　　　　Cavalry, 1 year.
1034.　6. SARAH-JANE, b. Nov. 13, 1850, d. April 14, 1855.
1035.　7. DARIUS-DAVIDSON, b. Sept. 11, 1854.
1036.　8. MARY-ELLEN, b. April 11, 1857.
1037.　9. IDA-CATHARINE, b. Nov. 11, 1859.

1038.　PERRY-PRATT,[381] (Samuel,[4] Abraham,[3] Joseph,[2] John,[1])
b. April 12, 1812 ; m. Lucinda, dau. of Isaac Moores of North Canaan, Conn., March 4, 1832.　She was b. Jan. 1, 1816, d. Dec. 22,
1865.　　　　　　　　　　　p. o. State Line, Berkshire Co., Mass.

1039.　1. MARIA, b. Aug. 3, 1833, d. March 26, 1863 ; m. Thomas C. Sweet, Attle-
　　　　borough, Mass.
1040.　2. ISAAC, b. Dec. 26, 1835 ; m. Anna Hodge.　　South Glastonbury, Ct.
1041.　3. DELANY, b. Dec. 28, 1837 ; m. Charles H. Taylor.

1042.   4. JEANETTE, b. Oct. 5, 1838, m. Benjamin Mun.   *Pittsfield, Mass.*
1043.   5. MARY, b. Dec. 4th, 1839, d. Oct. 4, 1841.
1044.   6. NELSON, b. Feb. 11, 1843.
1045.   7. JOHN, b. May 26, 1846.
1046.   8. GEORGE, b. Dec. 28, 1853.
1047.   9. SAMUEL, b. Oct. 1, 1857, d. Oct. 11, 1859.

1049.   ELIZABETH,[5][373] (*Samuel,*[4] *Abraham,*[3] *Joseph,*[2] *John,*[1]) b.
May 6, 1793, d. Oct. 9, 1861; m. 1st, Ebenezer Foot; 2d, Alexander
Jackson, Sept. 5, 1814. He was b. July 31, 1778, d. March 12,
1857.   *Jerusalem, Yates Co., N. Y.*

1050.   1. HANNAH, (by 1st husband,) b. May 20, 1812, d. April 7, 1862, unmar-
        ried.
1051.   2. MARY, b. Sept. 9, 1815, d. March 4, 1838, unmarried.
1052.   3. JOHN, b. Dec. 15, 1817, d. in North Carolina, m. Ann Holt.
1053.   4. ELECTA, b. Nov. 1, 1819, d. March 7, 1822.
1054.   5. ELIZA, b. March 5, 1822, d. Feb. 16, 1848; m. Abner-B. Jones, and had
        George and Mary.   *Pittsfield, Mass.*
1055.   6. EMILY, b. July 25, 1824, d. Sept. 30, 1846; m. Frederick Belter; no
        children.
1056.   7. AMY, b. Sept. 6, 1826; m. George Kingles, and had Allen, &c.
                                                 Stockbridge, Mass.
1057.   8. JULIA, b. May 18, 1829, m. Charles Bliven.
1058.   9. HENRY, b. Jan. 6, 1833, d. April 4, 1865; m. Susan Meek; no children.
1059.   10. LUTHER-TICHNOR, b. Aug. 30, 1835; m. Mary-Eliza Lynn, and had
        Franklin D., b. Oct. 30, 1867.   *Penn Yan, Yates Co., N. Y.*

1060.   CHARLES AVERY,[5][437] (*Jehiel,*[4] *Moses,*[3] *Moses,*[2] *John,*[1]) b.
Sept. 12, 1811; m. 1st, Sarah, dau. of Ralph Williams of Lodi, N. Y.,
Jan. 1, 1835; she was b. Dec. 6, 1813, d. May 29, 1840; m. 2d,
Emeline, dau. of Moses Slater of Monticello, Wis., Oct. 7, 1840.
She was b. Dec. 15, 1813. He was ordained as a preacher among the
United Brethren, Oct. 14, 1854. Has been circuit preacher, presiding
elder, agent for college, &c.   *Clinton, Summit Co., Ohio.*

1061.   1. LYDIA-ANN,[1271] b. in Brandt, N. Y., Nov. 29, 1835, m. Alfred-Brun-
        son Kerns.
1062.   2. RALPH-WILLIAMS, b. in Hanover, N. Y., March 3, 1837, d. Dec. 21, 1840.
1063.   3. CHARLES-JEHIEL,[1275] b. in Hanover, Jan. 24, 1839, m. Martha-Jane
        Loveland.
1064.   4. NELLIE-GRAY, b. in Brandt, Aug. 25, 1841, d. Nov. 11, 1863; m. Finney-
        Reform, son of Philo Loomis of Lodi, Ohio, Dec. 4, 1862. He was 1st
        Lieut. of Comp. K, 8th Ohio Vols., in war of rebellion; service about
        three years and three months.   *Lodi, Ohio.*
1065.   5. HERBERT-WILLIAMS, b. in Ridgeville, Ohio, April 4, 1845, d. Sept.
        25, 1849.   *Lodi, Ohio.*
1066.   6. EMMA-GERTRUDE, b. in Olmstead, Ohio, Aug. 4, 1852.

1067.   CHARLOTTE,[5][439] (*Jehiel,*[4] *Moses,*[3] *Moses,*[2] *John,*[1]) b. June
6, 1816; m. 1st, Daniel Crandall, Oct. 6, 1832; he was b. 1806,
d. 1835; m. 2d, William, son of William Bridges of St. Albans, Vt.,
Jan. 15, 1837. He was b. Jan. 16, 1814, d. 1846. He was a deputy
sheriff in Portage County, Ohio. She m. 3d, Asaph-Dickerson, son of
Justin Leonard of West Springfield, Mass., Jan. 8, 1849. He was b.
Nov. 29, 1802.   *Milwaukee, Wis.*

1068.   1. MARY-ELECTA, b. Sept. 9, 1833; m. David Richardson, and had Albert-
        Leonard.   *Suisun City, Cal.*
1069.   2. MIRABEAU-LAMAR, b. June 21, 1837; m. Ellen-Maria Ball, Dec. 26,
        1861, and had Grace-Antoinette, b. Jan. 30, 1863. In war of rebellion

he was in Comp. A, 1st Wisconsin Vols., from April 22, 1861, till discharged with Reg., Aug. 21, 1861. The Reg. was in action near Martinsburg, Va., July 2, 1861. In Sept. 29, 1863, he enlisted in 13th Wisconsin Light Artillery; was clerk of General Court Martial at New Orleans.

1070. 3. MARTHA-AUGUSTA, b. Dec. 30, 1839 ; m. April 24, 1860, John-Chapman West. Chief clerk in Post Office at Buffalo, N. Y. He was also in the army in the war of rebellion.
1071. 4. ADA-DICKERSON, b. April 27, 1850.
1072. 5. LILLIE-DICKERSON, b. April 7, 1852.
1073. 6. KATIE-DICKERSON, b. July 25, 1857.

1074. CATHARINE,[5][440] (*Jehiel,*[4] *Moses,*[3] *Moses,*[2] *John,*[1]) b. April 10, 1818, d. June 17, 1857 ; m. 1st, John-Fox Van Eman, March 23, 1837 ; he d. April 11, 1848 ; m. 2d, Isaac-Thomas Gaylord, May 8, 1851 ; he was b. Nov. 17, 1800.   *Talmadge, Summit Co., Ohio.*

1075. 1. EMELINE-AMELIA, b. Dec. 3, 1838, d. Feb. 10, 1859, m. Henry Vantin, May 16, 1858.   *Hudson, Ohio.*
1875. 2. MARIA-SLAFTER, b. Dec. 22, 1839, d. Oct. 14, 1862.
1077. 3. CORDELIA, b. April 27, 1843, d. March 17, 1845.
1078. 4. CATHARINE-CORNELIA, b. March 13, 1846.
1079. 5. ALMIRA-SARAH, b. Sept. 23, 1856.

1080. MARIA,[5][441] (*Jehiel,*[4] *Moses,*[3] *Moses,*[2] *John,*[1]) b. April 24, 1820, d. Jan. 17, 1868 ; m. William-Henry, son of Henry-James Phillips of Eaton, Ohio, Nov. 10, 1839. He was b. Sept. 17, 1809 ; is a Justice of the Peace.   *Laport, Ohio.*

1081. 1. WILLIAM-ALVA, b. July 28, 1840 ; m. Oct. 24, 1868, Maria-Elizabeth Nickerson.   *Cleveland, Ohio.*
1082. 2. LETITIA, b. March 29, 1825, d. Nov. 13, 1847.
1083. 3. EDGAR-AVERY, b. Sept. 30, 1848, d. July 6, 1864 ; in war of rebellion was in Comp. K,135 Ohio Vols.; killed near Martinsburg, Va., in a skirmish.
1084. 4. EDWARD-EMERSON, b. Dec. 30, 1850.
1085. 5. CORDA-CATHARINE, b. July 5, 1855.
1086. 6. LENA-MARIA, b. Jan. 28, 1859.

1087. MARY-ELECTA,[5][444] (*Jehiel,*[4] *Moses,*[3] *Moses,*[2] *John,*[1]) b. June 17, 1830 ; m. Henry Reddington, Aug 4, 1850. He was b. July 9, 1825.   *Manlius, Lasalle Co., Ill.*

1088. 1. EMILY-LYDIA, b. Nov. 6, 1853.
1089. 2. EDWARD-CHARLES, b. April 5, 1856.
1090. 3. LESLIE-JEHIEL, b. Feb. 21, 1858.
1091. 4. ELIZABETH-MARY, b. July 21, 1860.

1092. MARY-ELMIRA,[5][447] (*Moses,*[4] *Moses,*[3] *Moses,*[2] *John,*[1]) b. May 2, 1815, d. Sept. 8, 1856; m. Newman Dutcher, Aug. 21, 1842. He was b. May 3, 1813. He had by a former wife, Wheaton-M., who was in war of rebellion and killed at Jackson, Miss., 1863; also, Frederick-A., d. Dec. 7, 1864.   *Charles City, Floyd Co., Iowa.*

1093. 1. WALLACE, b. June 19, 1843, d. Sept. 14, 1849.
1094. 2. WILLIAM-ALBERT, b. Feb. 5, 1845 ; in war of rebellion served twenty-one months in Battery D, 1st Wis. Heavy Artillery; was in several battles ; though not wounded, was paralyzed in both legs, and is now (1869) at the National Asylum for disabled Volunteer Soldiers.   *Milwaukee, Wis.*
1095. 3. ELLEN-MARIA, b. Sept. 16, 1847, d. Sept. 5, 1849.
1096. 4. MARY-JANE, b. Sept. 5, 1849.
1097. 5. ABBY-PAMELA, b. April 10, 1852.
1098. 6. NEWMAN, b. Jan. 30, 1855.

1099. WILLIAM-GRAY,[5][448] (*Moses,*[4] *Moses,*[3] *Moses,*[2] *John,*[1]) b. Sept. 7, 1819; m. Catharine, daughter of Samuel Stoddard of Simsbury, Conn., Oct. 24, 1841. She was b. March 5, 1818, d. Dec. 29, 1867. Their children were as follows: *Monticello, Green Co., Wis.*

1100.   1. WILLIAM-HENRY, b. in Brandt, N. Y., Sept. 26, 1842, d. Jan. 16, 1863; in war of rebellion was in Comp. K, 22d Wis. Vols.; length of service five months.
1101.   2. ALZALON-IDA, b. in Sheffield, O., June 26, 1847; m. Philo, son of Nelson-A. Hitchcock of Exeter, Wis., Aug. 22, 1868. He was b. July 11, 1847; a preacher of the Second Advent faith.   *Exeter, Wis.*
1102.   3. ALMA-KATE, b. in Olmsted, O., May 23, 1851.
1103.   4. ELIZABETH-CARRIE, b. in Olmsted, O., June 3, 1854.

1104. ELIZA-ANN,[5][449] (*Moses,*[4] *Moses,*[3] *Moses,*[2] *John,*[1]) b. Aug. 8, 1822, d. Dec. 12, 1854; m. Harvey Richardson, April 22, 1839. Their children are as follows: *Olmstead Falls, Cuyahoga Co., Ohio.*

1105.   1. ANNA-ELIZA, b. in Brandt, N. Y., Aug. 29, 1840; m. William-Dewey Bennett, Aug. 14, 1859, and had Dewey-Leroy.   *Monticello, Wis.*
1106.   2. GEORGE-HARVEY, b. in Hanover, N. Y., Nov. 11, 1843; in war of rebellion in Comp. C, 3d Wis.; in battle of Antietam, wounded in both hands and discharged.
1107.   3. GILBERT-LEROY, b. in Olmstead, O., April 12, 1846.
1108.   4. ELECTA-LEONA, b. in Olmsted, O., June 6, 1849.

1109. JEROME-POND,[5][461] (*Adonijah,*[4] *Moses,*[3] *Moses,*[2] *John,*[1]) b. Oct. 8, 1817, d. June 11, 1867; m. 1st, in Thompsonville, Ct.; 2d, Margaret Axe, Oct. 2d, 1849. She was b. Feb. 6, 1820. She now (1868) resides at Moline, Ill. His children were as follows:

1109½.   1. ROBERT-W., by first wife.
1110.   2. LURA-LOUISA, b. Nov. 4, 1850.
1111.   3. ELIZABETH-TILLY, b. Feb. 6, 1853.
1112.   4. MARY-CLARISSA, b. Nov. 10, 1855.
1113.   5. MARTHA-CELIA, b. Nov. 26, 1858.
1114.   6. EMMA-OPHELIA, b. Oct 2. 1859.

1115. FRANCIS-MANSFIELD,[5] [462] (*Adonijah,*[4] *Moses,*[3] *Moses,*[2] *John,*[1]) b. Jan. 6, 1821; m. Elizabeth-Azubah, dau. of Erastus Wright, Feb. 11, 1844. She was b. Nov. 30, 1823. They had one child.
        Medina, N. Y.
1116.   1. MARTHA-ELIZA, b. Oct. 18, 1847, d. Sept. 17, 1849.

1117. FRANKLIN-AURELIUS,[5] [463] (*Adonijah,*[4] *Moses,*[3] *Moses,*[2] *John,*[1]) b. Feb. 11, 1823; m. Sophronia-Eunice, daughter of Edmund-Clark Hovey of Craftsbury, Vt., Dec. 5, 1850. She was b. Oct. 1, 1822, d. April 11, 1863. He was prepared for College at St. Lawrence Academy, Potsdam, N. Y.; graduated at Madison University, Hamilton, N. Y., in Class of 1850; received degree of A. M. at same, 1853; was ordained as Baptist clergyman, Nov. 14, 1850; has been settled at Mystic, Ct., New Rochelle, N. Y., Rome, N. Y., Keyport, N. J., and at Greenport, Long Island, and is now settled at
        Matawan, N. J.
1118.   1. IDA-ELIZA, b. in Groton, Ct., Nov. 24, 1852.
1119.   2. FRANK-HOVEY, b. in Rome, N. Y., May 16, 1855.
1120.   3. MYRON-EASTMAN, b. in Keyport, N. J., Dec. 18, 1857.
1121.   4. HENRY-GREWZEBACK, b. in Keyport, N. J., Aug. 1861, d. Dec. 29, 1863.

1122. ALMEDA-MALVINA,⁵[464] (*Adonijah,⁴ Moses,³ Moses,² John,¹*) b. Feb. 5, 1825; m. George-Washington, son of Stephen Bullard of Potsdam, Nov. 14, 1850. He was b. Aug. 26, 1823.

Madrid, N.Y.

1123. 1. ALFRED-MYRON, b. in Potsdam, N. Y., Nov. 24, 1851.

1124. ORRIN-REXFORD,⁵[466] (*Adonijah,⁴ Moses,³ Moses,² John,¹*) b. Nov. 7, 1830; m. Emily, daughter of Isaac Rexford of Malone, N. Y., June 19, 1854. She was b. Feb. 16, 1832. *Madrid, N.Y.*

1125. 1. Carrie-Louisa, b. April 29, 1858.

1126. LURA-LOUISA,⁵[467] (*Adonijah,⁴ Moses,³ Moses,² John,¹*) b. Aug. 23, 1833; m. John-Chubb, son of Benjamin Streeter of Stockholm, N. Y., May 15, 1865. He was b. Feb. 16, 1828.

Stockholm, Brasher Depot, N.Y.

1127. SAMUEL-BENJAMIN,⁵[500] (*Samuel,⁴ Moses,³ Moses,² John,¹*) b. Jan. 18, 1827; m. 1st, Maria-Olive, daughter of Austin Pease of Somers, Ct., March 25, 1848; she was b. Jan. 10, 1831, d. Dec. 29, 1865; m. 2d, Martha, daughter of Chester Chaffee of Thompson, Ct., March 26, 1867. She was b. Oct. 17, 1835. He is (1868) one of the selectmen of Tolland. *Tolland, Ct.*

1128. 1. SAMUEL-AUSTIN, b. Dec. 29, 1849.
1129. 2. ELLA-MARIA, b. Feb. 22, 1855.

1130. LEMUEL,⁵[501] (*Samuel,⁴ Moses,³ Moses,² John,¹*) b. Feb. 10, 1829; m. Mary-Jane, daughter of Gustavus Cushman of Stafford, Ct., June 8, 1854. She was b. June 28, 1835. He resides on the estate occupied by his grandfather, Moses Slafter. *Ellington, Ct.*

1131. 1. MARY-ANTOINETTE, b. Sept. 31, 1855.

1132. WILLIAM-ALBERT,⁵[502] (*Samuel,⁴ Moses,³ Moses,² John,¹*) b. Feb, 3, 1831; m. Elizabeth, daughter of David Wakefield of Somers, Ct., April 19, 1853. She was b. Oct. 28, 1831. In war of rebellion, enlisted in Comp. K, 22 Conn. Vols., Sept. 20, 1862; was in service nine months. Their children are as follows: *Thompsonville, Ct.*

1133. 1. EMMA-ADELAIDE, b. Feb. 17, 185–.
1134. 2. ELIZABETH, b. Aug. 12, 1857, d. in infancy.
1135. 3. WARREN-HENRY, b. Sept. 28, 1859.
1136. 4. ERMINA-BELL, b. Oct. 4, 1865, at Tolland.

1137. JANE-PHILENDA,⁵[504] (*Samuel,⁴ Moses,³ Moses,² John,¹*) b. Jan. 10, 1835; m. Rev. Charles-Frederick, son of Charles Newell of Ellington, Ct., Nov. 26, 1857. He was b. Aug. 21, 1836. He was ordained as a Methodist preacher, March 22, 1865. He has officiated at Square Pond, Gurleyville, Niantic, Windsorville, Wapping, Ct., and at Middleborough, Mass., and Scituate, Mass. Their children are as follows:

1138. 1. CHARLES-WILBUR, b. Dec. 28, 1859.
1139. 2. ERNEST-ALBERT, b. Sept. 7, 1862, d. Sept. 23, 1864.
1140. 3. ELMER-FREDERICK, b. Aug. 19, 1864.
1141. 4. GRACE-HARRIET, b. Nov. 4, 1866.

7

1142. JOHN-GREENLEAF,⁵[505] (*Samuel,*⁴ *Moses,*³ *Moses,*² *John,*¹) b. June 23, 1837; m. Emily-Jane, daughter of Ebenezer Harwood of Ellington, Ct., April 29, 1863. She was born in Stafford, Dec. 31, 1839.   *Stafford Springs, Ct.*

1143.   1. JOHN-ORLANDO, b. Dec. 19, 1864, at Tolland, Ct.
1144.   2. ALBERTUS, b. July 28, 1866.

1145. FANNY-CHARLOTTE,⁵[511] (*William,*⁴ *Moses,*³ *Moses,*² *John,*¹) b. Dec. 16, 1824; m. Henry-Curtis, son of Jedediah Aborn of Ellington, Ct., Oct. 13, 1850. He was b. Nov. 26, 1822.   *Square Pond, Ct.*

1146.   1. MILES-HENRY, b. July 24, 1854.   *Ellington, Ct.*

1147. HENRIETTA-ANN,⁵[512] (*William,*⁴ *Moses,*³ *Moses,*² *John,*¹) b. July 21, 1826; m. Ephraim-Harlem, son of Ephraim Dimmick of Stafford, Ct., April 20, 1851. He was b. April 27, 1826.
                                                    Square Pond, Ct.

1148.   1. MYRON-HARLEM, b. July 9, 1852.
1149.   2. GILES-SLAFTER, b. June 29, 1855.

1150. WILLIAM-DWIGHT,⁵[513] (*William,*⁴ *Moses,*³ *Moses,*² *John,*¹) b. March 16, 1828; m. Emeline-Catharine, daughter of William Thompson of Wales, Mass., Jan. 1, 1851.   *Tolland. Ct.*

1151.   1. MERRILL-DWIGHT, b. Jan. 17, 1855.
1152.   2. FANNY-ESTELLA, b. Oct. 8, 1857.
1153.   3. CHARLES-THOMPSON, b. Sept. 22, 1861.
1154.   4. DORA, b. Nov., 1864.

1155. BENJAMIN-FRANKLIN,⁵[515] (*William,*⁴ *Moses,*³ *Moses,*² *John,*¹) b. May 30, 1833; m. Marietta-Lura, daughter of Warren Richardson of Stafford, Ct., July 2, 1854.   *Square Pond, Ct.*

1156.   1. MARY-ANN, b. Dec. 16, 1863.

1157. GEORGE WASHINGTON,⁵[516] (*William,*⁴ *Moses,*³ *Moses,*² *John,*¹) b. July 27, 1836; m. Lora-Selenda, daughter of Lucius Aborn of Ellington, Ct., Nov. 10, 1855.   *Square Pond, Ct.*

1158.   1. ELLEN-CHARLOTTE, b. Oct. 12, 1856.
1159.   2. JEANNIE-IDA, b. July 5, 1864.

1160. CHAUNCY-FOX,⁵[518] (*Ariel,*⁴ *Moses,*³ *Moses,*² *John,*¹) b. March 10, 1830; m. Abby-Elizabeth, daughter of Garner Read of Willington, Ct., Feb. 26, 1854. She was born July 12, 1835. He removed from Ellington, Ct., to Iowa.   *Grove City, Cass Co., Iowa.*

1161.   1. CLARA-LILLIAN, b. May 16, 1855.

1162. CLARINDA,⁵[519] (*Ariel,*⁴ *Moses,*³ *Moses,*² *John,*¹) b. May 31, 1832; m. 1st, Jonathan-Parker, son of John Clark of Somers, Ct., Feb. 5, 1852; he died May 26, 1852. She m. 2d, William-Henry, son of Marcus Conover of Florida, N. Y., April 6, 1856. He was b. Jan. 29, 1816. Her children are as follows :

1163.   1. ELLA, b. April 27, 1857, d. Nov. 15, 1860.
1164.   2. MARY-DELLA, b. Sept. 29, 1862.
1164½. 3. ARIEL-MARCUS, b. Oct. 30, 1867.

1165. MARY,[520] (*Ariel,[4] Moses,[3] Moses,[2] John,[1]*) b. April 5, 1834; m. John Sanford, son of Charles Cromwell of Peru, N. Y., Dec. 16, 1858. He was b. April 20, 1833. *Grove City, Iowa.*

1166. 1. ELLA, b. Oct. 17, 1861.
1166½. 2. NORA, b. April 4, 1869.

1167. HARRIET-ELIZA,[521] (*Ariel,[4] Moses,[3] Moses,[2] John,[1]*) b. June 3, 1836; m. Charles-Hiram, son of Jedediah Aborn of Tolland, Ct., March 28, 1859. *Tolland, Ct.*

1168. 1. CHARLES-ARTHUR, b. Nov. 17, 1860.

1169. PAULINA,[522] (*Ariel,[4] Moses,[3] Moses,[2] John,[1]*) b. Nov. 26, 1839; m. John-Quincy, son of George-Sullivan Greenleaf of Springfield, Mass., March 26, 1860. He was b. Jan. 31, 1838. Their children are as follows: *Omaha, Nebraska.*

1170. 1. MINNIE-JOSEPHINE, b. July 6, 1861.
1170½. 2. LUELLA-MARIA, b. Oct. 17, 1866.

1171. HORATIO,[398] (*Anthony,[4] Anthony,[3] Moses,[2] John,[1]*) b. Feb. 1, 1807; m. 1st, Lucinda Fuller, Sept. 15, 1831; m. 2d, Julia Butler, Jan. 15, 1845. *Granby, Mass.*

1172. 1. HARRIET, d. young.
1173. 2. JULIA, d. young.
1174. 3. ALBERT,[1268] b. April 17, 1837, m. Harriet-Louise Joslyn.
1175. 4. EDMUND, d. young.
1176. 5. EMELINE, d. young.
1177. 6. EPHRAIM, d. young.
1178. 7. John, b. June 2, 1847.
1179. 8. EMELINE, b. Jan. 27, 1849, d. March 4, 1858.

1180. AMELIA,[400] (*Anthony,[4] Anthony,[3] Moses,[2] John,[1]*) b. Sept. 12, 1810, d. Sept. 24, 1863; m. Orrin Bramble of Springfield, Mass., 1829. He was born Sept. 15, 1807. Their children are as follows: *Springfield, Mass.*

1181. 1. HENRY, b. March 11, 1830, d. Feb. 14, 1864; in the war of rebellion he served in Comp. I, 37th Mass. Vols., from Aug., 1862, till he became ill, and died at Richmond, Va.; m. Henrietta Billings, Aug. 14, 1849, and had,—
(1.) Alice-Casey, b. June 20, 1850, d. Nov. 15, 1866.
(2.) Anzanette, b. March 25, 1852.
(3.) John-Zinskey, b, June 5, 1854.
(4.) Mary-Ruth, b. April 6, 1857.
(5.) Henry-Dickinson, b. Aug. 3, 1861.
(6.) Daniel-Orrin, b. April 29, 1864. *Springfield, Mass.*
1182. 2. FRANKLIN, b. Jan. 25, 1831; in war of rebellion he served in Comp. K, 27th Mass. Vols., from July 21, 1862, and re-enlisted in the same, and was discharged July 20, 1865; m. Julia-Ann Thayer, April 2, 1854, and had (1.) Franklin-Dwight, b. Feb. 17, 1855; (2.) Harriet-Elnara, b. Oct. 3, 1857. *Ludlow, Mass.*
1183. 3. MARY-FRANCES, b. March 22, 1833; m. Joseph-Lathrop Smith, June 1, 1859, and had Gratia-Amelia, b. Nov. 5, 1865. *Feeding Hills, Mass.*
1184. 4. ESTHER, b. March 13, 1835, d. July 16, 1848.
1185. 5. AMANDA-LAVANTIA, b. Jan. 18, 1837; m. Solomon-Drew Avery, July 9, 1853; in war of rebellion he enlisted in Comp. B, 10th New Hampshire Vols., Aug. 14, 1862; he was Brigade bugler at Yorktown; Post bugler at Point of Rocks; discharged June 10, 1865. Their children are (1.) Emma-Antoinette, b. Aug. 12, 1854; (2.) Alva-Viola, b. Feb. 7, 1856; (3.) Arthur-Drew, b. Sept. 25, 1857, d. Dec. 31, 1861. *Greenfield, Mass.*

1186. 6. ALMIRA, b. April 13, 1839, d. March 2, 1843.
1187. 7. MARCUS-MORTON, b. Jan. 6, 1842; m. Harriet-Sophia Willey, Jan. 17,
         1860, and had (1.) Frederick-Roland, b. Feb. 13, 1861, d. Aug. 6,
         1862; (2.) Minnie-Estella, b. Feb. 22, 1863.
1188. 8. CELIA-AMELIA, b. June 10, 1843; m. Alvin-Chilson, April 1, 1861, and
         had Esther, b. Aug. 18, 1867.   *Wilbraham, Mass.*
1189. 9. WILLIAM-MILLER, b. April 22, 1845, d. July 8, 1848.
1190. 10. ZOROASTER, b. Feb. 27, 1847, d. June 28, 1848.
1191. 11. WILLIAM-ELLERY, b. Aug. 18, 1848.
1192. 12. LUELLA-ISADORE, b. Nov. 10, 1850.

   1193. SARAH-FROST,[5][403] (*Anthony,*[4] *Anthony,*[3] *Moses,*[2] *John,*[1])
b. April 4, 1817; m. Alfred Trumbull, Sept. 1, 1839.
                                      Palmer Depot, Mass.
1194. 1. ALFRED, b. Jan. 19, 1843, d. in infancy.
1195. 2. SALMON-SIDNEY-PACKARD, b. Oct. 18, 1845.
1196. 3. ELLA-MELISSA, b. May 11, 1850.
1197. 4. LIZZIE-LIELIA, b. March 4, 1857.

   1198. RACHEL,[5][420] (*David-Frost,*[4] *Anthony,*[3] *Moses,*[2] *John,*[1]) b.
Oct. 5, 1820; m. George, son of Jabez Lyman of Royalton, Vt., May
23, 1848. The eldest two children were born in Williamstown, Vt.,
the third in Patch Grove, and the fourth in Tafton, Wis.
                          Bloomington, Grant Co., Wis.
1199. 1. CORYDON-DWIGHT, b. March 21, 1849.
1200. 2. CLARENCE-EDWARDS, b. May 7, 1850.
1200¼. 3. HARLAN-NEWELL, b. Nov. 9, 1858.
1200⅜. 4. ETTIE-ALMINA, b. March 9, 1862.

   1201. JAMES-GROW,[5][421] (*David-Frost,*[4] *Anthony,*[3] *Moses,*[2]
John,[1]) b. Jan. 11, 1822; m. Lucy-Malinda, daughter of Albina
Wheeler of Newport, N. H., Oct. 14, 1845; she was b. March 2,
1826, d. April 30, 1851; m. 2d, Julia-Augusta, daughter of Uriel
Blanchard of West Windsor, Vt., and widow of Horace-Ziba Lam-
kin, April 24, 1856. She was b. May 27, 1826.   *Montpelier, Vt.*

1202. 1. JAMES-CARLOS, b. in Royalton, Vt., Feb. 7, 1850.

   1203. CHARLOTTE-ELIZABETH,[4][422] (*David-Frost,*[4] *Anthony,*[3]
Moses,[2] *John,*[1]) b. Jan. 23, 1826; m. John, son of Elisha Wilde of
Royalton, Vt., Aug. 10, 1854. Their children were all born in Royal-
ton, Vt., and are as follows: *Royalton, Vt.*

1204. 1. JOHN, b. Dec. 1, 1855.
1205. 2. LUCY, b. June 7, 1856.
1206. 3. LEVI, b. June 29, 1860.
1206¼. 4. MARY, b. Dec. 12, 1862.
1206½. 5. EBEN, b. Oct. 1, 1864.

   1207. EUNICE,[5][426] (*Zebulon-West,*[4] *Anthony,*[3] *Moses,*[2] *John,*[1]) b.
July 13, 1809; m. 1st, Parsons-Gates Willey; he was b. Oct. 19,
1809, d. Sept. 30, 1844; m. 2d, Edwin-McRea Billings, Sept. 12,
1847. In the war of rebellion he was in Comp. A, 4th Mass. Cavalry,
and died at Jackson, Fla., after a service of nine months. Their
children are as follows: *Agawam, Mass.*

1208. 1. MARY-MINERVA, b. Jan. 24, 1829; m. James-Monroe Kelley, Jan. 24,
         1852.
1209. 2. PARSONS-GATES, b. April 20, 1831, m. Melinda Taft, July 28, 1853.
1210. 3. WILLIAM-SIMON, b. Nov. 23, 1832, m. Laura-Jane Dyer, Nov. 14, 1853.

1211. 4. EMILY-ANGELINE, b. Nov. 20, 1834 ; m. William Dugan, Oct. 20, 1855 ; in war of rebellion in 8th Reg. Conn. Vols.
1212. 5. EMELINE-ELIZABETH, b. Dec. 7, 1836; m. William-Wallace Hitchcock, March 19, 1855 ; he served three months in Comp. D, 37th Mass. Vols. ; wounded in battle of Wilderness and honorably discharged May 9, 1864.
1213. 6. HARRIET-SOPHIA, b. Jan. 11, 1838; m. Marcus-Morton Bramble, Jan. 19, 1860.
1214. 7. HENRY-DWIGHT, b. Jan. 13, 1839, d. Sept. 17, 1839.
1215. 8. NANCY, b. Oct. 28, 1840, d. Jan. 3, 1843.
1216. 9. JOHN-EDWIN, b. Oct. 27, 1848.
1217. 10. SARAH-EUNICE, b. May 23, 1851.

1218. LOVICE-ELIZA,[5][428] (*Zebulon-West,[4] Anthony,[3] Moses,[2] John,[1]*) b. March 22, 1813 ; m. 1st Samuel Eley, March 22, 1831 ; m. 2d, Samuel Phillips, July 13, 1851. Her children are as follows :
Williamsburg, N. Y.

1219. 1. SAMUEL, b. May 29, 1832.
1220. 2. WILLIAM-SCHENK, b. April 15, 1837 ; in war of rebellion in Comp. I, 31st New York Vols.
1221. 3. ANNA-ELIZA, b. Feb. 25, 1840.
1222. 4. GERTRUDE-EMMA, b. June 4, 1848.

1223. ANGELINA,[5][429] (*Zebulon-West,[4] Anthony,[3] Moses,[2] John,[1]*) b. April 23, 1815 ; m. William Ballou, and had the following children :
Ware, Mass.

1224. 1. THOMAS-HOWARD, b. in Springfield, Mass., July 19, 1839.
1225. 2. HANNAH-ELIZABETH, b. in Springfield, May 12, 1841.
1226. 3. JULIA-CAROLINE, b. in Belchertown, Aug. 18, 1843.
1227. 4. NANCY-ANN, b. in Springfield, June 18, 1845.
1228. 5. WILLIAM-EDGAR, b. in Springfield, April 15, 1847, d. July, 1848.
1229. 6. MARY-LOUISA, b. Aug. 11, 1850.
1230. 7. ELIZA-JANE, b. in Belchertown, May 1, 1852, d. 1853.
1231. 8. HENRY-FRANKLIN, b. in Ware, May 7, 1856.
1232. 9. WILLIS, b. in Ware, Jan., 1859.

1233. JESSE-FARNUM,[5][431] (*Zebulon-West,[4] Anthony,[3] Moses,[2] John,[1]*) b. Sept. 3, 1820 ; m. 1st Fidelia Burnet, Nov. 23, 1841 ; she was born March 17, 1824, d. June 5, 1852 ; m. 2d, Angenette Loomis, May 31, 1855. *Agawam, Mass.*

1234. 1. CHARLES-FARNUM, b. March 1, 1844 ; he is a gun-smith, Chicopee Falls, Mass.
1235. 2. HARRIET-ELLA, b. May 22, 1848.
1236. 3. MARY, b. Sept. 20, 1856, d. Aug. 11, 1857.
1237. 4. ELIZABETH-SARAH, b. July 24, 1862.

1238. ELIZABETH-BULLARD,[5][432] (*Zebulon-West,[4] Anthony,[3] Moses,[2] John,[1]*) b. April 22, 1822 ; d. Jan. 18, 1868; m. Benjamin-Daniel, son of William Tilden of Palmer, June 1, 1843. He was b. July 7, 1819. Their children are as follows :
North Wilbraham, Mass.

1239. 1. CHARLES-FAYETTE, b. in Longmeadow, Mass., Sept. 18, 1844 ; in war of rebellion he enlisted Sept., 1861, in Comp. B, 8th Conn. Vols., and served three years and six months.
1240. 2. ALBERT-ELMER, b. in Wilbraham, Oct. 20, 1847.
1241. 3. SARAH-JANE-SLAFTER, b. in Wilbraham, Dec. 14, 1849.
1242. 4. HENRY-DWIGHT, b. in Wilbraham, July 25, 1852.
1243. 5. MYRA-ELIZABETH, b. in Longweadow, Sept. 22, 1854, d. Jan. 31, 1866.
1244. 6. WILLIAM-ARTHUR, b. in Wilbraham, March 25, 1857.

1245. Flora-Elizabeth,[6][548] (*William,[5] John,[4] John,[3] Samuel,[2] John,[1]*) b. March 26, 1832; m. Gilbert, son of Isaac Baldwin of Frankenmuth, Mich., Feb. 15, 1851; he was b. July 28, 1828; in war of rebellion he served three years in Comp. I, 3d Michigan Cavalry. Their children are as follows: *Worth, Mich.*

1246. 1. Roisa-Lucy-Ann, b. June 16, 1852, d. June 16, 1852.
1247. 2. Rosalia, b. May 15, 1854, d. July 11, 1856.
1248. 3. George-Edwin, b. Nov. 3, 1856, d. June 25, 1863.
1249. 4. Almina-Louisa, b. Sept. 30, 1857.
1250. 5. Albert-Sidney, b. Nov. 20, 1861.

1251. Albert,[6][549] (*William,[5] John,[4] John,[3] Samuel,[2] John,[1]*) b. Sept. 15, 1833; m. Ruth, daughter of Davis Smith of Montrose, Mich., Feb. 28, 1855; she was b. March 23, 1836. In war of rebellion he enlisted, June 19, 1861, as a private; served as Orderly and Quarter-Master Sergeant till the 2d of Feb., 1863, when he was promoted to 2d Lieut. in Comp. E, 7th Mich. Infantry; he was killed at Gettysburg, July 2, 1863, while leading Comp. E, of which he was in command, into battle; he sleeps in the National Cemetery at Gettysburg, in Section G, No. 13; he left two daughters.
          Flushing, Genesee Co., Mich.

1252. 1. Mary-Mehetabel, b. Dec. 12, 1855.
1253. 2. Florence-Eveline, b. July 7, 1857.

1254. Oromel-Willis,[6][569] (*Thomas-Jefferson,[5] Sylvester,[4] John,[3] Samuel,[2] John,[1]*) b. Oct. 7, 1828; m. Caroline-Eliza, daughter of Thomas-Adams Cox of Vestal, New York, May 4, 1855; she was b. June 10, 1822. They have three children.
          Minnesota Lake, Minn.

1255. 1. Mary-Carrie, b. in Monticello, Minn., June 27, 1856.
1256. 2. Sophia-Rebecca, b. in Winona, Minn., June 17, 1858.
1257. 3. Lucy-Annette, b. in Quincy, Minn., Nov. 18, 1861.

1258. Carlos-Lewis,[6][570] (*Thomas-Jefferson,[5] Sylvester,[4] John,[3] Samuel,[2] John,[1]*) b. March 16, 1832; m. Lucy-Chamberlin, daughter of Ira and Annis (Holcomb) Tracy of Belmont, Alleghany Co., New York, March 16, 1864; she was b. April 15, 1832.   *Belmont, N.Y.*

1259. Edmund-Farwell,[6][573] (*Sylvester,[5] Sylvester,[4] John,[3] Samuel,[2] John,[1]*) b. Sept. 21, 1838, d. April 27, 1859; m. Lucy-Emily, daughter of Eben-Greene Bulkley of Guilford, Winnebago Co., Illinois, Dec. 3, 1857; she was b. Feb. 1, 1840; she has m. 2d, Clark Cheney.
          Lindenwood, Ill.

1260. 1. Edmund-Farwell-Clarence, b. in Guilford, Ill., Oct. 24, 1859.

1261. Emily-Diantha,[6][648] (*Asahel,[5] Calvin,[4] Eleazer,[3] Samuel,[2] John,[1]*) b. Oct. 25, 1834; m. Henry-Jacob, son of Nathan Tripp of Pomfret, Chautauque Co., New York, Dec. 18, 1856; he was b. Feb. 3, 1831. The following are their children: *Belvidere, Ill.*

1262. 1. Byron-Henry, b. Jan 6, 1858.
1263. 2. Ethel-Emily, b. Feb. 6, 1860, d. March 6, 1860.
1264. 3. Archie-Nathan, b. Sept. 21, 1861.

1265. MELVIN-CLARKSON,[6][649] (Asahel,[5] Calvin,[4] Eleazer,[3] Samuel,[2] John,[1]) b. Nov. 25, 1835; m. Sarah-Maria, daughter of John-Lawrence Rosecrans of Belvidere, Boom Co., Ill., Jan. 20, 1864; she was b. Jan 20, 1845.

1266. EURETTA-OLIVE,[6][650] (Asahel,[5] Calvin,[4] Eleazer,[3] Samuel,[2] John,[1]) b. Feb. 23, 1837; m. Thomas-Sir, son of John Rogers of Belvidere, Ill., formerly of Somersetshire, Eng., Sept. 6, 1859; he was b. Nov. 10, 1833. Their children are as follows: *Belvidere, Ill.*

1267. 1. FRANCIS-JAMES, b. April 2, 1864.
1267½ 2. EZRA MILTON, b. Dec. 8, 1868, d. April 8, 1869.

1268. ALBERT,[6][1174] (Horatio,[5] Anthony,[4] Anthony,[3] Moses,[2] John,[1]) b. April 17, 1837; m. Harriet-Louisa Joslin, Feb. 25, 1855. They have two children. *Chicopee Falls, Mass.*

1269. 1. EVA-BELL, b. April 6, 1857.
1270. 2. ELLA-LOUISE, b. Sept. 14, 1860.

1271. LYDIA-ANN,[6][1061] (Charles-Avery,[5] Jehiel,[4] Moses,[3] Moses,[2] John,[1]) b. Nov. 29, 1835; m. Alfred-Brunson, son of John Kerns of Canaan, Ohio, Sept. 9, 1858. He was b. Oct. 4, 1831. They have the following children: *Canaan, Wayne Co., Ohio.*

1272. 1. HERBERT-ALFRED, b. Jan 9, 1859.
1273. 2. HARPER-HARRISON, b. Sept. 2, 1860.
1274. 3. HARRIET-ELIZABETH, b. Nov. 1, 1862.

1275. CHARLES-JEHIEL,[6][1063] (Charles-Avery,[5] Jehiel,[4] Moses,[3] Moses,[2] John,[1]) b. Jan. 24. 1839; m. Martha-Jane, daughter of Elijah Loveland of Cincinnati, Ohio, March 28, 1861; she was b. Aug 7, 1842. *Dayton, Ohio.*

1276. 1. MINNIE-LUELLA, b. March 1, 1862, d. Nov. 5, 1863.

1277. THERON,[6][679] (Abraham,[5] Abner,[4] Joseph,[3] Joseph,[2] John,[1]) b. Sept. 7, 1805; m. Julia Ann, dau. of Levi Lobdell of Nassau, N. Y., April 9, 1833. She was b. April 21, 1812. They have the following children: *Princeton, Scott Co., Iowa.*

1278. 1. RACHEL,[1863] b. Jan. 19, 1834, m. John-Dickerson Stafford.
1279. 2. ANNA, b. Oct. 21, 1836, d. Oct. 31, 1852.
1280. 3. HARRIET, b. Feb. 21, 1839.
1281. 4 FAYETTE-LACEY, b. Nov. 8, 1841; in Comp. A, 14th Reg. Iowa, in war of rebellion.
1282. 5. JOHN-AUSTIN, b. Dec. 22, 1843.
1283. 6. ERASTUS-LOBDELL, b. Sept. 4, 1846.
1284. 7. ELEIDA, b. June 1, 1849, d. Jan. 20, 1855.
1285. 8. CLIFFORD-HENRY, b. Jan. 18, 1852.

1286. JOSHUA,[6][680] (Abraham,[5] Abner,[4] Joseph,[3] Joseph,[2] John,[1]) b. Feb. 11, 1806, d. June 12, 1864; m. Salome, dau. of Joel Burroughs of Essex, N. Y., Oct., 1828. She died March, 1829, without children. He married, 2d, Sarah, dau. of Comfort Benedict of Panton, Vt., Sept. 3, 1829. She was b. Aug. 24, 1811. They have the following children: *Pleasant Valley, Scott Co., Iowa.*

1287. 1. ANNETTE, b. April 17, 1831, m. Alonzo Chellis.
Pleasant Valley, Scott Co., Iowa.
1288. 2. WILLIAM-HENRY,[1923] b. May 6, 1837, m. Anna Seekins.

1289. 3. CELESTIA-CARKINS, b. April 29, 1841; m. Solomon-Oscar Hubbard, Sept. 5, 1866. He was born July 3, 1842, in Panama, N. Y. He enlisted in war of rebellion in Comp. G, 112th Illinois Vols.; he was with Gen. Burnside in Kentucky and Tennessee in 1863–4; with Gen. Sherman in Georgia in 1864; with Gen. Thomas in the campaign against Hood in Tennessee, 1864; with Gen. Schofield in North Carolina in 1865. He was in twenty-five "general engagements" and a hundred and ten skirmishes; he was made corporal Sept. 4, 1863, for " bravery and good conduct." They have one child, Grace-Lilian, b. April 6, 1868.   *Grinnell, Poweshiek Co., Iowa.*
1290. 4. ULISSES-KELLOGG, b. Aug. 3, 1844.   *Pleasant Valley, Mich.*
1291. 5. JOSEPHEINE, b. Sept. 15, 1846; m. Wesley, son of William Rambo, Nov. 23, 1864.   *Le Clair, Iowa.*
1292. 6. JULIUS, b. Sept. 25, 1848.
1293. 7. HILAH-ALMIRA, b. 1850, d. 1853.

1294. NATHAN,[6][682] (*Abraham,[5] Abner,[4] Joseph,[3] Joseph,[2] John,[1]*) b. Aug. 29, 1814; m. Roxana, dau. of Israel Goodale of Addison, Vt., Nov. 23, 1841. She was b. Oct. 13, 1813. He has been town clerk and postmaster of National, Clayton Co., Iowa, for several years.
National, Clayton Co., Iowa.

1295. 1. MARY-JANE, b. Nov. 17, 1844, d. May, 13, 1847.
1296. 2. VIOLA-ANGELA, b. Feb. 25, 1848, d. March 26, 1848.
1297. 3. ABRAM-JARED-LAVURN, b. Feb. 20, 1854, d. May 13, 1855.

1298. JONATHAN,[6][687] (*Isaac,[5] Joseph,[4] Joseph,[3] Joseph,[2] John,[1]*) b. May 7, 1793; m. Elizabeth-Dickson Wheaton, Jan. 8, 1826. Their children are as follows: *Ellington, N. Y.*

1299. 1. PERRY,[1854] b. Nov. 3, 1826, m. Martha Ingersoll.
1300. 2. JULIA, b. Nov. 18, 1828, m. David-Silas Chandler, April 11, 1861.
1301. 3. MARY,[1857] b. Sept. 1, 1830, m. William Palmer.
1302. 4. ALBERT,|1861] b. May 23, 1834, m. Emma Nye.
1303. 5. KIRKLIN, b. April 8, 1838; was in 7th Comp. Sharp Shooters in war of rebellion.
1304. 6. SUSAN, b. Nov. 23, 1839.
1305. 7. BENJAMIN, b. Oct. 14, 1841; was in Comp. G, 11th Illinois Cavalry, in war of rebellion.

1306. LOIS,[6][691] (*Isaac,[5] Joseph,[4] Joseph,[3] Joseph,[2] John,[1]*) b. July 8, 1801, d. July 9, 1844; m. Augustus, son of William Ross of Burrillville, R. I., June 3, 1819. He was b. Dec. 31, 1791.
Preston, Chenango Co., N. Y.

1307. 1. POLLY, b. May 31, 1820, m. Blin Harris, M. D.
1308. 2. WILLIAM, b. June 15, 1822.
1309. 3. JAMES, b. Oct. 3, 1824, m. Frances-Euphemia Mason.
1310. 4. EARLY-JUDSON, b. Sept. 13, 1826, m. Sarah-Elizabeth Bliven.
1311. 5. ISAAC, b. Nov. 21, 1828.   *Preston, N. Y.*
1312. 6. ALMIRA, b. Jan. 28, 1831.   *Preston, N. Y.*
1313. 7. LYDIA, b. July 18, 1833, m. John Noyes.
1314. 8. LOIS, b, March 15, 1836.   *Preston, N. Y.*
1315. 9. AUGUSTUS, b. March 15, 1838.   *Preston, N. Y.*

1316. AARON,[6][690] (*Isaac,[5] Joseph,[4] Joseph,[3] Joseph,[2] John,[1]*) b. Aug. 31, 1799; m. Sarah Scranton of Pharsalia, N. Y., Oct. 10, 1827. She was b. 1808, and had the following children:
Vicksburg, Kalamazoo Co., Mich.

1317. 1. AARON-MASON, b. Feb. 2, 1830.
1318. 2. POLLY-DIANA, b. Sept. 17, 1831.
1319. 3. CHARLES-ISAAC, b. Dec. 7, 1833.

1320. 4. GEORGE-RILEY, b. April 7, 1836, d. Aug. 30, 1836.
1321. 5. GREELEY-RILEY, b. Sept. 5, 1838 ; in war of rebellion was in Comp. I,
First Michigan Cavalry, three years.
1322. 6. JOSEPH-ANDREW, b. Jan. 17, 1840 ; was in war of rebellion several
years, in Comp. H, 6th U. S. Infantry.
1323. 7. LOIS-JEANETTE, b. Jan. 18, 1845.
1324. 8. PRECILLA-ADELL, b. May 12, 1848.
1325. 9. JOSEPHINE-VICTORIA, b. Nov. 22, 1851.

1326. ELIZA,[6][694] (*Isaac,[5] Joseph,[4] Joseph,[3] Joseph,[2] John,[1]*) b.
June 24, 1807 ; m. Alfred, son of Edmund Goodrich of Boston, March
18, 1827. He was b. July 15, 1804.
Cherry Creek, Chenango Co., N. Y.

1327. 1. JAMES-ALFRED, b. April 22, 1830.
1328. 2. CLARINDA-CYBELIA, b. May 13, 1832.
1329. 3. ALBERT-EMERSON, b. June 22, 1834.
1330. 4. ELIZA-ANN, b. May 15, 1837, d. April 19, 1847.
1331. 5. ISAAC-SLATER, b. Aug. 14, 1839, d. July 4, 1841.
1332. 6. PAMELA-MELINDA, b. April 28, 1842.
1334. 7. HANNAH-MELISSA, b. Jan. 17, 1845.
1335. 8. JOSEPH-SLATER, b. May 17, 1847.

1336. BENJAMIN,[6][686] (*Isaac,[5] Joseph,[4] Joseph,[3] Joseph,[2] John,[1]*)
b. March 26, 1789 ; m. 1st, Maria, dau. of Abraham Johnson of York,
Canada West, Jan. 2, 1816. She was b. May 24, 1801; she d. Nov.
19, 1834. He m. 2d, Mary, dau. of Dougald McLean of Killian, Ar-
gyleshire, Scotland, March 7, 1836. She was b. May 16, 1808. He
was in the 3d Reg., York (Canada) Militia, at the battle of Little York,
now Toronto, April 17, 1813.   *Buttonville, Canada West.*

1337. 1. ISAAC, b. Dec. 9. 1816.
1338. 2. WILLIAM, b. Aug. 18, 1818.
1339. 3. SAMUEL, b. May 4, 1820.
1340. 4. LOUISA, b. April 22, 1822.
1341. 5. ALBERT, b. April 15, 1824.
1342. 6. LYDIA,[1872] b. Feb. 10, 1826, m. Henry Wagner.
1343. 7. ABRAHAM, b. March 27, 1828.
1344. 8. BELFORD, b. Aug. 30, 1830.   *Polo, Ogle Co., Illinois.*
1345. 9. MARY,[1867] b. Aug. 9, 1832, m. Rev. Daniel Appleford.
1346. 10. JANE, b. Oct. 9, 1834, d. April 29, 1835.
1347. 11. CATHARINE,[1870] b. Feb. 10, 1837, m. Samuel Green.
1348. 12. JONATHAN, b. Sept. 10, 1838.
1349. 13. BENJAMIN, b. May 26, 1840.
1350. 14. SARAH, b. Dec. 31, 1841.
1351. 15. JOSEPH, b. Dec. 31, 1843.
1352. 16. LOIS, b. Jan. 7, 1846.
1353. 17. LEWIS, b. April 26, 1848, d. May 31, 1849.

1354. JOSEPH,[6][693] (*Isaac,[5] Joseph,[4] Joseph,[3] Joseph,[2] John,[1]*) b.
Jan. 8, 1805, d. Sept. 23, 1857 ; m. Lura, dau. of Simeon Webster
of Chenango Co., N. Y., Aug. 9, 1829. She was b. Jan. 23, 1805, d.
June 21, 1860.   *Poland, Chautauque Co., N. Y.*

1355. 1. AUSTIN,[1887] b. July 28, 1830, m. Exana-Althea Smith.
1356. 2. BRADFORD, b. Feb. 13, 1835 ; in war of rebellion was in Comp. K, 49th
N. Y. Vols.
1357. 3. DEVILLO, b. Feb. 19, 1839.   *Jamestown, N. Y.*
1358. 4. BERNARD-PHILETUS, b. Nov. 9, 1843, d. July 31, 1863; was in Comp.
B, 12th Reg., N. Y. Vols., in war of rebellion.

1359. Job,[6][685] (*Isaac*,[5] *Joseph*,[4] *Joseph*,[3] *Joseph*,[2] *John*,[1]) b. April 24, 1789, d. Sept. 19, 1862; m. Phila, dau. of Joseph Beckwith of Butternuts, Otsego Co., N. Y., Sept. 20, 1818. She was b. Feb. 23, 1801. The first seven of their children were b. in Preston, the others in Smyrna, N. Y.   *Smyrna, Chenango Co., N. Y.*

1360. 1. Anson-Zenas, b. Aug. 4, 1819, d. Feb. 6, 1822.
1361. 2. Horatio-Farrel,[1895] b. Dec. 18, 1820, m. Sarah-Melinda Babcock.
1362. 3. Amanda-Melvina,[1897] b. Dec. 4, 1821, m. Morris-Niles Brown.
1363. 4. Eliza-Ann,[1904] b. July 3, 1823, m. Thomas Bavin.
1364. 5. Louisa-Arvilla,[1907] b. Nov. 12, 1824, m. James-Munroe Colwell.
1365. 6. Samantha, b. Aug. 7, 1827, d. Aug. 10, 1840.
1366. 7. Andrew-Barton,[1909] b. May 12, 1829, m. Sarah Boynton.
1367. 8. Mara-Ann,[1914] b. May 8, 1831, m. Henry Holley.
1368. 9. Isaac-Orlando,[1918] b. Nov. 12, 1833, m. Mary-Ann Howe.
1369. 10. Clarinda-Emerancy, b. March 3, 1835, d. Sept. 15, 1840.
1370. 11. Lucetta-Angeline,[1921] b. June 25, 1842, m. Henry-Ornan Bartlett.

1371. Daniel,[6][692] (*Isaac*,[5] *Joseph*,[4] *Joseph*,[3] *Joseph*,[2] *John*,[1]) b. May 17, 1803; m. Sarah, dau. of Levi Fletcher of Coleville, N. Y., Sept. 6, 1827. She was born June 3, 1811.
Mount Brydges, Caradoc, C. W.

1372. 1. Charles-Bullen, b. July 11, 1829, d. Aug. 24, 1848.
1373. 2. Joseph-Daniel,[1891] b. Sept. 22, 1830, m. Louisa Allen.
1374. 3. James-Nash,[1893] b. June 5, 1832, m. Eleanor-Ann Brown.
1375. 4. Levi-Fletcher,[1882] b. Aug. 17, 1833, d. March 28, 1857, m. Eliza-Ann Garner.
1376. 5. Major-Benjamin,[1884] b. Dec. 14, 1835, m. Elizabeth Bates.
1377. 6. Isaac, b. Aug. 26, 1837, m. Feb. 9, 1865, Sophia Kemp.
Grand Rapids, Mich.
1378. 7. Sophia-Eliza,[1889] b. May 4, 1839, m. James-Gordon Cassie.
1379. 8. Lucy, b. July 8, 1841, d. Sept. 22, 1844.
1380. 9. Henry-Runion, b. July 23, 1843.
1381. 10. Simeon, b. May 18, 1845.
1382. 11. Charles, b. April 5, 1847.
1383. 12. Nancy-Abigail, b. Nov. 5, 1849.

1384. Nelson,[6][716] (*Jonathan*,[5] *Joseph*,[4] *Joseph*,[3] *Joseph*,[2] *John*,[1]) b. Sept. 25, 1805; m. Emily, daughter of Ford Kitchel of Rockaway, Morris Co., N. J., April 29, 1835. He was fitted for college at the academies at Plattsburgh, Fairfield and Belleville, N. Y.; graduated at Union College in class of 1831; studied divinity at Auburn Theological Seminary; was principal of the academy at Painesville, Ohio, two years; was also for several years in charge of other academies and high schools; has been superintendent of public instruction for Sacramento Co., Cal.; wrote and published a series of articles on the public school system of California. He has devoted much time to land surveying, and the aggregate number of acres surveyed by him is probably not less than two or three hundred thousand; he published the "Guide across the Plains," with a description of the country from Missouri to California; he published another small volume, called the "Fruits of Mormonism," or "A Fair and Candid Statement of Facts illustrative of Mormon Principles, Mormon Policy and Mormon Character," compiled by N. Slafter, A. M. He has the following children:
Sacramento City, Cal.

1385. 1. Susan-Almira,[1877] b. Feb. 15, 1837, m. E.-H. Hall.
1386. 2. Nelson-Kitchel, b. Sept. 11, 1838, d. Oct. 11, 1863.

1387. 3. FRANCES-EMILY, b. May 20, 1841 ; m. March 12, 1861, D.-W. Gilwicks.
1388. 4. ADALINE, b. Jan. 7, 1843 ; m. July 28, 1864, I.-W. Shanklin.
Rochester, N. Y.
1389. 5. CHARLOTTE, b. Nov. 27, 1844.
1390. 6. IRVING, b. Dec. 22, 1846, d. March 22, 1848.
1391. 7. MARTIN-IRVING, b. Dec. 27, 1849, d. Aug. 29, 1850.
1392. 8. HENRIETTA, b. Oct. 11, 1851.

1393. GEORGE-KING,⁶[719] (*Jonathan,⁵ Joseph,⁴ Joseph,³ Joseph,²
John,¹*) b. March 16, 1812 ; m. Maria Loomis, widow, dau. of Winthrop
Whedon of Kinderhook, N. Y., March 21, 1846. She was b. Sept.
25, 1815. *Aurora, Kane Co., Ill.*

1394. 1. BENJAMIN-FRANKLIN, b. Aug. 25, 1847.
1395. 2. LUCIAN, b. April 20, 1848, d. May 4, 1848.

1396. MARCUS-TULLIUS-CICERO,⁶[738] (*Israel,⁵ Joseph,⁴ Joseph,³
Joseph,² John,¹*) b. July 28, 1809 ; m. Maria, dau. of Jeremiah Mickel
of Carlisle, Schoharie Co., N. Y., March 24, 1831. She was born Nov.
26, 1810. *Fulton, Whitesides Co., Ill.*

1397. 1. AMANDA-ANN, b. May 4, 1832, d. Dec. 11, 1854 ; m. Samuel Lent of
Fair Haven, Ill., and had Abraham-Marcus.
1398. 2 ISRAEL, b. Nov. 13, 1834. In the war of rebellion he was in Comp. B,
75th Illinois Reg. ; he lost his left leg in the battle of Perryville ; he m.
Minerva Mickel, Nov. 2, 1853. *Sterling, Ill.*
1399. 3. EMILY, b. Feb. 8, 1836; m. Sept. 30, 1857, Edward-S. Pearsall.
Fulton, Ill.
1400. 4. SUSANNAH-ISADORE, b. May 15, 1838, d. Oct. 30, 1840.
1401. 5. HENRY-LARKIN, b. April 6, 1840; m. Delia Hammond. In the war of
rebellion he was in Comp. F, 93 Illinois Reg. ; he was in the battle of
Champion Hills; he lost the middle finger of his left hand ; was promoted to orderly sergeant of artillery. *Polo, Ogle Co., Ill.*
1402. 6. GERTRUDE, b. Feb. 28, 1842 ; m. Elijah Rood, Nov. 8, 1859.
Fulton, Ill.
1403. 7. MARY-JANE, b. March 6, 1844 ; m. George-Washington Rary, March 2,
1862. *Fulton, Ill.*
1404. 8. ALBERT-BENJAMIN, b. June 15, 1846. In the war of rebellion he was in
Comp. D, 34 Illinois Reg. ; he was in the battle of Nashville.
1405. 9. WILLIAM-ORLANDO, b. April 29, 1849.
1406. 10. JEREMIAH, b. Feb. 13, 1853.

1407. NATHAN,⁶[740] (*Israel,⁵ Joseph,⁴ Joseph,³ Joseph,² John,¹*) b.
Nov. 27, 1813 ; m. Eve, dau. of Malcolm McFarland of Bennettsville,
N. Y., Feb. 25, 1836; she was b. May 3, 1815.
Bennettsville, Chenango Co., N. Y.

1408. 1. ADELINE, b. Nov. 27, 1836; m. Rufus-F. Wilbur; was in Comp. D,
15th N. Y. Veteran Cavalry ; has been missing since the battle of the
Wilderness.
1409. 2. SARAH-JANE, b. June 13, 1839 ; m. Henry-W. Hoyt, Dec. 29, 1864.
Otego, Otsego Co., N. Y.
1410. 3. MARTHA, b. July 26, 1841.
1411. 4. FRANCES-OPHELIA, b. June 2, 1844.
1412. 5. JAMES-POLK, b. July 5, 1847.
1413. 6. CHARLES-TRACEY, b. June 25, 1849, d. May 31, 1850.
1414. 7. GEORGE-WILLIAM, b. May 14, 1851.
1415. 8. ORVILLE-LEROY, b. Sept. 25, 1854.
1416. 9. ALICE-JENETTE, b. March 5, 1857.

1417. ALBERT,⁶[743] (*Israel,⁵ Joseph,⁴ Joseph,³ Joseph,² John,¹*) b.
Sept. 9, 1821, d. May 14, 1864; m. Rhoda-Jane, dau. of Martin
Richardson of Sterling, Whitesides Co., Illinois, Oct. 19, 1854. He

was in Comp. D, 34th N. Y. Reg., was killed at the battle of Resaca,
Ga.   *Sterling, Whitesides Co., Ill.*

1418. 1. CHARLOTTE, b. Oct. 4, 1857.

1419. CHARLOTTE,[745] (*Israel,[5] Joseph,[4] Joseph,[3] Joseph,[2] John,[1]*)
b. Nov. 27, 1827 ; m. Hiram-Birdsall, son of Salmon Fuller of North
Sandford, Broome Co., N. Y., June 8, 1856 ; she was b. March 6, 1830.
He enlisted, Sept., 1864, for one year, in Comp. H, 1st N. Y. Veteran
Cavalry.   *North Sandford, Broome Co., N. Y.*

1420. 1. LAURA-ALMEDA, b. April 4, 1858.
1421. 2. ALMON-GERALDUS, b. July 15, 1859.

1422. JOSEPH,[739] (*Israel,[5] Joseph,[4] Joseph,[3] Joseph,[2] John,[1]*) b.
Aug. 14, 1811, d. April 22, 1847 ; m. Sarah, dau. of Henry Sylvius of
Stroudsburgh, Monroe Co., Pa., Jan. 26, 1832.
                                    North Sandford, Broome Co., N. Y.

1423. 1. LYDIA, b. June 23, 1833 ; m. Wm.-Lakin Axtell, March 18, 1857.
1424. 2 ALMON, b. July 21, 1835, d. April 23, 1846.
1425. 3. LOUISA, b. Oct. 6, 1837 ; m. Seth Blood, March 22, 1855.
1426. 4. OSCAR-JOSEPH, b. May 28, 1840 ; m. Margaret-Roger Axtell, July 17,
         1864.
1427. 5. JULIA-ANN, b. June 5, 1842 ; m. David Gibbs ; he was in Comp. G,
         30th N. Y. Vols., in war of rebellion.

1428. AARON,[753] (*Silas,[5] Abial,[4] Joseph,[3] Joseph,[2] John,[1]*) b.
March 20, 1810 ; m. Lucy Carter, dau. of James Bailey of Preston,
Pa., Aug. 15, 1847.   *South Foster, R. I.*

1429. 1. ISAAC RANDALL, b. July 16, 1848.
1430. 2. LUCY-ANN, b. Oct. 7, 1850.
1431. 3. MARY-ELIZABETH, b. March 7, 1853.
1432. 4. SUSAN-ELMA, b. Aug. 14, 1855.
1433. 5. HANNAH-ADAMS, b. June 27, 1857.

1434. SILAS,[754] (*Silas,[5] Abial,[4] Joseph,[3] Joseph,[2] John,[1]*) b.
April 21, 1812, d. ; m. Susannah, dau. of William Boswell of Foster, R.
I., April 2, 1835. She was b. May 24, 1818. She m. 2d, Hezekiah
French, and had Ida-L. and Mittie-Eveline. *South Killingly, Ct.*

1435. 1. DANIEL-SILAS, b. Dec. 6, 1837.   *Greenville, Ct.*
1436. 2. MARY-ANN,[1926] b. July 25, 1839 ; m. Darius-Lester Anderson.
1437. 3. ALMIRA-MELISSA,[1928] b. Jan. 21, 1841 ; m. Ed.-Everett Littlejohn.
1438. 4. DEBORAH-ARMINDA, b. Feb. 25, 1843, d. Sept. 30, 1849.
1439. 5. SUSAN-EMMA, b. Jan. 25, 1845 ; m. June 23, 1866, Alberton-Hosea Sals-
         bury, and had (1.) Emma-Estella, b. April 9, 1867 ; (2.) Minnie, b. July
         11, 1868.   *South Killingly, Ct.*
1440. 6. ALBERT-HENRY, b. May 22, 1847, d. Aug. 9, 1864. In the war of re-
         bellion he entered Comp. H, 3d Rhode Island Cavalry, on the 15th of
         April, 1864 ; became ill, and died in New Orleans on the 9th of Aug.,
         1864.
1441. 7. WILLIAM-SPENCER, b. Sept. 22, 1848, d. Oct. 5, 1849.
       Their first child, Henry-Silas, b. Aug. 15, 1836, d. at birth.

1442. AHIJAH,[756] (*Silas,[5] Abial,[4] Joseph,[3] Joseph,[2] John,[1]*) b.
Feb. 22, 1817 ; m. 1st, Eliza Pray, March 5, 1843. He m. 2d, Lucretia-Ann Tucker, Sept. 7, 1846. She was born Aug. 16, 1821.
                                    South Foster, R. I.

1443. 1. ALBERT-ANTHONY, b. April 1845, d. Aug. 1845.
1444. 2. AMY, b. July 23, 1847, d. Aug. 26, 1847.

1445. 3. HULDA-MARIA, b. Oct. 12, 1849.
1446. 4. MARY-ANN, b. Sept. 27, 1854.
1447. 5. ELLEN-ANTOINETTE, b. March 9, 1860.

1448. GEORGE,[6][757] (*Silas*,[5] *Abial*,[4] *Joseph*,[3] *Joseph*,[2] *John*,[1]) b.
April 11, 1819; m. Chalcedana, dau. of Jesse Shippee of Foster, Aug.
6, 1854. *South Foster, R. I.*

1449. 1. SELINDA, b. Aug. 21, 1855.
1450. 2. FRANKLIN-PIERCE, b. Nov. 15, 1858.

1451. SELINDA,[6][759] (*Silas*,[5] *Abial*,[4] *Joseph*,[3] *Joseph*,[2] *John*,[1]) b.
Nov. 10, 1823; m. Atwell-Anthony, son of William Williams of Fos-
ter, R. I., April 17, 1842. He was b. Dec. 30, 1820.
North Foster, R. I.
1452. 1. PHEBE-SELINDA, b. Sept. 27, 1862.

1453. HARRIET-AMANDA,[6][762] (*Silas*,[5] *Abial*,[4] *Joseph*,[3] *Joseph*,[2]
John,[1]) b. April 14, 1842; m. Jabez Chase, July 28, 1860.
Killingly, Ct.
1454. 1. JABEZ-MANSFIELD, b. Sept. 6, 1862.

1455. MILTON,[6][786] (*Paul*,[5] *Silas*,[4] *Joseph*,[3] *Joseph*,[2] *John*,[1]) b.
March 1, 1813; m. Elizabeth, dau. of Peter Bathrick of Bronson,
Ohio, Jan. 28, 1838. She was b. April 23, 1814. *Norwalk, Ohio.*

1456. 1. ASHER, b. Aug. 12, 1839; m. Dec. 3, 1862, Martha-Adeline Keeler.
Norwalk, Ohio.
1457. 2. ELIZABETH,[1940] b. May 6, 1843, d. July 4, 1864; m. Edward-Gregory
Husted. *Norwalk, Ohio.*

1458. SARAH,[6][787] (*Paul*,[5] *Silas*,[4] *Joseph*,[3] *Joseph*,[2] *John*,[1]) b. Aug.
30, 1817; m. Gilkey Morton, April 30, 1836. He was b. May 8,
1814. *Monticello, Lewis Co., Mo.*

1459. 1. THEODORE, b. May 5, 1837, d. Dec. 21, 1837.
1460. 2. LOUISA-ANNA, b. Sept. 27, 1838, d. 1839.
1461. 3. LUCY-ADELINE, b. Dec. 31, 1842.
1462. 4. HELEN-MARIA, b. Feb. 11, 1850.
1463. 5. CORA-MINERVA, b. July 11, 1854.
1464. 6. WILLIAM-HAMILTON, b. Oct. 27, 1856.
1465. 7. FRANKLIN, b. Dec. 17, 1859.

1466. BEULAH,[6][792] (*Silas*,[5] *Silas*,[4] *Joseph*,[3] *Joseph*,[2] *John*,[1]) b. in
Killingly, Ct., July 6, 1800; m. Hosea, son of John Martin of Killingly,
Ct., May 31, 1817. He was b. May 10, 1791. Her children were all
born in Killingly, Ct. *South Killingly, Ct.*

1467. 1. MALORA-ANN, b. June 14, 1818, d. Sept. 24, 1819.
1468. 2. WILLIAM-DANIELSON, b. Dec. 2, 1819, m. Mary-Maria Harrington, and
had (1.) Ellen, (2.) Ira. *Sterling, Ct.*
1469. 3. EMILY, b. Nov. 17, 1822; m. Wheaton Salsbury, Dec. 22, 1849; he was
born Aug. 26, 1821. Their children were (1.) George-Leonard, b. July
6, 1846, m. Marilla-Janette Cole, Oct. 4, 1868; (2.) Alberton-Hosea,
b. June 16, 1848, m. Susan-Emma Slater, June 30, 1866; (3.) Almedia-
Maria, b. Nov. 27, 1850; (4.) Henry-Burkley, b. Feb. 4, 1853; (5.)
Everett-Wilson, b. March 28, 1855; (6.) Erving-Adelbert, b. Aug. 21,
1857; (7.) Hiram-Elwood, b. Dec. 23, 1860; (8.) Charlotte-Evelyn, b.
May 18, 1863; (9.) William-Harrison, b. March 5, 1866.
Rockland, R. I.
1470. 4. MARY-SELINDA, b. Nov. 10, 1824, m. Joshua Rood.
South Killingly, Ct.

1471. 5. JOHN, b. Feb. 11, 1827 ; m. Freelove-Marinda Taylor, and had (1.) Amos-
       Olney, (2.) Horace, (3.) Jason-John.   *South Killingly, Ct.*
1472. 6. SILAS-SLATER, b. April 8, 1829 ; m. Jane Carr, and had (1.) William-
       Hosea, (2.) Mary-Jane.   *West Killingly, Ct.*
1473. 7. SUSAN-SLATER, b. Aug. 1, 1831, m. Jeremiah Boswell.   *Pomfret, Ct.*
1474. 8. HAZAEL-BURGESS, b. July 21, 1833 ; m. Jane-Greene, and had (1.) Charles-
       Edward, (2.) William.   *South Killingly, Ct.*
1475. 9. BRAYTON-SLATER, b. Feb. 5, 1836, m. Ellen-Arnold.
                                                           South Killingly, Ct.
1476. 10. ELLEN-MARSILVA, b. Feb. 27, 1838 ; m. Elisha Anderson, and had (1.)
       Lillie.   *South Killingly, Ct.*
1477. 11. HENRY, b. April 26, 1841.   *South Killingly, Ct.*

1478. SUSAN,[6][793] (*Silas,[5] Silas,[4] Joseph,[3] Joseph,[2] John,[1]*) b. in
Foster, R. I., Aug. 30, 1802 ; m. Otis, son of William Bastow of Killingly, Ct., Nov. 3, 1824. He was b. Oct. 2, 1792. Her children were
all born in Killingly, Ct.   *East Killingly, Ct.*

1479. 1. SILAS, b. Oct. 9, 1825, d. Oct. 14, 1825.
1480. 2. JULIA-ANN, b. April 19, 1827 ; m. Daniel-Putnam Spencer, and had (1.)
       Daniel-Otis, b. June 3, 1854 ; (2.) Byron-Barstow, b. Oct. 20, 1855 ;
       (3.) Irving-Putnam, b. July 12, 1859.   *East Killingly, Ct.*
1481. 3. MARY-WADE, b. May 20, 1829 ; m. Cromwell-Dyer Chase (he was b.
       May 16, 1827) and had (1.) Charles-Henry, b. Feb. 2, 1855 ; (2.) Mary-
       Dyer, b. May 24, 1857 ; (3.) Susan-Mahala, b. June 20, 1859.
                                                           Killingly, Ct.
1482. 4. PATIENCE-MILLARD, b. Jan. 12, 1831 ; m. Albert-Webb Greenslitt (b.
       Dec. 21, 1827) and had (1.) Frederick-Albert, b. Oct. 16, 1850.
                                                           East Killingly, Ct.
1483. 5. HENRY-CLAY, b. June 30, 1834.
1484. 6. OTIS-ALMOND, b. Dec. 23, 1835 ; m. Harriet-Augusta Gleason (she was
       b. Sept. 26, 1830) and had (1.) Franklin-Otis, (2.) Charles-Atwell,
       (3.) Susan-Caroline.   *Thompson, Ct.*
1485. 7. CHAUNCY-FITZ-CLEVELAND, b. May 3, 1842.   *Killingly, Ct.*
1486. 8. LOUISA-ELLIOTT, b. March 13, 1844.   *Killingly, Ct.*
1487. 9. THOMAS-PIERCE, b. Nov. 12, 1847.   *Killingly, Ct.*

1488. THOMAS,[6][794] (*Silas,[5] Silas,[4] Joseph,[3] Joseph,[2] John,[1]*) b. in
Killingly, Ct., May 15, 1804 ; m. Polly, dau. of Dr. Isaac Stowell of
East Killingly, Ct. ; she was b. April, 1804, d. April 19, 1829 ; m. 2d,
Sarah-Ann, dau. of Samson Chase of Killingly, April 15, 1832. She
was b. Dec. 9, 1814.   *Plainfield, Ct.*

1489. 1. POLLY, b. in Killingly, Ct., April 8, 1829 ; m. George-Durfee, and had
       (1.) Thomas-Vespasian.   *Putnam, Ct.*
1490. 2. RUTH-FRANCES, b. in Killingly, Ct., May 12, 1836 ; m. Daniel-Josiah
       Phillips.   *Plainfield, Ct.*
1491. 3. WALLACE-LYMAN, b. Oct. 27, 1840 ; served in war of rebellion in
       Comp. K, 1st Conn. Cavalry, one year and ten months, and in Comp.
       G, 26th Conn. Vols., nearly eleven months.

1492. ALMEDA-GREENLEAF,[6][795] (*Silas,[5] Silas,[4] Joseph,[3] Joseph,[2]
John,[1]*) b. in Killingly, March 17, 1806 ; m. James, son of James
Babson of Coventry, R. I., Oct. 11, 1826. He was b. Aug. 18, 1803.
Her children were born, 1, 3, Coventry, R. I. ; 2, 6, 7, 10, 11, Kil-
lingly, Ct. ; 4, 5, Smithfield, R. I. ; 8, Thompson, Ct. ; 9, Woodstock,
Ct. ; 12, Webster, Mass.   *Pomfret, Ct.*

1493. 1. ERASTUS-WALCOTT, b. Oct. 3, 1827 ; m. Adeline, dau. of William Pray
       of Foster, R. I., July 5, 1848. He served in war of rebellion in Comp.
       A, 12th R. I. Vols., ten months.   *Providence, R. I.*

1494. 2. Juliette-Slater, b. Sept. 9, 1829, m. Charles Gardner, Aug. 6, 1863.
Providence, R. 1.
1495. 3. Mary-Jane, b. Dec. 12, 1831; m. George-Washington, son of Ezekiel Walker of Coventry, R. I., June 5, 1853, and had Flora-Edith, b. July 26, 1865, d. Feb. 8, 1867. *Webster, Mass.*
1496. 4. Elisha-James, b. Feb. 20, 1834; m. Mary-Ann, dau. of James Chadwick of England, and had
(1.) Emma-Frances, b. in Killingly, Ct., Jan. 25, 1858.
(2.) Mary-Lucilla, b. and d. Oct., 1859.
(3.) Ellsworth-Chadwick, b. in Pomfret, Ct., April 5, 1862. He served in war of rebellion in Comp. A, 6th Conn. Vols., three years.
Plainfield, Ct.
1497. 5. Isaac-Holden, b. Dec. 19, 1835; m. Adeline-Elizabeth, dau. of Thomas Bradford of Canterbury, Ct., May 7, 1861, and had
(1.) Ella-Maria, b. in Windham, Ct., Oct. 25, 1863.
(2.) Charles-Bradford, b. in Killingly, Ct., June 15, 1868. He served in war of rebellion in Comp. K, 18th Conn. Vols., 2 months, and was discharged for ill health. *Danielsonville, Ct.*
1498. 6. Almeda-Avilla, b. March 15, 1838, m. Raymond-Noah Colvin, June 20, 1865. *Daysville, R. 1.*
1499. 7. Harriet-Ellen, b. Aug. 11, 1839, d. Feb. 28, 1841.
1500. 8. George-May, b. May 30, 1841; m. Sarah Gage of Woodstock, May 30, 1863, and had (1) Jennie-Estella, b. in Hartford, Ct., June 4, 1865.
Willimantic, Ct.
1501. 9. Henry-Whitman, b. Oct. 9, 1843; m. Jeannette-Elizabeth, dau. of John Murray of Killingly, Aug. 9, 1862. He enlisted, Aug. 9, 1862, in Comp. K, 18th Conn. Vols., and was discharged July, 7, 1865 : he was taken prisoner at the battle of Winchester, Va.; was confined in "Libby" and "Belle Isle;" was paroled, returned home; had "typhoid" and "chills and fever;" returned to his Reg. after about a year's absence, and was in two engagements in the valley of the Shenandoah. *Southbridge, Mass.*
1502. 10. Ellen-Anzela, b. April 7, 1845, m. George-Dallas, son of Erastus Smith of Foster, R. I., Feb. 14, 1864. *Pomfret, Ct.*
1503. 11. Estella-Elizabeth, b. Sept. 13, 1848.
1504. 12. Charles-Edgar, b. Jan. 20, 1853, d. Nov. 16, 1853.

1505. Brayton,[6][796] (*Silas,[5] Silas,[4] Joseph,[3] Joseph,[2] John,[1]*) b. in Killingly, Ct., July 10, 1808; m. Patience, dau. of Charles Millard of Warwick, R. I., Oct. 26, 1828, who was b. Nov. 7, 1805; was Justice of the Peace, 1855, in Killingly. *East Killingly, Ct.*

1506. 1. Brayton, b. June 9, 1829, d. June 19, 1829.
1507. 2. Alpheus-Brayton,[1930] b. Nov. 26, 1832, m. Ruth Matthews.
1508. 3. Josephine-Maranda,[1933] b. Oct. 2, 1835, m. Daniel-Metcalf Horton.
1509. 4. Helen-Maria, b. Nov. 10, 1837.
1510. 5. Edward-Burgess,[1938] b. April 5, 1841, m. Isadore Preston.
1511. 6. William-Augustus, b. Sept. 3, 1842.
1512. 7. Susan-Burgess, b. May 12, 1846.

1513. Hazael-Burgess,[6][797] (*Silas,[5] Silas,[4] Joseph,[3] Joseph,[2] John,[1]*) b. in Killingly, Ct., May 6, 1810, d. Oct. 5, 1866; m. 1st, Phebe, dau. of Asa Howe of Monson, Mass., March 26, 1834; she was b. Sept. 21, 1812, d. March 19, 1843; m. 2d, Esther-Wallace, dau. of Andrew Paine of Foster, R. I., March 10, 1844; she was b. April 29, 1809, d. June 23, 1848; m. 3d, Mary, widow of Thomas Heywood and dau. of John-Levi Miller, April 9, 1850; she was b. Nov. 19, 1816, d. Oct. 15, 1854. He was ordained as Baptist minister at Saratoga, Winona Co., Minn., Sept. 23, 1856; preached there till

1860; afterward preached in Tuscumbia and in the north part of Alabama, and was preaching in Killingly, Ct., 1866.

East Killingly, Ct.

1514.   1. ASA-BURGESS, b. Oct. 3, 1837, d. Nov. 20, 1860.
1515.   2. ABIGAIL-MARCY, b. Nov. 12, 1841, d. Jan. 27, 1843.
1516.   3. WILLIAM-TURNER, b. Dec. 12, 1844, d. June 6, 1861.
1517.   4. EMMA-NEWELL, b. July 6, 1846, m. George-Washington Wood, Jan. 1, 1864.
1518.   5. BRAYTON-HAZAEL, b. May 26, 1848.

1519. MARY-ELIZA,[6][798] (*Silas,[5] Silas,[4] Joseph,[3] Joseph,[2] John,[1]*) b. in Pomfret, Ct., Jan. 26, 1812; m. Asa-King, son of Asa Howe of Monson, Mass., April 28, 1835. He was born Dec. 6, 1810. Their children were born in Monson, Mass.   *Monson, Mass.*

1520.   1. LESTER, b. Aug. 28, 1838.
1521.   2. HARRISON-TYLER, b. Nov. 17, 1840, m. Jennie Thorp of Easthampton, Mass.   *Hartford, Ct.*
1522.   3. MARY-LOUISA, b. May 2, 1854.

1523. OTIS,[6][799] (*Silas,[5] Silas,[4] Joseph,[3] Joseph,[2] John,[1]*) b. in Pomfret, Ct., April 11, 1814; m. Alfreda, dau. of Rufus Bowen of Gloucester, R. I., Jan. 1, 1835. She was b. Jan. 1, 1813. He was Capt. of the 4th Comp. Light Artillery, Conn. Militia, commissioned May 27, 1840; is a machinist and resides in   *Lawrence, Mass.*

1524. PHEBE-ANN,[6] [800] (*Silas,[5] Silas,[4] Joseph,[3] Joseph,[2] John,[1]*) b. in Killingly, Ct., Nov. 14, 1817; m. Joseph, son of Isaac Clark of Gloucester, R. I., April 5, 1835ı He was born Nov. 19, 1811.
Wales, Mass.

1524½. 1. PHEBE-JANE, b. Feb. 3, 1837, d. March 3, 1845.
1525.   2. AMY-ANN, b. Oct. 14, 1838; m. 1st, John-Smith Andrews, who d. March 23, 1862, leaving a son, John-Alvin, b. April 6, 1862; m. 2d, Oliver-Ainsworth, son of Silas Perry of Wales, Mass., Dec. 3, 1862; he was b. Sept. 17, 1819. They have a daughter, Annie-Emily, b. April 14, 1868.   *Wales, Mass.*
1525¼. 3. ELIZABETH-FRANCES, b. July 31, 1840, d. Aug. 15, 1842.
1525½. 4. MARY-ELIZABETH, b. Sept. 24, 1843, d. March 30, 1845.
1526.   5. MARY-JANE-ELIZABETH, b. July 31, 1846, m. Dec. 28, 1866, Sanford-Barton Clark.   *Wales, Mass.*
1527.   6. JOSEPH-BRAYTON, b. Oct. 19, 1847.   *Wales, Mass.*
1528.   7. EVERETT-EUGENE, b. April 2, 1850; m. Sept. 4, 1868, Hattie-A. Olds; she was b. March 28, 1850.
1529.   8. SILAS-FRANKLIN, b. July 17, 1852.
1530.   9. CHARLES-ARBA, b. Dec. 16, 1855.
1531. 10. EMMA-ADELAIDE, b. Feb. 17, 1859.

1532. CHARLOTTE-TIFFANY,[6][801] (*Silas,[5] Silas,[4] Joseph,[3] Joseph,[2] John,[1]*) b. in Killingly, Ct., May 12, 1819; m. James, son of Samuel Hyde of Brooklyn, Ct., Sept. 8, 1839. He was born Sept. 8, 1818. Their children were born, 1, 3, 4, 5, Killingly, Ct.; 2, Brooklyn, Ct.; 7, at Riverpoint, R. I.   *Abington, Ct.*

1533.   1. GILES-FRANCIS, b. Oct. 28, 1841, d. June 16, 1864. He enlisted May 12, 1862, in Comp. K, 21st Conn. Vols.; was wounded àt Drury's Bluff, May 16, 1864; of the two soldiers detailed to carry him off the field, one was killed and the other wounded; thus abandoned, he was taken prisoner and carried to Richmond, where he died.
1534.   2. FREEDUS-MERRILL, b. Jan. 5, 1843, d. May 19, 1843.
1535.   3. SAMUEL-WOODWORTH, b. May 18, 1846.

1536. 4. ALMARIA-SLATER, b. June 20, 1848, d. Oct. 26, 1865.
1537. 5. EMMA-ANN, b. Oct. 16, 1850, d. Sept. 21, 1865.
1538. 6. CHARLOTTE-AMANDA, b. Sept. 20, 1852.
1539. 7. JAMES-FREDERICK, b. March 29, 1857.

1540. ALMARIA,[6][802] (*Silas*,[5] *Silas*,[4] *Joseph*,[3] *Joseph*,[2] *John*,[1]) b. in Killingly, Ct., Sept. 3, 1821, d. Feb. 23, 1848; m. John-Colby, son of Augustus Steere of Burrillville, R. I., Dec. 28, 1838. He was b. March 2, 1817. *Webster, Mass.*

1541. 1. MARGARET-SOPHIA, b. in Killingly, Ct., Sept. 19, 1840; m. Andrew-Jackson Cogshall, Sept. 7, 1856, and had (1.) George, b. Nov. 20, 1860; (2.) Emma-Idella, b. Sept. 5, 1861; (3.) Etta-Viola.
1542. 2. MARQUIS-EUSTIS, b. in Palmer, Mass., Jan. 19, 1844; m. Julia Balcom, and had (1.) Lena-Viola, b. Feb. 9, 1865.   *Douglas, Mass.*
1543. 3. DWIGHT-FULLER, b. in Webster, Mass., Jan. 6, 1848.

1544. ARBA-COVEL,[6][803] (*Silas*,[5] *Silas*,[4] *Joseph*,[3] *Joseph*,[2] *John*,[1]) b. in Killingly, Ct., April 19, 1824; m. Lucy-Clark, dau. of Frederick Avery of Jewett City, Ct., Aug. 25, 1844. She was b. Oct. 20, 1825. He was representative of the town of Holyoke in the General Court of Massachusetts in 1855; deacon of 2d Baptist Church in Holyoke, from 1855 to 1860; master of " Mount Tom Lodge," &c.
Whitinsville, Mass.

1545. MARY-ELIZA,[6][809] (*Stephen*,[5] *Silas*,[4] *Joseph*,[3] *Joseph*,[2] *John*,[1]) b. May 21, 1812; m. Daniel-Franklin, son of Daniel Rawson of Webster, Mass., May 1, 1838. He was b. Oct. 4, 1819. Their children were all born in Webster, Mass. *Webster, Mass.*

1546. 1. JOHN-FRANKLIN, b. June 10, 1839. In Comp. G, 51st Mass. Vols., in war of rebellion.
1547. 2. IRA SLATER, d. July 15, 1845.
1548. 3. SARAH-ELIZABETH, b. May 31, 1847.
1549. 4. MARY-ELLEN, b. Jan. 1, 1850.
1550. 5. SAMUEL-EFFING, b. Jan. 18, 1854, d. Jan. 5, 1856.

1551. ESTHER-ANN,[6][810] (*Stephen*,[5] *Silas*,[4] *Joseph*,[3] *Joseph*,[2] *John*,[1]) b. Dec. 14, 1813; m. George-Washington, son of George Smith of Smithfield, R. I., Aug. 14, 1834. He was b. May 3, 1814. The eldest three children were b. in Slatersville, and the fourth in Woonsocket, R. I. *Woonsocket, R. I.*

1552. 1. GEORGE-WASHINGTON, b. Aug. 15, 1835; m. May 1, 1854, Caroline-Augusta Shearman, and had Stephen-Slater, b. Jan. 11, 1855.
1553. 2. HERBERT-SLATER, b. Nov. 18, 1841; m. July 19, 1863, Nellie Thorndike. *Woonsocket, R. I.*
1554. 3. WILLIAM-DEFOREST, b Aug. 16, 1849.
1555. 4. EDWIN-ALDEN-GROSVENOR, b. Aug. 25, 1861.

1556. STEPHEN,[6][811] (*Stephen*,[5] *Silas*,[4] *Joseph*,[3] *Joseph*,[2] *John*,[1]) b. Aug. 17, 1817; m. Sally-Blake, dau. of Capt. James Carrol of Smithfield, R. I., Nov. 28, 1839. She was b. May 1, 1816. He commenced the study of medicine in 1852 with Dr. Metcalf Marsh of Slatersville; began to practice in 1858 in Slatersville; removed to Whitinsville, Jan., 1864. In Nov., 1865, commenced the practice at Glendale, R. I., his present residence. *Slatersville, R. I.*

1557. 1. JAMES-STUART, b. in Slatersville, R. I., April 23, 1841. In war of rebellion he enlisted in Comp. I, 7th R. I. Vols., Aug. 13, 1862; discharged Oct. 25, 1862, for disability. He enlisted in U. S. Veteran

8

Reserve Corps, Aug., 1864, was appointed corporal, served one year and was discharged for disability. He was commissioned 2d Lieut. of 2d R. I. Veteran Vols., but was not able to procure a discharge from the U. S. V. R. Corps until the regiment was out of service. He was assistant postmaster at Slatersville, 1857, '8, '9, and was a recruiting officer in R. I., 1862. Librarian of the Public Library at Milford, 1868.
Milford, Mass.

1558.   2. EMMA-LAWTON, b. in Whitinsville, Mass., Aug. 4, 1850, d. Oct. 5, 1851.
1559.   3. EMMA-LAWTON, b. in Slatersville, R. I., Jan. 14, 1856.

1560. SARAH-FANNY,[6][812] (*Stephen,*[5] *Silas,*[4] *Joseph,*[3] *Joseph,*[2] *John,*[1]) b. Sept. 2, 1820, d. May 24, 1860; m. George, son of William Dirk of Smithfield, R. I., May 1, 1845. Her children were born where she now resides.   *Slatersville, R. I.*

1561.   1. SARAH-WILLIAMS, b. Aug. 26, 1846.
1562.   2. FRANCES-VERNON, b. Jan. 12, 1853.

1563. HENRY-PELEG,[6][813] (*Stephen,*[5] *Silas,*[4] *Joseph,*[3] *Joseph,*[2] *John,*[1]) b. Dec. 26, 1822; m. Emily, dau. of George Carpenter of Uxbridge, Mass., Jan. 25, 1855. She was born Dec. 16, 1823. His children were born at Uxbridge.   *Uxbridge, Mass.*

1564.   1. EMILY-MARIA, b. June 15, 1859.
1565.   2. ALICE-TAFT, b. Dec. 31, 1861.

1566. RHODA-ANN-WINSOR,[6][814] (*Stephen,*[5] *Silas,*[4] *Joseph,*[3] *Joseph,*[2] *John,*[1]) b. April 18, 1825; m. John-Learned, son of Thurlow Stimpson of Leicester, July 31, 1845. He was b. April 8, 1824. Their children were born in Slatersville.   *Slatersville, R. I.*

1567.   1. MARY-ELIZABETH, b. April 8, 1847.
1568.   2. ELLA-SLATER, b. Jan. 6, 1854.

1569. WAKEMAN-RICE,[6][832]   (*John,*[5] *Silas,*[4] *Joseph,*[3] *Joseph,*[2] *John,*[1]) b. Feb. 21, 1815; m. Sarah-Ann, dau. of Jacob Probasco of Sherman, Ohio, Jan. 24, 1839. She was b. Feb. 22, 1823.
Norwich, Ohio.

1570.   1. ZALMON-BAILEY, b. Aug. 20, 1843.
1571.   2. ALVILDA-GEORGIANA, b. Sept. 21, 1845, m. Clinton Ashley.
1572.   3. LEWIS-CLIFFORD, b. Sept. 27, 1856.

1573. CYNTHIA,[6][833] (*John,*[5] *Silas,*[4] *Joseph,*[3] *Joseph,*[2] *John,*[1]) b. March 21, 1819; m. Ira, son of Noah Wood of Pittsfield, N. Y., May 8, 1836. He was born Jan. 1, 1804.   *Havanna, Ohio.*

1574.   1. DAVID-AMES, b. June 13, 1837.
1575.   2. LUCINA-AUGUSTA, b. July 19, 1839, d. July 26, 1847.
1575½. 3. FRANKLIN, b. Oct. 6, 1841; in Comp. I, 19th Ohio, sergeant from Aug. 12, 1862, to June 9, 1865, in war of rebellion.
1576.   4. CYNTHIA-JANE, b. March 20, 1844.
1577.   5. WILLIAM-TURNER, b. Jan. 9, 1846, d. June 28, 1850.
1578.   6. EUGENIA-ZITELLA, b. July 20, 1850.
1579.   7. MARY, b. Sept. 6, 1853, d. Sept. 6, 1853.
1580.   8 CAROLINE-LEVANTINE, b. Oct. 6, 1858.

1581. BEULAH,[6][837] (*John,*[5] *Silas,*[4] *Joseph,*[3] *Joseph,*[2] *John,*[1]) m. James-Gardiner, son of John Mead of Greenwich, Ohio. He was born March 11, 1819,   *New London, Ohio.*

1582.   1. JAMES, b. Nov. 21, 1853, d. Nov. 21, 1853.

1583. Almira,[6][827] (*John*,[5] *Silas*,[4] *Joseph*,[3] *Joseph*,[2] *John*,[1]) b. Dec.
3, 1806; m. 1st, James, son of John Murry of Ireland, March 19,
1824; he was b. March 31, 1800, d. Sept. 15, 1840; m. 2d, Jonas
Rischel, b. Feb. 1, 1786, d. 1865.   *Sherman, Ohio.*

1584. 1. John, b. Jan 31, 1825; m. Feb. 1, 1849, Amanda-Malvina, dau. of
        Richard Allison of Leonidas, Mich.; she was b. May 31, 1831; res. New
        Buffalo, Mich. Their children are,—
        (1.) Cecelia, b. Jan. 15, 1850.
        (2.) Cordelius, b. Jan. 16, 1853, d. Oct. 20, 1854.
        (3.) Viola-May, b. May 22, 1860.
        (4.) Ginevra-Amanda, b. Dec. 15, 1863.
1585. 2. Naomi, b. Nov. 26, 1826; m. Josiah-Dean, son of George Gallup of
        Northmoreland, Pa., Feb. 5, 1843; res. Clay, O. He was b. Nov. 5,
        1810. Their children are,—
        (1.) Parmenas-Lewis, b. June 28, 1845, d. Oct. 9, 1852.
        (2.) Dorlesca-Narcissa, b. May 12, 1847; d. March 22, 1868; m. June
        20, 1862, Obadiah, son of John Craiglow of Clay, O.; in war of
        rebellion he enlisted Sept. 13, 1861, discharged July 2, 1862.
        They had Charles-Sylvester, b. June 24, 1863, and Dorlesca-
        Malvina, b. Nov. 19, 1867.
        (3.) Electa-Almira, b. Aug. 7, 1850.
        (4.) James-Murry, b. Sept. 3, 1853.
        (5.) George-Benadan, b. April 12, 1856.
        (6.) Luella-Medora, b. July 1, 1858.
        (7.) Josiah-Dean, b. June 30, 1863; (8.) Mary-Cordelia, b. March
        23, 1868.
1586. 3. Nancy, b. Sept. 23, 1829; m. William-Albert, son of Josiah Holbrook of
        Townsend, O., Aug. 19, 1849. He was b. March 12, 1823; enlisted in
        war of rebellion Sept. 3, 1861, in Comp. A, 3d Mich. Cavalry, 4th Ser-
        geant, discharged, Aug. 25, 1862; res. Clay, O. Their children are,—
        (1.) Luella-Almira, b. June 10, 1850, d. Aug. 29, 1857; (2.) Naomi-
        Medora, b. Nov. 22, 1856; (3.) Cynthia-Jane, b. Oct 9, 1865.
1587. 4. James, b. Jan. 16, 1832; m. Mary-Cordelia, dau. of Lemuel Youngs of
        Reed, O., Dec. 23, 1855. She was b. Feb. 2, 1830.   *Sherman, Ohio.*
1588. 5. Eleazer-Arnold, b. July 12, 1837, d. April 28, 1865; m. Orra-Adelia,
        dau. of Russell Owen of Lyme, O., Oct. 11, 1861. She was b. Oct. 12,
        1840, d. Dec. 21, 1862; res. Sherman, Ohio.

1589. Jane-Lucretia,[6][835] (*John*,[5] *Silas*,[4] *Joseph*,[3] *Joseph*,[2]
John,[1]) b. Dec. 25, 1821; m. Otis, son of Hosea Shippee of Springfield,
Ind., Oct. 5, 1838. He was b. May 12, 1814.   *Springfield, Ind.*

1590. 1. Mary-Jane, b. Sept. 4, 1840.
1591. 2. Almira, b. March 22, 1842; m. Albert-Wright Ballou; he enlisted in
        Comp. B, 73d Ind. Vols., March 21, 1862, discharged May 13, 1863;
        drafted, and served in Comp. I, 23d Reg., from Sept. 21, 1864, to May
        30, 1865.
1592. 3. Luryntha-Ann, b. April 25, 1847.
1593. 4. Beulah-Elvira, b. Oct. 31, 1850.
1594. 5. Lucina-Augusta, b. Oct. 31, 1853, d. April 26, 1860.
1595. 6. Henrietta, b. March 9, 1857.
1596. 7. Hiram, b. March 9, 1857.

1597. Abraham,[6][836] (*John*,[5] *Silas*,[4] *Joseph*,[3] *Joseph*,[2] *John*,[1]) b.
Aug. 28, 1824; m. Esther-Ann, dau. of Stephen Turwillager of Springfield, Ind., Dec. 25, 1843. She was b. May 2, 1820. *Springfield, Ind.*

1598. 1. George-Washington, b. June 9, 1845; enlisted in Comp. B, 123 Ohio,
        July, 1862, served three years.
1599. 2. Delos-Nelson, b. Feb. 20, 1847; enlisted March, 1862, in Comp. B,
        128 Ind., served three years.
1600. 3. Wakeman-Rice, b. Feb. 22, 1852.
1601. 4. Charles-Otis, b. Dec. 29, 1860.

1602. SILAS,[6][838] (*John*,[5] *Silas*,[4] *Joseph*,[3] *Joseph*,[2] *John*,[1]) b. Oct. 20, 1827; m. Julia-Minerva, dau. of Edward St. John of Greenwich, O., May 18, 1856. She was b. Dec. 7, 1824. *New Buffalo, Mich.*

1603. 1. JEANETTE, b. June 29, 1857.
1604. 2. IRA-CREVOLA, b. Dec. 30, 1858.
1605. 3. GEORGE-ARNOLD, b. Feb. 18, 1861, d. Sept. 27, 1862.

1606. GEORGE-WASHINGTON,[6][839] (*John*,[5] *Silas*,[4] *Joseph*,[3] *Joseph*,[2] *John*,[1]) b. Dec. 28, 1829; m. Harriet-Ann, dau. of William Turwillager of Scipio, N. Y., Jan. 4, 1851. She was b. Dec. 10, 1827. *New Buffalo, Mich.*

1607. 1. HOSEA-SHIPPEE, b. July 27, 1855.

1608. DAVID-AMES,[6][834] (*John*,[5] *Silas*,[4] *Joseph*,[3] *Joseph*,[2] *John*,[1]) b. Aug. 21, 1818; m. Adaline, dau. of Oliver Shippee of Springfield, Indiana, Dec. 13, 1838. She was b. March 7, 1821. *Springfield, Ohio.*

1609. 1. ELIZABETH-NAOMI,[1943] b. Sept. 28, 1842; m. Martin-Van-Buren Stites.
1610. 2. JOHN-HENRY, b. June 24, 1845; in war of rebellion he was in Comp. B, 128 Indiana Vols.; enlisted Dec. 25, 1863, discharged Oct. 9, 1865.
1611. 3. IRA-CREVOLA, b. Sept. 23, 1850, d. Sept. 14, 1856.
1612. 4. RICHARD-THOMAS-CUMINS, b. June 21, 1853.
1613. 5. DAVID, b. Dec. 31, 1858.
1614. 6. JOSEPHUS-DAVIS, b. May 28, 1860.

1615. JOHN,[6][829] (*John*,[5] *Silas*,[4] *Joseph*,[3] *Joseph*[2] *John*,[1]) b. Feb. 9, 1810; m. 1st, Harriet, dau. of Jonathan Butler of Fitchville, Ohio, March 20, 1840; she was b. Dec. 28, 1813, d. Jan. 28, 1841; m. 2d, Mary-Ann, dau. of William Everngin of North Fairfield, Ohio, Nov. 20, 1842; she was b. March 21, 1825, d. Nov. 25, 1855; m. 3d, Isabella-Parker, dau. of Thomas Crow of Chatham, U. C., Aug. 9, 1856; she was b. May 22, 1822. He enlisted in Comp. B, 123 Ohio Vols., Aug. 18, 1862, discharged June 30, 1865. *North Fairfield, Ohio.*

1616. 1. HARRIET,[1948] b. Feb. 14, 1843, m. Samuel Moore.
1617. 2. WILLIAM-AMES, b. Aug. 15, 1844; he enlisted in war of rebellion in Comp. B, 123d Ohio Vols., Aug. 18, 1862, discharged June 12, 1865.
1619. 3. SILAS, b. June 9, 1846, d. Oct. 31, 1848.
1620. 4. JEANETTE, b. June 2, 1848, d Sept. 25, 1851.
1621. 5. RICHARD-THOMAS, b. Aug. 17, 1857.
1622. 6. FRANKLIN-JOHN, b. Jan. 6, 1860.

1623. ALZADA,[6][828] (*John*,[5] *Silas*,[4] *Joseph*,[3] *Joseph*,[2] *John*,[1]) b. Jan. 25, 1808; m. Richard, son of John Commins of Livingston, N. Y., March 24, 1842; he was b. May 14, 1806, d. Sept. 16, 1861; m. 2d, Frederick, son of Christopher Halcoe of Germany, July 14, 1863. He was b. Aug. 15, 1815. *New Buffalo, Mich.*

1624. ABIGAIL-CAROLINE,[6][831] (*John*,[5] *Silas*,[4] *Joseph*,[3] *Joseph*,[2] *John*,[1]) b. Feb. 13, 1814; m. Hosea, son of Hosea Shippee of Springfield, Ind., Oct. 4, 1838. He was b. June 2, 1806. *Springfield, Ind.*

1625. ALVIRA,[6][841] (Joseph,[5] Silas,[4] Joseph,[3] Joseph,[2] John,[1]) b. March 9, 1823 ; m. Alvin, son of William Bates of Edinburgh, Saratoga Co., N. Y., Oct. 12, 1848. He died Sept. 19, 1862.
Lapeer, Lapeer Co., Mich.

1626. 1. WILLIAM-ARNOLD, b. Aug. 24, 1851 ; he enlisted, Jan., 1867, in Comp. G, 4th U. S. Light Artillery.
1627. 2. CATHARINE-ELIZA, b. April 20, 1853.
1628. 3. EMMARANCY, b. Dec. 16, 1854.
1629. 4. RHODA-ARMINDA, ⎫
1630. 5. ROBY-CORINDA, ⎭ b. Oct. 1, 1857.
1631. 6. PHEBE-JANE, b. Jan. 21, 1859, d. Aug. 10, 1861.

1632. JOSEPH-WILLIAM,[6][843] (Joseph,[5] Silas,[4] Joseph,[3] Joseph,[2] John,[1]) b. Feb. 11, 1825 ; m. Mary-Ann, dau. of Stephen Fedder of Clifton Park, Saratoga Co., N. Y., March 30, 1844. She was b. June 13, 1826. He enlisted in Comp. F, 8th Mich. Cavalry, April 8, 1865, discharged Oct. 8, 1865. *Lapeer, Lapeer Co., Mich.*

1633. 1. CATHARINE-MARIA, b. June 24, 1845, d. March 17, 1846.
1634. 2. PLINY-GURNSEY, b. Sept. 13, 1846.
1635. 3. CYNTHIA-ELIZA, b. April 19, 1848.
1636. 4. STEPHEN, b. March 23, 1850.
1637. 5. JOHN-GERRET, b. Sept. 16, 1851.
1638. 6. VITIA, b. Dec. 24, 1854.
1639. 7. SARAH-JANE. b. Feb. 10, 1856.
1640. 8. JEANETTE, b. June 15, 1860.

1641. SILAS,[6][846] (Joseph,[5] Silas,[4] Joseph,[3] Joseph,[2] John,[1]) b. May 30, 1831 ; m. Amanda, dau. of Barnabas Terry of Pontiac, Mich., March 17, 1853. She was b. May 9, 1836. *Lockport, N. Y.*

1642. 1. GEORGE, b. Sept. 7, 1854.
1643. 2. ISAAC, b. March 31, 1857.
1644. 3. CHARLES, b. Feb. 17, 1859.

1645. HELEN,[6] [849] (Joseph,[5] Silas,[4] Joseph,[3] Joseph,[2] John,[1]) b. March 19. 1840, d. Oct. 4, 1866; m. William-Henry, son of William Duncan of Pownal, Vt., Oct. 4, 1856. He was b. May 9, 1827.
Lapeer, Mich.

1646. 1. AMBROSE-JAMES, b. Nov. 26, 1857, d. Dec. 19, 1857.
1647. 2. EMMARETTA-CORDELIA, b. Jan. 3, 1859.
1648. 3. CATHARINE-VANDECAR, b. March 25, 1861.
1649. 4. CHARLES-HENRY, b. May 5, 1863.
1650. 5. MINNA-AMANDA, b. June 19, 1865.

1651. CHAUNCEY,[6][855] (Joseph,[5] John,[4] Joseph,[3] Joseph,[2] John,[1]) b. May 2, 1795 ; m. Margaret, dau. of James Kenedy, Jan. 22, 1822. She was b. Dec. 21, 1797. *Upper Jay, Essex Co., N. Y.*

1652. 1. DAVID,[1952] b. Feb. 8, 1823, m. Catharine Goucher.
1653. 2. ELIZA,[1967] b. Dec. 13, 1824, m. Edmund-Pierpont Aiken.
1654. 3. SARAH-ANN, b. Jan. 22, 1827 ; m. Alvanus-Kilburn, son of Benjamin Whitman of Upper Jay, N. Y., Feb. 9, 1854 ; he was b. Dec. 9, 1825.
Lewis Centre, N. Y.
1655. 4. MELISSA, b. Dec. 29, 1828, d. Nov. 7, 1834.
1656. 5. NAPOLEON-BONAPARTE,[1963] b. Jan. 13, 1830, m. Mary Palmer.
1657. 6. PAMELA-ERMINA,[1960] b. Dec. 21, 1832, m. Charles-Michael Wells.
1658. 7. JOSEPH, b. July 25, 1834, d. Nov. 4, 1864 at Morganzia, La., in U. S. service, having enlisted Dec., 1863, in 2d New York Veteran Cavalry.
1659. 8. MINERVA, b. July 29, 1836, d. Oct. 5, 1838.
1660. 9. HELEN-MARY, b. Aug. 15, 1839.

1661. ABIGAIL,[6][856] (*Joseph,*[5] *John,*[4] *Joseph,*[3] *Joseph,*[2] *John,*[1]) b. June 10, 1797; m. Eli-Beckwith, son of Eli Hull of Keene, N. Y., Sept. 1818, and had the following children:

1662.   1. CHARLOTTE-DIADEMIA, b. Dec. 17, 1821; m. William-Smith, and had (1.) Servilla-Clara, (2.) Leverett-Card, (3.) Allen-Munroe, (4.) Julia, (5.) Charles, (6.) Bianca-Ignisa.   *Ashford, Wisconsin.*
1663.   2. ELI, b. July 7, 1823, d. March 7, 1854; m. Leonora-Ann Glines, and had (1.) Ella-Melissa (2.) Juan-Solonois, (3) Alice.   *Auburn, Wis.*
1664.   3. SALLY, b. March 7, 1824; m. Eleazer-Howe Glines, and had (1.) Araminta-Ann, (2.) Benjamin-Beckwith, in Comp. H, 32 Wis. Vols., (3.) Lucy-Marion, (4.) Laura-Luella, (5.) Eugene-Howard, was in Comp. B, 4th Wis. Cavalry, (6.) Merton, (7.) Maurice, (8.) Martin-Eli, (9.) Millard.   *Ashford, Wis.*
1665.   4. ALDEN, b. March 16, 1826; m. 1st, Lucy-Ann Nichols, 2d, Marietta Crownhart, and had by her (1.) Orson-Fillmore, (2.) Chloe-Arabella.   *Ashford, Wis.*
1666.   5. HARRIET, b. April 6, 1830; m. Ransom-Heminway, and had (1.) Florence-Angelia, (2.) Milton, (3.) Edith, (4.) Ervan.   *Ashford, Wis.*
1667.   6. JOSEPH-SLATER, b. April 1, 1832; m. 1st, Lucretia-Armeda Martin, and had (1.) Effie-Abigail; 2d, m. Sarah-Ann Martin, and had (2.) Viola-Armeda, (3.) Eleanor-Ann.   *Ashford, Wis.*
1668.   7. LYMAN, b. April 26, 1834; m. Caroline-Leahy, and had (1.) Minnie-Jane, (2.) Mabel-Caroline.   *Fond du Lac, Wis.*
1669.   8. FANNY-ARLETTE, b. May 11, 1838; m. George-Washington Chapman, and had (1.) Leon-Willis, (2.) Lester-Wilbur, (3.) Lewis-Walter.
                                                                Milo, Ohio.
1670.   9. MARTIN-BECKWITH, b. May 30, 1841; m. Irene Parsons; in war of rebellion he was in Comp. E, 6th Wis. Vols.   *Ashford, Wis.*

1671. LYMAN,[6][858] (*Joseph,*[5] *John,*[4] *Joseph,*[3] *Joseph,*[2] *John,*[1]) b. March 15, 1802; m. 1st, Mary, dau. of John Hamilton of Elizabethtown, N. Y., April 9, 1826; she was b. Dec., 1804, d. May 16, 1833; m. 2d, Sarah, dau. of Caleb Ingals of Keene, N. Y., Jan. 16, 1842; she was b. April 16, 1807.   *Wilmington, Essex Co., N. Y.*

1672.   1. HARRIET, b. Aug. 4, 1827, m. Robert-Bullard Gilmore, Nov. 17, 1847.
1673.   2. ERMINA, b. Dec. 24, ——, d. July, 1833.
1674.   3. LYMAN, b. May 10 1833, d. Aug., 1833.

1675. DEWITT-CLINTON,[6][862] (*Joseph,*[5] *John,*[4] *Joseph,*[3] *Joseph,*[2] *John,*[1]) b. July 16, 1812; m. Roxa, dau. of John Thomas of Halifax, Vt., Feb. 17, 1840. She was b. July 19, 1814.
                                                Adams Centre, Jeff. Co., N. Y.

1676.   1. WILLIAM-HENRY, b. April 3, 1841; in war of rebellion was in 2d N. Y. Artillery, Comp. H.
1677.   2. JOHN-DUNN, b. March 9, 1842, d. Feb. 26, 1846.
1678.   3. LUCY-DEBORAH, b. Nov. 19, 1843, d. Feb. 21, 1844.
1679.   4. LYDIA-MARIANA, b. Sept. 27, 1845.
1680.   5. CHESTER-GILBERT, b. Oct. 5, 1849.
1681.   6. ROWLAND-THOMAS, b. Dec. 12, 1853.
1682.   7. CHARLES-EDGAR, b. April 25, 1856, d. May 23, 1856.
1683.   8. IDA-ELLA, b. Jan. 22, 1858.

1684. GEORGE-WASHINGTON,[6][861] (*Joseph,*[5] *John,*[4] *Joseph,*[3] *Joseph,*[2] *John,*[1]) b. June 15, 1810; m. 1st, Harriet Trumbull, Jan., 1832; 2d, Candace-Arabella Temple, Nov. 11, 1840; she was b. March 9,

1816. He has been a Methodist preacher many years, and is now, 1865, located at   Coloma, Waushara Co., Wisconsin.

1685. 1. EDGAR, b. Sept. 23, 1832, m. Alvira Randall.
1686. 2. EGBERT, b. Nov. 14, 1833.
1687. 3. ALMEDA-ESTHER, b. Oct. 13, 1836, m. William Brown.
1688. 4. HARRIET-JEANETTE, b. Aug. 19, 1842.
1689. 5. ABBOTT-HARWOOD, b. Feb. 27, 1857.

1690. JOHN-MADISON,[6][903] (*John,[5] John,[4] Jo! eph,[3] Joseph,[2] John,[1]*) b. April 22, 1811; m. Wealthy, dau. of Abel Wilder, April 22, 1841. She was b. Sept. 1, 1816. He was a major in the militia.
                                                                         Granville, Ohio.
1691. 1. JOHN-FRANKLIN, b. May 17, 1842, d. Jan. 12, 1843.
1692. 2. FRANKLIN-AUGUSTUS, b. Nov. 6, 1843; he is now (1869) an undergraduate of " Denison University," Granville, Licking Co., Ohio, of class of 1871.

1693. MARY-MARIA,[6][907] (*John,[5] John,[4] Joseph,[3] Joseph,[2] John,[1]*) b. April 23, 1824, d. May 30, 1851; m. John, son of Thomas-Murphy of Waterloo, Iowa, Nov. 11, 1849.   *Waterloo, Iowa.*

1694. 1. ALICE-MARIA, b. May 15, 1851.

1695. HARRIET-CAROLINE,[6][904] (*John,[5] John,[4] Joseph,[3] Joseph,[2] John,[1]*) b. Dec. 22, 1812; m. Admiral-Nelson, son of Jeremiah Webb of Greenwich, N. Y., Nov. 2, 1830. He was b. Dec. 27, 1808. Her eldest two children were b. in Bainbridge, N. Y., the others in Chardon, Ohio.   *Chardon, Ohio.*

1696. 1. JOHN-SLATER, b. May 31, 1831.
1697. 2. STEPHEN-JAY, b. Dec. 25, 1832, d. Feb. 11, 1839.
1698. 3. JERRIE-CHUSSION, b. May 3, 1835; m. Alzina-Marancie Warriner, May 2, 1861, and had (1.) Addison-Emmet-Verner, b. March 11, 1862, (2.) Grace-Angusta, b. Aug. 8, 1866.   *Claridon, Ohio.*
1699. 4. HARRIET-LOUISA, b. Oct. 29, 1837, d. Oct. 13, 1859.
1700. 5. HERMAN-JAY, b. Jan. 9, 1840; m. Henrietta-Matilda Westcott, June 3, 1860, and had (1.) Caroline-Duella, b. June 10, 1861, (2.) Theron-Edward, b. Feb. 2, 1863, (3.) daughter.   *Chardon, Ohio.*
1701. 6. SARAH-AUGUSTA, b. Oct. 24, 1841; m. Pembroke-Mortimer Cowles, Aug. 30, 1868. He served as a private in Comp. F, 19th Ohio Vols. Militia, from April 20, 1861, three months; 3d color-sergeant in 42 Ohio Vols., from Sept. 24, 1861, three years and one month; commissioned 1st Lieut. in Comp. A, 196 Ohio Vols., from Feb. 7th, ten months; in all four years and one month.   *Chardon, Ohio.*

1702. DELIA-LISCOMB,[6][920] (*Ira,[5] John,[4] Joseph,[3] Joseph,[2] John,[1]*) b. Jan. 23, 1811, d. Oct. 15, 1842; m. the Rev. Sherman-Bond, son of Norman Canfield of Chardon, Ohio, Nov. 3, 1836. He was b. Dec. 25, 1810. He was educated by a partial course at Yale College, New Haven; spent one year in study of the law, then studied theology; was or :ained to the ministry of the Presbyterian Church in May, 1837; was settled in Bainbridge, Ohio, two years; in Ohio city, from 1839 to June, 1844; was pastor of the 2d Presbyterian Church in Cleveland, Ohio, about ten years. On May 1, 1854, became pastor of the first Presbyterian Church in Syracuse, N. Y., and is now (1865) in the same charge. The honorary degree of A. M., was early conferred upon him by the Western Reserve College, and the degree of D. D was conferred upon him by Hamilton College in 1857. He published a sermon on the "American Crisis," delivered on the day of the National Thanksgiving, Nov. 24, 1864. She had one child by this marriage.

Syracuse, N. Y.

1703. 1. SHERMAN-DWIGHT, b. Oct. 26, 1840. He entered Hamilton College in 1860. In 1862 he enlisted in the 24th New York Independent Battery; was in the battles of Kingston and Whitehall. He was recommended for promotion, and commissioned 1st Lieut. in Comp. A, 145th New York Infantry. Before taking command, however, he volunteered and fought as a private in the third day's battle at Gettysburg. He afterward joined his regiment, but acted in the several offices of captain, adjutant and major, till his regiment was disbanded in Dec., 1863. He resumed his studies in Hamilton College, and was graduated in July, 1864, and is now, 1865, engaged in the study of law.

1704. SARAH-ANN,[6][921] (*Ira,[5] John,[4] Joseph,[3] Joseph,[2] John,[1]*) b. Nov. 12, 1812; m. John, son of Duncan McArthur of Jay, N. Y., Dec. 29, 1836. He was b. Dec. 25, 1808, d. Sept. 22, 1843. She m. 2d, Robertson, son of Bergen Huff of Lyons, N. Y., June 21, 1846. He was b. Jan. 2, 1802. *Hartsgrove, Ashtabula Co., Ohio.*

1705. 1. EARL-PIERCE, b. Jan. 4, 1838; m. Orlena Curtice, and had (1.) Alta, born March 14, 1861. He enlisted Aug., 1861, in Comp. B, 29th Ohio Vols., and discharged April, 1862.
1706. 2. ELLEN, b. Nov. 22, 1841.
1707. 3. JOHN-BYRON, b. Feb. 6, 1844. He enlisted Aug., 1861, in Comp. B., 29th Ohio Vols.; wounded at battle of Cedar Mountain, a Minie ball passing through his body; in December he was discharged.
1708. 4. JAMES-ROBERTSON, b. March 2, 1848.
1709. 5. JULIETTE-MAY, b. March 2, 1855.

1710. MELISSA,[6][922] (*Ira,[5] John,[4] Joseph,[3] Joseph,[2] John,[1]*) b. April 16, 1814, d. Feb. 4, 1858; m. William, son of George Aldrich of Pierpont, Ohio, Sept. 1, 1840. He was born July 30, 1816.

Forest City, Iowa.

1710½. 1. CHARLES, b. Sept. 22, 1841, d. March 21, 1842.
1711. 2. EDWIN-NEWELL, b. Nov. 12, 1843. In the war of the rebellion he was in Comp. K, 142d Indiana Vols., from Oct. 18, 1864, to Oct. 18, 1865. He participated in five battles and fifteen skirmishes; was wounded in the right arm near the shoulder; he was taken by the rebels and escaped after an imprisonment of three months. *Forest City, Iowa.*
1712. 3. ERMINA, b. Nov. 29, 1845; m. Oct. 12, 1862, Charles-Hudson Luckore, and had (1.) Sherman-Hudson, b. Sept. 17, 1864; (2.) Winfield-Judson, b. April 14, 1866; (3.) William-Albertus, b. July 27, 1868.
Forest City, Iowa.
1713. 4. WINFIELD-SCOTT, b. May 27, 1847.
1714. 5. OSSIAN, b. March 17, 1850.
1715. 6. NEWTON-SEIR, b. Aug. 2, 1852, d. Feb. 10, 1858.
1716. 7. RICHARD, b. Jan. 4, 1854.
1716½. 8. ARRIE, b. Feb. 4, 1858, d. Feb. 10, 1858.

1717. CYPRIAN,[6][923] (*Ira,[5] John,[4] Joseph,[3] Joseph,[2] John,[1]*) b. Sept. 21, 1816; m. Elizabeth, dau. of Dea. Levi Brown of Elizabethtown, Essex Co., N. Y., Feb. 11, 1838. She was b. April 22, 1811.

Acadia, Allen Co., Ohio.

1718. 1. JULIA, b. Oct. 23, 1844, m. Harrison Hayes.

1719. IRA,[6][926] (*Ira,[5] John,[4] Joseph,[3] Joseph,[2] John,[1]*) b. Aug. 16, 1822; m. Radamtha, dau. of Hezekiah Segur of Connaut, Pa., Aug.

22, 1842. She was b. Sept. 27, 1824. He was ordained to the Free-will Baptist ministry, March 25, 1859 ; he was acting chaplain in the 7th Kansas Cavalry from Sept. 6, 1861, to Feb. 6, 1862 ; in recruiting service from Feb. 6, 1862, to May 29, 1862, in Jefferson Co., Kansas, and from Sept. 1, 1862, to Nov. 30, 1862, in Ashtabula Co., Ohio, and in the same county from June 1, 1863, to May 30, 1864 ; was two months company quarter-master sergeant and acting regimental quarter-master sergeant in the 7th Kansas Cavalry. *East Trumbull, O.*

1720. 1. DELIA-LISCOM, b. May 22, 1844.
1721. 2. GEORGE-HENRY, b. Dec. 31, 1847, d. March 4, 1851.
1722. 3. CHESTER-LISCOM, b. June 8, 1849.
1723. 4. ROSINA, b. Dec. 2, 1853.
1724. 5. CLARA, b. Nov. 10, 1861.

1725. HENRY,[6][927] (*Ira,[5] John,[4] Joseph,[3] Joseph,[2] John,[1]*) b. Nov. 18, 1825 ; m. Phebe Barnham, widow, dau. of John Parch of Elkader, Iowa, Oct. 4, 1857. She was b. Nov. 8, 1835.
Elkader, Clayton Co., Iowa.

1726. 1. MUNROE, b. July 25, 1858.
1727. 2. FRANK-LISCOM, b. Aug. 19, 1860.
1728. 3. SARAH-ELIZABETH, b. Feb. 12, 1863.

1729. JANE-ANN,[6][929] (*Ira,[5] John,[4] Joseph,[3] Joseph,[2] John,[1]*) b. June 7, 1829 ; m. Andrew, son of Amos Curtice of Pierpont, Ohio, Nov. 6, 1853. He was b. Aug. 3, 1829. He enlisted in Comp. B, 29th Ohio Vols., Sept. 19, 1862, discharged Dec. 4, 1863 ; he enlisted again in the 2d Ohio Light Artillery, Sept. 2, 1864, discharged Aug. 9, 1865. He now holds the office of supervisor and school director.
Pierpont, Ohio.

1730. 1. WALTER-LEROY, b. May 21, 1854.
1731. 2. LUCIAN-ALPHONZO, b. June 10, 1857.
1732. 3. MORTON-AUGUSTUS, b. March 8, 1861.

1733. BENJAMIN-PERRY,[6] [932] (*Benjamin,[5] Benjamin,[4] John,[3] Joseph,[2] John,[1]*) b. June 25, 1805 ; m. 1st, Philantha, dau. of Stephen Moore of Fenner, Madison Co., N. Y., Oct. 19, 1828 ; she was b. 1800, d. Nov. 7, 1837 ; m. 2d, Martha, dau. of David Gillett of Campbelltown, Steuben Co., N. Y. ; she was b. April 13, 1813, d. ; m. 3d, Deborah-Malvina Blackman, widow, dau. of Silleck Weed of Chautauque Co., N. Y., Nov. 19, 1864 ; she was b. Nov. 29, 1828.
Erie, Erie Co., Pa.

1734. 1. AMELIA-OSBORN, b. Aug 10, 1829.
1735. 2. ICHABOD, b. Feb. 20, 1836, d. March 10, 1836.
1736. 3. CHARLES-PERRY, b. Dec. 3, 1838.
1737. 4. JAMES-BYRON, b. Dec. 13, 1841, d. Nov. 28, 1843.
1738. 5. MARION-JANE, b. Jan. 3, 1844.
1739. 6. ALBERT-FRANCIS, b. Nov. 14, 1846, d. Dec. 20, 1847.
1740. 7. SARAH-ELLEN, b. Sept. 5, 1851.
1741. 8. CARRIE, b. Aug. 5, 1854.

1742. LEVI,[6][933] (*Benjamin,[5] Benjamin,[4] John,[3] Joseph,[2] John,[1]*) b. Oct. 12, 1806 ; m. Julia, dau. of Elijah Kress of Clarence, Erie Co., N. Y., Sept. 27, 1831. She was b. May 19, 1809, d. April 9, 1863. He was postmaster at Platea, Erie Co., Pa., during the administra-

tion of Presidents Taylor and Fillmore.   The eldest four of his children
were born in St. Thomas, Canada, the others in Girard, Pa.

Albion, Erie Co., Pa.

1743.   1. HORTENSE-EUGENIA,[1984] b. Oct. 10, 1833, m. Daniel-Webster Horton.
1744.   2. RENALDO-FARR, b. Oct. 23, 1835, d. Oct. 30, 1852.
1745.   3. SARAH-LORENA, b. Aug. 31, 1838, d. Jan. 10, 1839.
1746.   4. AMELIA EVELINE, b. April 15, 1840, m. Wm. Hayes, April 17, 1864.
Albion, Pa.
1747.   5. MARY-ALCESTA, b. Oct. 11, 1842.
1748.   6. JULIA-SUSANNAH, b. April 20, 1846.

1749. ELIAS,[6][934] (*Benjamin,[5] Benjamin,[4] John,[3] Joseph,[2] John,[1]*)
b. July 2, 1808; m. Emeline, dau. of Samuel Topliff of Barnard, Vt.,
July 4, 1830.   She was b. Feb. 12, 1808.   He has been a justice of
the peace and constable in the town of Alden, N. Y., several years.
His eldest child was born in Ellington, his second in Alexander, and
the others in Alden, N. Y.   *Alden, Erie Co., N. Y.*

1750.   1. AMY-ANN, b. March 17, 1831, d. April, 1834.
1751.   2. FAYETTE-TOPLIFF, b. March 31, 1832, d. May, 1834.
1752.   3. ABBY-MARIA, b. Aug. 15, 1837.
1753.   4. ANGELIA-EMELINE-TOPLIFF, b. Aug. 7, 1845.

1754. HORACE,[6][936] (*Benjamin,[5] Benjamin,[4] John,[3] Joseph,[2]
John,[1]*) b. Jan. 30, 1812; m. Catharine, dau. of Robert Large of
Girard, Erie Co., Penn., May 22, 1842.   She was b. Aug. 24, 1823.
His elder children were born in Girard, Pa., the others at the place of
his present residence.   *Hebron, McHenry Co., Ill.*

1755.   1. EUGENE-BURDELL, b. Aug. 3, 1843, d. April 20, 1864 ; in war of rebel-
          lion he was in Comp. F, 95th Illinois Infantry.   He enlisted Feb. 17,
          1864, and died in service.
1756.   2. FANNY-EVELINE, b. Dec. 26, 1844.
1757.   3. JOSEPH-HORACE, b. Sept. 9, 1849 ; in war of rebellion he was in Comp.
          D, 95th Ill. Infantry ; he was in the service eleven months ; was at Nash-
          ville when Hood was defeated ; was in the fourteen days fight at Span-
          ish Fort, the chief defence of Mobile.
1758.   4. SARAH-CERELIA, b. Sept. 7, 1851.
1759.   5. BENJAMIN-FRANKLIN, b. Feb. 27, 1854.
1760.   6. MARY-CATHARINE, b. July 2, 1857.
1761.   7. HOMER-CLARKE-LARGE, b. Sept. 20, 1858.
1762.   8. SUSAN-ISABELLA, b. Feb. 18, 1862.
1763.   9. ELLEN-CORNELIA, b. Aug. 23, 1863.
1764. 10. WILLIAM-SNAVELLY, b. Sept. 13, 1864.

1765. SANFORD,[6][938] (*Benjamin,[5] Benjamin,[4] John,[3] Joseph,[2]
John,[1]*) b. July 19, 1816; m. Catharine, dau. of James Porter of
Girard, Erie Co., Pa., Jan. 27, 1848.   She was b. Jan. 27, 1827.   He
has been a justice of the peace, town clerk, town treasurer, &c.
His children were born in Girard.   *Girard, Erie Co., Pa.*

1766.   1. LUCY-JANE, b. Jan. 6, 1849.
1767.   2. EDWIN-CLARENCE, b. April 20, 1851.

1768. FANNY-WELLS,[6][939] (*Benjamin,[5] Benjamin,[4] John,[3] Joseph,[2]
John,[1]*) b. July 14, 1818; m. David-Darius, son of Jotham-Judd
Barnes of Girard, Erie Co., Pa., April 28, 1844.   He was b. March 12,
1820.   Has been constable, &c.   *Platea, Erie Co., Pa.*

1769.   1. HOMER-SLATER, b. Oct. 6, 1856.

1770. ERASTUS,[6][940] (*Benjamin,[5] Benjamin,[4] John,[3] Joseph,[2] John,[1]*) b. Aug. 13, 1820; m. Adelia-Maria, dau. of the Rev. Daniel Richey of Albion, Erie Co., Pa., June 23, 1853. She was b. July 6, 1830. Has been an officer in the M. E. Church many years; has no children of his own, but has an adopted daughter, Esther-R. Slater.

Girard, Erie Co., Pa.

1771. DENNISON,[6][941] (*Benjamin,[5] Benjamin,[4] John,[3] Joseph,[2] John,[1]*) b. Sept. 9, 1822; m. Lydia-Jane, dau. of Lyman Badger of Girard, Erie Co., Pa., Feb. 20, 1855. She was b. April 9, 1834.

Platea, Erie Co., Pa.

1772. 1. BENJAMIN-FREMONT, b. Nov. 27, 1855.
1773. 2. SEYMOUR-BADGER, b. Dec. 16, 1857, d. Feb. 13, 1860.
1774. 3. AMY-BELL, b. March 15, 1861.

1775. DANIEL-HOPKINS,[6][944] (*Daniel,[5] Benjamin,[4] John,[3] Joseph,[2] John,[1]*) b. Aug. 19, 1804, d. Sept. 28, 1855; m. Joannah, dau. of Perley Hopkins of Eaton, Madison Co., N. Y., May 28, 1829. She was b. Dec. 10, 1808.

Juda, Green Co., Wisconsin.

1776. 1. SUSANNAH, b. Feb. 26, 1830, d. July 26, 1854, m. Amos Carpenter.
1777   2. LUCRETIA, b. Oct. 8, 1831, m. Charles-Wilkes Read.

Juda, Green Co., Wis.

1778. 3. ALVIRA, b. Aug. 22, 1833, d. July 26, 1834.
1779. 4. CORNELIA, b. Sept. 25, 1835, d. July 9, 1839.
1780. 5. FLORETTA, b. May 3, 1838, d. July 23, 1839.
1781. 6. HARRISON-LEWIS, b. June 1, 1840; in the war of rebellion he was in Comp. B, 1st Colorado Cavalry, and was stationed at Fort Garland in Colorado Territory.
1782. 7. ELIZA-ANN, b. Nov. 10, 1842.
1783. 8. MINERVA-ELIZABETH, b. April 19, 1846, d. Aug. 15, 1847.
1784. 9. ARNOLD-HOPKINS, b. Feb. 16, 1848, d. July 20, 1860.
1785. 10. EZEKIEL, b. March 18, 1851.

1786. HANNAH-SELINDA,[6] [945] (*Daniel,[5] Benjamin,[4] John,[3] Joseph,[2] John,[1]*) b. Jan. 5, 1806, d. June 1, 1844; m. William-Vincent, son of John Hubbard of Eaton, N. Y., Oct. 8, 1829. He was b. July 14, 1808, d. Feb. 10, 1859; has been inspector and superintendent of schools. *Richland, N. Y.*

1787. 1. CLARK, b. May, 1844, d. Aug., 1844.

1788. RHODA-LUCINDA,[6][948] (*Daniel,[5] Benjamin,[4] John,[3] Joseph,[2] John,[1]*) b. Dec. 28, 1812, d. Sept. 5, 1844; m. Daniel-Joseph, son of Elias Burdick of Albion, N. Y., May 3, 1838.

South Richland, Oswego Co., N. Y.

1789. 1. BRAYTON, b. in Richland, N. Y., Dec. 17, 1841; in the war of rebellion was in Comp. K, 110th N. Y. Vols.; he is now (1865) jail-keeper at Key West.

1790. BRAYTON,[6][946] (*Daniel,[5] Benjamin,[4] John,[3] Joseph,[2] John,[1]*) b. June 12, 1807; m. Philena, dau. of Oliver Wescott of Foster, R. I., afterwards of Richland, N. Y., Jan. 12, 1832. She was b. Jan. 1, 1811. His children were born in Richland, N. Y.

Daysville, Oswego Co., N. Y.

1791. 1. MELISSA-HELEN,[1987] b. Dec. 16, 1832, m. Charles-Edward Russell.
1792. 2. LUCINDA-ANN,[1990] b. June 11, 1835, m. John-Allen Russell.
1793. 3. LOVIRA,[1995] b. Jan 22, 1837, m. Warren-George Smith.
1794. 4. EMILY-ELVIRA,[1996] b. Feb. 8, 1839, m. William-Henry Russell.

1795.　5. Frederic-William,[1999] b. March 29, 1841, m. Abbie-Westcott.
1796.　6. Calista-Jane,[1997] b. July 28, 1843, m. Daniel Dean.
1797.　7. Allen-Brayton, b. Aug. 14, 1845.
1799.　8. Lewis-Russell, b. Jan. 27, 1848.
1800.　9. Veeder-Franklin, b. Jan. 3, 1851.

1801.　Susannah,[6][947] (*Daniel*,[5] *Benjamin*,[4] *John*,[3] *Joseph*,[2] *John*,[1])
b. Feb. 26, 1810; m. Capt. William, son of Henry Easton of Provi-
dence, R. I., Nov. 23, 1828. He was b. Nov. 1, 1801. They have
had no children.　　　　　　　　　　　　　　　　*Providence, R. I.*

1802.　Almira,[6][950] (*Daniel*,[5] *Benjamin*,[4] *John*,[3] *Joseph*,[2] *John*,[1])
b. Oct. 25, 1818, d. Feb. 23, 1849; m. Lewis, son of Elisha Russell
of Richmond, Oswego Co., N. Y., Dec. 31, 1835. He was b. Oct. 14,
1815.　　　　　　　　　　　　　　　　　　　　　*Erie, Penn.*

1803.　1. Brayton, b. in Girard, Feb. 1, 1849.

1804.　Allen-Johnson,[6][951] (*Daniel*,[5] *Benjamin*,[4] *John*,[3] *Joseph*,[2]
John,[1]) b. Sept. 9, 1825; m. Minerva-Elizabeth, dau. of Washington
Luther of Girard, Erie Co., Penn., Oct. 7, 1847. She was born Oct.
10, 1828.　　　　　　　　　　　*Elysian, LeSueur Co., Minnesota.*

1805.　1. Harvey-Ellis, b. in Girard, Pa., Jan. 14, 1849.
1806.　2. Mary-Lelinda, b. in Richmond, Ill., April 18, 1851.

1807.　Elizabeth,[6][963] (*Stephen*,[5] *Stephen*,[4] *Abraham*,[3] *Joseph*,[2]
John,[1]) b. May 19, 1811; m. Nathaniel, son of Henry Ellis of Tomp-
kins Co., N. Y., May 1, 1834. He was b. May 25, 1814, d. Oct. 18,
1855. Their children are as follows:
　　　　　　　　　　　　　Saugatuck, Allegan Co., Mich.

1808.　1. William-Henry-Harrison, b. Aug. 2, 1835, d. Oct. 5, 1839.
1809.　2. David, b. Oct. 8, 1837, d. March 5, 1841.
1810.　3. James-Riley, b. July 17, 1839, d. June 8, 1841.
1811.　4. Stephen, b. March 12, 1842.
1812.　5. Frances-Marion, b. Oct. 29, 1844, d. April 27, 1856.
1813.　6. Warren, b. March 4, 1847.
1814.　7. Charles-Ira, b. July 13, 1849.
1815.　8. Lorenzo, b. Nov. 19, 1850, d. Oct. 9, 1852.

1816.　Stephen-Meret,[6][964] (*Stephen*,[5] *Stephen*,[4] *Abraham*,[3] *Jo-
seph*,[2] *John*,[1]) b. Feb. 25, 1813; m. Miriam, dau. of Henry Ellis of
Seneca Falls, N. Y., Sept. 13, 1833. She was b. March 7, 1812.
　　　　　　　　　　　　　Salem Centre, Allegan Co., Mich.

1817.　1. Oliver,[1973] b. July 9, 1834, m. Sarah McIntosh.
1818.　2. Martha-Louisa,[1976] b. March 11, 1836, m. Clark Gillespie.
1819.　3. Zilpha-Arminta,[1978] b. Nov. 25, 1837, m. Alva Ash.
1820.　4. Luther, b. April 8, 1841.
1821.　5. Lucinda-Adeline, b June 10, 1844.
1822.　6. William-Riley, b. Oct. 30, 1846.
1823.　7. Mary-Jane, b. June 21, 1850.

1824.　Ellery-Sylvester,[6][965] (*Stephen*,[5] *Stephen*,[4] *Abraham*,[3]
Joseph,[2] *John*,[1]) b. Oct. 1, 1815; m. Pluma Harding of Candor, Tioga
Co., N. Y., June 15, 1845.　　　　*East Candor, Tioga Co., N. Y.*

1825.　1. Minerva, b. June 5, 1847.

1826. Anson-Brown,[6][967] (*Stephen,[5] Stephen,[4] Abraham,[3] Joseph,[2] John,[1]*) b. May 19, 1818; m. Diantha, dau. of Rufus Howland of Rutland, Jefferson Co., N. Y., July 20, 1841. She was b. Jan. 21, 1816.

Barnes Corners, Lewis Co., N. Y.

1827. 1. Elizabeth-Maria, b. May 23, 1842.
1828. 2 Sarah-Malvina, b. Feb. 16, 1844.
1829. 3. Rufus-Adelbert, b. Feb. 19, 1846, d. April 9, 1864. He was in Comp. L, 10th New York Artillery, in the war of rebellion.
1830. 4. Lucia-Ann, b. Sept. 12, 1849.
1831. 5. Veretta-Selinda, b. Oct. 16, 1851, d. Feb. 9, 1864.
1832. 6. Ida-Selinda, b. Dec. 30, 1852.
1833. 7. Frank-Adelbert, b. June 5, 1855.
1834. 8. Charles-Jay, b. Dec. 12, 1858.

1835. Minerva,[6][968] (*Stephen,[5] Stephen,[4] Abraham,[3] Joseph,[2] John,[1]*) b. Jan. 21, 1820; m. 1st, Loren-Daniel, son of Daniel Whipple, Jan. 2, 1840; he was b. Oct. 14, 1819, d. April 1, 1851; m. 2d, Robert-Ambrose, son of Robert McDonald, May 1, 1859. He was b. April 16, 1820. *Saugatuck, Allegan Co., Mich.*

1836. 1. Stephen-Rodolphus, b. Oct. 21, 1841.
1837. 2. Francis-Ellery, b. Nov. 8, 1843. He was in Comp. G, 6th Michigan Heavy Artillery, in the war of rebellion.
1838. 3. Emma, b. March 1, 1849, d. April 1, 1851.

1839. Albert,[6][969] (*Stephen,[5] Stephen,[4] Abraham,[3] Joseph,[2] John,[1]*) b. Feb. 16, 1822; m. Arrena, dau. of William Updike of New Jersey, Oct. 28, 1844. She was b. March 13, 1823.

Saugatuck, Allegan Co., Mich.

1840. 1. Alonzo-Franklin, b. April 17, 1846.
1841. 2. Charles-Eugene, b. April 28, 1848.
1842. 3. Arthur-Newton, b. Jan. 6, 1850.
1843. 4. Clarissa-Lavinia, b. April 1, 1852.
1844. 5. Eunice-Emily, b. Aug. 7, 1854.
1845. 6. Nathan-Norwood, b. March 26, 1857.
1846. 7. Marietta, b. May 27, 1860.
1847. 8. Stephen-Albert, b. Sept. 22, 1864.

1848. Eunice,[6][970] (*Stephen,[5] Stephen,[4] Abraham,[3] Joseph,[2] John,[1]*) b. Feb. 16, 1824; m. Lorenzo-Dow, son of Oliver Evans of New Hampshire, Feb. 6, 1849. He was b. Jan. 14, 1824, d. April 3, 1859.

Saugatuck, Allegan Co., Mich.

1849. 1. Loren, b. April 6, 1850.
1850. 2. Mary-Emma, b. May 7, 1853, d. Oct. 4, 1854.
1851. 3. Minerva-Albena, b. June 6, 1858.

1852. Stephen-Deanton,[6][996] (*Joseph,[5] Stephen,[4] Abraham,[3] Joseph,[2] John,[1]*) b. Aug. 20, 1830; m. Mary-Ann-Elvira, daughter of James Alexander of East Houndsfield, N. Y., Dec. 5, 1852. She was b. Sept. 12, 1831. *East Houndsfield, N. Y.*

1853. 1. James-Herbert-Herschell, b. Nov. 8, 1854.

1854. Perry,[7][1299] (*Jonathan,[6] Isaac,[5] Joseph,[4] Joseph,[3] Joseph,[2] John,[1]*) b. Nov. 3, 1826; m. Martha, dau. of Peter Ingersoll of Ellington, Chautauque Co., N. Y., May 10, 1849. She was b. 1829, d. Sept. 15, 1862. *Ellington, Chautauque Co., N. Y.*

1855. 1. John, b. March 26, 1857.
1856. 2. Charles, b. March 5, 1861, d. Sept. 2, 1862.

1857. MARY,[7][1301] (*Jonathan,*[6] *Isaac,*[5] *Joseph,*[4] *Joseph,*[3] *Joseph,*[2] *John,*[1]) b. Sept. 1, 1830; m. William, son of Warren Palmer of Randolph, Cattaraugus Co., N. Y., July 3, 1851.   *Wataga, Knox Co., Ill.*

1858.   1. SIDNEY-LUVERNE, b. June 12, 1854.
1859.   2. KIRKLIN, b. May 2, 1856.
1860.   3. CORA-ELIZA, b. April 2, 1858.

1861. ALBERT,[7][1302] (*Jonathan,*[6] *Isaac,*[5] *Joseph,*[4] *Joseph,*[3] *Joseph,*[2] *John,*[1]) b. May 23, 1834; m. Emma, dau. of Joseph Nye of Ellington, Chautauque Co., N. Y., May 10, 1859.
Ellington, Chautauque Co., N. Y.
1862.   1. Effiegene, b. June 13, 1861.

1863. RACHEL,[7][1278] (*Theron,*[6] *Abraham,*[5] *Abner,*[4] *Joseph,*[3] *Joseph,*[2] *John,*[1]) b. Jan. 19, 1834; m. John-Dickerson, son of John Stafford of LeClair, Scott Co., Iowa, Feb. 1, 1857.   He was born Nov. 12, 1827.   *Princeton, Scott Co., Iowa.*

1864.   1. EDGAR-LEROY, b. March 24, 1858.
1865.   2. GEORGE-HENRY, b. Aug. 25, 1862, d. Feb. 24, 1864.
1866.   3. DICK LEWIS, b. Dec. 4, 1864.

1867. MARY,[7][1345] (*Benjamin,*[6] *Isaac,*[5] *Joseph,*[4] *Joseph,*[3] *Joseph,*[2] *John,*[1]) b. Aug. 9, 1832; m. Rev. Daniel, son of the Rev. William Appleford of Drummondville, C. W., Sept. 29, 1859.   He was b. Dec. 28, 1833.

1868.   1. WILLIAM-BENJAMIN, b. Nov. 19, 1860, d. April 29, 1863.
1869.   2. ANNIE-MARIA, b. June 23, 1862, d. May 8, 1863.

1870. CATHARINE,[7][1347] (*Benjamin,*[6] *Isaac,*[5] *Joseph,*[4] *Joseph,*[3] *Joseph,*[2] *John,*[1]) b. Feb. 10, 1837; m. Samuel Green, Aug. 15, 1863. He was b. Feb. 29, 1836.   *Greenwood, Pickering Co., C. W.*

1871.   1. Child, not named, b. June 28, 1864.

1872. LYDIA,[7][1342] (*Benjamin,*[6] *Isaac,*[5] *Joseph,*[4] *Joseph,*[3] *Joseph,*[2] *John,*[1]) b. Feb. 10, 1826; m. Henry, son of William Wagner of Markham, C. W., Jan 23, 1845.   He was b. June. 23, 1817.
Reach Utica, C. W.

1873.   1. BENJAMIN, b. June 20, 1846.
1874.   2. WILLIAM, b. Dec. 20, 1847.
1875.   3. MARY, b. Nov. 19, 1849.
1876.   4. JOSEPH, b. Aug. 7, 1852.

1877. SUSAN-ALMIRA,[7][1385] (*Nelson,*[6] *Jonathan,*[5] *Joseph,*[4] *Joseph,*[3] *Joseph,*[2] *John,*[1]) b. Feb. 15, 1837; m. H. E. Hall of Byron, Genesee Co., N. Y., May 12, 1859.   *Byron, Genesee Co., N. Y.*

1878.   1. CLARENCE-HENRY, b. May 14, 1860.
1879.   2. LANSING-SLATER, b. May 14, 1860, d. Nov. 30, 1860.
1880.   3. GENEVIEVE, b. Dec. 22, 1862, d. July 13, 1863.
1881.   4. HUBBARD, b. May 9, 1864.

1882. LEVI-FLETCHER,[7][1375] (*Daniel,*[6] *Isaac,*[5] *Joseph,*[4] *Joseph,*[3] *Joseph,*[2] *John,*[1]) b. Aug. 17, 1833; m. Eliza-Ann Garner of Scotland, June 5, 1856.   *Mount Brydges, Caradoc, C. W.*

1883.   1. LEVI-BENJAMIN, b. Nov. 23, 1857.

1884. MAJOR-BENJAMIN,[7][1376] (*Daniel*,[6] *Isaac*,[5] *Joseph*,[4] *Joseph*,[3] *Joseph*,[2] *John*,[1]) b. Dec. 14, 1835, d. July 23, 1864; m. Elizabeth, dau. of Edward-Stubbs Bates of Kent Co., Michigan, Dec. 26, 1860. He d. at Chattanooga, Tenn., in the army.

Grand Rapids, Kent Co., Mich.

1885. 1. EDWARD, b. June 8, 1862.
1866. 2. MATILDA-JANE, b. May 31, 1864.

1887. AUSTIN,[7][1355] (*Joseph*,[6] *Isaac*,[5] *Joseph*,[4] *Joseph*,[3] *Joseph*,[2] *John*,[1]) b. July 28, 1830; m. Exana-Athea, dau. of Edgar Smith of Poland, Chautauque Co., N. Y., March 12, 1856. She was b. April 20, 1834. *Jamestown, Chautauque Co., N. Y.*

1888. 1. ELLIOT-FRANKLIN, b. Jan. 7, 1859.

1889. SOPHIA-ELIZA,[7][1378] (*Daniel*,[6] *Isaac*,[5] *Joseph*,[4] *Joseph*,[3] *Joseph*,[2] *John*,[1]) b. May 4, 1839; m. James-Gordon, son of James Cassie of Reach Utica, C. W., Dec. 17, 1860.

Reach Utica, N. Ontario Co., C. W.

1890. 1. SARAH-ANN, b. April 9, 1862.

1891. JOSEPH-DANIEL,[7][1373] (*Daniel*,[6] *Isaac*,[5] *Joseph*,[4] *Joseph*,[3] *Joseph*,[2] *John*,[1]) b. Sept. 22, 1830; m. Louisa, dau. of Gregory Allen of California, Dec. 27, 1853. *Mount Brydges, Caradoc, C. W.*

1892. 1. DANIEL HENRY, b. Nov. 22, 1857.

1893. JAMES-NASH,[7][1374] (*Daniel*,[6] *Isaac*,[5] *Joseph*,[4] *Joseph*,[3] *Joseph*,[2] *John*,[1]) b. June 5, 1832; m. Eleanor-Ann, dau. of James Brown of Caradoc, C. W., May 6, 1857. *Mount Brydges, Caradoc, C. W.*

1894. 1. MARY-ANN, b. Feb. 22, 1858.

1895. HORATIO-FARREL,[7][1361] (*Job*,[6] *Isaac*,[5] *Joseph*,[4] *Joseph*,[3] *Joseph*,[2] *John*,[1]) b. Dec. 18, 1820; m. Sarah-Melinda, dau. of Lodowick Babcock of Pharsalia, N. Y., Aug. 14, 1844. She was b. March 1, 1823. *North Pharsalia, Chenango Co., N. Y.*

1896. 1. PLUMA-URANIA, b. May 24, 1846.
1897. 2. ALICE-MAY, b. Dec. 8, 1859.

1897. AMANDA-MELVINA,[7][1362] (*Job*,[6] *Isaac*,[5] *Joseph*,[4] *Joseph*,[3] *Joseph*,[2] *John*,[1]) b. Dec. 4, 1821; m. Morris-Niles, son of Jonas Brown of Hinsdale, Cattaraugus, N. Y., Oct. 20, 1842. He was b. Jan. 31, 1820. *Haskell Flats, Cattaraugus Co., N. Y.*

1898. 1. CHARLES-JEROME, b. Aug 28, 1843, d. July 26, 1865. In the war of the rebellion he was in Comp. K, 65th N. Y. Vols. ; he died in U. S. hospital of typhoid fever.
1899. 2. FRANCIS-BARTON, b. Feb. 18, 1845.
1900. 3. EDMUND-ORLANDO, b. Nov. 1, 1847.
1901. 4. LOUISA-AMANDA, b. Nov. 5, 1849.
1902. 5. MARY-ANN, b. Oct. 1, 1851.
1903. 6. EMILY-PHILA, b. Nov. 7, 1853.

1904. ELIZA-ANN,[7][1363] (*Job*,[6] *Isaac*,[5] *Joseph*,[4] *Joseph*,[3] *Joseph*,[2] *John*,[1]) b. July 3, 1823; m. Thomas, son of Richard Bavin of Smyrna, Chenango Co., N. Y., Oct. 9, 1843. He was b. Sept. 1, 1818.

Loganville, Sauk Co., Wis.

1905. 1. AMANDA-AMELIA, b. April 13, 1849.
1906. 2. ELLA-ALMANZA, b. June 16, 1855.

1907. Louisa-Arvilla,[7][1364] (*Job,*[6] *Isaac,*[5] *Joseph,*[4] *Joseph,*[3] *Joseph,*[2] *John,*[1]) b. Nov. 12, 1824; m. James-Monroe, son of Asa Colwell of Sherburne, Chenango Co., N. Y., Dec. 14, 1842. He was born Jan. 2, 1820.   *Sherburne, Chenango Co., N.Y.*

1908. 1. Emily-Amelia, b. April 11, 1847.

1909. Andrew-Barton,[7][1366] (*Job,*[6] *Isaac,*[5] *Joseph,*[4] *Joseph,*[3] *Joseph,*[2] *John,*[1]) b. May 12, 1839; m. Sarah, dau. of Jonathan Boynton of Smyrna, Chenango Co., N. Y., Nov. 2, 1854. She was b. Jan. 25, 1825.   *Smyrna, N. Y.*

1910. 1. Delbertie-Emily, b. in Smyrna, N. Y., Sept. 9, 1855.
1911. 2. Boynton, b. in Hinsdale, N. Y., April 26, 1858.
1912. 3. Luna-Bell, b. in Hinsdale, N. Y., Aug. 9, 1862.
1613. 4. Effie-Luvan, b. in Hinsdale, June 27, 1864.
1913½. 5. Clinton-Jerome, b. in Springfield, Iowa, June 19, 1866.

1914. Mary-Ann,[7][1367] (*Job,*[6] *Isaac,*[5] *Joseph,*[4] *Joseph,*[3] *Joseph,*[2] *John,*[1]) b. May 8, 1831; m. Henry, son of Paris Holley of Smyrna, Chenango Co., N. Y., Oct. 2, 1851. He was b. June 7, 1830.
            Smyrna, Chenango Co., N. Y.

1915. 1. Tuvette, b. Dec. 28, 1853.
1916. 2. Clara-Ann, b. Oct. 25, 1857.
1917. 3. Duane, b. Oct. 21, 1859.

1918. Isaac-Orlando,[7][1368] (*Job,*[6] *Isaac,*[5] *Joseph,*[4] *Joseph,*[3] *Joseph,*[2] *John,*[1]) b. Nov. 12, 1833; m. Mary-Ann, dau. of William Howe of Haskell Flats, Cattaraugus Co., N. Y., March 14, 1861. She was b. May 25, 1833.   *Plover, Sauk Co., Wis.*

1919. 1. Orlando-Howe, b. Dec. 31, 1862.
1920. 2. Lena, b. Oct. 5, 1864.

1921. Lucetta-Angeline,[7][1370] (*Job,*[6] *Isaac,*[5] *Joseph,*[4] *Joseph,*[3] *Joseph,*[2] *John,*[1]) b. June 25, 1842; m. Henry-Ornan, son of Patrick Bartlett of Smyrna, Chenango Co., N. Y., March 18, 1860. He was b. May 20, 1837.   *Plymouth, Chenango Co., N. Y.*

1922. 1. Erving, b. Oct. 22, 1861.

1923. William-Henry,[7][1288] (*Joshua,*[6] *Abraham,*[5] *Abner,*[4] *Joseph,*[3] *Joseph,*[2] *John,*[1]) b. May 6, 1837; m. Anna, dau. of John-Austin Seekins of LeClaire, Scott Co., Iowa. She was b. May 13, 1840. In the war of the rebellion he was in Comp. B, 5th Iowa Vols.
            Pleasant Valley, Scott Co., Iowa.

1924. 1. Elmina-Lucinda, b. May 8, 1861.
1925. 2. Henry-Elmer, b. Nov. 19, 1862.
1925½. 3. Nettie-May, b. May 27, 1866.

1926. Mary-Ann,[7][1436] (*Silas,*[6] *Silas,*[5] *Abial,*[4] *Joseph,*[3] *Joseph,*[2] *John,*[1]) b. July 25, 1839; m. Darius-Lester Anderson, April 1, 1860. He was born April 18, 1839.   *South Killingly, Ct.*

1927. 1. Eudora-Minnie, b. June 29, 1863.
1927¼. 2. William-Asa, b. July 22, 1868.

1928. Almira-Melissa,[7][1437] (*Silas,*[6] *Silas,*[5] *Abial,*[4] *Joseph,*[3] *Joseph,*[2] *John,*[1]) b. Jan 21, 1841; m. Edward-Everett, son of William-

Henry Littlejohn of Albany, April 27, 1855. He was b. March 19, 1839. *Albany, N. Y.*

1928½. 1. HENRY-EVERETT, b. Feb. 18, 1857, d. Feb. 21, 1857.
1929. 2. WILLIAM-EVERETT, b. May 9, 1863.
1929½. 3. IDA-MYRA, b.

1930. ALPHEUS-BRAYTON,⁷[1507] (*Brayton,⁶ Silas,⁵ Silas,⁴ Joseph,³ Joseph,² John,¹*) b. Nov. 26, 1832; m. Ruth, dau. of John Matthews of Killingly, Ct., June 25, 1855. She was b. Dec. 14, 1832.
South Providence, R. I.

1931. 1. LORAETTA-RUTH, b. Jan. 20, 1857.
1932. 2. ALPHEUS-BRAYTON, b. June 4, 1862.

1933. JOSEPHINE-MARANDA,⁷[1508] (*Brayton,⁶ Silas,⁵ Silas,⁴ Joseph,³ Joseph,² John,¹*) b. Oct. 2, 1835; m. Daniel-Metcalf, son of Jonathan Horton of Oswego, N. Y., June 25, 1855. He was b. July 8, 1828. He enlisted Aug. 10, 1862, in 110th N. Y. Vols., and was discharged, from ill health, after a service of one year and ten months. He enlisted again, Aug. 26, 1864, and served as a sergeant till the end of the war, being ten months and eleven days.
Hannibal, Oswego Co., N. Y.

1934. 1. CARRIE-EVELINE, b. July 27, 1859.
1935. 2. IDA-JANE, b. Oct. 6, 1860.
1936. 3. ALICE-MARTHA, b. Sept. 2, 1862.
1937. 4. ELLEN-MARIA, b. Nov. 10, 1864.

1938. EDWARD-BURGESS,⁷[1510] (*Brayton,⁶ Silas,⁵ Silas,⁴ Joseph,³ Joseph,² John,¹*) b. April 5, 1841; m. Isadore, dau. of the Rev. Michael-Merrill Preston of Killingly, Ct., Jan. 1, 1862. She was b. Sept. 26, 1844. *Providence, R. I.*

1939. 1. ALICE-MARIA, b. Aug. 20, 1863.

1940. ELIZABETH,⁷[1457] (*Milton,⁶ Paul,⁵ Silas,⁴ Joseph,³ Joseph,² John,¹*) b. May 6, 1843; m. Edwin-Gregory, son of Edwin Husted of Norwalk, Ohio, Nov. 20, 1861. He was b. Jan. 4, 1835.
Norwalk, Ohio.

1941. 1. ARTHUR-LEGRAND, b. Dec. 28, 1862.
1942. 2. CHARLES-ELMER, b. June 26, 1864, d. July 17, 1864.

1943. ELIZABETH-NAOMI,⁷[1609] (*David-Ames,⁶ John,⁵ Silas,⁴ Joseph,³ Joseph,² John,¹*) b. Sept. 28, 1842; m. Martin-Van-Buren, son of John-Newton Stites of Springfield, Ind., April 7, 1861. He was b. Jan. 29, 1837. *Springfield, Ind.*

1944. 1. MARTIN-CREVOLA, b. Feb. 1, 1862, d. March 15, 1864.
1945. 2. JOHN-NEWTON, b Dec. 25, 1862.
1946. 3. GEORGE-WASHINGTON, b. April 14, 1864.
1947. 4. LOTTIE-ISADEN, b. April 18, 1865.

1948. HARRIET,⁷[1616] (*John,⁶ John,⁵ Silas,⁴ Joseph,³ Joseph,² John,¹*) b. Feb. 14, 1843; m. Samuel, son of Samuel Moore of Mishawaka, Indiana, Dec. 29, 1857. He was b. July 3, 1828. He enlisted in the war of rebellion, Aug. 4, 1862, in Comp. B, 73d Indiana Vols., and was discharged, July 1, 1865. *Springfield, Ind.*

1949. 1. JAMES-MEAD, b. June 6, 1859, d. June 15, 1864.
1950. 2. JOHN-SLATER, b. June 17, 1861, d. June 13, 1864.
1951. 3. CORA, b. April 9, 1866.

9

1952. DAVID,[7][1652] (*Chauncy*,[6] *Joseph*,[5] *John*,[4] *Joseph*,[3] *Joseph*,[2] *John*,[1]) b. Feb. 8, 1823; m. Catharine, dau. of Sidney Goucher of Upper Jay, Essex Co., N. Y., Jan. 16, 1845. She was b. March 22, 1825.   *Upper Jay, Essex Co., N. Y.*

1953. 1. GEORGE-DAVID, b. Sept. 28, 1845, d. Sept. 13, 1864, in hospital at New
          Orleans; he was in Comp. M, 2d New York Veteran Cavalry, in war of
          rebellion.
1954. 2. ADALBERT-SIDNEY, b. June 20, 1847.
1955. 3. FLORENCE-JANE, b. April 27, 1850.
1956. 4. MARGARET-ELIZABETH, b. April 9, 1852, d. March 5, 1854.
1957. 5. WELLINGTON-LANGDON, b. July 3, 1857.
1958. 6. FRANKLIN-ALBERTUS, b. May 3, 1859, d. April 18, 1860.
1959. 7. FRANCES-ELIZABETH, b. Aug. 13, 1862.

1960. PAMELA-ERMINA,[7][1657] (*Chauncy*,[6] *Joseph*,[5] *John*,[4] *Joseph*,[3] *Joseph*,[2] *John*,[1]) b. Dec. 21, 1832; m. Charles-Michael, son of Michael Wells of Jay, Essex Co., N. Y. He was b. May 7, 1830; he was in Comp. M, 118th N. Y. Vols., in the war of the rebellion.
        Jay, Essex Co., N. Y.

1961. 1. EVANGELINE, b. Sept. 28, 1857, d. May 28, 1863.
1962. 2. EUGENE-HERBERT, b. March 2, 1859, d. March 20, 1864.
1963. 3. FLORA-ANN, b. July 8, 1861, d. March 17, 1864.

1963. NAPOLEON-BONAPARTE,[7][1656] (*Chauncy*,[6] *Joseph*,[5] *John*,[4] *Joseph*,[3] *Joseph*,[2] *John*,[1]) b. Jan. 13, 1830; m. Mary, dau. of William Palmer of Upper Jay, N. Y., Dec. 8, 1853. She was b. May 15, 1839. He was in 2d New York Veteran Cavalry in the war of the rebellion. Their children are as follows: *Lewis Centre, Essex Co., N. Y.*

1964. 1. GILSON-MELVILLE, b. Nov 18, 1855.
1965. 2. WILLIE-McCLELLAN, b. June 20, 1861, d. June 20, 1862.
1966. 3. WILLIE-MARK, b. May 13, 1863.

1967. ELIZA,[7][1653] (*Chauncy*,[6] *Joseph*,[5] *John*,[4] *Joseph*,[3] *Joseph*,[2] *John*,[1]) b. Dec. 13, 1824; m. Edmund-Pierpont, son of Samuel Aiken of White Hall, N. Y., Oct. 5, 1845. He was b. Nov. 23, 1811. He was in 2d Conn. Heavy Artillery in the war of the rebellion.
        Jay, Essex Co., N. Y.

1968. 1. ATWOOD-ALVANUS, b. March 28, 1847; he was in Comp. A, 2d Conn.
          Heavy Artillery, in the war of the rebellion.
1969. 2. GEORGE-ROBINSON, b. April 7, 1848.
1970. 3. HENRY-MELVILLE, b. Dec. 17, 1850.
1971. 4. EDDA-LANOR, b. Sept. 1, 1851, d. March 13, 1854.
1972. 5. ALMEDA-ANN, b. Sept. 24, 1853.

1973. OLIVER,[7][1817] (*Stephen-Merit*,[6] *Stephen*,[5] *Stephen*,[4] *Abraham*,[3] *Joseph*,[2] *John*,[1]) b. July 9, 1834; m. Sarah McIntosh, Oct. 14, 1860. She was born May 16, 1843. *Saugatuck, Allegan Co., Mich.*

1974. 1. MARY-MARTHA, b. Dec. 9, 1861.
1975. 2. MIRIAM-ABIGAIL, b. Oct. 12, 1864.

1976. MARTHA-LOUISA,[7][1818] (*Stephen-Merit*,[6] *Stephen*,[5] *Stephen*,[4] *Abraham*,[3] *Joseph*,[2] *John*,[1]) b. March 11, 1836; m. Clark Gillespie, Oct. 10, 1853. He was born Oct. 10, 1825.
        Saugatuck, Allegan Co., Mich,

1977. 1. FANNY-ISADORE, b. May 24, 1856.

1978. ZILPHA-ARMINTA,[7][1819] (*Stephen-Merit*,[6] *Stephen*,[5] *Stephen*,[4] *Abraham*,[3] *Joseph*,[2] *John*,[1]) b. Nov. 25, 1837 ; m. Alva, son of William Ash of Saugatuck, Mich., Nov. 25, 1855. He was born Feb. 10, 1833. *Saugatuck, Allegan Co., Mich.*

1979. 1. FREDERICK-M., b. Nov. 24, 1856.
1980. 2. ELLA, b. July 20, 1860.
1981. 3. ALVA-EDWIN, b. Sept. 24, 1864.

1982. JULIA,[7][1718] (*Cyprian*,[6] *Ira*,[5] *John*,[4] *Joseph*,[3] *Joseph*,[2] *John*,[1]) b. Oct. 23, 1844 ; m Harrison, son of Alanson Hayes of Marion, Ohio, Nov. 7, 1860. He was b. May 16, 1840 ; he was in Comp. I, 34th Ohio Zouaves, in the war of the rebellion. (See No. 878.)
Miles Point, Carrol Co., Mo.

1983. 1. HARRISON-CLIFFORD, b. June 4, 1862.

1984. HORTENSE-EUGENIE,[7][1743] (*Levi*,[6] *Benjamin*,[5] *Benjamin*,[4] *John*,[3] *Joseph*,[2] *John*,[1]) b. Oct. 10, 1833 ; m. Daniel-Webster, son of Samuel-F. Horton of Branford, Ct., Oct. 19, 1858. He was b. Jan. 21, 1837, d. Feb. 14, 1863. He was Capt. of Comp. A, 51st N. Y. Vols.; quartermaster of 51st N. Y. Vols.; commissary of 2d Brigade, 2d Div., 9th Army Corps, on the staff of Gen. Ferrerro; received a wound at the battle of Newbern, which caused his death.
Albion, Erie Co., Pa.

1985. 1. LIZZIE, b. July 3, 1859.
1986. 2. DAVID-WRIGHT, b. March 31, 1861.

1987. MELISSA-HELEN,[7][1791] (*Brayton*,[6] *Daniel*,[5] *Benjamin*,[4] *John*,[3] *Joseph*,[2] *John*,[1]) b. Dec. 16, 1832 ; m. Charles-Edward, son of Elisha Russell of Richland, Oswego Co., N. Y., Oct. 4, 1851. He was born Dec. 14, 1828 ; in the war of the rebellion he was in Comp. G, 184th New York Vols. *Port Ontario, Oswego Co., N. Y.*

1988. 1. HENRIETTA, b. Oct. 15, 1852.
1989. 2. SUSAN-ALMIRA, b. Feb. 2, 1864, d. Jan. 7, 1866.

1990. LUCINDA-ANN,[7][1792] (*Brayton*,[6] *Daniel*,[5] *Benjamin*,[4] *John*,[3] *Joseph*,[2] *John*,[1]) ; m. John-Allen, son of Daniel-Smith Russell of Mexico, Oswego Co., N. Y., April 6, 1854. He was born Aug. 31, 1827.
South Richland, Oswego Co., N. Y.

1991. 1. JOHN-ALLEN, b. May 31, 1856.
1992. 2. LUCINDA-ESTELLE, b. Nov. 20, 1857.
1993. 3. EMILY-MARIE, b. Feb. 15, 1860.
1994. 4. LEVA-JANE, b. May 18, 1862.

1995. LOVIRA,[7][1793] (*Brayton*,[6] *Daniel*,[5] *Benjamin*,[4] *John*,[3] *Joseph*,[2] *John*,[1]) b. Jan. 22, 1837 ; m. Warren-George, son of Conrad Smith of Salisbury, Herkimer Co., N. Y., Oct. 4, 1862. He was born March 13, 1838 ; he was in Co. B, 57th New York Volunteers, in the war of the rebellion. *Port Ontario, N. Y.*

1995½. 1. CELIA-MAY, b. March 2, 1865.

1996. EMILY-ELVIRA,[7][1764] (*Brayton*,[6] *Daniel*,[5] *Benjamin*,[4] *John*,[3] *Joseph*,[2] *John*,[1]) b. Feb. 8, 1839 ; m. William-Henry, son of Jacob Russell of Richland, Oswego Co., N. Y., Feb. 14, 1861. He was born Feb. 5, 1828. *South Richland, Oswego Co., N. Y.*

1996½. 1. BRAYTON, b. June 30, 1866.

1997. CALISTA-JANE,[7][1796] (*Brayton*,[6] *Daniel*,[5] *Benjamin*,[4] *John*,[3] *Joseph*,[2] *John*,[1]) b. July 28, 1843 ; m. Daniel, son of William Dean of Richland, N. Y., Feb. 28, 1864. He was born March 22, 1844.

Port Ontario, N. Y.

1998. 1. WILLIAM-MORRIS, b. April 9, 1865.

1999. FREDERICK-WILLIAM,[7][1795] (*Brayton*,[6] *Daniel*,[5] *Benjamin*,[4] *John*,[3] *Joseph*,[2] *John*,[1]) b. March 29, 1841 ; m. Abbie, dau. of William Westcott of Ellisburg, Jefferson Co., N. Y., Aug. 29, 1865; she was born July 26, 1847. In the war of the rebellion he was sergeant in Comp. B, 12th New York Cavalry, and was in service about three years.   *South Richland, N. Y.*

2000. 1. CORA, b. in Ellisburgh, N. Y., Dec. 17, 1866.

SUMMARY.

The number of the descendants of John Slafter, whose names are recorded on the foregoing pages, is THREE THOUSAND FIVE HUNDRED AND SEVENTY-SEVEN.

Of these TWELVE are graduates of Colleges. TEN are under-graduates of Colleges, eight of whom did not complete their course, and two are now (1869) members.

SIXTEEN were in the early wars of the country.

ONE HUNDRED AND SIXTY-FIVE enrolled themselves and took part in the defence of the government in the war of the great rebellion.

The number of those who have married descendants of the emigrant ancestor, whose names may be found in this volume, is ONE THOUSAND AND TWENTY.

APPENDIX.

JAMES SHAFTER.

By the will of Benjamin Slafter, of the second generation, it appears that his father, the emigrant ancestor, had ten children, and at the time the will was made, 1756, they were either living, or were supposed to have living issue, as he left the reversion of his estate to his nine brothers and sisters and their heirs. In the body of this work, as will appear on page 4th, we have only included nine children, not having found absolute evidence to identify the tenth. Many circumstances, however, point to James Shafter, the ancestor of the Hon. Oscar-Lovell and the Hon. James-McMellen Shafter, of San Francisco, as the son of John Slafter, our emigrant ancestor. The tradition in relation to the origin of this family, is, that James Shafter came to this country, or was here, early in the 18th Century, that he and his wife died leaving two young children, a son named after his father, James, and a daughter, Mary. The two children were adopted by a farmer residing in or near Framingham, Mass. The daughter in the process of time became the wife of a Mr. Chubb, and removed to Vermont. The son married Miss Esther McMellen, and became a resident of Dudley, Mass. Here tradition begins to be supported by the public records. In Dudley the name of James Shafter is found on a tax bill in 1763. About this time he removed to Richmond, N. H. He was soon after, probably in 1766, killed by the fall of a tree. His son James afterwards settled in Athens, Vermont. As we shall give the names more fully in the several generations hereafter, we need not enter into any farther details at this time.

Among the circumstances which indicate that James Shafter was the son of John Slafter may be mentioned the similarity of the name.

In the extensive and exhaustive researches which we have made among English surnames, we do not find anywhere the name of Shafter, nor do we find it in this country except as belonging to this family. From this circumstance we infer that in its present form it is of modern origin. The names Shafter and Slafter are so near alike that they are frequently confounded. The writer has often been addressed by those not entirely familiar with his name, as if it were spelled with an h instead of an l. James Shafter, being left without father or mother when a small child, might easily have had the *l* of his father's name changed to *h*, especially as his guardian may have been an entire stranger to his father.

There is another circumstance which renders the supposed connection of the families not improbable. The second James Shafter, who was left an orphan as before stated, was born not far from 1730, and, if our theory be correct, was the grandson of John Slafter. By turning to the record of the birth of John Slafter's grand-children, it will be seen that the first was born in 1714 and the last in 1747, so that his birth in 1730 was about midway between the first and the last, and therefore the time of his birth renders it not inconsistent that his father should have been the son, as we have supposed, of John Slafter. The theory or supposition of this connection harmonizes with all the known facts. The reasons may be briefly re-stated as follows:

1. The similarity of the names is such that the *h* might easily have been substituted for *l*, especially in the case of orphan children, where there was no one to correct the error.

2. The name Shafter not being found in England or this country, except in this case, would indicate that it may have been first applied in its present form of spelling to James Shafter of Dudley, and that the name of his ancestors probably had a different spelling.

3. John Slafter is known to have had ten children, only nine of whom can be otherwise accounted for.

4. James Shafter of Dudley, the first of the Shafter family of whom we have any distinct knowledge, was a contemporary of the grand-children of John Slafter, and might therefore have been his grandson.

From the above facts it seems to us that there is a very strong proba-bility that James Shafter of Dudley was the grandson of John Slafter. The evidence is not absolute, and therefore we have not introduced the genealogy of his family into the body of this work. As the local and family history of New-England shall come to be more generally devel-oped, records which have thus far eluded our search, may, and we trust will come to light, that will clear up the question and leave upon it no shadow of doubt.

The following is an outline of the descendants of James Shafter; a more thorough investigation would undoubtedly give many dates and facts which are here wanting. The following were obtained from the late Hon. William-R. Shafter of Townshend, Vermont:

1. JAMES SHAFTER and wife, according to tradition, were settled in or near Framingham, Mass. They both died, leaving two young chil-dren, as follows:

2.   1. JAMES,[4] b. about 1730.
3.   2. MARY, b. about 1732. She, according to tradition, married —— Chubb, and removed to Vermont.

4. JAMES,[2] b. about 1730, d. about 1766; m. Esther McMellen; resided first in Dudley, Mass., but about 1763 removed to Richmond, N. H. He was killed accidentally by the fall of a tree. Their chil-dren were the following:

5.   1. SIMON; is said by tradition to have been a captain in the Continental Army in the Revolutionary War, and to have died of small-pox at Valley Forge.
6.   2. LOIS; m. —— White of Weathersfield, Vt.,
7.   3. MARY; m. Ellis Thayer of Newfane, Vt.
8.   4. ESTHER; m. Benjamin Thrasher of Athens, Vt.
9.   5. JAMES,[13] b. Sept. 15, 1759, d. Jan. 9, 1816; m. Abigail Johnson.

10. 6. Prudence ; m. Jeremiah Barrows of Richmond, Vt.
11. 7. Lydia ; m. Enoch Phillips, and resided in Essex, N. Y.
12. 8. Charity ; m. Jabez Whipple of Athens, Vt.

13. James,[9] b. Sept. 15, 1759, d. Jan. 9, 1816 ; m. Abigail John-son, and settled in Athens, Vt. He was in the battles of Bunker Hill, Bennington, Saratoga, and perhaps others ; he represented the town of Athens in the Legislature of Vermont many years. Their children were as follows :

14. 1. Atlanta ; m. Caleb Hall of Springfield, Vt., and had (1.) Abby, (2.) James, (3.) John, (4.) Martha, (5.) Edward.
15. 2. William-Rufus,[18] m. 1st, Mary Lovell, m. 2d, Fanny Lovell, m. 3d, Eliza-Spaulding Jewett.
16. 3. John-Lock ; m. Ruth Dean of Athens, Vt., and had (1.) Charity, (2.) Mary-Ann, (3.) Atlanta, (4.) Experience-Ellen, (5.) Hannah, (6.) John-Dean, (7.) Fanny.
17. 4. Mary ; m. Don Lovell, and had (1.) George-Grout, (2.) Lewis-Shafter, (3.) Mary, (4.) Homer, (5.) Abby, (6.) Fanny.

18. William-Rufus,[15] b. about 1786, d. March 1, 1864 ; m. 1st, Mary Lovell, m. 2d, Fanny Lovell, m. 3d, Eliza-Spaulding Jewett. He resided in Townshend, Vt. ; was a justice of the peace and a judge of the county court. His children .were by his first wife, and were as follows : *Townshend, Vt.*

19. 1. Wealthy-Lauretta ; m. Roswell Ransom and had (1.) Elizabeth-Fletcher, (2.) Mary-Lovell, (3.) Helen-Lauretta, (4.) Frances-Maria, (5.) Gertrude, (6.) James-Newton, (7.) Albert.   *Galesburgh, Mich.*
20. 2. Oscar-Lovell ; graduated at Law School of Harvard College ; practised Law in Vermont ; is now a judge of the Supreme Court of California ; m. Sarah Riddle, and had (1.) Emma, (2.) Alice-Maud, (3.) Mary, (4.) Alice-Maud, (5.) Alice-Maud, (6.) Alice-Maud, (7.) Hugh-Neal, (8.) Sarah, (9.) Bertha, (10.) Eva, (11.) Infant.   *San Francisco, Cal.*
21. 3. Hugh-Morris ; m. Eliza-Sumner, and had (1.) William-Rufus, (2.) Ann-Eliza, (3.) James-Newton, (4) John-Nelson.   *Galesburgh, Mich.*
22. 4. James-McMellen ; practised Law in Vermont and in California ; member of State Senate in California, &c., &c. ; m. Julia-Granville Hubbard, and had Payne-Jewett, graduated at University of California, and member of Law School of Harvard University, (2.) James, (3.) Chester-Hubbard, (4.) Julia-Ruth.   *San Francisco, Cal.*
23. 5. William-Newton ; m. Bessie Lapham, and had (1.) Mary, (2.) William-Oscar, (3.) Infant.   *Sheboygan, Wis.*
24. 6. Mary Lovell ; m. Philip-Henry Edminster, and had (1.) William-Wood, (2.) Jessie-May, (3.) James-Henry, (4.) James, (5.) James-Lovell.
       Townshend, Vt.

GRADUATES OF COLLEGES,

WHO ARE DESCENDANTS OF JOHN SLAFTER.

CHARLES WRIGHT, . . .	Williams College, . .	1803.
NELSON SLATER, . . .	Union College, . . .	1831.
CHARLES JEWETT, . . .	Middlebury College, .	1834.
THOMAS WRIGHT, . . .	Williams College, . .	1835.
CORODEN SLAFTER, . .	Madison University, .	1838.
JOHN-GODFREY SAXE, . .	Middlebury College, .	1839.
EDMUND-FARWELL SLAFTER, .	Dartmouth College, .	1840.
ABRAHAM-BROOKINS GARDNER,	Union College, . . .	1842.
CARLOS SLAFTER, . . .	Dartmouth College, .	1849.
FRANKLIN-AURELIUS SLATER, .	Madison University, .	1850.
SOLOMON WRIGHT, . . .	Williams College, . .	1859.
SHERMAN-DWIGHT CANFIELD, .	Hamilton College, . .	1864.

UNDER-GRADUATES OF COLLEGES.

THOMAS-JEWETT WRIGHT, .	Williams College.
EDGAR-MANDLEBERT BURTON,	U. S. M. A. at West Point.
JOHN-FARWELL SLAFTER, .	Norwich University.
HINCKLEY-WRIGHT WILLIAMS,	Amherst College.
OLIVER-HAZARD-PERRY BENNETT,	Williams College.
ORRIN-CRANMER BATES, . .	Williams College.
DANFORD-HENRY KNOWLTON, .	College of the City of New York.
MINER-ROCKWELL KNOWLTON,	College of the City of New York.

LEVERETT-HULL WALKER, now (1869) a Cadet U. S. M. A., West Point.

FRANKLIN-AUGUSTUS SLATER, now (1869) in Denison University, Ohio.

ROLL OF HONOR.

THE NAMES OF THE DESCENDANTS OF JOHN SLAFTER WHO HAVE BEEN IN THE
MILITARY SERVICE OF THEIR COUNTRY.

The references are to the consecutive numbers in the body of the work, where an account of their service may be found. In some cases the account is not so full as could be desired. The facts sent in have, however, been fully embodied. The names of those marrying descendants who have been in the military service are not in these lists, but will be found, with proper notices, in the body of the work.

The following are the names of those who participated in the wars of the country anterior to the late rebellion, viz., the French war of 1756, the American Revolution of 1776, and the English war of 1812. It is presumed that other members of the family were in these wars, but their service has not come to the knowledge of the compiler.

DEXTER, ASAHEL	. .	200	SLATER, JOSEPH . . .	854
MANN, THOMAS-JEWETT	'	80	SLATER, NATHAN . .	952
NICHOLS, ALBION	. .	188	SLATER, STEPHEN . .	962
NICHOLS, ASA-HUNTINGTON .		189	THATCHER, SAMUEL . .	196
SLAFTER, JOHN . . .		96	WELLMAN, JOSEPH . .	13
SLATER, BENJAMIN	. .	931	WELLMAN, OLIVER . .	13
SLATER, ELISHA	. .	958	WELLMAN, PETER , .	12
SLATER, JOSEPH	. .	299	WELLMAN, TIMOTHY . .	14

WAR OF THE REBELLION.

We are happy to place upon this ROLL OF HONOR the names of the noble young men, descendants of our emigrant ancestor, who hastened to join the loyal army to suppress the late rebellion.

Some of them fell upon the field of battle. Some returned to their homes with constitutions shattered and broken, to linger and die. Others are maimed and crippled for life.

But the sacrifice was willingly made and was inspired by the loftiest sentiments that belong to our nature, and its memory will live perpetually in the hearts of their kindred and friends.

AIKEN, ATWOOD-ALVANUS	1968	BABSON, ISAAC-HOLDEN	1497
ALDRICH, EDWIN-NEWELL	1711	BARNEY, BYRON-BURTON	83
BABSON, ELISHA-JAMES	1496	BATES, WILLIAM-ARNOLD,	1626
BABSON, ERASTUS-WALCOTT	1493	BRAMBLE, FRANKLIN	1182
BABSON, HENRY-WHITMAN	1501	BRAMBLE, HENRY	1181

BRIDGES, MIRABEAU-LAMAR	1069	JEWETT, ERASTUS	84
BROWN, ALONZO-EMERY	865	JEWETT, JESSE	84
BROWN, CHARLES-JEROME	1898	JONES, ISRAEL	871
BROWN, CHARLES-NORMAN	865	JONES, PIERPONT-EDWARDS	871
BROWN, FRANKLIN-ROLDON	865	JONES, WILLIAM-HENRY	871
BROWN, GEORGE-WASHINGTON	534	LAMB, WILLIAM-HENRY	177
BROWN, HIRAM-GILBERT	865	LENT, ABRAHAM-MARCUS	1397
BROWN, JOHN	532	LUSE, HENRY-HUMPHRIES	956
BROWN, MARTIN-HORACE	865	MATOON, ALBERT-GILMORE	68
BROWN, RODNEY-SLAFTER	533	MCARTHUR, EARL-PIERCE	1705
BURDICK, BRAYTON	1789	MCARTHUR, JOHN-BYRON,	1707
BURGESS, GILES-JEWETT	87	MUZZY, JAMES-SAMUEL	875
BURTON, JOHN-HOWES	83	NEEDHAM, EDWARD-ELMORE	82
CANFIELD, SHERMAN-DWIGHT	1703	NICHOLS, BENJAMIN-TOWNSEND	190
CHANDLER, STEPHEN-EDWIN	590	NICHOLS, JAMES-WELLINGTON	189
CHAPPELL, WILLIAM-HENRY	881	NICHOLS, ROLLA-ALONZO	193
COLEMAN, GEORGE-HENRY	884	PAULK, NOAH-WEBSTER	395
COLEMAN, THEODORE-ALFRED	884	PAULK, JOHN-LOVIN	395
CORRIN, JAMES-HENRY	208	PHILLIPS, EDGAR-AVERY	1083
CORRIN, JOHN	208	RAWSON, JOHN-FRANKLIN,	1546
DAVIS, WALTER-SHAFFER	285	RICHARDSON, GEORGE-HARVEY	1106
DERBY, ALONZO-FARWELL	527	RICHARDSON, MILES-CLINTON	192
DERBY, ORIN-ALVIN	527	RICHARDSON, WILLIAM-WARNER	192
DUNNING, ABRAM-HERBERT	82	ROBINSON, ALBERT-CORODEN	248
DUNNING, WILLIAM-HENRY	82	RUSSELL, WM.-HENRY-HARRISON	196
DUTCHER, WILLIAM-ALBERT	1094	SHAW, PHILANDER-MOSES	726
ELEY, WILLIAM-SCHENK	1220	SLAFTER, ALBERT	1251
FREEMAN, CLEMENT-OLIVER	898	SLAFTER, ALBERT-ALPHONZO	652
FULLER, EDWARD-PERRY	915	SLAFTER, ALONZO	552
FULLER, ELLIOT-LEVERETT	911	SLAFTER, JUDSON	560
FULLER, HILAND-HALL	911	SLAFTER, WILLIAM-ALBERT	1132
GILBERT, MILES-HALL	197	SLAFTER, WILLIAM-BUNCE	630
GLINES, BENJAMIN-BECKWITH	1664	SLATER, ALBERT	1417
GLINES, EUGENE-HOWARD	1664	SLATER, ALBERT-BENJAMIN	1404
GRAY, RICHARD-JAMES	213	SLATER, ALBERT-HENRY	1440
GRAY, SIMON-PHILIP	213	SLATER, BENJAMIN	366
HAMMOND, JOHN-MADISON	891	SLATER, BENJAMIN	1305
HAYES, ALEXIS-POPE	880	SLATER, BERNARD-PHILETUS	1358
HAYES, DAVID-SMITH	882	SLATER, BRADFORD	1356
HAYES, HARRISON	1982	SLATER, BRAYTON	1789
HAYES, NAPOLEON-BONAPARTE	732	SLATER, CALVIN-GREEN	845
HAYES, NELSON	882	SLATER, DELOS-NELSON	1599
HENDRICK, ALBERT-EVERTON	362	SLATER, DILLON-POMROY	863
HULL, MARTIN-BECKWITH	1670	SLATER, EUGENE-BURDELL	1755
HYDE, GILES-FRANCIS	1533	SLATER, FRANCIS-ELLERY	1837
JEWETT, ALBERT-BURTON	84	SLATER, FREDERIC-WILLIAM	1999
JEWETT, CHARLES-ELAM	79	·SLATER, GEORGE-DAVID	1953
JEWETT, EDWIN-SCOVELL	79	SLATER, GEORGE-LEVI	863

SLATER, GEORGE-WASHINGTON	1598
SLATER, GREELEY-RILEY	1321
SLATER, HARRISON-LEWIS	1781
SLATER, HENRY-LARKIN	1401
SLATER, IRA	1719
SLATER, ISRAEL	1398
SLATER, JAMES	1029
SLATER, JAMES-STUART	1557
SLATER, JOHN	863
SLATER, JOHN	955
SLATER, JOHN	1615
SLATER, JOHN-HENRY	1610
SLATER, JONATHAN	715
SLATER, JOSEPH	840
SLATER, JOSEPH	1658
SLATER, JOSEPH-ANDREW	1322
SLATER, JOSEPH-HORACE	1757
SLATER, JOSEPH-WILLIAM	1632
SLATER, KIRKLIN	1303
SLATER, MAJOR-BENJAMIN	1376
SLATER, NAPOLEON-BONAPARTE	1963
SLATER, PHILIP	1033
SLATER, ROYAL-GAY	435
SLATER, RUFUS-ADELBERT	1829
SLATER, SAMUEL	863
SLATER, SAMUEL	1003
SLATER, SIMON	847
SLATER, STEPHEN	962
SLATER, TRUMAN	1031
SLATER, WALLACE	863
SLATER, WALLACE-LYMAN	1491
SLATER, WILLIAM-AMES	1617
SLATER, WILLIAM-HENRY	1923
SLATER, WILLIAM-HENRY	1100
SLATER, WILLIAM-HENRY	1676
SLAUGHTER, FAYETTE-LACEY	1281
SMITH, DWIGHT-KELLOGG	783
STAFFORD, GEORGE,	712
STETSON, JAMES-HENRY	12
TAYLOR, EZEKIEL-VALOROUS	352
TAYLOR, HIRAM-MOSES	349
TAYLOR, WARREN	349
TAYLOR, JOSEPH	345
THATCHER, BERTRAM-CASTNER	197
THATCHER, JOSEPH-TRUESDALE	197
THATCHER, MILES-HALL	197
THATCHER, WM.-WASHINGTON	197
THOMPSON, HENRY-EUGENE	291
TILDEN, CHARLES-FAYETTE	1239
TURNER, STANLEY-WILLIAM	774
WARREN, ELON-GALUSHA	627
WATERS, SAMUEL	1016
WATERS, WILLIAM	1011
WAY, LOAN-DENNIS	82
WHIPPLE, FRANCIS-ELLERY	1837
WILLES, MATTISON	494
WILLES, SYLVESTER	493
WILSON, JOHN-NEWTON	543
WOOD, FRANKLIN	1575½

INDEX NO. I.

The Christian or given names of the descendants of the emigrant ancestor, John Slafter, in the male line, comprising all who bear the patronymic under the varied forms of Slafter, Slaughter and Slater. The references are to the consecutive numbers at which the name occurs. The figures on the left of the name indicate the year of birth; those on the right the consecutive number.

10

INDEX NO. II.

The surnames of the descendants of the emigrant ancestor, John Slafter, in the female line, comprising all who do not bear the patronymic. The references are to the consecutive numbers at which the family bearing the name may be found, with their several Christian names.

INDEX NO. III.

The names of those who have married descendants of the emigrant ancestor, John Slafter. The references are to the consecutive number under which the name occurs.

Crooke, Joseph-Stephens	535	Fenton, Dorothy	23
Crossman, Freelove	952	Fenton, Eunice	105
Crow, Isabella-Parker	1615	Fenton, Horace	68
Crownhart, Marietta	1665	Fenton, Lovina	109
Cummings, Abraham,	747	Fisher, Lydia	277
Curtice, Andrew	1729	Fisher, Pamela	746
Curtis Stephen	57	Fitch, Amos	414
Cushman, Horace	76	Fletcher, Sarah	1371
Cushman, Mary-Jane	1130	Floyd, John-Adams	12
		Foote, Sarah-Ann	79
D.		Foster, Freeman	12
Dagget, Rebecca	459	Foster, Eliza-Ann	454
Darling, Christiana	363	Foster, Ira	189
Darling, Mary-Ann	57	Foster, Sarah	425
Daken, Henry-Smith	1005	Fowler, Abraham-Gardner	86
Davenport, Sarah	173	Fox, Mary	517
Davis, Joshua	365	Fox, Prudence	347
Davis, Mary-Ann	410	Franklin, Arad-Hitchcock	889
Dawkins, Alpheus	68	Frazer, Robert-Lyon	84
Day, Alanson	977	Freeman, Anna	88
Day, Priscilla	13	Freeman, Mary	105
Dean, Daniel	1997	Freeman, Oliver-Perry	898
Dean, Jerusha	892	Frost, Alpha	409
Delano, Nelson	976	Frost, Experience	149
Derby, George-Alvin	527	Frost, Hannah	425
Dexter, Daniel	199	Fuller, Hiram-Birdsall	1419
Dexter, Jerusha	268	Fuller, Lucinda	1171
Dibell, Olive	1001	Fuller, Luther	908
Dickson, Horace	819	Fuller, Maria	397
Dimmick, Ephraim-Harlem	1147	Fuller, Mary-Emilia	86
Dirk, George	1560	Fullington, Julia-Alice	578
Dorris, Susan	189	Fulton, Fanny	878
Doty, Josephine	83		
Downes, Emeline	87	**G.**	
Drury, Sarah-Keith	79	Gage, Ophelia-Brunette	631
Drury, Zephaniah-Keith	82	Gage, Sarah	1498
Dudley, Mary	863	Gage, Susannah	737
Duncan, William-Henry	1645	Gamble, Lucinda	82
Dunham, Eber	86	Gallup, Josiah-Dean	1585
Dunn, Mary	918	Garfield, Lyman	852
Dunning, Abraham	82	Gardner, Charles	1494
Durfee, George	1560	Gardner, David	81
Dustin, Newell	82	Gardner, David-William	81
Dutcher, Newman	1092	Garner, Eliza-Ann	1882
Dyer, Arnold	353	Gault, Eliza-Clay	1013
		Gaylord, Isaac-Thomas	1074
E.		George, Harvey	12
Eaton, Bethia	62	George, Jesse	12
Eaton, Mary	16	Giffin, Achsa	84
Easton, William	1801	Gibbs, David	1427
Edwards, Theodocia	473	Gilbert, Julia	1011
Eldridge, Esther	612	Gillespie, Clark	1976
Eldridge, Royal-Chapman	614	Gillett, Eliza-A.	891
Eley, Samuel	1218	Gillett, George	157
Elkins, Horace	529	Gillett, Martha	1733
Ellis, Miriam	1816	Gillett, Mary-Ellen	79
Ellis, Nathaniel	1807	Gilmore, Robert-Bullard	1672
Elmer, Silas-Wright	79	Glass, Emily	983
Ensign, Hannah	82	Gleason, Harriet-Augusta	1484
Evans, Lorenzo-Dow	1848	Glines, Eleazer-Howe	1664
Evarts, Elizabeth-Frances	83	Glines, Leonora-Ann	1663
Everngin, Mary-Ann	1615	Godfrey, James-Henry	86
		Goldsmith, Burlin-Nelson	705
F.		Goodale, Roxana	1294
Fairbanks, Harriet-Green	12	Goodrich, Alfred	1326
Fanning, Patrick	616	Goodwin, Mary-Ann	352
Farley, Mehitable	66	Gorham, Nancy	346
Farnham, Eliza-Ann	543	Gott, William-N.	57
Farnsworth, Relief	308	Goucher, Catharine	1952
Fedder, Mary-Ann	1632	Gove, Sarah	902
Fellows, Harvey	550	Grant, Cornelia	68

Johnson, Sarah-Miranda	646
Johnston, John-Compton	525
Jones, Harriet	81
Jones, Israel	871
Jones, Levi	57
Jones, Sarah	880
Joslyn, Harriet-Louisa	1268
Judd, Edward-Root	906

K.

Keeler, Martha-Adeline	1456
Kellogg, Fanny	510
Kellogg, William-H.	712
Kelly, Mary-J.	895
Kelsey, Mary-Ann	749
Kemp, Sophia	1377
Kendrick, A.	79
Kent, Louisa-Relief	471
Kenedy, Margaret	1651
Kephart, Orman	885
Kerns, Alfred-Brunson	1271
Kettle, Mary	825
Keyes, Joseph	86
Kibbee, Austin-Graves	491
Kimball, Elizabeth-Freelove	915
King, Ann-Eliza	822
King, Lois	299
King, Lovina	824
Kirby, William	997
Kirch, Sarah-Louisa	79
Kitchel, Emily	1384
Knickerbocker, Mary	672
Knowlton, Danford	489
Knox, Mary	68
Kress, Julia	1742
Kull, John-Michael	664

L.

Ladd, Nathaniel	19
Lamb, Nathan	172
Lampman, Bradford	83
Landers, Hiram	888
Landon, Eliza	79
Large, Catharine	1754
Lattin, Lucy	412
Leahy, Caroline	1668
Leeds, Elizabeth-Tripp	12
Lent, Samuel	1397
Leonard, Asaph-Dickerson	1067
Lewis, Asa	450
Lewis, Daniel	364
Lewis, Sophia	83
Lilly, Maria-Lucretia	653
Lincoln, Alanson	81
Lincoln, Lewis	80
Lincoln, Levi	81
Liscom, Sally	919
Little, Alzina	82
Littlejohn, Edward-Everett	1928
Lobdell, Julia-Ann	1277
Lombard, Jacob	864
Loomis, Angenette	1233
Loomis, Finny-Reform	1064
Loomis, Maria	1393
Lovejoy, Almira	12
Loveland, Martha-Jane	1275
Lovett, William	81
Lucas, Ann-Calista	555
Luckore, Charles-Hudson	1712
Luse, Robert	956
Luther, Minerva-Elizabeth	1804
Lyon, Louisa	453

M.

Mallory, Leverett	897
Maguire, Constant	361
Maine, Maria	594
Mann, Anna	677
Mann, Ephraim	80
Martin, Hosea	1466
Martin, Lucretia-Armeda	1667
Martin, Sarah-Ann	1667
Mansfield, Rebecca	459
Markham, Lydia	350
Marcey, Freeman	481
Mason, Frances-Euphemia	1309
Mason, Nancy	80
Matthews, Ruth	1930
Mattoon, Calvin-Stebbins	68
Mattoon, Willis	68
May, Sally	705
Maynard, Achsa	68
Maynard, Mary	451
Maynard, Moses	68
McArthur, John	1704
McCandless, Sarah-Ann	957
McDermett, Catharine	80
McDonald, Robert-Ambrose	1835
McEving, Louisa	82
McFarland, Eve	1407
McIntosh, Sarah	1973
McKinney, Cynthia	82
McLean, Mary	1336
McLeod, Sarah	83
Meacham, Henry	499
Meacham, Mary-A.	892
Mead, James-Gardiner	1581
Meigs, Sandford-Tullar	84
Merchant, Janette-L.	81
Metcalf, Daniel-Horton	1508
Metcalf, William-Williams	68
Merethew, Hannah	958
Michael, Catharine	80
Mickel, Maria	1396
Mickel, Minerva	1398
Millard, Patience	1505
Miller, Martin-Luther	539
Miller, Mary	1513
Mitchel, Eli-Brooks	83
Mix, Stephen	57
Moffit, Delana	372
Moffit, Matthew	133
Money, George	362
Moore, Samuel	1616
Morgan, Emeline	87
Morgan, Rachel	86
Morgan, Zylpha	982
Morse, Marvel	12
Morton, Apelone	384
Morton, Zilkey	1458
Moses, Royal	723
Munger, Waldo	189
Munsell, Cynthia	435
Murphy, John	1693
Murray, Stephen	864½
Murray, Jeannette-Elizabeth	1501
Murry, James	1583
Muzzy, Samuel	875
Myers, Joseph	80
Myers, Simon	80

N.

Nash, William-Phelps	79
Needham, Silas	82